# The Pro Arte Quartet

Robert Maas, Germaine Prévost, Laurent Halleux, and Alphonse Onnou. Listening to a Quatuor Pro Arte recording. Courtesy of the Tully Potter Collection.

# The Pro Arte Quartet

## A Century of Musical Adventure on Two Continents

John W. Barker

UNIVERSITY OF ROCHESTER PRESS

The University of Rochester Press gratefully acknowledges generous support from the Pro Arte Centennial Fund.

First published 2017
Reprinted with corrections 2018

University of Rochester Press
668 Mt. Hope Avenue, Rochester, NY 14620, USA
www.urpress.com
and Boydell & Brewer Limited
PO Box 9, Woodbridge, Suffolk IP12 3DF, UK
www.boydellandbrewer.com

ISBN-13: 978-1-58046-906-7

**Library of Congress Cataloging-in-Publication Data**

Names: Barker, John W., author.
Title: The Pro Arte Quartet : a century of musical adventure on two
   continents / John W. Barker.
Description: Rochester : University of Rochester Press, 2017. | Includes
   bibliographical references and index.
Identifiers: LCCN 2017027062 | ISBN 9781580469067 (hardcover : alk.
   paper)
Subjects: LCSH: Pro Arte Quartet. | Musical groups.
Classification: LCC ML421.P765 B37 2017 | DDC 785/.7194—dc23 LC
   record available at https://lccn.loc.gov/2017027062

A catalogue record for this title is available from the British Library.

This publication is printed on acid-free paper.
Printed in the United States of America.

*Front cover image:* Pro Arte Quartet, 1928. Alphonse Onnou, Robert Maas, Germain Prévost, Laurent Halleux. Courtesy of the University of Wisconsin–Madison, Mills Music Library. *Back cover image:* Pro Arte Quartet, May 2011. David Perry, Suzanne Beia, Sally Chisholm, Parry Karp. Photograph by Rick Langer. Courtesy of the University of Wisconsin–Madison, Mills Music Library.

*This book is dedicated to the twenty-seven musicians who have served in the quartet over a century.*

# Contents

*Illustrations follow p. 158.*

# PREFACE

A centennial naturally invites celebration. The centennial of a string quartet, however, is an unprecedented occasion for celebration. The survival of any quartet for any length of time requires a very special chemistry that allows the fusion of four distinctly musical personalities into a transcendent, coherent entity. And it also requires the submission of individual careers to the interests of full-time ensemble playing. Finally, it requires the flexibility to assimilate new members as personnel changes take place.

Many quartets have endured for years, even decades. The replacement of any one member by a newer one inevitably requires adjustment and rededication. Some quartets have survived even recurrent turnovers in membership. But only one string quartet has managed to survive not only membership changes but also further crises, challenges, and transformations, to endure as a continuously active ensemble, under the same name, for a full century. That is the ensemble that began in Brussels, Belgium, as the Quatuor Pro Arte and continues to this day as the Pro Arte Quartet, based in its home in the School of Music of the University of Wisconsin–Madison.

Justifiably, that home institution generated a prolonged celebration of the centennial, in the years 2012–14, featuring concerts and the commissioning of new works. The crowning episode was a return-to-roots tour of the original homeland, Belgium, in the spring of 2014. This book represents a final contribution to the celebration.

My involvement in that final project was the work of Sarah Schaffer, the quartet's manager. She chaired superbly the advisory committee that planned the centennial and on which I myself served. Sarah has been a mentor, collaborator, and inspiration to me in this prolonged project, from its conception to its realization. She carefully and painstakingly read through a preliminary draft of the book, giving excellent advice; and she has given invaluable help in assembling the illustrations. Accordingly, I must give her much of the credit for what is good in the resulting volume, and absolve her from any of its faults or failings.

As a scholar of the history of centuries long past, I am not used to dealing with living descendants of, or participants in, the actual life of such an organization as the Pro Arte Quartet. I must therefore acknowledge forthwith the help, advice, and encouragement I have received from the present members of the ensemble: David Perry, Suzanne Beia, Sally Chisholm, and Parry Karp. Mr. Karp in particular, as the member of longest service in the quartet's history, has been particularly valuable as a consultant.

I owe great debts to several past members, such as Norman Paulu and Richard Blum. But two of these in particular have been special benefactors: Lowell Creitz and Martha Francis Blum.

For the many decades of the quartet's residence in Madison, the maintenance of files and records on its activities has been very inconsistent. The first continuing manager of the group, Helene Stratman Blotz, conscientiously collected the quartet's concert programs. That practice lapsed badly in subsequent hands, but Creitz was extraordinarily diligent in keeping a steady log of his performances, in and beyond the quartet. He has been most generous in giving me access to this log, which is an indispensable source for the years 1955–76. After him, less diligence was displayed, and the simple filings of programs has been patchy (though Parry Karp and David Perry have kept their own files of programs).

In Martha Blum I have a most important predecessor. A lively observer, as well as a fine musician, after her retirement from the quartet, she undertook to research and write its history. With institutional financial support, she set to work on what would commemorate the fiftieth anniversary of the quartet's establishment in Madison. She interviewed appropriate people (both here and abroad) and did extensive study of the correspondence of Elizabeth Sprague Coolidge. She poured so much of the results into drafts meant for a full-scale volume. Alas, the ultimate outcome was a reduction into a thirty-nine-page digest that was combined with an anniversary commemoration of the Music School's wind quintet. But, in all these forms, her devoted work has provided me with much inspiration and substance.

More recently, I have become acquainted with the work of the Belgian scholar Anne Van Malderen. For her monumental doctoral dissertation (Université Catholique de Louvain, 2012), she did extraordinarily extensive research on the history of the quartet in its Belgian identity (1912–47) and produced a rich historical and analytical study. As she was writing it, she graciously supplied me with advance copies of her monumental dissertation. In my treatment of those years, I have depended heavily, and gratefully, on her work.

Not one of my own direct contacts, but an early resource for all who study the Pro Arte Quartet is a remarkable set of recollections by the longest-surviving member of the original Belgian foursome, Germain Prevost. These were captured on audiotape in a remarkable interview with him, conducted in San Francisco by Norman and Cathy Paulu in 1979. Together with a CBC film they made with him two years earlier in Vancouver, BC, Prevost's personal reflections bring the quartet's early history vividly to life. The University of Wisconsin's archives also contain interviews and testimonials, including recollections by another of the quartet's violists, Bernard Milofsky, that have been vital to this project.

I owe a great personal debt to Tully Potter, one of the world's leading experts in the history of recorded music. I have found particular inspiration in his magisterial biography, *Adolf Busch: The Life of an Honest Musician* (2010). A stimulating contact person of great patience and generosity as well as wit, he has been of essential help in formulating the discography in appendix E, and in assisting with the illustrations.

Among others I must acknowledge with special thanks are Jeanette Casey and Tom Caw of the Mills Music Library and David Null of the University of Wisconsin Archives, for their generous aid in giving me access to their collections. Further thanks are due to Susan Halpert of the Houghton Library at Harvard University. Thanks are also due to Robert Graebner, for assistance with photography and program files.

Added to all these must be my wife, Margaret, for her regular helpfulness in a number of ways—including reading and commenting upon the manuscript.

I must, however, express my concerns about a procedural decision I have had to make. As a professional scholar, I have been raised with sworn allegiance to the note, foot- or end-. For a book such as this, however, aimed at both a specialized and general readership, I have had to hesitate. Extensive notes would add gravely to the length of the book. More crucially, a great deal of serious citational apparatus would be impossible to follow, given the character of so much of the source material involved. These are conversations, notes, unofficial files with no systematic organization, and even archival files with little in the way of numbering and placement that could be referred to with any meaning. A good deal of the useful material remains in chaotic files stored in cartons, many residing temporarily on desks and floors. Where specific kinds of material (letters, reviews, etc.) are referred to, I have tried to give minimal identification within the text, in the hope that readers might derive some guidance to them. I list below the major sources I have used, which may also provide some guidance to readers interested in delving into them.

An ex post facto resolution of the foregoing solution would be the gathering together of as much as possible of all this unsecured material, together with already archived materials, into a comprehensive Pro Arte archive that would be accessible to future researchers. Such a venture is now under consideration, and may eventually be housed in the Mills Music Library at the University of Wisconsin's Memorial Library, though not for some time, given the requirements of space, personnel, and financing, elements that are increasingly scarce these days.

Given the mazes and complexities of resources drawn upon for this book, it is inevitable that some mistakes or inaccuracies have been committed. For these I must apologize. I can only hope that the broad picture I have tried to give will alert music lovers to the remarkable history of this historic ensemble. I might add that the century-long story of a string quartet poses challenges as to what material to include, what to leave out, and how to organize what is assembled. Readers may find that my structural pattern, chapter by chapter, produces endless processions of data about performances and repertoire. But a quartet is a performing group: performing is what it is about—where and when and what. A simplistic anecdotal approach hardly does justice to the realities of its life. I hope, therefore, that a clear setting forth of so much of the available data will give the reader insights into the day-by-day, week-by-week, month-by-month, year-by-year realities of the quartet's busy life over the course of a century, as well as helping future researchers.

A comment is due on the photographs assembled as visual documentation of the quartet's membership. Over the course of the century, one may reckon twenty-three different configurations of membership, as the personnel changed over a century. It is not possible to document visually every one of those configurations, but the images assembled do present eighteen of the twenty-three. More to the point, those eighteen manage to include all of the individual players who have played with the quartet, with only two exceptions—the original cellist, Lemaire, and the short-term substitute violinist Won Mo Kim.

For help in securing these images, I am indebted to many, including Robert Graebner, Tully Potter (and his assistant, Richard Burch), and Anne Van Malderen. Particularly helpful have been Sarah Schaffer, and Marina Menendez of the Distillery Studio. Special thanks must go to David Null's diligent assistant Catherine H. Phan and, again, to Jeanette Casey of the University of Wisconsin Mills Library.

A word as to treatment of our quartet's name. It was formulated in French, of course, as the Quatuor Pro Arte. It was identified thus in its initial years of operation. But with international exposure, and especially in its involvements with English-language venues, audiences, and managements, it readily adopted the parallel name of the Pro Arte Quartet. Thus, the name in either language is usable for the group up to 1940. The group's label became bilingual even before it made the transition from a French-speaking base to an English-speaking one. I have tried to honor the original Belgian identity in my own uses in the book, but after the transition, the Anglo-American form inevitably comes to triumph. Additionally, at times I have resorted to the abbreviations of QPA and PAQ, as convenient. I add that I have subtly varied the spelling of violist Germain Prévost's name, using the accented form of his surname during the account of his QPA years, but dropping that for the time after he had settled in the United States.

# Basic Sources

- Correspondence, conversations, and interviews with a number of people, drawn extensively upon their recollections or information. These people include: Suzanne Beia, Martha and Richard Blum, Patrick Chatelin (grandson of Georges Charbonneaux), Sally Chisholm, Susan Cook, Lowell Creitz, Walter Gray, Bonnie Hampton, Rose Mary Harbison, Parry Karp, Norman Paulu, David Perry, and Tully Potter.
- Archives of the University of Wisconsin, and of the University's School of Music (in Mills Music Library).
- Archival files, mainly kept by Helene Stratman Blotz, presently held by Parry Karp.
- Martha Blum's article, "The Pro Arte Quartet: 50 Years" (in the publication cited in the bibliography), and her drafts and papers (Mills Library).
- Correspondence of Elizabeth Sprague Coolidge, in the Elizabeth Sprague Coolidge Foundation collection at the Library of Congress; with transcriptions thereof by Martha Blum.

- Papers of Rudolf Kolisch, in the Houghton Library of Harvard University.
- Anne Van Malderen's dissertation, "Historique et réception des diverses formations Pro Arte (1912-1947): apport au répertoire de la musique contemporaine" (PhD diss., Université catholique de Louvain-la-Neuve, 2012). Accessible for download at https://dial.uclouvain.be/pr/boreal/object/boreal: 114941.

# LISTS OF QUARTET MEMBERSHIP

## Alphabetical

Basso, Robert (vln II, 1960–64)
Beia, Suzanne (vln II, 1995—present)
Blum, Martha Francis (vln II, 1974–88)
Blum, Richard (vla, 1957–91)
Brosa, Antonio (vln I, 1940–44)
Chisholm, Sally (vla, 1991—present)
Creitz, Lowell (vc, 1955–76)
Evans, C. Warwick (vc, 1940–41)
Friedlander, Ernst (vc, 1943–55)
Gottlieb, Victor (vc, 1941–42)
Halleux, Laurent (vln II, 1912–43)
Karp, Parry (vc, 1976—present)
Kim, Jae-Kyung (vln II, 1988–95)
Kim, Won Mo (vln II, 1964–67)
Kolisch, Rudolf (vln I, 1944–67)
Lemaire, Fernand Auguste (vc, 1912–18)
Maas, Robert (vc, 1921–40)
McLeod, John (vln II, 1973–74)
Milofsky, Bernard (vla, 1947–57)
Moore, Thomas (vln II, 1967–73)
Onnou, Alphonse (vln I, 1912–40)
Paulu, Norman (vln I, 1967–95)
Perry, David (vln I, 1995—present)
Prevost, Germain (vla, 1912–47)
Quinet, Fernand (vc, 1918–21)
Rahier, Albert (vln II, 1943–60)
Sopkin, George (vc, 1942–43)

## Chronological, by Instrument

| Violin I | Violin II |
|---|---|
| Onnou, Alphonse (1912–40) | Halleux, Laurent (1912–43) |
| Brosa, Antonio (1940–44) | Rahier, Albert (1943–60) |
| Kolisch, Rudolf (1944–67) | Basso, Robert (1960–64) |
| Paulu, Norman (1967–95) | Kim, Won Mo (1964–67) |
| Perry, David (1995—present) | Moore, Thomas (1967–74) |
| | McLeod, John (1973–74) |
| | Blum, Martha Francis (1974–88) |
| | Kim, Jae-Kyung (1988–95) |
| | Beia, Suzanne (1995—present) |

| Viola | Violoncello |
|---|---|
| Prevost, Germain (1912–47) | Lemaire, Fernand Auguste (1912–14) |
| Milofsky, Bernard (1947–57) | Quinet, Fernand (1918–21) |
| Blum, Richard (1957–91) | Maas, Robert (1921–40) |
| Chisholm, Sally (1991—present) | Evans, C. Warwick (1940–41) |
| | Gottlieb, Victor (1941) |
| | Sopkin, George (1941–43) |
| | Friedlander, Ernst (1943–55) |
| | Creitz, Lowell (1955–76) |
| | Karp, Parry (1976—present) |

## Personnel Configurations

Grouped by years of the first violinists; names in score order, vln I, vln II, vla, vc.

### Onnou (1912–40)

| | |
|---|---|
| 1912–18 | Onnou, Halleux, Prévost, Lemaire |
| 1918–22 | Onnou, Halleux, Prévost, Quinet |
| 1922–40 | Onnou, Halleux, Prévost, Maas |
| 1940 | Onnou, Halleux, Prévost, Evans |

## Brosa (1940–44)

| | |
|---|---|
| 1940–41 | Brosa, Halleux, Prévost, Evans |
| 1941–42 | Brosa, Halleux, Prevost, Gottlieb |
| 1942–43 | Brosa, Halleux, Prevost, Sopkin |
| 1943 | Brosa, Rahier, Prevost, Sopkin |
| 1943–44 | Brosa, Rahier, Prevost, Friedlander |

## Kolisch (1944–67)

| | |
|---|---|
| 1944–47 | Kolisch, Rahier, Prevost, Friedlander |
| 1947–55 | Kolisch, Rahier, Milofsky, Friedlander |
| 1955–57 | Kolisch, Rahier, Milofsky, Creitz |
| 1957–60 | Kolisch, Rahier, R. Blum, Creitz |
| 1960–62 | Kolisch, Basso, R. Blum, Creitz |
| 1962–64 | [Kolisch], Basso, R. Blum, Creitz ("University of Wisconsin Piano Quartet": Steffens) |
| 1964–67 | [Kolisch], W. Kim, R. Blum, Creitz ("University of Wisconsin Piano Quartet") |

## Paulu (1967–95)

| | |
|---|---|
| 1967–73 | Paulu, Moore, R. Blum, Creitz |
| 1973–74 | Paulu, McLeod, R. Blum, Creitz |
| 1974–76 | Paulu, M. Blum, R. Blum, Creitz |
| 1976–88 | Paulu, M. Blum, R. Blum, Karp |
| 1988–91 | Paulu, J. Kim, R. Blum, Karp |
| 1991–95 | Paulu, J. Kim, Chisholm, Karp |

## Perry (1995–present)

| | |
|---|---|
| 1995–present | Perry, Beia, Chisholm, Karp |

# INTRODUCTION

# Quartet Contexts

The world of music making into which the Pro Arte Quartet was born and in which it operated was well established at the ensemble's inception. The instrumental types and ensemble combinations had been clearly established over generations, as had the forms of ensemble writing. A repertoire of working literature was also being developed, and our quartet made important contributions to this. Its rise and flourishing were accompanied by the operations of many continuing quartet ensembles of significant stature—its siblings and rivals—in an ever-changing kaleidoscope of groups, many of which fell by the wayside as the Pro Arte continued to thrive.

These factors provide an important backdrop to our story of the Pro Arte Quartet, and so it is perhaps useful at the outset to say a few words about them, to establish a context.

◈   ◈   ◈

What has become accepted over some two-and-a-half centuries as the "string quartet" is a somewhat eccentric combination of instruments, if one thinks about it. We expect a vocal ensemble or a chorus normally to consist of the soprano-alto-tenor-bass combination of voice parts (SATB). As it evolved, however, this particular mustering of the violin family amounts to two trebles (or sopranos), an alto and a baritone, but no true bass. On paper, that combination might seem somewhat top-heavy. Nevertheless, it is, in function, quite flexible. The second violin can pair with either the first or with the viola; the viola can also pair with the cello, while the latter, with its wide range, can both reach high in pitch and offer a full-bodied bass line. It is a remarkably adaptable combination, a fact that has doubtless contributed to its enduring acceptance.

The flexibility of the string quartet formulation is furthered, of course, by the frequent introduction of a fifth instrument, for quintet combinations. The piano is the most common such addition, but wind instruments (such as clarinet) have also found favor. The addition of another stringed instrument, either another viola or another cello, has helped produce some extraordinarily fine string quintets. The addition of both has generated the string sextet, which allows fascinating rethinking of the quartet texture. While the string-quartet configuration can thus be carried beyond itself, that conventional foursome has remained the firm focus of our chamber music.

In the latter half of the eighteenth century, experiments with the quartet configuration were pursued by a number of composers, chief among whom, by far, were Haydn and Mozart. Through their work, quartet compositions were recognized as a substantial idiom. By the early nineteenth century, musicians and audiences began thinking generally of musical compositions not just as ephemeral creations of momentary but fleeting attraction, but rather as candidates for inclusion in an incremental literature of "standard works"—an eventual "repertoire." Such was certainly the case as composers discovered in the string quartet at once the most rewarding and the most challenging of instrumental idioms.

It should go without saying that these composers have written not only string quartets but also quartets for string trio and another instrument, and many quintets, with either stringed or other instruments as the fifth partner. Such works are a supplemental dimension to the basic repertoire of string-quartet music. There are, of course, many other works that, if not "basic" or as yet "mainstream," are drawn upon for programming variety. And the Pro Arte Quartet, throughout its history, made a point of encouraging and performing a wide range of new compositions. But the broad repertoire sketched by composers from Haydn onward was the steady resource that provided the group with its pool of programming choices—as will be clear in what follows.

❧  ❧  ❧

As the idiom's working repertoire evolved, so also did the emergence of professional performing groups with sets of players committed to corporate careers. At first, groups had a certain *ad hoc* and ephemeral character. Later, as they became associated with the work of living composers, some groups became more stable. Franz Schuppanzigh (1776–1830), the Viennese violinist was a pioneer in creating group continuity with his string quartet, which collaborated with Beethoven in the latter's late quartets. Later counterparts would be two groups in the Soviet Union, the Beethoven Quartet (1931–90) and the Borodin Quartet (1945–present) that, in their heydays, were close collaborators with Shostakovich.

Of the continuing ensembles that emerged in the latter part of the nineteenth century, an important one was the Viennese Hellmesberger Quartet (1849–91). France generated the Armingaud Quartet (1855–ca. 1870), in which the composer Lalo played second violin. But the premier one was surely the Joachim Quartet (1869–1907), founded and led by the great violinist Joseph Joachim (1831–1907). This group was a pioneer in giving exclusively quartet concerts, and in touring. Only slightly less venerable was the durable Rosé Quartet (1882–1938). Both the foregoing collaborated with Brahms in his last years. Meanwhile, the United States was graced by the pioneering Kneisel Quartet (1885–1917).

Belgium itself was a thriving scene of quartet activity. The great violinist Eugène Ysaÿe founded a quartet under his name in 1886, as did his successor at the Conservatory, César Thomson, in 1898. Mathieu Crickboom, who played second violin in the Ysaÿe Quartet, founded his own Quatuor Crickboom (1892). Other Belgian groups were the Quatuor Zimmer (1896), in Brussels, and the Quatuor Charlier (1904), in Liège. There was also a Brussels Quartet, made up of German players. These ensembles provided a lively background and inspiration for the young prodigies who created the Quatuor Pro Arte.

Roughly contemporary with the Pro Arte's creation was the Flonzaley (1902–28), the first group to perform a complete cycle of the Beethoven quartets. In England a trail-blazing group was the London Quartet (1908–34). The era of World War I produced the Budapest Quartet (1917–67), one of the most successful and enduring of its type, The Léner Quartet (1918–40s), and the particularly fine Busch Quartet (1919–44, 1946–51), were internationally acclaimed. These were followed in postwar Germany by the Amar Quartet (1921–29), in which the composer Hindemith played viola, and by the Kolisch Quartet (1922–39); also by the Brosa Quartet (1925–38), the Galimir Quartet (1927–93), and the Curtis Quartet (1927–81), as well as the

Prague Quartet (1920–55), the Virtuoso String Quartet (1923–36), the Wiener Konzerthaus Quartet (1934–62), and the Hungarian Quartet (1935–72).

Even in the years of World War II, new groups appeared: the Loewenguth (193?–197?) and Pascal (194?–197?) Quartets; the Végh (1940–81), and the Parrenin (1944–198?). The war's aftermath saw a rapid proliferation of string quartets internationally. To cite them all would be impossible, but there are many noteworthy ones active in performing and recording. Of new groups founded in the United States, the Paganini (1945–66) and Fine Arts (1946–present) benefited from Pro Arte losses; yet another was the LaSalle (1946–87). Noteworthy have been the Juilliard Quartet (1946–present) and the Amadeus Quartert (1947–87). Of the same vintage were the Quartetto Italiano (1945–80), the Smetana Quartet (1945–89), the Tátrai Quartet (1946–present), the Janáček Quartet (1947–present), and the Hollywood Quartet (1947–61). Short-lived and Haydn-focused was the Schneider Quartet (1952–55).

The decade of the 1960s saw further blossoming with the Talich (1964–present), Guarneri (1964–2009), Kodály (1965–present), Lindsay (1965–2005), Melos (1965–2005), Gabrieli (1966–present), Fitzwilliam (1968–present), Panocha (1968–present), Cleveland (1969–95), and Tokyo (1969–2013) quartets. The following decades continued the proliferation, with the Alban Berg (1970–2008), Chilingirian (1971–present), Takács (1975–present), Orlando (1976–97), Martinů (1976–present), Emerson (1976—present), Orion (1987–present), Angeles (1988–present), Brentano (1992–present), Pavel Haas (2002–present), St. Lawrence (1989–present), Jerusalem (1993–present), Belcea (1994–present), Pacifica (1994–present), and Casals (1997–present) Quartets. (The Kronos Quartet, founded in 1973, is devoted quite specifically to avant-garde music and is thus somewhat marginal to our focus.)

The foregoing is, of course, only the most cursory digest of an enormous array of ensembles operating over the course of some three or four centuries. A more comprehensive listing of quartets formed from 1914 onward may be found online at Paul Rapoport's QuartetWeb/Performing Groups, while Anne Van Malderen has compiled a listing of 188 quartets organized since Schuppanzigh's in 1804.

Nevertheless, this survey may serve to represent ensembles that have been forerunners, contemporaries, and in many ways competitors to the Pro Arte Quartet over the course of more than a century (1912–present).

❧　❧　❧

The organization of what follows is chronological. As with any human activity, the life of a string quartet evolves, and it does so over the passage of time. Transformations come as a function of both intragroup dynamics and external circumstances. The processions of performance dates and locations traced in these chapters may seem tedious, and yet they reflect the natural life of a performing group. The players lived that life, and we must live it with them to understand and appreciate their history.

The divisions of that history can be tied to the successive phases of leadership by the individual first violinists. This may appear an arbitrary decision, but it does, in fact, reflect the very distinct characteristics of the quartet's formations and changes over the years. The extent of "control" that different first violinists asserted may have varied, but the influence of each has nevertheless been considerable. From Onnou to Brosa to Kolisch to Paulu to Perry, significant changes of directions and character may be discerned. The changes that developed during the tenures of the two longest-serving first fiddlers were so considerable that it is worth dividing the years of each of their incumbencies into two successive chapters.

Each chapter is subdivided into distinct categories of operation. First, there is a narrative of the ensemble's activities and experiences. This may at first seem like a monotonous catalogue of dates and places. But this reporting reflects the fact that a string quartet is a performing group, with the progression of concerts and events in the group's strenuously busy life. For the original Quatuor Pro Arte, this narrative is organized by years, since the group traveled relentlessly, almost around the calendar, with periods of rest only at certain intervals that did not always correspond to seasons. Their schedule really transcended seasons. On the other hand, for the group's life of residence at the University of Wisconsin, the Pro Arte Quartet was fitted quite directly into the pattern of booking seasons and two-semester academic years.

The second section of each chapter examines, to the extent surviving data allow, the working repertoire of the quartet, phase by phase, pointing up differences that emerged between various configurations and over time.

The third section of each chapter (except the first) enumerates and evaluates the recordings undertaken and bequeathed by each successive quartet phase. Such segmented treatment is complemented by comprehensive discographic listings in appendix E.

A century of history inevitably must be broken down into digestible units, and this format, it is hoped, will allow for a meaningful absorption of a great deal of what that century has witnessed in the life of one evolving performing group.

# THE ONNOU YEARS, I

# (1912–31)

## Formation, Definition, and Patronage

The Brussels Conservatory of Music was founded in 1832 as an academy of the state, contemporaneously with the creation of the independent Kingdom of Belgium as that state. Among its earliest directors were the Belgian musicologists François-Joseph Fétis (1784–1871) and François-Auguste Gevaert (1828–1908), whose successive regimes covered the first seventy-six years of the school's existence, long dominating the musical life of Brussels.

A violin department was established under Lambert Massart. His successor (1843–52) was the eminent violinist and composer Charles-Auguste de Bériot (1802–70), who established what came to be called the Franco-Belgian school of violin playing, based on the traditions and style of Paganini. This school of the violin emerged as the only rival on the international scene to the so-called Russian School of St. Petersburg. The influence of each "school" was great and widespread.

Massart's pupil Henri Vieuxtemps led that faculty department in his turn, and was teacher of Eugène Ysaÿe, who followed the Polish virtuoso Hendryk Wieniawski. Succeeding Ysaÿe as director was César Thomson. In subsequent generations, the violin faculty included André Gertler and Arthur Grumiaux. (Since 1967, the Conservatory has been divided into two institutions, one for instruction in French, the other in Flemish.)

With such a faculty, the Conservatory nurtured several generations of gifted young musicians, who were drawn to it as providing the foundation of their careers. Among them were those who became founders of the Quatuor Pro Arte.

๑   ๑   ๑

The eldest of them was Germain Prévost, who was born in 1891. His father was a tanner, but the family was actively musical and encouraging. Arthur, the first of the three sons, trained as a clarinetist and became an important figure in Belgian musical life. Germain was the second son, and in his turn became an admired (and money-earning) clarinetist. He studied violin, and at age thirteen he began to teach himself the viola, which was to become his true love. With such diverse foundations, Germain secured entry to the Brussels Conservatory in 1909, at age eighteen, as a clarinet student. Through great diligence he worked up his skills on the viola and advanced rapidly. Though his professional identity as a violist became settled, he never let his clarinet skills lapse completely—and there are stories of his jumping into a substitute-clarinet role at the drop of a hat.

In 1910 Prévost met, among other Conservatory students, the young violinist Alphonse Onnou. The latter, born in 1893, was the son of a tailor who did his best to sustain the boy's quickly emerging talent. In his early violin training, Onnou met another gifted student of the instrument, even younger than he—Laurent Halleux, born in 1897, and a protégé of César Thomson. Onnou entered the Conservatory in 1909, and Halleux followed soon after. Onnou quickly became a star student: Prévost was as deeply impressed by his musicianship and technique as by his personal modesty.

In 1912, at age nineteen, Onnou took first prize in violin at the Conservatory. In that same year, amid their studies, Onnou, fifteen-year old Halleux and twenty-one-year old Prévost, along with an eighteen-year-old cellist named Fernand Auguste Lemaire, began working informally as a string quartet. (Not yet a partner was the eleven-year-old cellist Robert Maas.) That tentative initiation by these precocious young players is one reason for taking 1912 as the inaugural year of the Quatuor Pro Arte—a point to which Onnou would give endorsement in a later statement.

Outside of the Conservatory, two of these brilliant students made their first public appearance in 1913, in a quartet organized by the violinist Désiré Defauw (1885–1960). Defauw would eventually turn to conducting, becoming Belgium's leading maestro, and would even serve a few years on the Chicago Symphony's podium. But in 1913, he joined with Onnou in creating the Quatuor Defauw, with himself as first violin, Onnou as second, Prévost as violist, and Jacques Gaillard as cellist. (As an example of professional inbreeding, Gaillard would, in 1922, become the father-in-law to QPA cellist Robert Maas.) The Quatuor Defauw made its first public appearance in the spring of 1914, as part of a concert series devoted to exploring new music. (For playing in these "subversive" concerts without proper permission from the Conservatory, Prévost was punished with a month's suspension.)

The Quatuor Defauw operated only infrequently, and the next landmark in the creation of the Quatuor Pro Arte had already come in March of 1913, when Onnou mustered an ensemble with himself as first violinist, sixteen-year-old Halleux as second, Prévost as violist, and, apparently, Lemaire (who had just won the Conservatory's first cello prize) as fourth member. The group had no formal name as yet, but their program of new music by contemporary Belgian composers foreshadowed their eventual commitment to such literature. And that concert has made 1913 the alternate year for the origin of the Quatuor Pro Arte.

&#x204B; &#x204B; &#x204B;

At this point it is appropriate to introduce an important patroness who might be called "the first Elizabeth" among the quartet's benefactresses. This is the Queen of Belgium, Elisabeth (in the French spelling of the name). Born a Bavarian duchess in 1876, she had trained in her early years as a violinist, becoming an accomplished musician under Ysaÿe's personal guidance. In 1900 she married the Belgian prince who would become King Albert I (r. 1909–34). Joined by her husband, she was a staunch promoter of cultural activities, becoming greatly beloved. She continued to play the violin privately through her life, especially in chamber music.

The emerging Quatuor Pro Arte was only one of the activities that Elisabeth pursued, and in their formative years she made efforts at protecting the members. She seems to have taken a particular interest in Prévost, eventually inviting him to the royal palace to play with her in quartets. Prévost described her as "a lovely lady, very regal, but she had only tiny tone." In 1932, she arranged that the QPA should be designated the official quartet of the Belgian court.

Her lifelong devotion to her personal instrument generated a musical foundation she helped create, and that was named in her honor, the Queen Elisabeth Violin Competition. Organized in 1937, it quickly became prestigious and internationally influential. Other instrumental categories were soon added to her competition. Long-lived, she died in 1965.

❧   ❧   ❧

The two World Wars were virtual frames for the original Quatuor Pro Arte. The First War threatened—but failed—to disrupt, or at least forestall, the quartet's genesis. The Second War would contribute to the winding down and redefinition of the Brussels ensemble.

Each of the four players had different experiences during the years of World War I. Because of a tubercular condition, Onnou was exempted from military service. He spent the time mainly in German-occupied Brussels, playing in theaters—as did his colleagues in their poststudent years—in order to scratch out a livelihood. But he held onto his idea of a continuing group, keeping up contact with the members, and undertaking quartet performances as often as he could.

At the outset of the war, in 1914, Defauw fled to England, where he was soon to found a new string quartet. Prévost followed him that November, meeting Defauw (who gave him some financial help), and also the fugitive Polish pianist Artur Rubinstein. Lemaire appears to have worked with Defauw, but continued connections with Onnou. Apparently Lemaire played with Onnou's group from 1914, though he seems to have traded off the cello chair intermittently with Fernand Quinet. There is only sketchy word of Halleux, but it appears that he, too, remained in Brussels during the war, and may have done some work with Onnou.

It was Prévost, however, who had the liveliest wartime experiences. Fired by patriotism, and despite a family exemption, he chose to leave England and enlist in Belgian forces to fight the Germans. Leaving his viola behind in London, he returned to Belgium, received military training, and was at the front in 1915. He used a furlough in 1916 to go to London and reclaim his viola. As a necessary safeguard, he entrusted it to his brother, Arthur, who was by this time a military bandmaster with Belgian forces. Germain was invited to play in some concerts for soldiers. Word of his presence spread and caught the attention of Queen Elisabeth, who had a summer villa at La Panne, near the front.

Prévost found himself summoned out of the trenches to play in spontaneously formed quartets, of which one in 1915 involved Ysaÿe.

The following spring, Ysaÿe was again present at La Panne, playing first violin to the queen's second. Prévost was summoned to be violist. Whether on this or another occasion (in 1918), he tried to resist the summons on the argument that his uniform was badly soiled from his trench fighting. He was ordered to the palace anyway, where he was given clean clothes upon entry. For his services, the queen offered to have him transferred from active fighting, but he insisted he would continue doing his duty. Seven months before the war's end, when invited to join a military orchestra and string quartet, he agreed, but only on condition that he be allowed to return to the trenches when fighting resumed. His bravery and his devotion to his comrades won him several medals and the eventual rank of sergeant.

In 1918, Prévost was concertizing with his groups in Brussels. The military-generated Quatuor Gadeyne was of excellent quality, but not all members found consistent attendance feasible. Onnou was brought in. Onnou had been working with Halleux, and at this point he invited Prévost to join their quartet—in effect, to rejoin the nascent Pro Arte group. Prévost recalled that he agreed, with the stipulation that the group must rehearse every day, even Sunday. This was accepted. Less is known about the cellist, Lemaire. He may have had health problems, but he seems to have been involved in the group until 1918, when this chair was officially occupied by Fernand Quinet, then twenty (and winner of the Conservatory's cello prize in 1914). Lemaire remained active in French musical life into the 1930s.

Meanwhile, it was apparently in 1917 that the persisting Brussels group settled on what would be come their definitive name. Despite some competition between Onnou and Halleux, clearly Onnou was the guiding member, in intellect and personality. Suggestions were made that the quartet should take his name as the first violinist, a common practice with such ensembles. He rejected this with an argument interesting for its future implications. As Prévost has testified, Onnou said, "No, because I can die and the group must go on. We must find a neutral name." A professor at the Conservatory suggested the Latin term *pro arte*, and this was soon adopted by the members of the group.

Their financially precarious situation was given a military solution. Onnou, Halleux, and Quinet, who had not done military service during the war, still had to fulfill their obligations. Prévost's brother, Arthur, was the nation's leading military bandmaster. Through him an arrangement was made with a culture-loving general, Baron Victor Buffin, that the three should perform their service—without military training or armed activities—as an official military string quartet, attached to Buffin's army of occupation in Germany. They became the Quatuor à Archet du 1er Régiment des Guides. They concertized widely, mainly in programs of contemporaneous music, much to the fascination of the Germans in their audiences (as Prévost recalled). They also performed for the royal family at La Panne. They received military stipends until 1926, but the pay was not so generous that the quartet members could escape their supplemental employment in movie houses and theater pits—where, in off-duty hours they would hold their quartet rehearsals, for lack of other venues.

Under these circumstances, the quartet went through final stages of definition. As the Quatuor Pro Arte, they were performing regularly, mainly in Brussels but also around Belgium. For one concert in 1920, Onnou yielded the first chair to Halleux. Such "interchangeability," remarked upon as a novelty, was resorted to frequently for some years. (At their discretion, Onnou would take first place in Romantic and modern literature, Halleux in the more Classical and traditional repertoire.) And it was in 1920 that the quartet became involved with a personality who would place them in a new and higher level of visibility.

❧  ❧  ❧

Paul Collaer (1891–1989) was an exceptional figure in Belgian cultural life. In his early years he studied music at Michelen Conservatory, won prizes, and began at age twenty to concertize as a pianist. At the same time, he began studies in the sciences, at first in physics, earning a doctorate in natural sciences in 1919. He soon became a professor of chemistry at the Mechelen Athenaeum.

Continuing his musical activity, he shared with a number of others the feeling that Belgium had been isolated from the newest cultural developments by World War I. With that in mind, he created in 1921 an organization called Les Concerts Pro Arte. Extended annually, they lasted, under Collaer's direction, until 1934. Their activities extended to involvement with exhibitions of new art.

The Quatuor Pro Arte was already operating with that name, though only in conjunction with their military functions. The coincidence of name only complemented the great affinity the group had with Collaer's intentions. Above all, these musicians fully sympathized with his promotion of the newest music. Though Collaer was only a few years older than most of the Pro Arte players (and the same age as Prévost), he was in a position to give them their first platform of prominence, at a time when, newly blossoming, they could most use it. The Quatuor Pro Arte players were therefore participants from the first concerts, appeared in them regularly, and served all the way to the end of this concert institution.

After his concert series, Collaer moved on in 1937 to become director of the Flemish division of the Belgian Radio, a post he held until 1953. From this influential position he was able even more fully to champion the newest music, while at the same time he contributed greatly to the revival of sixteenth-century Italian music, by Monteverdi and others.

Collaer continued to expand his interests. During World War II he had plunged into research on ethnomusicology, which became his ultimate specialty. He organized international conferences in this field. He held functions in the International Institute for Comparative Music Studies in Berlin. He was responsible for the creation of the Circle internationale d'études ethno-musicologiques. With funding from UNESCO, he founded a department of ethnomusicology at the Musée royal de l'Afrique centrale, near Brussels. On the basis of his wide and deep experience, he wrote and published actively.

Paul Collaer and violist Germain Prévost were to be the longest-lived survivors of the Quatuor Pro Arte's world. Both born in the same year (1891), the two were in contact as late as 1975. At that time Collaer apparently requested of Prévost information about the emergence of the quartet. On September 4 of that year, despite ill health and vision difficulties, Prévost wrote by hand a substantial reply, in which he traced his own and his colleagues' activities from 1912 to 1918. Prévost closed with regrets that his constrained finances made it impossible for him to go to Belgium to confer more fully with Collaer. Other contacts between them might be presumed as well. Prévost died in autumn 1986, at age ninety-five. The still more durable Collaer outlasted him by three years, dying at age ninety-eight.

✄  ✄  ✄

The Quatuor Pro Arte first appeared in Les Concerts Pro Arte on January 24, 1921, as part of an elaborate and varied program. The quartet's contribution was Darius Milhaud's Quartet no. 2. This was the first step in what would become a long and close association of the group with this composer. It was extended shortly afterward when Milhaud's Quartet no. 5 was to be given its local premiere in a concert of new French works at the Conservatoire, sponsored by the French embassy. As Prévost remembered it, one of the Conservatory quartet's members refused to play the music, and an appeal was made to Onnou's ensemble that they take over the program. They had only three days in which to prepare this, amid the obligations of their bread-and-butter jobs, but they mastered the scores, notably Milhaud's. The concert was a triumph. Milhaud himself was present and was greatly impressed—marking the group's establishment of cordial contacts with that composer.

The quartet was attracting attention. Collaer's Concerts Pro Arte provided both exposure and publicity. Committed as they were to the newest music, these concerts could be controversial. Prévost later recalled: "Every concert was a scandal, a scandal. Police in the concert. Ooh la la. That was something. People came to see the fights." More staid opportunities also opened. On two occasions in 1921, and on one more in 1922, they were invited to private concerts given at the home of Henri Le Boeuf, an important writer committed to promoting new music.

Amid all this, a final personnel change was made. The cellist Quinet chose to withdraw from the quartet during the summer of 1922. His reasons apparently combined matters of intra-group tensions, poor health, and a desire eventually to make a transition from performer to composer. Negotiations over his replacement were pursued to success in September, with the addition of Robert Maas, then twenty-one years old. He had completed his Conservatory studies two years earlier, winning its cello prize. He first appeared publicly with the quartet in a concert of December 14, 1922. His incorporation into the group now established the membership configuration that would constitute the Quatuor Pro Arte for the next seventeen years, their Belgian years of glory. In that sense, 1922 represents the final landmark year to which we may date the group's creation.

In their concertizing, they made their initial move outside Belgium, first to Paris in 1922, then to Geneva the following year. In Paris that December, in a program entirely of music by Igor Stravinsky, the quartet played his Concertino for String Quartet. It had been composed in 1920 on commission from the Flonzaley Quartet, which, however, had found it too difficult. Prévost would later tell a droll story about the quartet's encounter with Stravinsky over it, dating it to 1920.

When the composer appeared, descending a spiral staircase, he looked "just like the drawing of him by Picasso."

> Yes, he was very cold at first. We'd come to play his Concertino for String Quartet and see if he would accept that we took it with us on tour. The Flonzaley Quartet had commissioned the concertino, and paid a very big sum, but Stravinsky gave them only an eight-minute piece, and it was only rhythm, no melody. Oh, the Flonzaley was an old-fashioned quartet, they didn't have the technique for that piece. But it was our cup of tea.

> Stravinsky said to us, "I've made my own performance of the concertino on this pianola and I'll play it for you." Ooh la la. Our first violinist, Onnou, he whispered to me, "I hope that bloody machine doesn't work." And, by golly, it didn't. Please, we said, let us play *our* interpretation, and we did. Stravinsky didn't say a word. He returned up that spiral staircase. And then he came back down and was very warm for a change. He said, "Gentlemen, I accept you play my concertino, it is wonderful how you do it, and I want you to have the manuscript parts. But I want 100 francs every time you play it."

> We accepted, although that 100 francs every performance was a risk for us. Quartet fees were low in the 20s, we always traveled third class, carrying all our bags.

The Pro Arte next played it as part of their most extended venture until then, at the first concert of the new International Society for Contemporary Music (ISCM) in Salzburg, Austria, on May 8, 1923, to enthusiastic acclaim. They played it again in Paris in December 1923, and again triumphantly in another all-Stravinsky program on January 14, 1924, at a Pro Arte Concert in Brussels. Their command of the piece won the deep admiration of the composer himself, thus adding another important contact with a contemporary master. And the piece continued to be an active part of their repertoire in their ever-expanding tours (Paris, Geneva, Vienna, Saint-Nazaire, Monte-Carlo, Barcelona, Milan, Rome, Zurich) though 1924.

The quartet's appearances at their early launching pad, Les Concerts Pro Arte in Brussels, won them a good deal of notice from international critics. Such early reputation was only enhanced by their appearance at the ISCM festival in 1923. It was just months before that ISCM debut that a crucially important contact was made, with no less than the "second Elizabeth," the woman who was to become their most important supporter and promoter.

⊰  ⊰  ⊰

Elizabeth Sprague Coolidge (1864–1953) was one of the three great musical patronesses of the first half of the twentieth century, along with the Princesse de Polignac and Gertrude Clark Whittall—and perhaps the most important of them.

While the Civil War was in its last stages, in the year before Lincoln's assassination, she was born in Chicago to the Sprague family, which had become fabulously wealthy from their S&W (Sprague and Warner) food business. Her father, Albert Arnold Sprague, was an enthusiastic patron of Chicago's musical life, especially opera. She herself showed early musical talent, trained as a pianist, and at a young age even appeared as a soloist with the Chicago Symphony under Theodore Thomas. In 1891 she married Frederic Shurtleff Coolidge. He was no relation to the man who became the thirtieth President of the United States; much later, when one of her commissions was mistakenly attributed to the wife of Calvin Coolidge, she jokingly called herself "the other Mrs. Coolidge." She did not know that president, but she did become close friends with the thirty-first president, Herbert Hoover, and with his wife.

"ESC," as she was sometimes called, withdrew from public performance as a result of a persistent stage fright and of the onset of her partial deafness, which appeared first in her twenties and deepened thereafter. She nevertheless delighted in private chamber music playing. She also made some efforts as a composer, which continued over the years—as her "consolation," as she said. We know of some early songs of hers, and from later years a string quartet (1915), a trio for piano and strings (1930), and a sonata for oboe and piano (1947). Two movements of the quartet were transcribed for orchestra by Frederick Stock and performed in 1916; and the entire composition was recorded by her namesake quartet in 1942.

In 1915–16, the deaths in close succession of her father, her husband, and her mother left Mrs. Coolidge an independent heiress of great wealth. She then began to pursue her destiny as a patroness. Her benevolences were directed toward a number of worthy causes, but most specifically to musical ones, and above all to chamber music. A particular focus was the Library of Congress's Music Division. In 1925 she created the Elizabeth Sprague Coolidge Foundation, whose various purposes included the commissioning of new musical works, and the arrangement of concerts and festivals in which they would be performed. She even went so far as to fund the building of a theater at the Library of Congress for such purposes. All this was supplemented by her institution in 1932 of the Elizabeth Sprague Coolidge Medal "for eminent services to chamber music."

The most spectacular fruits of all this were her awards and support—both from the Foundation and from her own pocket—to literally hundreds of composers. The list of them is a who's-who of composers of the first half of the twentieth century, both famous and now-forgotten ones, and a large number of their resulting works have become acknowledged and regularly played masterpieces. She was noteworthy in not limiting her support only to music fitting her tastes. Frequently she actually did not like new scores she had fostered. She was famous in her later decades for attending premieres and turning off her hearing aid. "I can pay for it, but I don't have to listen to it" was her typically forthright explanation. On one occasion—recalled by later quartet member, violist Bernard Milofsky—when asked "why she put her money into music and not into art, she replied, 'Young man, I may be deaf, but I'm not blind.'"

It was to her greatest love, chamber music, that she devoted her most passionate support. She and her husband had built a home in Pittsfield, Massachusetts, in the Berkshire hills. In 1918 she instituted the South Mountain Chamber Music Festival there, and later at the Temple of Music nearby. At these gatherings, young and new ensembles were heard, and interacted. Mrs. Coolidge gave support to a series of string quartets in which she invested often-fleeting hopes. Among the ensembles receiving her largesse were the Berkshire, Coolidge, Gordon, Kolisch, Lenox, Letz, London, and Roth Quartets. To many of them, she had become the "Goddess of Chamber Music."

As she aged, Mrs. Coolidge seemed more and more regal in manner. Prévost recorded his first impressions of her as being "like a statue": garbed in a powerfully conservative, elegantly plain dress, with a lace collar, and a big hat. He said he was afraid of her.

≈ ≈ ≈

Among contemporary composers whose music the Quatuor Pro Arte had sampled was Alfredo Casella, who invited the quartet to participate in a pair of concerts in May 1923 at the American Academy in Rome, where he was music director. The Academy was to be a beneficiary of Mrs. Coolidge's support, while Italy in general was her favorite country

for travel through most of her life. She attended these concerts, and
there she first encountered the Pro Arte. As Casella himself quipped, it
was "love at first hearing." This reaction was only reinforced when she
heard the group again in Salzburg at the ISCM concerts that August.
These encounters constituted a landmark not only in the quartet's history, but also in Mrs. Coolidge's life—and she was at the time just short
of her fifty-eighth birthday.

Not only their playing but also the personality of Onnou himself
struck sympathetic chords and drew her into a deeply personal bond.
In fact, it was she who put an end to sporadic chair swapping: Onnou
would be first violin, and that was that. A further advantage for Onnou
was that, unlike other members of the quartet, he spoke some English,
which facilitated his communication with Mrs. Coolidge. Often disap-
pointed with other quartets she had sponsored, she found in the Pro
Arte what she was looking for: the perfect vehicle for her advancement
of chamber music at the very time when her involvements in Pittsfield
were collapsing. She offered to support the Pro Arte's concerts, quickly
becoming their booking manager and agent as well, in cooperation
with their Brussels manager, Gaston Verhuyck.

Through her efforts, the quartet was set up for a series of ten concerts, in March and April of 1924, in eight Italian cities (Milan, Brescia,
Bari, Rome, Genoa, Florence, Venice, and Padua). The latter six of
these concerts offered a single program of two works. One was a Concerto for String Quartet, op. 40, by Casella, who had asked personally
that they give the work its premiere run. The other work was nothing
less than Arnold Schoenberg's landmark piece of avant-gardism, *Pierrot
Lunaire*, op. 21. The Pro Arte had already been digging into Schoenberg's works, and had performed the first two of his quartets. It had
even dabbled with parts of this revolutionary opus 21, but in these six
concerts the quartet joined with other Viennese musicians under the
composer's direct leadership. (The Florence performance on April
1 was attended by the cancer-ridden Giacomo Puccini, just months
before he died of heart failure, on November 29, 1924, in Brussels.)

Through the following two years, the Quatuor Pro Arte continued
to concertize widely in Belgium, France, Switzerland, and Italy, while
also maintaining their deep involvement with Collaer's Les Concerts
Pro Arte. Long gone were the days of jobbery in Brussels theaters: constant travel and total commitment to the quartet on the part of all four
men were now the realities of life. At their most active, we are told,
they required some twenty-three large suitcases, which they handled

themselves. A problem for them at many hotels was laundry service. Though they did not always travel together on land, they did so by sea. They might have looked forward to some relaxation on ocean crossings; however, they found that ship captains would often ask them to perform on board.

Scope for their travels was expanded further when, through Verhuyck's contacts, the quartet made two appearances in London in mid-November 1925. Within weeks, they performed their first concerts in Portugal and Spain. But most momentous was the launching of their appearances in the United States.

From her very first contacts with the quartet, Mrs. Coolidge had wanted to involve them in the inauguration of the new concert hall she had financed at the Library of Congress in Washington, DC. They had not been able to participate in her first festive inauguration in 1925, but it was arranged for them the following year—the invitation processed through Belgian and American diplomatic offices. On September 23, 1926, the quartet embarked on the SS *Fennland*. Setting the precedent, they agreed to present two shipboard concerts, on September 30 and October 2. Their programs were a mix of Mozart, Borodin, Glazunov, and Milhaud. But they were launched, appropriately—and perhaps with an eye to New World prospects—by Dvořák's "American" Quartet, op. 96, which the group had only recently added to their repertoire. (Any copyright issues involved with some selections were negated by the fact that the concerts were given mid-ocean, not in any one country.)

Completing what would be their first sailing to North America (for an eventual total of thirty-three crossings), the quartet disembarked in New York on October 5, and sped to Washington to participate in the Second Coolidge Chamber Music Festival, thus catching up with her determination that the group be introduced to (and in) her new facilities at the Library of Congress. The QPA played for four successive concerts (October 7–10), devoted variously to quartets and sonatas. The composer they played the most was the Belgian Albert Huybrechts, one of whose pieces was a Coolidge Prize winner. César Franck's D-Major Quartet was played in two of the programs. Standing apart from Gallic choices was Beethoven's Quartet, op. 135. The Pro Arte's playing was highly praised in the group's first reviews in the United States.

From Washington, the quartet rushed back to New York to give a concert at the New York Public Library on October 12; then on to

Boston to perform on October 17 at its Public Library; then to New York again for two concerts on October 24 and 28 for the year-old League of Composers. They continued down to Baltimore where, at the Peabody Conservatory, they combined Beethoven's opus 95 and Dvořák's opus 96 with a Malipiero work. In Richmond, Virginia, their November 2 concert won a critic's recognition of them as "one of the most wondrous quartets in the world."

On November 5, 1926, by way of New York, the indefatigable four-some moved on to the American Midwest, for concerts in Detroit (November 8) and St. Paul (November 11), the latter a private per-formance in the home, appropriately, of a Northern Pacific Railway magnate. These were but short hops as the quartet rode westward. There was a stop in Denver (November 14). On November 17, the quartet reached the Pacific coast at Portland, Oregon, where there was an apparent stop (November 20), but then sped down to California. There they gave concerts in Palo Alto (November 22) and San Fran-cisco (November 27, 28). Doubling back eastward, they made appear-ances in Denver (December 1), and Kansas City, Missouri (December 3), then pushed on to Boston for a concert (December 7) and thence to Montreal (December 9), in their first plunge into Canada. It was back to Washington for another appearance at the Coolidge Audito-rium (December 10), followed by a quick appearance (December 13) in Albany, New York. In New Haven, Connecticut, they gave a concert at Yale University (December 14) that was followed by a single concert in New York the next day. A dip down to Philadelphia allowed them a brief experience of the "gigantesque" Grand Court of the John Wana-maker department store (December 29) as a prelude to an appearance (December 30) in the Wanamaker Auditorium in New York. (For its monster organ, Rodman Wanamaker would commission from Bel-gian composer Joseph Jongen his *Symphonie concertante* for organ and orchestra, op. 81, which, ironically, was not played on its intended instrument until 2008.)

With that, the first North American tour by the Quatuor Pro Arte ended. The players boarded the SS *Majestic* on January 1, 1927 (no shipboard concert required), and reached Belgium on January 7. The next day, they were back in Brussels for an appearance with Les Con-certs Pro Arte. Even in our present age of rapid travel, especially by air, it seems astonishing that the quartet could have covered so much ground in a mere eighty-seven days. The achievement wins admira-tion for stamina and sturdy health alone. (The players, it might be remembered, were passing from their late twenties to their early thirties.) Above all, the Quatuor Pro Arte now moved from international to intercontinental status.

Early in 1927, the quartet added points in the Netherlands to their itinerary. The year marked the centenary of the death of Ludwig van Beethoven, which prompted numerous commemorations, and the Quatuor Pro Arte was not to be left out. They had performed Beethoven quartets in previous years, but only sparingly. The hesitation may have been partly due to Onnou's determination to master these works completely; he was once quoted as saying that he would have the group rehearse scores new to them for a year before putting them before the public. A centenary proposal from Barcelona provided the centerpiece for a four-week tour of Spain.

The initial stops, with non-Beethoven programs, were in Barcelona itself (February 22) and Valencia (February 23), followed by a group of three Beethoven quartets (op. 59, no. 2, op. 132, and op. 127) in Tarragona (February 23). Only on February 26, 1927, back in Barcelona, did the quartet perform what would be the first of a future total of twenty-seven Beethoven cycles done by these Belgians. The performances were spread over five concerts, in the following layout:

> February 26: Op. 18, no. 1; op. 127; op. 59, no. 2
> February 27: Op. 18, no. 3; op. 130; op. 133; op. 59, no. 3
> February 28: Op. 18, no. 2; op. 135; op. 18, no. 4; op. 95
> March 1: Op. 18, no. 6; op. 132; op. 74
> March 2: Op. 18, no. 5; op. 131; op. 59, no. 1

This arrangement followed a pattern conventional among quartets generally, with each concert offering works from each of Beethoven's compositional "periods" (early, middle, late). This first cycle also established the quartet's commitment to playing the opus 130 with its original finale, the *Grosse Fuge*, op. 133. The quartet rounded off this Spanish tour with stops at Bilbao (March 4–5–6) and Cordoba (March 7), before returning to Brussels by way of Marseille (March 11) and Geneva (March 15)—all of these programs without any Beethoven.

In late March and early April 1927, the quartet again participated in Les Concerts Pro Arte in Brussels. After a few months they were in Frankfurt (July 18–19). In October they were in Paris, Rome, and Geneva, and then gave performances in Brussels and Liège. The following month, however, Mrs. Coolidge arranged another visit to

England, with stops in London (November 6), Oxford (November 8), and Sherborne (November 10). After appearances around France, the quartet was back in Spain once again, appearing in Barcelona (November 23, 27, 29), Tarragona (November 30, December 1), Saragossa (December 2), and Bilbao (December 5, 6). Nor was the Pro Arte finished for the year: over to London they went to give a concert sponsored by the Belgian embassy there (December 12). Yet more: concerts in Brussels, Marseille, and Brussels again (Les Concerts Pro Arte) to round out the year.

Barely rested, one guesses, after giving a Brussels concert on New Year's Day 1928, the quartet sailed (January 3–12, 1928) for their second tour of the United States, again a thorough and comprehensive one. The group began with a concert in New York on the day of their arrival, and then, from January 8 through March 26, they made appearances in nearly twenty cities (Washington, DC; Hattiesburg, Mississippi; and Louisville, Kentucky, in the eastern states; Duluth alone in the Midwest; San Francisco, Berkeley, El Palomar, and Palo Alto in California; Eugene and Portland in Oregon; Tacoma, Spokane, Seattle, and Astoria in Washington state; Los Angeles, Pasadena, and Redlands again in California; then back east to Buffalo, New York, Washington, DC, Philadelphia, and New York. The final stops hold some interest. In Washington on March 22, the quartet made a command appearance in Calvin Coolidge's White House, with a program of Haydn (op. 20, no. 4), Debussy, and the American Louis Gruenberg. In Philadelphia, they were once more in Wanamaker's Grand Court, and in New York at the Wanamaker Auditorium, both familiar venues from the first visit. For both Wanamaker concerts, the quartet was able to play on a set of instruments by Matteo Goffriller, rarities belonging to the Rodman Wanamaker Collection. The homeward voyage began on March 28, on SS *The American Banker.*

Meanwhile, during the Pro Arte's absence on tour, Les Concerts Pro Arte in Brussels replaced them (March 14, 1928) with the Wiener Streichquartett, newly founded by Rudolf Kolisch, in their first international appearance outside of Vienna. Therewith appears momentarily on our scene the violinist who would later take over Pro Arte Quartet itself.

Amid various assignments, the quartet returned to England not once but three times in 1928 (in June, and then November and December), continuing to build an enthusiastic following. Their three stops, besides London, were in Chelsea, Bournemouth, and Oxford, plus Haslemere. Through 1928, besides regular appearances in Belgium and France, by way of Marseille and Toulon, the quartet made a stay in northern Italy (December 8–14) giving concerts in Genoa, Milan, Rome, Florence, and Turin.

After a stop in Hamburg (January 10, 1929), the Pro Arte fully launched the new year with another visit to England (January 14–19: Kensington, London, Newcastle, Gloucester, Painswick). The foursome was only briefly back at home before they set forth on their third tour of North America. They boarded the *Île-de-France* on January 24. On January 28, the day before their arrival in New York, they played the seemingly unavoidable shipboard concert. This time there was no tarrying in New York at the outset. After a journey by train of 24 hours, on February 3 our intrepid players began a forty-eight-day tour of the American Midwest in Chicago.

Their itinerary took them to Ann Arbor and East Lansing in Michigan, and Cleveland, Columbus, and Oberlin in Ohio; turning back east, they gave concerts in Philadelphia and Boston, with a Canadian trip north to Montréal and Québec; then back to the Midwest— Denver, Kansas City, and Chicago—before a swing back eastward to Rochester, New York, and thence to Smith College in Northampton, Massachusetts, and Sweet Briar College in Virginia. Only then did the tour reach its climax in New York City. At its Town Hall, the quartet presented the second of their Beethoven Quartet cycles. The format consisted of six concerts this time (March 18–22, 1929), with the contents in a new organization:

Op. 18 no. 1; op. 59, no. 3, op. 127
Op. 74; op. 18, no. 2; op. 131
Op. 18, no. 3; op. 133; op. 59, no. 1
Op. 95; op. 18, no. 6; op. 132
Op. 18, no. 5; op. 130
Op. 18, no. 4; op. 135; op. 59, no. 2

In this format, the Pro Arte detached the *Grosse Fuge*, playing it separately from the opus 130, which they gave with its replacement finale. A partial reason for this arrangement may have been to accommodate a non-Beethoven intrusion into the series, the Piano Quintet by César Franck, with no less than Walter Gieseking as pianist. At any rate, the cycle won warm praise from critics.

Upon their return to Europe, the quartet undertook a major project as part of a string-quartet festival in Reims (April 30—May 5, 1929);

they performed a series of six concerts of twenty-three works surveying the literature from a Vivaldi arrangement and Haydn to Jerzy Fitelberg (including three works dedicated to the group), all of which won great acclaim. Another bold venture was a series of six concerts (October 1–21) in Germany, Czechoslovakia, and Austria—Hamburg, Munich, Berlin, Aussig (or, in Czech, Ústí nad Labem), Vienna. It is said that Richard Wagner's ninety-two-year-old widow, Cosima, was present for the Munich concert (October 10). On October 21, in the last of these cities, the group played the new Quartet no. 4 of Bartók, a composer whose works they had already been championing. Bartók himself called by telephone from Budapest, where he had listened by radio, and offered to dedicate the work to the Pro Arte when it was published.

October of 1929 continued to be busy. The new Bartók string quartet was brought to Les Concerts Pro Arte (October 25), and then there were two concerts in Geneva sponsored by Mrs. Coolidge. Between October 31 and November 11, the quartet was again in England (Cambridge, Blackpool). Before November was ended, they were in Turin. Then, for their first venture to Ireland, one concert (November 25) in Dublin. The month of December, 1929, was devoted to a good dozen concerts in fifteen different European cities in four countries ((Italy, Switzerland, France, and Belgium).

The beginning of 1930 found the Pro Arte members at sea once again (January 14–25), on the steamer SS *Montrose*, for their fourth North American tour. They gave the usual onboard concert on the first night. Arriving in Canada, they gave one performance in Québec (January 28) before moving on to launch another continent-crossing itinerary (February 2—March 16), with appearances in New York, Indianapolis, Philadelphia, Nashville, and Columbus, before taking up, after five days in California (Sacramento, Oakland, Santa Ana, Pasadena, Santa Barbara, and Los Angeles), a final appearance in Chicago. In this series, the stop at Mills College in Oakland (March 3) was to be the foursome's first encounter with an institution soon to be of great importance to them. After a private concert in New York, the Pro Arte members boarded the *Aquitaine* for the voyage home (March 20–26).

The spring of 1930 was occupied with concerts in Brussels and Reims, and climaxed with one in London (July 3). In September 1930 the quartet participated in an ISCM program in Liège. Another Austro-German tour—Munich, Vienna, Frankfurt, Nürnberg, Berlin— occupied most of October (1–18). They made a brief venture into Czechoslovakia at Pilsen (October 18). Early November found them in Switzerland (Saint-Gall, Morat, Geneva, Vevey, and Winterthur). The Pro Arte participated in a historical survey entitled Le Quatuor après Schumann (The Quartet since Schumann) in Liège (November 18–22) and swept through the British Isles (York, London, Westminster, Exeter, and Dublin) in December (4–15). Then they brought the year to a close with their third cycle of the Beethoven Quartets, their first in Brussels, in five concerts (December 25–29), using the same organization as for their first cycle in Barcelona in 1927. The king and queen attended the complete series, and local critics were ecstatic.

January of 1931 was marked by the definitive abandonment of a project that had been discussed since 1927: a tour of South and Central America. It was never to be. The quartet participated in sessions of Les Concerts Pro Arte in the early weeks of 1931. Then, for nearly two weeks in February (16–27), they gave concerts in a new sphere of outreach, Scandinavia (Copenhagen, Carlsberg, Ålborg, Stockholm). After some time in France, the group was in England for three concerts (March 10, 12, 16: Blackpool, Bangor, London). More work in Les Concerts Pro Arte drew them back to Brussels, but Reims figured importantly in the spring, especially for a series of four concerts (June 8–9, 11–12) as part of a Haydn-Mozart Festival there. The bicentennial of Haydn's birth was soon to come, while the one-hundred-and-seventy-fifth anniversary of Mozart's birth was at hand, making this combination timely. But the inclusion of seven of Haydn's quartets in this series, and the increasing programming of them by the group, foreshadowed a commitment to such literature that was soon to come.

In October the quartet made a tour of Central Europe (10–23: Vienna, Karlsbad, Reichenberg, Frankfurt). Due to growing political unrest there, this was to be the Pro Arte's last booking in Austria. November 1931 launched important new ventures, to be taken up in the next chapter.

# Repertoire

In the twenty-eight years of the Quatuor Pro Arte's existence as a Belgian ensemble—as divided arbitrarily between this and the next chapter—they developed into a relentlessly touring group. Consequently, the picture of their range of repertoire is central to understanding their evolving character. A definitive analysis of this repertoire is not likely, given the pitfalls and gaps in the surviving information. Many concerts were not documented, or lacked indication of the program contents. Nevertheless, thanks to Anne Van Malderen's indefatigable accumulation of data, it is possible to sketch a discernible picture of the quartet's performing patterns. This attempt at making such a sketch has therefore been dependent upon her work. The numerical computations are made entirely by the present author, who assumes full responsibility for any flaws, underestimations, or miscalculations in what follows.

Taking the quartet through their evolving configurations (including their military years) for this chapter's time span of 1911–31, it may be reckoned roughly that the group gave, or participated in, some 663 concert events. (This computation omits the many occasions in which members of the group performed in solo sonata functions; also omitted are many occasions when the group performed as part of the Pro Arte Concerts orchestra or large ensemble. Considered here, however, are trio performances involving the group, as well as augmented quartet and quintet appearances.)

The quartet's repertoire developed, as did the group's personality and experiences. From the outset, the players were deeply interested in the music of their own time. They also felt an obligation to promote new music by their own countrymen. Their programs are thus constantly marked by performances, many of them premieres, of music that they might repeat a few times or might not, but that rarely became part of their continuing repertoire. Most of these Belgian composers have not achieved enduring international recognition, and so their names now are no more than that for us today. Some twenty-eight of them might be noted: Adolphe Biarent, E. Bonnal, Michel Brusselmans, Désiré Defauw, L. Delcroix, L. Delune, Léon Du Bois, Paul Gilson, J. Hüttel, Albert Huybrechts, Joseph Jongen, C. Leirens, Guillaume Lekeu, R. van Leyden, Martin Lunssens. P. Menu, J. Perceval, F. Peyrot, Marcel Poot, Fernand Quinet (our early cellist), François Rasse, B. Reichl, Joseph Ryelandt, H. Sarly, K. Stimmer, Victor Vreuls, J. de Walque, and Théophile Ysaÿe. Of these, we might single out Lekeu (one work five times) and Jongen (six works in nineteen performances), a few of whose works have achieved some circulation and notability. Our players were also sympathetic to kindred French composers of relatively minor standing today, such as André Caplet, Maurice Delage, Charles Koechlin, and Paul Le Flem. One lone Dutchman, Willem Pijper, was minimally represented. Also embraced, however, were such Swiss contemporaries as Conrad Beck and Jean Binet.

Welcome was extended to the Latvian composer Jāzeps Vītols, as well as to the Poles Grzegorz Fitelberg and Karol Szymanowski.

From an early point, the players felt compelled to spread awareness of the music of the French school, music by composers of past, current, and oncoming generations. Even one of Gounod's now-neglected string quartets was given five performances. Of course, partly with patriotic sentiments, the group strongly embraced the Franco-Belgian César Franck, whose String Quartet and Piano Quintet (performed in our time period thirty-three and twelve times, respectively) would become among the group's staples. Less attention was given to Ernest Chausson, four of whose works received a combined total of ten performances. The group was closer to Gabriel Fauré, whose late attention to chamber music was directly contemporary with the Pro Arte's early years: his two Piano Quartets received two performances each, his Quartet a full ten, and his Piano Quintet five.

Two French composers were taken up in particular. Claude Debussy's *Danse sacrée et danse profane* received a mere two performances, but his Quartet in G Minor was played 121 times, just in this time period, and thus was established early as the ensemble's most favorite work by far. Maurice Ravel's Introduction and Allegro and his Trio for Piano and Strings were given four and six times respectively, but his Quartet in F received seventy-two performances, as a serious but distant competitor.

Of the older generation of Russian composers, Nikolai Rimsky-Korsakov was represented in only six performances, and Anatol Liadov the same. The daring Alexander Scriabin was accorded only four presentations of one minor piece. Of the works of Alexander Glazunov, only a marginal one, his suite of *5 Novelettes*, received no less than thirty-two documented performances, testifying to the quartet's enduring devotion to it.

As their ensemble became established, the Pro Arte closely followed the creativite output of their direct contemporaries. Important among these were the Parisian composers who came to be known as *Les Six*. And of these, by far the most immediately connected to the Pro Arte was Darius Milhaud, a close friend of Paul Collaer, and actively involved in the musical life of Brussels. The quartet members cultivated him from an early point, and worked with him recurrently. It was apparently for them (both Collaer and the QPA) that Milhaud made in 1926 an arrangement of his 1923 ballet, *La création du monde*, which they performed some six times during this period, while also participating in performances of the full score at least four times. The QPA was also devoted to the composer's earlier string quartets: they favored nos. 2 (six times), 4 (fourteen), 6 (eleven), and 7 (forty-three)—in all, eighty-two performances of five works. (The Pro Arte would go on to commission two more quartets from Milhaud.) As for the Swiss-born Arthur Honegger, against some twelve performances of three of his works there some twenty-four presentations of his Quartet no. 1. Though the quartet became involved with music of Francis Poulenc, that was only marginally, since the composer never wrote a work specifically for their ensemble. Georges Auric drew the quartet's attention—again, marginally. To this circle's number might be added Florent Schmitt, who inspired only a single performance.

A particular Swiss composer stands out in the Pro Arte's commitments: Ernest Bloch. While more attention would be given him later, up to 1931 his Piano Quintet would merit twelve documented performances. By comparison, Swiss composer, Ernst Levy's Second Quartet was played only twice.

One national group of composers with whom the Pro Arte established strong contacts were Italians. Notable, and from an early point, was Alfredo Casella. The group was involved twice in playing his *Sérénade,* while they gave five performances of his *Five Pieces for String Quartet,* and fourteen presentations of his Concerto for String Quartet, which he dedicated to the Pro Arte. Franco Alfano was given only three presentations, while a trifle by Ildebrando Pizzetti merited only one. Far more important was Gian Francesco Malipiero, the first three of his quartets given continuing attention: no. 1, twenty-five times; no. 2, nine, and no. 3, one. And Vittorio Rieti was accorded two performances of his *Madrigals* and no less than twenty-one of his First Quartet.

The Pro Arte also took serious interest in the work of at least three English composers. The Oboe Quintet of Arthur Bliss was accorded some five performances. Frank Bridge's Third Quartet was given three renderings. Eugene Goossens' Sextet received two performances, and his First Quartet four, but his *Phantasy Quartet* was played nineteen times.

Of Germans, most important was Paul Hindemith: his Quartet no. 4 was given eighteen performances as against five for the Fifth Quartet and two for the First Trio. Ernst Toch's Eleventh Quartet was given four readings, while a work by the unfortunately named Karl Marx received one. The Hungarian Ernst von Dohnányi received only two performances, while Zoltán Kodály's Second Quartet was given four presentations. A quartet by the Czech-born German composer Hans Krása and Václav Štěpán's Piano Quintet were each played twice. Later to acquire greater significance, the Czech Bohuslav Martinů drew four performances for his Quartet no. 2, and five for his Viola Quintet. The Pole Ludomir Michal Rogowski achieved one representation, while Russian-born cosmopolitan Nikolai Tcherepnin had another. The Polish-born Alexandre Tansman's Second Quartet was performed three times.

Though not a major contributor to the mainstream literature of the string quartet, Igor Stravinsky became important for the Pro Arte in early interactions and in two works with which they became identified: the *Three Pieces*, in whose extraordinary demands the group delighted (fifty-seven times), and the Concertino (fifty-nine times). The early Prokofiev was recognized only in his *Overture on Jewish Themes* (four times).

The Quatuor Pro Arte did not plunge as deeply into the Second Viennese School as the group's later configurations would. Nevertheless, its composers were by no means neglected in the early years. Indeed, Onnou himself had a great admiration for this particular modernist school. Pianist Gunnar Johansen recalled that, in one conversation he had with Onnou, the latter insisted that there were only two really important composers: Beethoven and Schoenberg! The group was actively involved in fourteen early performances of Arnold Schoenberg's notorious *Pierrot Lunaire*, while taking on his Second Quartet four times, and his Third twice. Alban Berg was represented by his Quartet (three times), his Chamber Concerto (once), and his *Lyric Suite* (once). Anton Webern's *Five Movements*, op. 5 were given eighteen performances. To this group might be added Ernst Krenek, represented by his Fourth and Fifth Quartets, one time each.

Even American composers attracted the quartet's attention. Two works by the little-remembered Daniel Stanley Smith were played, while Leo Sowerby was accorded one representation, as was a piece by Charles Martin Loeffler. Louis Gruenberg's *Four Indiscretions* was given ten performances and Leo Ornstein's Piano Quintet was played thrice, as was Nikolai Berezowski's *Thème et variations fantastiques*. Though not a conventional composer for string quartet, Aaron Copland won three performances of his piano trio *Vitebsk*.

Before finally turning to the Pro Arte's investment in the "basic repertoire," we might note an unintended survey of some "pre-basic" pioneers, in pieces mostly adapted for modern string quartet: Claude

LeJeune, Jean-Baptiste Loeillet (one, seven times), François-André Philidor, Jean-Philippe Rameau, and J. S. Bach. Notable in this group however, is Antonio Vivaldi: an arrangement of his Concerto op. 5, no. 3 was favored recurrently some nineteen times.

Which finally brings us to that basic repertoire of string-quartet literature with which the Pro Arte would necessarily come to terms in their early decades.

The obvious starting point would be Joseph Haydn, with whose quartets the Pro Arte would become uniquely identified through its incomplete recording project soon to be considered. While the group was not as deeply experienced in the Haydn quartets as they would later become, the players by no means neglected these works. References are made to performances of thirty-seven quartets not specifically identified. Beyond those, it would seem that a total of seventy-nine performances were given of twelve quartets. Documented reports indicate that the group sampled all but seven (opp. 1, 2, 3, 9, 42, 50, 55) of the sixteen published quartet sets. Four of the twelve were performed only once, but all the others a range of several times. Clearly the most favored was op. 71 no. 1 (twenty-five times), followed by op. 74, no. 3 (seventeen times) and op. 77, no. 1 (ten times), op. 76, no. 2 (nine times), op. 54, no. 2 (seven times). Opus 64, no. 5 and op. 74, no. 1 were played four times each, as with two more from opus 76 (nos. 3, 4).

Wolfgang Amadeus Mozart's quartets were more intensely explored. A total of one hundred and twenty-eight performances were given of eight works. The earliest ones were approached gingerly: K. 160 and K. 171 each twice, K. 173 four times. Otherwise, interest was focused on the final nine quartets. By far the most favored were K. 428 (twenty-six times), and K. 421 (twenty-four times), followed by K. 575 (eighteen times), K. 387 (fifteen times), K. 465 and K. 590 (ten times each), and K. 458 (eight times). Lesser attention was given to the Flute Quartet K. 285 (once), to the Piano Quartet K. 478 and the Clarinet Quintet K. 581 (each three times), or the String Quintet K. 516 (twice).

The Pro Arte's engagement with Ludwig van Beethoven's quartets was to be more fully defined, of course, as the group moved through their full thirty-five cycles up to 1940. The initial four cycles given up to 1931 had only begun to affect the formulation of their repertoire. By that year, nevertheless, the quartet gradually worked their way into the Beethoven oeuvre, mastering all eighteen of the full array of these works, in a total of one hundred and nineteen performances. Several personal favorites emerged along the way: op. 59, no. 2 (nineteen times); op. 95 (eighteen times); op. 74; and op. 18, no. 2 (twelve times each). The players chose to present opus 130 fourteen times in its original form, restoring the *Grosse Fuge*, op. 133, as its original finale. (It also gave the Fugue itself separately at least three times.) Only once did they present the "posthumous" form of opus 130, with its substitute finale. The remaining ten quartets were performed from one to four times each.

Franz Schubert's works were approached more cautiously, but still affectionately. Other than D. 93 (once), only the late works were seriously addressed. The *Quartettsatz*, D. 703, was presented only once at first, but the "Rosamunde" Quartet, D. 804, eight times, and *Tod und das Mädchen*, D. 810, sixteen times. In addition, the great Quintet D. 956 was managed six times.

Giuseppe Verdi's sole quartet was played eight times. The Pro Arte was slow to approach Mendelssohn's chamber works, venturing only two of them up to 1931. By contrast, Robert Schumann's chamber works were amply taken up, in fifty-four performances of five works: the Trio for Piano and Strings, op. 80, was done twice; of the opus 41 Quartets, no. 1 was given five times, no. 2 ten times, and no. 3 no less than twenty-eight times; and the Piano Quintet was accorded nine performances.

Of the two quartets of Bedřich Smetana, no. 1 was played four times. Alexander Borodin's First Quartet was played twice but, by contrast, the Second was given forty-one readings, establishing it as another of the quartet's long-term favorites. Tchaikovsky merited only a single performance of his Quartet no. 3.

The Pro Arte was slow and cautious in coming to the chamber works of Johannes Brahms, a composer for whom Onnou himself had a private distaste. Up to 1931 they played the Quartet op. 51, no. 1 six times, and the op. 51 no. 2 twelve times. Beyond those performances, there were six of the Piano Quintet, and one each of the Clarinet Quintet and of the Sextet No. 1. Hugo Wolf's *Italian Serenade*, later to be a favorite, was done only once at this point. But at least the mature quartets of Antonín Dvořák would early attract the group's attention. While the opus 51 quartet gained two performances, the opus 96 ("American") quartet launched its continuing devotion from the group with twenty-seven performances by 1931.

A "modernist" whose works our ensemble followed closely was Béla Bartók, whose compositions would certainly take their place in the canonic literature. With promptitude, the group played the first four of his quartets, respectively, fourteen, four, four, and nineteen times—the last of these, no. 4, being specifically dedicated to the Pro Arte.

Once again, all these numbers are somewhat tentative, since many concerts were reported without specifications of their programs, while there were likely to have been performances not properly documented at all. From what problematic data is available, however, we have already estimated a plausible, and impressive, figure of six hundred sixty-three performances during the generously defined spread of 1912–31. Within those, we could perceive a possible figure of 193 individual works presented. Still, even with these tentative figures, we can have some picture of just how ambitious the Pro Arte's working repertoire seems to have been in the early decades.

# 2

# THE ONNOU YEARS, II

# (1932–40)

## Reputation, Landmarks, and Crisis

By the end of 1931, the Quatuor Pro Arte had reached the full pla-
teau of eminence; their ensemble was perfectly integrated, notable
for precision and clarity. The four members played as one, instinc-
tively, as a token of their total commitment to chamber music playing.
Each of them undertook ventures (often as part of the group's concerts) into the realm of sonatas and occasional solo pieces. But they
had long given up any sideline of orchestral playing, they no longer
had to do theater work for subsistence, and their full commitment was
to the group's identity and operations. They were more of a family to
each other than they were to their own natural families.

All of them were married, and all but Onnou had children. Their
balance of local performances in Brussels with relentless rounds of
touring kept them exceedingly active from season to season. This
became their burden: their travels on tight schedules strained the
energies they wished to put into their performances, so as to sustain
their group reputation. Yet they would attend postconcert receptions
or linger to mingle with the audiences at the cost of reduced sleep
before early departures the next mornings. As the years passed, the
players could only spend a month at home in Brussels during the
summers, and perhaps a brief time at Christmas. Otherwise, they con-
sumed most of their lives "on the road," living out of their luggage.
Milhaud observed of their life that their schedule allowed them no

time to visit the great museums and monuments of the European cities where they played: "They know only the concert hall, the train station, and the hotel room where they rehearse tirelessly."

They were all in generally good health, and of mature ages. All but one of them (Onnou) were somewhat balding, prompting Tully Potter to call the group "Poirot Lunaire"—thereby committing a pun that combined the image of Agatha Christie's famous (balding) Belgian detective with the title of the Schoenberg work with which they were early involved.

We might well pause here to say something about these four men as individuals.

Alphonse Onnou (1893–1940) was age thirty-eight in 1931. The instrument on which he settled was one built for him in 1929 by René Aërts of Brussels, designed after a violin by the Guadagnini clan. Gifted with extraordinary technical facility, he was also a musician of deep understanding, clearly the intellectual anchor of the group. He was also notable as a "quick study" of scores, with a remarkable memory. At the same time, he was a warm human being, with a wonderful sense of humor. Though quiet in manner, he possessed resources of calm authority and tact that also made him the emotional anchor of the group, preventing tensions from growing out of hand. The other three men were deeply devoted to him. He was the only one of the four to investigate a role as concerto soloist, and that only briefly. First, he played Beethoven's Violin Concerto in Brussels: twice in 1935 (November 23, 24) with the Brussels Symphony Orchestra under Hermann Scherchen; and once (February 8, 1940) with the Belgian Radio Orchestra under Franz André. Both occasions had been organized to pay tribute to Onnou. In 1934 he played a Wieniawski tidbit as well.

Two anecdotes point up two of Onnou's predilections. He was an avid chain-smoker. Toward the end of one concert in Stockton, California, Onnou was puzzled to hear giggling, not only from the audience but also from his fellow players. It seems that, during intermission, he had carelessly stuffed an open pack of cigarettes into his trouser pocket. As he played, they began to trickle out one by one. Recognizing the humor of it, he readily joined in the laughter. Another of Onnou's delights was drinking beer and buying beer for his friends. Once, when the quartet played with German colleagues, they all met to celebrate after the concert. Onnou and his colleagues ordered a toast at their own expense. This was so well received that they ordered a second round of beer, again at their own expense. When the Germans called for a third round, however, the foursome quietly stole away.

Laurent Halleux (1897–1964) was age thirty-four in 1931. His instrument was a 1930 violin by Emile Laurent, after the Guadagnini family. Quiet, gentle, even shy, he was a superbly qualified player. As noted, in the quartet's earliest years, he would assume the first violin part in Mozart and the earlier composers, while Onnou took the first chair for Romantic and modern works. It was Mrs. Coolidge who, particularly favoring Onnou, insisted that the latter permanently be the first violinist. Halleux accepted this gracefully, and he brought special sensitivity to the often-underestimated second-violin role. His playing style was noted as particularly sweet, with a silvery elegance, perhaps augmenting Onnou's slightly more restrained tone as a unifying stability.

Germain Prévost (1891–1987) was age forty in 1931—the oldest of the players and, ironically, to be the most long-lived. His instrument was a 1702 viola by Carlo Bergonzi. As against the seriousness of the other players, Prévost projected a colorful, even flamboyant personality, addicted to tension-breaking wit and even practical jokes. The story is told that, before one concert, the two violinists detected a strange odor coming from their instruments. It proved to be Limburger cheese, delicately spread on their chin rests, and Prévost's grin revealed the author of the prank. But he is remembered by his students for his warmth and skills. He was particularly active in playing chamber music beyond the quartet realm. Concerned about the relatively small literature for his instrument, he commissioned some for it, at least one piece in memory of Onnou. The many recollections he has left us provide us with a quite vivid picture of the quartet's early history.

Prévost's role in rescuing the nascent quartet from World War I limitations was the result of his relationship with his older brother, Arthur Prévost, who was director of Belgian military musical life. As we shall see, Germain played a crucial role in steering the quartet through their survival after Onnou's death.

Robert Maas (1901–48) was age thirty in 1931, the youngest member of the group. His instrument was a 1729 cello by Domenico Montagnana. Of a serious personality, he nevertheless had a poetic bent and his love for travel made him the least troubled by the relentless life of touring. He could easily match Onnou's technique and was regarded as one of the outstanding quartet cellists of his day. His brother, Marcel Maas, was a fine pianist who often collaborated in Pro Arte concerts.

Agnes Albert, who played privately with them in quintets, provided vivid characterizations of the four men: "Onnou was a wonderfully kind and jolly person; it was all at a tremendously high level with him. Halleux was rather reticent. Prévost was the most individual member of the group, almost Gallic in his originality and fantasy and totally irrepressible in his enthusiasm. Maas was very gentle, like a giant; he was the tall one—the others were rather small men. Playing with them was marvelous—no quartet players were like them. It was one sound, very unified."

Clearly, these four men made a superbly balanced, stylistically integrated ensemble. As early as 1925 a British critic stated: "One has never heard them surpassed, and rarely equalled, in volume and beauty of tone, in accuracy of intonation, and in perfection of balance between the parts." Some fifteen years later, a famous comment was made by one of the group's admirers and collaborators, the pianist Gunnar Johansen: "I consider the Pro Arte Quartet as the finest organization of its kind in existence, the perfect quadrangle that makes a perfect circle."

✧ ✧ ✧

The 1931–32 season was to prove a pivotal one in at least two ways, among some others. First, there was the launching of the Pro Arte's recording activity. Second, through Mrs. Coolidge, there was the involvement with the annual summer programs of Mills College in California.

It was an important step for the Quatuor Pro Arte, at the peak of their maturity, to become involved with the recording industry at an early stage of that industry's development. A commercial market for recordings of short pieces of varying categories had quickly developed, despite the economic restraints brought by the Great Depression. A public appetite for recordings of "serious" (i.e., "classical") music was slower to develop. Beyond a plethora of single-side tidbits, both complete symphonies and complete operas had been ventured early on, in spite of the initial limitation of two minutes and then, of four to five minutes of time to each 78-rpm side. These extended recordings resulted in multi-disc albums of enormous bulk and weight. (A 1903 recording of Verdi's *Ernani*, even heavily cut, ran to forty single-sided discs.)

Beyond spatial concerns, there were sonic limitations. From the late 1880s, as pioneered by Thomas Edison and others, recordings were made and issued on cylinders. Edison produced them until 1929. But in 1894 Emile Berliner's flat gramophone discs went on the market, and the more efficient technology of their duplication gave them progressive superiority over the cylinders (which were also more cumbersome to store). Both media, however, employed the same recording process, known as "acoustical," in which sound was awkwardly captured in sonic horns and transferred directly into record grooves. By 1925, the new technology of "electrical" recording had been launched. That allowed the capturing of sound by microphones for electrical processing into the groves of wax discs (eventually of shellac). This process greatly expanded the frequency range for a fuller, more natural sound.

One of the titans (perhaps the first) in the history of recording classical music was Fred (Frederic William) Gaisberg (1873–1951). An American by birth (in Washington, DC), Gaisberg was trained as a pianist: in 1889, still a teenager, he made cylinder recordings as an accompanist, and in 1894 he toured the United States with the great soprano Nellie Melba as her pianist. But he was also interested in the evolving recording medium, and became a sales manager and technician for the original Columbia Company, an Edison branch. He knew and worked with Berliner, and was involved with the very beginnings of the acoustical 78-rpm disc. He gradually phased out his performing career to become a "recording expert," a position foreshadowing the later designation of "recording producer."

Gaisberg's experience as a professional musician was the foundation of his wide acquaintance with leading performers of the day and his growing round of travels as an "artist recruiter." His first recordings of Enrico Caruso in 1902 were only the most famous examples of his preserving the voices of many of the great singers of the later nineteenth and early twentieth centuries; later, many of the most eminent instrumentalists joined the procession. The fabulous success of Gaisberg's Caruso recordings expanded the audience for classical music through celebrity attractions. He had settled in London, where he was now a key figure in the employ of the Gramophone Company (founded 1898), which went through various changes to become known as His Master's Voice (of the listening dog logo) or HMV. In 1931, HMV merged with Columbia to become Electric and Musical Industries (EMI), affiliated primarily (though not exclusively) with the American RCA Victor

Company. Patient, tactful, and charming, Gaisberg had become the ideal mentor to and supervisor of recording artists.

Having shifted decisively to the new electrical process and wax disc technology, EMI in 1929 acquired the property on Abbey Road, in St. John's Wood, London, as its new domestic recording venue, a set of studios fitted with the latest electronic facilities. It was officially inaugurated when, on November 12, 1931, Sir Edward Elgar conducted his "Land of Hope and Glory." Its studios have since become identified by an unenlightened public solely as the site of the Beatles' recording activities; but it has been, over eighty years, the venue of some of the greatest recordings of classical music ever made. In 2011, as part of the expiring EMI company as a whole, it was sold to Universal-Warner-Sony BMG.

New opportunities were ironically furthered by the decline in sales amid the Great Depression, prompting the idea of recording series sold by subscription, with the advance collection of fees supporting the recording sessions. Gaisberg's assistant, Walter Legge, a passionate lover of German lieder, organized the Hugo Wolf Society as sponsor for a series of issues of that composer's songs, launched also in the autumn of 1931. The project was such a great success that its continuation was guaranteed. It also encouraged imitation, resulting in the monumental Beethoven Sonata Society series for which Artur Schnabel recorded the complete piano sonatas of that composer.

Gaisberg took readily to this idea. A great admirer of the violinist Fritz Kreisler, he organized the Beethoven Violin Sonata Society series in which that one player recorded the full cycle. Gaisberg was interested in chamber music, which was making only a slow progress onto records. The Léner Quartet was one that made some acoustic recordings, as did the early Budapest Quartet. The latter group was taken up by Gaisberg, and made their first electrical recordings for HMV. Gaisberg conducted negotiations with Adolf Busch with plans to record him in solo works but also to use his Busch Quartet in a number of works. Excited by the Society ventures taking shape, Gaisberg hoped for a Beethoven Quartet series. That did not come to full fruition, though a number of fine recordings of works by Beethoven, Schubert, and others did.

The eighty-three string quartets of Joseph Haydn were as yet little represented in recordings. To be sure, the Viennese Fitzner Quartet had undertaken this cycle on the brink of World War I, but in the old and inadequate acoustic method. Accordingly, one of the projects that Gaisberg envisioned, as early as 1930, was a presentation of all of Haydn's surviving quartets in a new cycle. This was to be associated with the work of Walter Wilson Cobbett (1847–1937), a successful business man who was also an amateur violinist and musicologist, patron and promoter of chamber music, publisher and author—in many ways a kind of British counterpart to Mrs. Coolidge.

One of Gaisberg's last projects was a comprehensive new performing cycle of the Haydn Quartets, based on Cobbett's edition of these works, and as sponsored by HMV itself. Seeking performers to realize this project, Gaisberg followed his now personal pursuit of stylistic consistency by having only one group do the complete job, rather than farming it out to a number of groups. A deal with the Pro Arte was discussed apparently as early as April of 1931. Gaisberg undertook it on the understanding that the Pro Arte players knew the complete Haydn repertoire. He was assured by the quartet members, with a little bending of the truth, that this was so. In point of fact, there is documentation that they had played only about fifteen in public—though Prévost later thought they had known twenty-eight.

The Pro Arte gave a concert in London on November 18, 1931, consisting of three Haydn quartets. Moreover, the group was known to be committed to a series of Haydn Bicentennial Festival concerts in Brussels in mid-December. On the strength of these facts and the enthusiastic reception of the November 18 concert, Gaisberg settled the deal and the contract was signed on November 23.

Immediately after performing their fourth Beethoven cycle at Cambridge (November 24–28) the plucky players undertook their first recording sessions. These took place at first not in the new Abbey Road facilities, but in those of Queen's Small Hall. Held on November 30, December 1 and 2, these sessions captured a total of four quartets, drawn from four different opus sets. They also generated a famous incident. The players had understood that they would deal with four scores they knew, one of them being op. 20, no. 4. Instead, they found on their desks the music for op. 20, no. 2, which they had never played before. Prévost pointed this out to Onnou with alarm, but Onnou hissed, "Shut up, we will play it!" And they did, from sight. Fortunately, by this time the Pro Arte players were masters of sight-reading. Their spontaneous choice of tempos for the work became gospel for many performers of it thereafter. Prevost recalled that, after these sessions, the group repaired to the nearest pub to play darts and to "get drunk in fifteen minutes."

In 1932, the Haydn Quartet Society was organized as the umbrella under which the Pro Arte's Haydn recordings would be issued. The eventual output was eight volumes of seven two-sided discs per set containing three or four quartets each. Though the Pro Arte players were hardly Haydn specialists, these recordings gave them authoritative status for long thereafter, and were an enormous factor in spreading their reputation ever more widely. It is interesting, however, that recent books on the history of recordings all but totally ignore the Pro Arte Haydn project. Even Gaisberg himself, in his autobiography, had nothing whatsoever to say about the Pro Arte and Haydn, perhaps because of his preoccupation with big-name star performers over ensembles.

In the eight years that followed, the quartet worked in a series of fifteen sets of sessions totaling forty-one days. They managed to record twenty-seven Haydn quartets, plus two falsely attributed to him, plus twenty-three pieces by fifteen other composers—a grand total of fifty compositions. They did this strictly as a sideline to their touring. The sessions were fitted in amid concerts they were giving in London, or sometimes at the conclusion of a season. They were virtually never rehearsed, but done "on the run," drawing often upon repertoire with which they were immediately working in concerts.

All this was testimony to the four men's dogged energy. They and the HMV technicians admired and trusted each other for their skills. According to one anecdote, after a long recording session, the quartet players were conversing with a studio technician while packing up their instruments. When the technician revealed that he had never heard of Bartók before, the musicians promptly sat down, unpacked their instruments, and played through a complete Bartók quartet for him. Reports vary as to whether it was no. 1 or no. 4. The latter had been dedicated to them, and both were in their active repertoire, though the former might seem to be the more likely choice. How better could the members of the Quatuor Pro Arte demonstrate their self-sacrificing ardor for their music?

 ✇   ✇   ✇

Carrying on the momentum of their initial Haydn recordings, as well as honoring their prior commitment, the Pro Arte gave in Brussels the two concerts that were their contribution to the Haydn Festival, on December 17 and 21, 1931: playing four quartets each, including two of the three they had just recorded (and among them the op. 2

no. 2 poison pill). The new year began with a round of concerts in France and Belgium, plus a series of twelve concerts in Denmark (January 12–29, 1932), that prompted the quartet's first involvement with the music of Carl Nielsen—doubtless in memory of that composer's death the previous October. Concerts in Belgium and Italy in February were capped by a stay in March in Spain, mainly for the fifth of the Pro Arte's Beethoven Quartet cycles, given in Madrid (March 4–10) in the five-concert format first set in 1927. In Marseille on March 20, they appeared in the world premiere of Martinů's Concerto for String Quartet and Orchestra, written for and dedicated to them. The growing frequency of Haydn quartets in the group's programming was emphasized by their participation of a new round of Haydn Bicentennial Festival concerts in Brussels (April 4–15). This was followed a day later (April 15) by a concert in Antwerp, in which the Pro Arte replaced the Roth Quartet in an all-Haydn program.

Soon after, in late April 1932, the quartet embarked on the SS *Berengaria* for their fifth visit to the United States. They stopped in Boston for a pair of morning-afternoon concerts on May 1, one of which included their first attention to the quartets of the American Roy Harris. They then did two days of broadcasting in New York (May 9–10). The east coast was not their real destination, however, but rather California, across the continent, which they reached in late May of 1932. There they gave concerts in Los Angeles and Santa Barbara, and especially at Claremont's Pomona College. By mid-June, they had reached their intended destination: Mills College in Oakland.

❧ ❧ ❧

Mills College is a small liberal arts institution founded in 1852 and designed exclusively for young women. It early identified itself with a strong program of music teaching and performance, welcoming an eventual roster of some of the leading performers and composers over the years. Mrs. Coolidge, a graduate of Stanford University and personally fond of the state of California, was generous in her patronage of several educational institutions there, including Mills. She was a personal friend of its Dean of Music, Luther Marchant, and during the 1920s began support of its summer music program—amid her arranging of work for a number of ensembles there and elsewhere. She took to residing at Mills each summer, even studying with its composition and harmony professor, Domenico Brescia, at age 67. There had been some feelings of jealousy of her support of programs in other institutions, but Mrs. Coolidge smoothed over problems by offering to sponsor the Pro Arte's residence there in the summer of 1932. (The group had already performed there once in March 1930.) Discussions were pursued as to just how much of a teaching obligation the players would bear, but terms were agreed upon, and the quartet arrived at the college on June 17, 1932. Between June 19 and July 27 they gave a total of thirteen concerts (one of which was actually at Stanford University), with a break for a concert (July 12) at Dominican College in San Rafael. Maas's brother Marcel also came with the quartet, contributing piano performance and instruction.

The residence was a complete success. The college's faculty was immensely impressed by the Pro Arte's artistry, while the players entered into their teaching duties with enthusiasm. It was clear that they would be welcomed back in successive summers. The terms of their contract were important in setting the models for what would be established at the University of Wisconsin eight years later. The introduction of teaching into their activities would also foreshadow the quartet's future transformation in Madison. More immediately, the Pro Arte's almost regular participation in the Mills College summer sessions would become an important anchor to the United States for them.

&#x204A;  &#x204A;  &#x204A;

Directly from Oakland the quartet returned east and boarded the SS *Mauretania* for the return voyage. They gave two shipboard concerts, on August 6 and 7, the programs including two Haydn quartets (among them their favored op. 33 no. 3). They were soon back at work. They spent four days in London in early October for the second round of their HMV recording sessions, their first in the Abbey Road Studio 3. In that, their Haydn assignment was softened to take advantage of the then-young Artur Rubinstein's presence with a Brahms piano quartet. (Full of himself, Rubinstein demanded fifty percent. But he backed down when Onnou refused to play on those terms.) Also in these sessions, the Pro Arte ventured a recording they never finished of the "Voces intimae" Quartet by Jean Sibelius—a work they never played in public. (That test take was destroyed.) After a stop in Cardiff, the quartet was off to Denmark for eight concerts (October 18–November 2), mostly in Copenhagen, including their final two performances of a Nielsen Quartet (no. 4).

Then it was off to Great Britain for concerts (November 7–January 1) in Edinburgh, Bradford, London, and Cambridge. Their centerpiece was the sixth Beethoven Quartet cycle in London (November 17–22, 1932), in the five-day format of 1927, while the capstone was a series of what were described as "Five Historical Recitals" in Cambridge (November 26–30). December and early January were spent mainly on the continent. The quartet returned to London for two days (February 7, 8, 1933) at HMV's Abbey Road studios for the third round of recordings—this one including a Bloch piano quintet with Casella. March was marked by the seventh Beethoven Quartet cycle (opp. 14–21, still on the five-day format), held in Brussels as part of a celebration of the quartet's twentieth anniversary. A background to such festivities was the designation of the Pro Arte as the official quartet to the Belgian royal court the previous year—doubtless giving Queen Elisabeth new opportunities to join in playing with the members.

In the midst of all this occurred a poignant episode. Georges Charbonneaux was a wealthy patron of Reims who had sponsored a number of concerts, both public and private, in his city—including the six-concert series on the history of the string quartet (April 30—May 8, 1929). Charbonneaux was himself a competent pianist, often playing quintets privately with the group. The obviously very cordial relationship between them was soon given dramatic confirmation. Gravely ill, Charbonneaux had been in southern France but, in need of surgery, moved to Paris in the first week of March 1933, staying at the Hotel St. James. According to his grandson, Patrick Chatelin, apparently on March 6—between their Epernay concert (March 4) and the beginning of their Beethoven cycle in Brussels (March 7)—the Quatuor Pro Arte visited Charbonneaux and played for him the Cavatina from Beethoven's opus 130 quartet. Charbonneaux went on to his operation on March 11: on the next day he seemed to be recovering, but then died in the afternoon of March 13; his funeral was held on March 16. The quartet was not able to make an appearance in his home city until March 22, at which time, it is said, the group again played the Beethoven Cavatina, either as part of the program or as an addition, as their last gesture toward their deceased patron and friend.

Many decades later, the original QPA's ailing violist Prévost might well have thought back to that tribute when parallel gestures were made to him by the later Pro Arte Quartet, in his last declining years in California.

Concluding March of 1933 with its concert in Reims and one in Marseille, the quartet spent much of April rushing through Italy (Bergamo, Rome, Palermo, Milan, Mantua, Rimini, Verona, Padua). By late April they were in Spain (Barcelona, Oviedo, Bilbao, Madrid), returning to Italy (Rome, Asolo) in mid-May. In London for a concert in tribute to Elgar (May 16, 1933), they used the opportunity for more HMV recording sessions: the fourth, on two separate days (May 18, 25) mainly devoted to the Franck Quartet. Sandwiched in between was one appearance in a Shakespeare tribute at Stratford-upon-Avon (May 21).

With a barely caught breath, the quartet took ship (the *Europa*) on June 2, 1933, for their sixth visit to the United States. Going immediately by train from New York, they arrived mid-month for their second summer at Mills College, their exclusive destination of this trip. There, in Oakland, between June 18 and July 16, they presented six concerts, plus an inserted one at Palo Alto (July 14). Their programs included a work by Copland and one by Domenico Brescia (Mrs. Coolidge's composition teacher). The quartet returned home for the rest of the summer, but by autumn the players were ready for yet another—their seventh—sailing to the United States. Their first activities were in Chicago, where they gave three concerts (October 18, 20, 22), whose programs made a point of including American works—one quartet each by George W. Chadwick, John Alden Carpenter, and Roy Harris. Between October 28 and November 11, they were at points on the eastern seaboard (Pittsfield, New York, Boston, Harvard University, Wellesley, and Yale University at New Haven). One of the New York events was a private one, at the home of Morton Gould.

The quartet was back in England in time for their eighth Beethoven Quartet cycle in Cambridge (November 29, 30, December 1, 2, 4; five-concert plan). This was followed by a busy round, the fifth, of recording sessions for HMV (December 8, 11, 12)—the last day combined with a public concert!

After Christmas at home, and a charity concert on January 1, 1934, the quartet plunged into more Beethoven with a single three-quartet concert in Hamburg, as arranged by prior contract. But the new Nazi regime had suspended such contracts and, on their way homeward, the players were arrested by the police at Aachen, causing an outcry in the press. Assurances from the conductor Wilhelm Furtwängler won their release. That was enough for them to vow no further concerts in Germany, a vow the quartet kept. From Hamburg they proceeded to Copenhagen for the ninth full Beethoven Quartet cycle (January

10, 12, 16, 19, 22, 23, 26, on the six-concert plan first used in 1929). But those six concerts were punctuated with quick digressions to cities around Denmark and Sweden. From January 31 to February 16, they were in the British Isles with stops in Bristol, Dublin, Cardiff, Bangor, Edinburgh, Glasgow, and London. Amid those, they found time to fit in their sixth (January 31) and seventh (February 11, 14, 15) recording sessions at Abbey Road, working in both cases with the great pianist Artur Schnabel.

Amid concerts in late February and mid-April (Luxemburg, Strasbourg, Marseille, Brussels), there came another landmark event in the quartet's history. On April 19, 1934, Paul Collaer's Concerts Pro Arte gave a final presentation, closing a distinguished history of a dozen years. Onnou had been deeply involved in their organization from the start, and his quartet had participated regularly in their events. Mrs. Coolidge took the occasion to launch her replacement operation, the Concerts Pro Arte–Coolidge, whose origins she liked to trace back to 1923. The label had already been used for many of the concerts by the quartet she had sponsored, but it became the exclusive one for the group's events—at least those in the United States—beginning with one in June 1934 during the ensuing California residence.

That was the ultimate goal of the quartet's seventh voyage to the United States. Commencing activities on the eastern seaboard, the group focused (May 12–19, 1934) on several American educational institutions (Bryn Mawr College in Pennsylvania, Princeton University in New Jersey, and the Peabody Conservatory in Baltimore). They made a quick stop for a concert in Washington (May 22), augmented by a visit to Mrs. Coolidge's apartment there. As she loved to do, she sat them down to play quintets with her at the piano. (She was also particularly fond of playing sonatas with Onnou. She had corresponded with Onnou as early as March to make just such plans, and more.) Having taken a large studio suite in Los Angeles, she proposed that, when they were all in California, the quartet could work with some students in it. She also projected times for Sunday excursions around the shore areas before settling in at Mills College.

Mrs. Coolidge, in fact, had a capacious touring car in which she loved being driven around by her handyman and chauffeur, one Sherman. She particularly enjoyed going on drives with "her boys," the four Belgians—or the "Brussels bunch," as she also called them.

After two concerts in Pasadena and a preliminary one at Mills, the quartet settled in for the third of their summer residences at the college. As part of that, they contributed a series of six concerts (June 17, 24, July 1, 8, 15, 22, 1934), each devoted to a "national" literature (respectively, German, Belgian, Italian, French, Russian, Austrian). These were interlaced with the group's tenth Beethoven Quartet cycle (June 22, 29, July 6, 13, 20, 27, six-concert plan), at Stanford University in Palo Alto. Those concerts were the first presented under the sponsoring label of the Concerts Pro Arte–Coolidge. This summer's activity ended with three concerts in San Francisco (July 29–31).

Returned home, the Pro Arte launched into a summer–autumn schedule that prefigured a veritable Beethoven Quartet orgy. First, there was a series of five concerts (August 10, 12, 15, 16, 20, 1934) for the Belgian radio. It was then off to Great Britain in November for a round of four concerts (Leeds, Aberdeen, Woking, Cambridge, Oxford). Amid these, the group fitted in two more rounds of recording sessions for HMV: the eighth, of three days (October 29–31), and the ninth, of three extended days (November 2, 3, 19), the latter involving Artur Schnabel again. There was even a quick trip to Reims (November 14). December saw a concert in Paris and two in Madrid.

January of 1935 was devoted to concerts at two Belgian universities: Antwerp (January 4, 14) and Ghent (13, 16). By late January, the quartet was off for their eighth visit to the United States. Along with quick stops at Bryn Mawr (January 24, February 2), there appear to have been seven concerts in Washington. Mrs. Coolidge had made her personal plans for this stay. She had urged Onnou to come a day early, so that the two of them could do some sonata playing, followed by "some quintet fun together" with all four Belgians. Two concerts in New York (February 18, 22) marked this relatively brief transatlantic visit. They were back in Brussels in early March, and then slipped over to London for a concert on March 9, preceded by their ninth round of HMV recording, during four busy days at Abbey Road (March 6–9).

Then the group returned to Beethoven Quartets, on a grand scale and in another innovative fashion. First, the Pro Arte now organized their cycles in six-concert units, abandoning earlier formats and presenting the quartets in chronological order by opus numbers (again with the *Grosse Fuge* separated from opus 130). This seems to have worked well for the other novelty: what were called "overlapping" (*imbriquées*) concerts, in leapfrogging sequences around five cities. This was apparently the idea of manager Verhuyk. Effectively, this represented as many full cycles: the group's twelfth at Liège (March 18, 25, April 1, 8, 29, May 6), the thirteenth at Antwerp (March 19, 26,

April 2, 9, 30, May 7), the fourteenth at Brussels (March 20, 27, April 3, 10, May 2, 8), the fifteenth at Louvain (March 21, 28, April 4, 11, May 1, 9), the sixteenth at Ghent (March 22, 29, April 5, 12, May 3, 10). The players seemed to keep track of where they were sufficiently to graft into the same six dates of the Brussels performances a cycle of six "History of the String Quartet" concerts, plus an extra Concert Pro Arte–Coolidge event in Brussels (March 30). All that constitutes thirty-six concerts over six weeks.

Nor did they pause for breath, it would appear. After two Bartók performances at the Sorbonne (May 11, 12, 1935), they gave two more concerts in Paris, mainly devoted to works commissioned by or dedicated to Mrs. Coolidge. And then they were off to the United States again for their ninth visit there, with California as the only destination. (This time, Onnou brought his wife along.) For this 1935 summer (June 23–July 31), the quartet again resorted to the "overlapping" technique, presenting twelve concerts at Mills College in Oakland, but also four at Stanford in Palo Alto, specifically to serve the Coolidge California Students Concerts, another of Mrs. Coolidge's benevolences. At one of the Oakland concerts (July 7), the quartet gave the American premiere of Berg's *Lyric Suite*. (A report of their playing the Mozart Clarinet Quintet on July 10 with Benny Goodman is somehow a confusion, as is discussed in appendix A.)

After some rest, the quartet resumed operations with a pair of concerts (October 22, 25, 1935) in Copenhagen, before spending much of November in London for the seventeenth Beethoven Quartet cycle, using the now-established six-concert chronological format by opus numbers. While in London, the players stole time (November 16, 18, 19) for their tenth round of HMV recording sessions, working again with Schnabel. These they followed with concerts in London, Newcastle, and Blackpool. Back in Brussels, Onnou gave his first two performances of the Beethoven Violin Concerto (November 23, 24). The quartet then gave two successive Beethoven cycles at French universities during December: the eighteenth at Aix-en-Provence, the nineteenth at the Sorbonne in Paris. The year 1935 was rounded off with a concert each in Marseille and Bordeaux.

There was yet more Beethoven to pursue in January 1936. The twentieth quartet cycle was presented in Brussels, under Pro Arte–Coolidge auspices, again in the six-concert, opus-number format (January 6, 8, 10, 11, 15, 17), amid which concerts in Liège and Ghent were interwoven, followed by more appearances through the month at Louvain, Liège, and Ghent. We observe that, between August 1934 and January 1936, the Pro Arte played a total of nine complete Beethoven Quartet cycles. Until 1939, and notably in the year 1936, most of the group's appearances were via the Concerts Pro Arte–Coolidge sponsorship.

February 1936 was largely devoted to four concerts in Chelsea, England, for a Mozart-Haydn Festival. Then, on the 29th of the month, the quartet set sail for their tenth visit to the North America: lasting well over five months, it was to be the longest. On the eastern seaboard the group made one stop (March 10) at the Washington's Library of Congress, another (March 14) at New Brunswick, New Jersey, in which they played the Concerto for String Quartet and Orchestra that Martinů wrote for them. After concerts in Boston (March 15) and Washington (March 17), the Pro Arte began April in New York, giving two performances of the Martinů Concerto with the New York Philharmonic (March 8, 9), followed by a chamber concert (March 13.) There is a vague reference to a possible appearance at Swarthmore College at the beginning of May.

The quartet did make a trip to Chicago in early May for the purposes of making a recording of Mozart's Clarinet Quintet with no less than Benny Goodman—a previously misunderstood event, and one that was unproductively aborted (see appendix A). Almost immediately, the Pro Arte set forth for an unusually prolonged stay in California. It was launched at the California Institute of Technology in Pasadena with the Pro Arte's twenty-first Beethoven Quartet cycle, running for six concerts (May 9, 16, 23, 30, June 6, 13, 1936) in the opus-number format. There were spaces in between those concerts for appearances at the University of Redlands in San Bernardino, Pomona College at Claremont, and the University of California at Berkeley. From June 21 to July 29 the group was again at Mills College in Oakland for their third summer of residence there. The focus of that stay was yet another Beethoven Cycle, their twenty-second, played this time on their original five-concert plan of 1927 (June 24, July 8, 15, 22, 29). Interspersed with these concerts were others, at Mills (July 13, 19, 26), for the Coolidge California Students program at Berkeley (June 25) and at Stanford University in Palo Alto (July 2, 9, 16, 23). The 1936 tour concluded with stops in Portland, Oregon (July 31), and Seattle (August 3).

Following a brief summer rest, the Pro Arte opened the autumn season in Prague (October 19) but then spent the better part of

November 1936 in London, first for a pair of concerts (9, 10) in which the players joined with their protégés the Griller Quartet for Mendelssohn's Octet. Then they devoted three busy days (November 15, 18, 19) to their eleventh round of recording sessions for HMV at Abbey Road. There was a concert back in Belgium, at Frameries (November 22), after which they swooped down to Rome's American Academy where, at Mrs. Coolidge's invitation, they gave the first performance of Samuel Barber's new Quartet op. 11—the source of the latter popular *Adagio for Strings.* A Rome Prize resident of the Academy, Barber had just finished the work in its initial two-movement form. He had intended it for the Curtis Quartet, and was not happy with the idea. Having heard a Schubert recording made by the Pro Arte, he did not like the group—and as it turned out, Barber was unhappy with their performance. The Quatuor Pro Arte never programmed it again. (The Curtis Quartet did manage to play it in 1937, in its original first two-movement form. Only in 1943, with the troublesome finale resolved, was the full premiere given at the Library of Congress by the Budapest Quartet.)

There was time for an intense session, the twelfth (December 13), of recording for HMV in London, as pressure was put on the group to extend the Haydn series. The quartet then took ship again for their eleventh journey to the United States. This was to have been another wide tour under the Pro Arte–Coolidge umbrella. But, because of Onnou's troubled health at the time, the engagements were reduced to little more than a Beethoven Quartet cycle, the twenty-third, in Chicago (scheduled again in the five-concert plan: January 26, 30, 31, February 1, 4, 1937). There are reports of a supplemental concert in Chicago (selected Beethoven quartets) and another in Evanston, Illinois, but all engagements planned for the spring were canceled.

The quartet's energies had been exhibiting a discernible slowing in recent months, despite what was certainly a busy schedule. Onnou's health was intermittently problematic, occasionally requiring some weeks of reduced activity. Nevertheless, the Pro Arte carried on without serious loss of momentum.

We hear of the quartet back in full fettle by the spring of 1937. In June they were on the Atlantic for their twelfth voyage to the United States. On board the liner *Normandie* they gave one shipboard concert (June 12) in which they played their favorite Debussy Quartet, while Marcel Maas played piano pieces. On the west coast, via Seattle, the group reached California for their sixth summer at Mills College.

There they gave thirteen concerts between June 27 and August 4, offering varied repertoire. Pianist Maas also contributed six recitals of his own.

The autumn of 1937 was devoted to the second Beethoven Quartet cycle of the year, the group's twenty-fourth, offered in Lausanne, in a reversion to the six-concert plan of 1929 (on October 20, 21, 27, 28, 30, November 2, 1937). Amid these, the group intercalated five concerts (October 22, 26, 29, November 1, 3) of miscellaneous repertoire. Then, on the same date (November 12) the group gave two separate performances of their Martinů concerto. The year was rounded out by two days of recording sessions for HMV, their thirteenth set, at Abbey Road (November 15, 16, 19). During the second of these two days, a recording was made of them playing Mozart's serenade *Eine kleine Nachtmusik*, a work they are reported never to have presented in public performance.

Between December 31 and January 7, the Pro Arte began the year 1938 by launching their thirteenth visit to the United States. After a single concert in New York (January 9), they took up their twenty-fifth Beethoven Quartet cycle, this time at Wellesley College (January 10–19), on the six-concert plan of 1929. The quartet played at the Folger Shakespeare Library in Washington (January 20) and then moved westward, with a stop in Chicago for three concerts (February 5, 7, 9), whose programs included some novel ventures into "early" quartet music.

From Chicago, it was on to California. This was not related to the summer program at Mills College, but was sparked by a tenth-anniversary celebration there of its Music Building, which Mrs. Coolidge had funded. For the occasion, Onnou and Maas joined with Mrs. Coolidge in a performance of her own Trio in F Major—one of the very rare occasions when she appeared with the Pro Arte in public. (She had, in fact, hoped to perform with the group at Mills the previous summer, but was prevented by ill health.)

It was more Beethoven next, with their twenty-sixth and twenty-seventh Quartet cycles, given in another of those "overlapping" patterns, delivered alternatively in Claremont at Pomona College on the six-concert plan of 1929 (February 25, 26, March 4, 5, 11, 12), and at UCLA in Los Angeles on the five-concert format of 1927 (February 27, March 3, 8, 10, 13). Sailing from New York (March 19), the quartet returned home for a month of rest—although they seem to have given one performance in Geneva on April 14 (where the members apparently played Mrs. Coolidge's Trio again, if without her) and another in Paris on April 25. There were concerns, especially from Mrs. Coolidge about Onnou's recurrent health troubles with phlebitis.

By May 1938 the Pro Arte was back in action, and for a set of important celebrations: the quartet's twenty-fifth anniversary, for one, and the anniversary of the Concerts Pro Arte–Coolidge for another, plus the respective tenth anniversaries of the Palais des Beaux Arts and of the Société Philharmonique de Bruxelles. The festivities were pre-figured by the last of the private concerts the Pro Arte would give in honor of the important patron Henry Le Boeuf, who had sponsored or hosted many of the group's performances. The festivities proper included nine concerts in which the quartet participated (May 5–20). At the first of these, the Pro Arte offered their Martinů concerto (plus Marcel Poot's *Ballade* for the same forces) with the Philharmonic Soci-ety under Franz André. At another (May 18), the Pro Arte presented the world premiere of a work, the *Cantata de l'infant et de la mère*, that Darius Milhaud had composed for, and dedicated to them. On May 21 a grand banquet was given, specifically to honor the Pro Arte, attended by former and present members with their families, and individuals important in the quartet's past; Onnou himself delivered a speech reflecting on the group's history.

Not resting on their laurels, the quartet sailed (June 2–7, 1938) for the United States, their fourteenth such journey. Upon arrival in New York, they appear to have made a recording (of Rieti) for the Victor company. Onnou alone went to Washington, where he met with Mrs. Coolidge as the group's representative to discuss future concert plan-ning. The others went on to the west coast where Onnou joined them for concerts in Portland, Seattle, and Los Angeles. Though documen-tation is scarce, the quartet appears to have played a reduced role (July 2–22) in the 1938 summer session at Mills College. They gave concerts at other California points in late July and early August before traveling eastward for their twenty-eighth Beethoven Quartet cycle at Princeton University, in five successive days (August 9–13) on the 1927 plan.

The quartet sailed homeward (August 13–16, 1938), bypassing an invitation that Mrs. Coolidge had made to participate in a festival she had planned in September at Pittsfield—where Onnou might have played Bach beside Rudolf Kolisch. After some rest, the quartet made what would be a final round of performances in Denmark (October 14, 19, 23). An appearance planned as a twenty-fifth anniversary com-memoration in Prague, however, had to be canceled.

There were eight concerts (October 25–November 4, 1938), all but one in Switzerland, mostly focused on either of two works—Hans Schaeuble's Quartet no. 2 or Robert Schumann's Piano Quintet. The last of these was an anniversary celebration by a pair of French patrons. But almost immediately, the group went to England. On November 5 the Pro Arte was at the HMV studios for a one-day session, the fourteenth, to record more Haydn. But their main business was the twenty-ninth Beethoven Quartet cycle, given at Chelsea November 15, 18, 22, 25, December 6, 9), on the six-concert plan of 1929. There was also time to slip in concerts at Cambridge (December 2, 4) and at Manchester (December 7), with successive concerts in London (December 12, 13, 15). Clustered around the very last of those was the fifteenth—and what would prove the last—of the Pro Arte's HMV recording sessions (December 15, 16, 1938), in which another Haydn quartet was balanced against the only Beethoven quartet (op. 59 no. 2) that the group had the opportunity to put on discs. The Pro Arte then capped the year with concerts in Paris and Reims (December 18–22).

As 1938 passed to 1939, Onnou and Mrs. Coolidge discussed the ever-more disturbing situation in Europe in their correspondence. They made concert plans. She laid out, in the face of her somewhat diminishing financial situation, how her Coolidge Concerts would be funded in the future: she would cover half the costs, and the host organization—usually to be some educational institution—would take responsibility for the other half. She urged Onnou and the quartet to continue the affiliation with Mills College, because, given financial uncertainties, "they may need that income." She concludes: "I hope you are feeling a little less depressed, as I am myself doing, and I am sure that once again when we work together in our chosen and beloved fields of chamber music we shall find so much of objective interest that we shall forget any subjective inquietude. It will be delightful to compare notes once again."

Musically, the quartet's year 1939 began with concerts in Paris (January 3), Cannes (January 4), and Marseille (January 5). Their programs pointed to the event that fully opened (as it would close) the year. This was a Beethoven Quartet cycle in Brussels, this one the thirtieth, in the five-concert format of 1927 (January 6, 7, 9, 11, 13). It was followed immediately by another appearance in Marseille (January 14), after which the Pro Arte moved on for a series of eight concerts in as many cities in Italy (January 16–26: Genoa, Naples, Rome twice, Milan twice, Trieste, Verona). There appears to have been a concert in

Rotterdam on January 31. Though it could not be known at the time, these would be the quartet's last appearance in these cities, with the sole exception of Brussels.

From February 5 to 10, 1939, the group made a seriously storm-tossed Atlantic crossing on the *Queen Mary* for their fifteenth journey to the United States. Their first concerts were, in effect, preliminary events. On February 12 they performed in New York, for the National Broadcasting Company, a program of three Haydn quartets, plus a trio of his, with pianist Myra Hess participating. This was followed by a concert in Boston (February 15), then one in Washington DC (February 22) and another at Cornell University (March 1).

All that was indeed a prologue to a celebration that Mrs. Coolidge had planned for the group in her auditorium at the Library of Congress, back in Washington. This was to be the American counterpart to the celebration in Belgium of the Pro Arte's twenty-fifth anniversary. There were six concerts in this series (March 16, 18, 23, 25, 30, April 1, 1939), whose programs deliberately matched those of the Brussels anniversary festival. These concerts were broadcast over the radio, but, more important, they were recorded in the first capturing of the quartet's sound on magnetic tape. In the midst of this series, the quartet gave two concerts (March 20, 21) at the Peabody Conservatory in Baltimore, and then went to Chicago (March 28) to fit in the two works for string quartet and orchestra, the Concerto by Martinů and the *Ballade* by Poot, joined by the Chicago Symphony under Frederick Stock.

The Washington anniversary series was the occasion for several recognitions. At the last concert, on April 1, Onnou was given the Coolidge Medal for distinguished service to chamber music, an annual award that Mrs. Coolidge had developed. And the quartet as a whole was given, in late April, the *First Citizenship* award, which guaranteed them free entry into the United States at their pleasure.

Flush with the acclaim these events brought them, the quartet made their first and only appearance in Charleston, South Carolina (April 9), and then moved on to another new—and eventually significant—destination, the University of Wisconsin at Madison. There the Pro Arte gave two concerts (April 11, 12, 1939) with programs of Beethoven, Debussy, Mozart, Brahms, Hoffstetter/Haydn, and Schubert that happened to contain some of the players' favorite works by these composers. The local audience was enchanted. When Mrs. Coolidge wrote to Carl Bricken, director of the University's School of Music, suggesting the return of the quartet for a Beethoven cycle the following spring, he replied with eager agreement. He followed his cable with a letter (April 17) expressing unbridled enthusiasm—a response significant for what would come.

But the Pro Arte's chief destination now was Kansas City. There they gave the ensemble's thirty-first Beethoven Quartet cycle, in six consecutive days (April 14–19, 1939) using the format of 1929. This was followed directly by two concerts (April 20, 21) at the University of Kansas at Lawrence. After that came a string of far-flung concerts, not clearly documented, at Long Beach, California (May 7), Los Angeles (May 9, 16, 23, 30), Colorado Springs (June 2, 3), and Baltimore (June 4).

The Pro Arte had been scheduled to participate in the summer session at Mills College. But the mounting fears about impending war in Europe, Maas's emerging health problems over an obscure infection, and the idea of staying on for six months away from their families prompted Onnou to argue for a cancellation of the Mills commitment. There was a further reason: they had been requested by their government to participate in the 1939 World's Fair in New York that spring. Already designated as the official string quartet to the Belgian Royal Court, they were obvious cultural ambassadors for their country. The Pro Arte appeared in two concerts (the government officials had wanted four) at the Exposition's Belgian Pavilion, June 5 and June 8. The second concert included in their program not only the beloved quartets of Debussy and Franck but also a short work by no less than Carl Bricken.

The engagements at the Mills sessions that summer were thus canceled. The Pro Arte's place was taken by the Budapest Quartet, and by a series of recitals by pianist Marcel Maas. The Pro Arte set sail for Europe on June 10, and remained inactive for the next two months. (There is a report of a six-concert Beethoven Quartet cycle, which would have been the group's thirty-second one, given at Pittsfield, Massachusetts, September 30–October 15; but it seems rather to refer to the work of the Kolisch Quartet.) Activity was resumed, in Brussels, with a concert on October 26, 1939, followed by the group's official thirty-second Beethoven Quartet cycle, on the six-concert format of 1929, but on Thursdays, extended over eight weeks (November 30, December 7, 14, 21, January 18, 25)—the wide spacing of the concerts possibly made in view of Maas's health problems. This would prove to be the Pro Arte's final cycle in Europe, and the last concerts in which Maas would appear as a member of the group.

On February 8, 1940, Onnou gave his third performance of the Beethoven Violin Concerto, with Franz André conducting the Belgian National Orchestra, in a concert intended as a tribute to the beloved violinist. Thereafter, the Pro Arte prepared for what would be their sixteenth (and last) tour of the United States. Meanwhile, momentous changes were in progress.

∾   ∾   ∾

Carl Bricken was a musician of wide talents and experience. After basic studies at the New England Conservatory and Yale University, he spent a good deal of time in Europe. He studied piano in Vienna, but traveled widely. Back in the United States, he studied composition at the University of Chicago. (As already noted, the Pro Arte tactfully took up one of his compositions after their 1939 concerts in Madison.) It was in Chicago that he encountered Mrs. Coolidge. He and his wife Dorothy became her strong friends. They shared many enthusiasms, including admiration for the Quatuor Pro Arte. It was through Bricken's associations with Mrs. Coolidge that the quartet was engaged for their first appearance in Madison in April of 1939.

Bricken had been brought to the University of Wisconsin in Madison in 1938, to become head of its School of Music. His sponsor, Clarence A. Dykstra, who had become president of the university the year before, was a musical enthusiast himself, and saw Bricken as the man who could elevate the music program. To that end, Dykstra gave Bricken full authority to make appointments and develop policies.

One of the first things that Bricken did was to bring to the faculty the brilliant Danish pianist Gunnar Johansen. For this purpose, Bricken was able to utilize the status of Artist in Residence at an American university. That status had been pioneered at Madison first in the field of art. With a combination of state money and support from the local Brittingham Foundation, the painter John Stuart Curry was established with this title—curiously, however, through the School of Agriculture. Curry operated in a specially built one-room studio for the decade of 1936–46. (Later, this position was to be held by the painter Aaron Bohrod, 1948–73).

The appointment of Johansen as Artist in Residence was the first adaptation of this status to music. It followed a series of twelve "historical recitals" that Johansen gave at Madison in the spring of 1939—at about the same time that the Pro Arte first appeared there. The offer

from the University of Wisconsin had been made simultaneously with
one by Cornell University. Despite the more advantageous location of
Ithaca, New York, as well as a higher remuneration, Johansen chose
Madison, to a considerable extent on the understanding that the University of Wisconsin was seeking to bring the Pro Arte back to Madison
for some kind of continuing status in the following year. Johansen was
well acquainted with the quartet. He had heard the foursome play at
Mills College, and was an enthusiastic admirer of their artistry, with
which he eagerly anticipated collaboration. It is thus clear that, already
by the middle of 1939, the idea of establishing some kind of Pro Arte
residence in Madison was in the air.

On December 14, 1939, Bricken wrote to Mrs. Coolidge "about an
idea that has been close to my heart for a long time." He expressed the
hope that sufficient financing could be found

> to invite the Pro Arte Quartet to the faculty of the School of Music for
> one semester of the year as their place of residence and as a taking-
> off point for their concert appearances, the plan to be very flexible
> and their duties here to be consistent with their reasonably restricted
> schedule as to their concert appearances during the period of, say,
> the first semester of the year.
>
> I propose this in particular because of the lack of opportunity in the
> past for good string playing and study in the state, since most of the
> emphasis has been placed on band.
>
> We would, of course, want the quartet to make appearances here in
> Madison, at the university, and in certain strategic points in the state,
> also to do a light schedule of teaching and coaching string sections
> in the orchestra. It might be an excellent time to encourage them
> to bring their families to this country, and to give them some respite
> from the worries that have undoubtedly oppressed them during the
> past few years.

Bricken notes that he has not yet broached this idea to the quartet
members themselves, feeling that he must first seek Mrs. Coolidge's
blessing, and perhaps even her financial contribution.

What was proposed was an expansion of the Mills College summer
programs. The suggestion of the quartet's relocation in America would
fit Mrs. Coolidge's own concern about freeing the players from their
increasingly grim European situation. After all, with the German invasion of Poland on September 1, 1939, World War II had now begun. By

this time, too, she was feeling some financial pinch, so that she would welcome having the quartet being given a secure perch of their own, less dependent upon her money. For some time, she had been thinking that some sort of American institutional (educational) affiliation would be a sensible goal for the ensembles she had been supporting, and a way of drawing American universities into the support of her beloved chamber music. The initial proposal was for a putatively temporary residence, of at least one year. But it might be the beginning of something more.

Mrs. Coolidge was, indeed, immediately negative about the possibility of making any financial contributions of her own. With a modestly positive reaction to the basic idea, she advised putting the matter directly to the quartet members, notably Onnou. Apparently the idea was taken seriously by them, and Mrs. Coolidge wrote on January 9 of her hopes for an affectionate reunion with him. (She had come to address him as "Dear [or Dearest] Alphonse," signing her letters as "Elizabeth." In his turn, he had been less consistent and more circumspect about forms of address.)

≼ ≼ ≼

As the quartet made their preparations for ocean crossing, they faced a crisis, and the first change in personnel since 1921. Maas had been put in a hospital, where Onnou visited him. His illness (actinomycosis) was the result of an infection he acquired—it is said, by munching on some polluted grass—that was misdiagnosed as the then-dreaded "foot and mouth" disease. Accordingly, he was denied entry permission by the US Immigration Service. On February 5, 1940, Onnou wired Mrs. Coolidge to report the loss of their cellist, and asked her if she could find a replacement. The second week of February was a mad scramble to deal with this. The American cellist Frank Miller was contacted, but, though interested, was not available. Mrs. Coolidge quickly contacted C. [Charles] Warwick Evans, who had previously been cellist with the London Quartet, one of the ensembles to which she had given warm support. He was then in California with his wife, the cellist Lysebeth Le Fèvre, who was herself a very fine musician, a handsome and flamboyant personality. They were a lively couple, sometimes combative but also devoted, described as a kind of "Mutt and Jeff." (Evans was, in fact, a physically towering figure, perhaps even more so than Maas.) Evans agreed, eventually committing to twenty-seven concerts with the Pro

Arte. Mrs. Coolidge also had secured her various contractors' agreements to accept the group with the new cellist: Bricken did this immediately, preserving the original contract, and others fell into line. For their part, the players accepted this "outsider"—in status not only a stranger but a non-Belgian—with the understanding this was only a temporary arrangement and that Maas would eventually rejoin them.

In late February, while making the crossing on the liner *Rex* for what would be their sixteenth (but incomplete) visit to the United States, the players agreed to go forward with the Beethoven cycle and the other commitments. They even talked about a Brahms cycle at the Library of Congress in the autumn. Warwick Evans traveled from California and met the Belgians when they arrived in New York on March 17. (A concert scheduled there for March 3 had been canceled due to all the delays). The absorption of a new member into an existing string quartet is no easy matter, and rehearsals must have had a great intensity. Evans found, in fact, that his stylistic ideas about the music involved differed from those of the Belgians. But he generously decided to go along with their approach, and to give his best to them. These four were all seasoned professionals; and, again, the Belgians were still confident that eventually Maas would rejoin them. Mrs. Coolidge herself, on March 23, wrote to ask after Onnou's again-uneven health and to inquire how the rehearsals were going.

Well enough, it would seem, for the new foursome to tackle their prescheduled concerts. The month of April was spent making the rounds of two Massachusetts colleges (Mount Holyoke, Smith) and Yale University. There is even a report of a pair of concerts in Washington, DC, under Coolidge auspices. Meanwhile, dramatic efforts were afoot in Madison to find financing for the quartet's autumn residence there. Bricken wrote to Mrs. Coolidge on April 23, 1940, that both he and President Dykstra were hard at work finding money to support a residence of three years, no less, by the quartet at the University of Wisconsin. "There is nothing that either President Dykstra or I should rather do than have the Pro Arte here on the faculty of our music school," Bricken wrote. Some definite prospects for financial donations were, he reported, already at hand.

On April 25, Mrs. Coolidge wrote to Onnou that the quartet had an offer from a sister patroness. Mrs. Gertrude Clarke Whittall had proposed some engagements that would clash with the idea of a second year in Madison. Mrs. Coolidge discouraged acceptance of this plan, but wrote that, whatever developed, the Belgians could bring their families over to settle in Washington. She assured Onnou that she would see to it that the quartet was properly provided for. (She also urged Onnou to cable some money to help Maas.)

The Pro Arte had moved on to a series of three concerts (May 2–4) at the University of Kansas at Lawrence as decision making was proceeding. Bricken was pressing for acceptance of his latest proposals, but Mrs. Coolidge telegrammed Onnou advising him to "please accept nothing" for another week. Two days later, she sent another telegram to Onnou, suggesting that the quartet accept the "alternative plan" of a six-month engagement in Madison, while then taking the Whittall offer (a good and assured one) for 1941–42. They could all meet in Chicago on May 28 to discuss plans, including family arrangements. Apparently Bricken was still diddling over the contract, and she advised Onnou to tell him to "take it or leave it" as to the latest proposals.

By this time, amid all these negotiations, the Pro Arte were in Madison. They arrived on May 5, welcomed by an unseasonable snowstorm and low temperatures, to fulfill their commitment for a Beethoven Quartet cycle, their thirty-third—in the opus-number format. There had been discussion of a possible two-week format, and this was modified into an extended series of six concerts every other day (May 6, 8, 10, 12, 14, 16), as part of the Memorial Union Spring Fest series, part of a yearlong celebration of the Union's new concert hall, with the quartet as a "star attraction." Instead of using their established 1929 format of programming, for some reason the quartet reverted to chronological pattern by opus numbers. Bricken's wife, Dorothy, recalled that there was deep concern about selling enough tickets so late in an already busy season.

On May 14, close to the end of the cycle, Mrs. Coolidge wrote to Onnou, saying that Bricken had informed her that the Madison concerts were "going magnificently." She acknowledged that the players were fatigued by their performing and by the continued indecision about their future on the part of the university. She regretted that she could not meet them in Chicago, after all, but would do so in the impending sessions at Mills College. Indeed, she anticipated a free period of some ten days when she could once again take them on scenic drives in her open car.

But when she wrote that message, a dramatic turn of events had already come to pass. The first two concerts were played against the background of headlines announcing crises in Europe. At the intermission of the third concert, on May 10, President Dykstra mounted the stage, signaling the musicians to wait. To a shocked audience, he announced that Belgium had just been invaded by the Germans, leaving the Pro Arte stranded. Dykstra announced that the University of Wisconsin would give the Pro Arte Quartet a refuge and a new, official place of residence, and would do its utmost for their families.

The quartet players had not known of the war news until that moment. For the three Belgians, it must have been almost unimaginably shocking. They were anguished for their country. They also had to face the facts that not only could they be cut off from it but that their families, and Maas, were potentially trapped there, while their city was being bombed. With a combination of bravery and mesmerism, the players did the only thing they could think of doing. They played the rest of the concert, and they played the remaining ones.

For a long time, it was assumed that Dykstra's announcement that the Pro Arte would become a "quartet in residence" was a sudden and spontaneous one, a product entirely of that dramatic moment. Clearly, though, that was not the case. The plans had been in the works for months, and the German invasion had simply accelerated them. This Madison myth of the Pro Arte still persists to the present.

The sympathy and admiration generated for the quartet were reflected in a report that Bricken sent to Mrs. Coolidge on May 22, barely a week after the series ended:

> The members of the Pro Arte left last Saturday, after one of the most inspiring and beautiful series of six Beethoven concerts that I have ever heard and certainly that Madison has ever heard. The whole festival, of which the Pro Arte supplied the bulk of the quantity and quality of the program, was a tremendous success.

> . . . We were all aware of the terrific emotional and mental strain the men in the Pro Arte were undergoing. I don't believe there was a single person who sat in their presence who was not aware of the enormous self-control and dignity that they displayed. They have won their places deep in the heart of this whole community and university, and I feel privileged to have the opportunity to write to you.

And Gunnar Johansen expressed his feelings in pithy eloquence: "If those three brave Belgians can play through the concert tonight while they know Brussels and their families are being destroyed, it is but another proof that music stands for something far greater than we are."

The three Belgians in the quartet had the instant impulse to return home and join the fight against the Germans. But they were deterred as discussion continued over their alternative course: settling in Madison. Almost immediately after the Madison concerts, the quartet filled a series of engagements at the University of Kansas (May 19, 21, 23). From there they proceeded to Los Angeles, where they joined Mrs. Coolidge. On May 28, Dykstra sent Onnou a letter outlining the terms of the quartet's contract with the University of Wisconsin. The Pro Arte would be in residence in Madison from October 1, 1940, to April 1, 1941. They would participate in the School of Music's programs and activities as agreed with the director. They would give twenty-five concerts around the state and nearby points in Minnesota—expenses provided by the university, but profits to go to the university. They would be officially identified as the Pro Arte Quartet of the University of Wisconsin. The quartet would be allowed to accept engagements on its own during gaps in the academic calendar. It would undertake teaching of up to three students per member; they would join Johansen in a music appreciation course; and they would assist in training string students for the University orchestra. A further proposal was that each member of the quartet would give solo recitals, but Bricken at first exempted Prévost from this, on the argument that there was too little solo literature for the viola. Angry, Prévost proceeded to solicit new works of this kind, notably from Milhaud, who responded immediately—winning the triumphant violist a reminder and a vindication of his exclusion.

A special feature of these terms was the requirement to play concerts outside of Madison, around the state. This was a direct application of what had emerged for University leaders as the "Wisconsin Idea" or "outreach" concept, as part of the University Extension program. Its rationale was summed up in the slogan "the boundaries of the University are the boundaries of the state" or "extending the campus of the University to the borders of the state." The concept was that the University must share its resources with the entire population of Wisconsin, and not just reserve them for the narrow confines of the Madison campus.

On May 31, Onnou communicated the ensemble's acceptance of the proposed contract, as the university's official string quartet. An article in the *Wisconsin State Journal* of June 16, 1940, revealed the financial arrangements that would secure the residency. The Pro Arte, it proclaimed, had been "bought" for the University through private donations. To cover the costs of the first year of the residency, four loyal and prosperous alumni, already generous donors to its causes, had come together: the distinguished former diplomat Joseph E. Davies, the regent Frank J. Sensenbrenner, the Chicago lawyer George I. Haight, and the philanthropist Thomas E. Brittingham. Each had pledged $2,250, totaling $10,000—considerable sums in the currency of that time. To finance the second year of residence, President Dykstra was seeking an even larger amount ($16,000) in subsidy.

As this was going on, the Pro Arte pursued their latest commitments. At the Mills College summer session in 1940, they contributed thirteen concerts between June 23 and July 31. In the midst of all that, on July 19, Onnou fell ill, and only his stubbornness allowed him to finish the concerts. The group moved on to Chicago's Ravinia Park, to present what would be their thirty-fourth Beethoven Quartet cycle (and their last one) on six consecutive days (August 5–10), reverting to the 1929 format. That Onnou mustered the strength to carry out this assignment is a further testimony to his dedication. Indeed, in the newspaper reports of the series, personnel attention was focused rather upon Evans, as a replacement for Maas. Inclement weather at first restricted audience size, if not enthusiasm. In the *Chicago Daily Tribune*, the day after the first concert of the series, critic Edward Barry praised the quartet's "great variety of beauty and detail. In general, the performance was marked by an exquisite transparency and purity of tone and by an admirable precision and unity."

Writing in the same journal in August 7, the day after the second concert, critic Cecil Smith had a few reservations:

> The audience received the Pro Arte players enthusiastically, and derived obvious pleasure from their performance. Without wishing to belittle their extraordinary accomplishment in mastering the entire imposing Beethoven quartet literature, I must own that I found certain deficiencies in their playing. On the whole their approach to these early [op. 18] quartets was a surface one, somewhat lacking in dynamic intensity, and often either overlooking or failing to solve problems of tempo, of structural relationships, and even of phrasing and intonation.

Two days later, when he reviewed the fourth concert in the series, Smith was too pleased with the music to make any fuss over the performance. His reservations two days before could have reflected several factors: his own ideas about Beethoven style and playing; an effect of the Pro Arte's working with the substitute cellist; or some effect of Onnou's health problems. Whatever the case, it should be noted that these concerts were the last ones in which Onnou would play in the quartet that he had fathered.

Back in Madison, Onnou began some tests to establish what his condition represented, but the results were inconclusive at this point. Meanwhile, the quartet members found themselves bogged down in more fruitless efforts to bring Maas out of Belgium. It was becoming clear that he could still not be expected to reclaim the cello position—though some hopes persisted for the further future. Arrangements had to be made with Evans to extend his participation in the quartet. This was settled by September, and his return to Madison was fixed for October 7.

While the quartet was finishing their Beethoven cycle at Ravinia, news came on August 10 that Onnou's wife, Jeanne, had reached New York, after a tortuous passage out of Belgium. She was the only one of the quartet's family members who had yet managed to reach the United States. Ambassador Davies, among others, was doing his best on their behalf. Onnou was in Madison to welcome his wife when she finally arrived there on August 16. Jeanne Onnou's arrival, however, brought new travails. Worried about the Onnou home in Brussels, she had arranged for Alphonse's mother and sister to take residence in it. She spoke no English, and felt herself in an alien world. But she and her husband, as did the other Belgians, began the search for housing in their new home city. The Onnous and Halleux settled on apartments in Kennedy Manor, an elegant complex not far from the campus, while Prevost found lodging elsewhere.

The reunion of the Onnous was gravely darkened, of course, by the continuing decline of Alphonse's health. By late September he was in Madison General Hospital for a full round of testing. Mrs. Coolidge wrote to him in great concern. Bricken visited him regularly, as did Prevost—who was able to smuggle into his room forbidden bottles of beer.

Given Onnou's failing health, it became clear that he could no longer be counted on to play with the quartet, at least for the present. As a result, a concert scheduled in Milwaukee for October 16 was canceled. The planned Beethoven Quartet cycle (which would have been their thirty-fifth), scheduled for Madison in November, was at first postponed to January and then canceled. As a token replacement, the other three players, with Johansen, and a double-bass player, offered a program of piano quartets by Mozart and Brahms, plus Schubert's "Trout" Quintet, on November 3, under the designation of "Pro Arte Quartet Ensemble."

Meanwhile, the saga of Onnou's health continued—a sad story made more poignant by the picture given in the correspondence of Bricken and Mrs. Coolidge. Through October, Onnou's condition fluctuated. Deeply concerned, Mrs. Coolidge thought that he might go to Boston to see two world-class specialists, for care she could arrange. On October 17 Bricken telegraphed her that blood smears had been sent to the specialist in Boston, Dr. George Richard Minot. That same day, Mrs. Coolidge wrote an affectionate letter to her "dear friend" Alphonse, suggesting that he might make the trip to Boston to be attended by Dr. Minot and Dr. Kessel, both Nobel Prize winners. In Boston, too, she could attend on him. Toward his needs, she included a personal check for $400.

In mid-October, Bricken wrote to Mrs. Coolidge to address realities with painful bluntness:

> This letter . . . is to tell you something that lies sorely on my heart and mind. It concerns Alphonse. His doctor came to tell me yesterday that he will not play again with his quartet, and that it is only a matter of a little time that he has to live.
>
> Some time ago, after your last visit here, the physician's report was ominous, but we all hoped that his illness was not acute. Yesterday, after the latest microscopic examination of the blood cells, it is now definitely established that the trouble is leukemia and it is fatal.
>
> I have tried so hard to bear up under this dread. I can no longer deceive myself. As you so wisely said before, we must face facts. A difficult problem faces me. I don't know whether to tell Alphonse or not. It seems brutal to leave Mrs. Onnou at the sudden mercy of complete ignorance of the facts.
>
> On the other hand, the very existence of the Pro Arte is in the balance. It seems to me that Alphonse must be consulted first. The problem of a permanent replacement is immediate and no easy decision to make, since nobody can replace Onnou.
>
> I have pulled no punches. The truth lies hard and bare on these pages. As I read them over, my respect and affection for Alphonse has grown, so that it makes it all the more difficult to see as clearly as I should. The Pro Arte must go on and that is the objective that makes the load bearable. Please write me.

Hopes persisted that Onnou might last a year, and he was mostly out of the hospital, at home. But the truth was beginning to dawn on him. Through Bricken, he begged Mrs. Coolidge to come to him immediately. On October 22 she reached Chicago and asked Bricken to make arrangements for her in Madison. She continued on, presumably by train—Prevost had the recollection that she made the trip entirely by taxi, but that may have meant just from the Madison train station. In Madison she was able to spend some time with Onnou. Apparently she was the one assigned to tell him of his fate, as best she could. The next day, October 23, she wrote to her friend at Mills College, Luther Marchant:

> We are, of course, trying to keep him from the complete knowledge of it, but it is my sad duty to go to him and tell him that the doctors have all pronounced that he must not expect to play for at least a year. This, I hope, will soften the blow for him, but for us it means that he has not long to live. The night before last he had such paroxysm of pain and was so desperately ill that he has sent for me and, of course, I am hurrying to do what I can for my dearest friend.

With Onnou, Bricken, and the other two Belgians, she could at least discuss ideas for the quartet's future.

After her departure, she was kept in contact with developments by Bricken and his wife, and by Beth Evans, the cellist's wife, with whom she had become friendly. She also began making arrangements to provide financial donations to Onnou and his wife. On November 5, Bricken wrote:

> Our dear friend Alphonse is not at all well, and Sunday morning Dr. Middleton [local physician] talked to me in such a way as to tell me in a general manner that he was afraid that our worst fears were being realized, even before they expected them.
>
> I am afraid that this means that Alphonse is sinking now. What more can be said? It is one of the tragic mysteries of life that I can't understand, but feel in the end that it is inevitable we can do no more than accept it. I am going over today with a lawyer friend to see if we can help Madam Onnou straighten out the simplest essentials. . . .
>
> I cannot tell you how much your visit meant and still means. I cannot tell you how much lasting affection all of us have for you. You must know this and we send you, all together, our warmest love.

Three days later, Bricken wrote Mrs. Coolidge that Onnou had made a will, and had created a joint bank account with his wife. "He knows the truth and is most philosophical." Bricken also talked with Dr. Hugh

Payne Greeley, a local specialist: "He tells me that Alphonse may possibly carry on for perhaps a month. It is enough to say now that he is pretty low." Informed by Jeanne Onnou that her husband could no longer see to read, Mrs. Coolidge wrote a letter to Alphonse, to be read to him, full of the most extended expressions of admiration and affection for him—conveyed for perhaps the last time. On November 15, Bricken wrote to her that

> Our friend Alphonse seems, for some remarkable reason, to have spent three excellent days and nights. His eyes seem clearer. He seems to have slept well, and he talks with great clarity.
>
> I am amazed at his resilience. We both know the quality of his heart. In fact, I handed him your letter without having to read it to him. I was happy that this could be so. . . .
>
> Wouldn't it be marvelous if Alphonse really overcame every conceivable conviction on the part of those who know most about him, and lived in spite of what seems to be inevitable? You know, I still feel this may be possible and I can't help but say this to you in this closing paragraph because I want you to feel that way, too. There is something beyond our limited comprehension in which I still believe. My enormous love to you.

But last desperate hopes were unavailing. On the night of November 19, 1940, at 10:35 p.m., Onnou died. Hearing immediately of the "expected but shocking news of dear Alphonse Onnou," Mrs. Coolidge noted: "You can imagine what a bereavement it is. I want to help the Pro Arte Ensemble as a memorial to one of the dearest periods of my life." She automatically assumed all the medical expenses, and contributed to the funeral. On November 22, Onnou's funeral was held at St. Paul's Catholic chapel, just off the campus. In tribute, the School of Music canceled all its classes that day.

A moving description of these events is provided in a long letter that Bricken wrote to Mrs. Coolidge, in two installments, on November 23:

> This letter is a day later than I had wanted to get it off, because of the many little responsibilities and duties attendant to the arrangements for the final rites for Alphonse, which were held yesterday morning. Your flowers looked exquisite on top of his casket, with a beautiful heart from his wife on one side and a lovely violin from the Pro Arte Quartet on the other. The inscriptions on these were very simple, but

very touching. The services were held at the University Catholic chapel with a generous attendance, representing our student body and all of the members of our faculty.

He has been temporarily placed in a vault for easy shipment to Belgium whenever it will be possible.

Madam Onnou intends to stay here until something like an intelligible role or a definite development takes place between the relationship with this country and Germany. I doubt whether she could easily go back home in any case at this time and, as she says, she is not well enough nor capable of going back alone with her dear husband's remains.

If I could speak easily of my own feelings to anyone it would be to you, but I think you will understand how I feel, even though I cannot very well put it into words. Alphonse's illness was of slowly increasing development. On Tuesday night [the 19th] Dorothy and I had gone to a concert at which our presence was necessary here at the University Club. Prevost, Halleux, and Brosa [the new first violinist] were also there. We all had at the end of the program, and during the program, a rather remarkable intuition that something would happen that night. It was not therefore any surprise when Madam Onnou hastily called the club and asked us to come over quickly.

Fortunately, Dorothy and Beth Evans had asked for a priest that afternoon, who arrived at the same time as we did and none too soon. As I recall, we got to the house at about five minutes past 10:00 and the priest immediately prepared to give Alphonse extreme unction.

The poor fellow, as bad off as he was, he did not then, I am convinced, know that this had been his last rites. It seems that he was suffering and that a hypodermic was essential, which had very intelligently and timely been given by the excellent nurse who had been there for two nights.

He quieted down, but his breathing was very labored. He was mostly conscious, however, so it was very obvious that the end was near. Dr. Greeley, bless him, said also that it would not be long and came prepared to spend the night. He also attended the funeral, by the way.

During the priest's administration Alphonse looked around and said, in a startled way, "What's going on here?" In the room with him were his wife, the nurse, Halleux, Prevost, Evans, and myself. Dr. Greeley arrived almost immediately after and knew that it would not be very much longer.

I shall never forget him standing beside Alphonse, a benign figure, in fact, so merciful that my heart went out to him. He very gently stroked Alphonse's wrist and watched his wife most intently. In two minutes after his last words, Alphonse looked at the ceiling and died. In his last moments he said to Prevost, "Germain, you are more embarrassed than we are," meaning apparently he and his wife, "I want to die."

I have never experienced anything like it and I shall never forget it. Alphonse Onnou died as nobly as he lived. I am not sure, nor will I ever be, that I had any right to be there at his passing, but believed, and still believe, that I should be there for your sake.

Everyone here who has been in any slight way connected with this tragic saga has been superb, even the nurse, the doctors, the owners of Kennedy Manor where he lived, and, yes, even the janitor remarked how many good friends they have here. The janitor, by the way, came to the funeral.

I see now ahead a period of reconstruction for the quartet, a period of intensive work to help them forget their irretrievable and irreplaceable loss. You say rightly that it will never again be the Pro Arte Quartet, but it can be a superb quartet and now is a difficult period of readjustment which I feel certain will soon be achieved.

I do not know what else to tell you. When I see you again there will be little things, and things that you will want to know, which I can tell you in conversation.

It was decided that the idea of returning Onnou's remains to Belgium was not feasible, and he was buried on April 11, 1941, at Forest Hill Cemetery, where the grave may still be seen. Not only did Mrs. Coolidge assume all of Onnou's medical expenses, but she also made compassionate efforts to assist Onnou's devastated widow. Jeanne Tréfois Onnou was, in her ways, a stubborn woman. She had resented Mrs. Coolidge's domineering relationship with, and control of, Alphonse. But Mrs. Coolidge did all she could, on her side, to offer expressions of consolation. More, she arranged to send Jeanne monthly checks toward basic expenses. Jeanne was in frequent—and apparently warm—correspondence with Mrs. Coolidge. Mrs. Onnou was plagued by bad health, which Mrs. Coolidge thought was possibly the result of strains from Madison's climate, but she was in fact already seriously deteriorating. Mrs. Coolidge felt that she could help Jeanne in contacting the ex-presidential Hoovers with an eye to a possible resettlement in California;

and, later, she dismissed the widow's idea of a fund-raising concert on her behalf in Madison. Mme Onnou did manage a trip to Italy in 1941.

Jeanne Onnou never learned English, which put her in tremendous difficulty. She was, indeed, an exile in a strange land. Used to a quasi-aristocratic life at home, she could not understand the different flavor of equalitarian American society. Dorothy Bricken found her demanding and "a pain in the neck." Mrs. Coolidge and others did what they could to order some books in French for her. A particular burden fell upon Beth Evans, who took up the task of providing regular help and companionship in French. Mrs. Onnou did not like the shopping in Madison, and so Beth had to drive her frequently to Milwaukee to satisfy her requirements. And, all along, the widow's health grew ever worse. She was able to find treatment in the Morningside Sanitarium: the physician who treated her said that "hers is the worst case I have ever seen." Some other local friends did what they could. Carl Bricken reported on September 29, 1942, that Jeanne could not live much longer. Mrs. Coolidge saw the situation as truly pathetic, and wrote to Bricken on October 2, 1942:

> I am glad to have direct news of poor Mrs. Onnou.
>
> And, like you, I feel that she has very little to live for, and should not be sorry to know that she is out of her misery. I have felt that her case was one of the most forlorn and almost tragic that I have ever known, and I have done what I could to interest some of her husband's friends in giving her a helping hand. But my efforts have resulted only in sympathetic words and no really substantial assistance . . . although I do not think her a particularly fine or interesting character, she is a poor, unfortunate human being who does not deserve all the suffering which has been put upon her.

Release came within the month. Jeanne Onnou died on October 27, not quite two years after Alphonse's death. Her funeral was held two days later, also at St. Paul's chapel, and she was buried in Forest Hill Cemetery, next to her husband.

ꝏ  ꝏ  ꝏ

Alphonse Onnou was only forty-seven when he died. With him passed a remarkable musician and a splendid human being. He was the only one of the twenty-seven musicians who have played with the Pro Arte

Quartet to have died "in harness," still an official and active member of the group.

## Repertoire

Using incomplete data, it may be suggested that in the nine years 1932–40 the Quatuor Pro Arte gave, at a minimum estimate, some 617 concerts.

For that nine-year period, the repertoire assumed was quite distorted, by comparison with the figures of 1912–31. This resulted from one simple factor: the embracing of Beethoven Quartet cycles as the veritable backbone of the group's activities. The thirty-one cycles in this time period constituted an estimated 177 concerts, apportioning all other repertoire to only 440 concerts. But, beyond the cycles, individual Beethoven quartets also bulked large in the 617 documented concerts.

Presumably with their intensified involvement in these works thanks to the cycles, the players incorporated almost all seventeen of the working components into concerts, often many times over. The opus 18 set was perhaps the least represented area of the literature: no. 2 three times; no. 3 eight times; no. 4 six times; no, 5 only once; no. 6 three times. Of the opus 59 set, no. 2 was performed five times, but no. 3 an impressive twelve times. Opus 74, the group's apparent favorite, rated twenty-three appearances, while opus 95 was granted only two. Of the late quartets: opus 127, three times; opus 130 (original form), sixteen times; opus 130 (revised form), four times; opus 131 and opus 132, thirteen times each; opus 133 and opus 135 only once each; and the *Grosse Fuge* individually, twice. As always, such figures probably would be higher if we had data from the inadequately documented concerts.

Another shift should have come as a result of the Pro Arte's involvement in recording the quartets of Haydn. Surprisingly, the number of the ensemble's concert presentations did not increase beyond the pre-1932 numbers: 111 performances of nineteen quartets, as against the earlier 115 performances of eleven documented quartets. Nevertheless, the range of selections was wider, as at least the documented concerts suggest, and the choices were generally in line with what was being recorded. Of op. 1, no. 1 (once), and no. 6 (twice); of op. 20, no. 2 (eight times, perhaps in atonement for the recording switch) and no. 5 (once); of op. 33, nos. 2 (twelve times), 3 (ten times), and 6 (once); of op. 54, no. 1 (four times) and no. 2 (20 times!); of op. 64, nos. 4, 5, and 6 (two, five and three times, respectively); of op. 71, only no. 1 (once); of op. 74, only no. 3 (eleven times); of op. 76, nos. 1, 2, and 5 (one, seven, and two times, respectively); of op 77, no. 1 (thirteen times), and no. 2 (seven times). The spurious "Haydn" op. 3, no. 5 (actually by Hoffstetter) was done no less than eleven times.

The principal sacrifice made to this overbalance of Beethoven (if not overflow of Haydn) was in attention to deserving Belgian composers. Although the group had highlighted compositions by their countrymen through 1931, thereafter we can specifically identify performances of works by only three Belgians: Jean Absil (three pieces once each), Joseph Jongen (one work twice) and Marcel Poot (ditto). Among lesser-known French composers, we find only Marguerite Béclard d'Harnoncourt (one work twice) and Jean Cartan (one work five times). The Swiss Hans Schaeuble appears twice. Passing appearances are made by the German Conrad Beck (one work thrice), the Polish-born Alexandre Tansman (once), and the Russian-American Nicolai Berezowsky (one work thrice); plus Gdal Saleski (one). A bit less obscure are the Italians Gian Francesco Malipiero (his Quartet no. 3 seventeen times), Ildebrando Pizzetti (his Quartet no. 2 four times), Ottorino Respighi (his *Concerto a cinque* twice), and Vittorio Rieti (his Quartet no. 1 six times); and the Dane Carl Nielsen (his Quartet no. 4 four times).

A category of composers that continued to thrive was Englishmen. Thus, we have Arnold Bax (twice), Lennox Berkeley (his Quartet no. 3 twice), Frank Bridge (Quartet no. 3 twice), Edward Elgar (his Quartet twice and Piano Quintet once), and Eugene Goossens (*Phantasy Quartet* thrice), plus the Irishman Charles Wood (once).

One clear direction of repertoire growth was with regard to American composers, to some extent reflective of the quartet's constant tours around the United States. Samuel Barber's Quartet was performed once and never played again. Variously posted were Italian-born Domenico Brescia (thrice), Carl Bricken (once), John Alden Carpenter (thrice), George Whitefield Chadwick (his Quartet no. 4 twice, Quartet no. 5 once), Albert Sprague Coolidge (Elizabeth's son: his Trio four times), Aaron Copland (*Two Pieces*, twice), Louis Gruenberg (four times), Roy Harris (Quartet no. 1 four times and Quartet no. 2 seven times, plus a Trio once), Mary Howe (once), Frederick Jacobi (his two string quartets each twice), H. J. Mills (once), Harold

Morris (once), Walter Piston (Quartet no. 1 twice, Quartet no. 2 five times), David Stanley Smith (Quartet no. 6 seven times), and Randall Thompson (thrice).

The Pro Arte continued to champion twentieth-century "modernists," though they were becoming more "mainstream" as time passed. They remained loyal to the two important members of the Parisian *Les Six*, especially to Darius Milhaud. The group appeared in three renditions of his *Création du monde*, in the composer's piano-and-quartet adaptation. Of his Quartets, no. 2 (twelve times!), nos. 5 and 7 (thrice each), no. 8 (eight times), and no. 9 (five times). The Quartets of Arthur Honegger were also prominent: no. 1 (twice), no. 2 (three times), and no. 3 (nine times). Rather in the background was Ernest Bloch (his Piano Quintet no. 1 six times). The works of Bohuslav Martinů appeared quite regularly: above all the Concerto for String Quartet and Orchestra that he wrote for the Pro Arte (eleven times); of his Quartets, no. 2 (four times) and no. 5 (thrice), plus three other chamber works (once each). Paul Hindemith's Quartets were also addressed: no. 4 (sixteen times!) and no. 5 (four times). Igor Stravinsky was not forgotten: his *Three Pieces* (eleven times), and of course the *Concertino* (seven times).

The composers of the Second Viennese School continued to be supported by the quartet. Thus, Arnold Schoenberg's Quartets no. 2 (four times) and no. 3 (eight times); and Alban Berg's *Lyric Suite* (nine times). Anton Webern seemingly did not place in this period.

At the other extreme, the Pro Arte did dabble in some "early" literature: a transcription by Sydney Back of a piece by the Elizabethan John Bull (once); a chamber piece by François Couperin (once); the durable transcription of Antonio Vivaldi's Concerto op. 3, no. 5 (fifteen times); a quintet by Luigi Boccherini (once); the Quartet no. 7 (twice) by Haydn's younger contemporary Nicolas-Marie Dalayrac; plus Bach, in the form of five transcriptions of chorale-preludes, and of seven *contrapuncti* from his *Kunst der Fuge*.

The drawing upon the "basic" or "mainstream" string-quartet literature may be addressed alphabetically by composer. Sturdy support for the quartets of Béla Bartók: no. 1 (five times), no. 4 (seven times), no. 5 (twelve times). Alexander Borodin's Quartet remained a staple (eight times). Johannes Brahms received uneven attention: of the opus 51 Quartets, nos. 1 (twenty-three times!) and 2 (five times), and op. 67 (once); of the Piano Quartets, op. 25 (thrice), op. 26 (once); the Piano Quintet (five times). Claude Debussy's Quartet, their all-time top-scorer, was filled out with fifty-three more performances! Antonin Dvořák's opus 96 Quartet was downgraded to a mere eight performances, while the second of his youthful quartets (B-flat, B. 17) was a lone novelty.

Gabriel Fauré was represented only by his two Piano Quintets (once each). But César Franck's Quartet remained another top favorite (thirty-five times), if his Piano Quintet (thrice) less so. Alexander Glazunov's *Five Novelettes* slipped down to seven appearances, while there were three others of his works (one four times). Felix Mendelssohn appeared only by way of his Octet, played once with the Griller Quartet.

Wolfgang Amadeus Mozart won expanded attention, if with variable depth. Of a total of twenty-five works reported, there were one hundred and forty-seven documented performances. Of those totals, there were fifteen quartets, played 112 times. (There are reports also of some seven unidentified quartets.) Of the quartets, their appeal to the group seems to have varied widely. K. 458 was the most frequently played (twenty-three times), followed by K. 465 (twenty times), K. 575 (fourteen times), K. 387 (ten times), K. 428 (nine times), and K. 499 (eight times). Beyond those, performances seem to have been few: K. 464 (four times), K. 421 (twice), followed by K. 80 and K. 590 (once each). But the Prelude and Fugue K. 546 was given eight readings. The piano quartets fared moderately well: K. 478 six times and K. 493 twice. The string quintets appeared variously, dependent of course upon the availability of the second violist: K. 516 (eight times) and K. 515 (six times) led the list, followed by K. 614 (four times), K. 593 (thrice), K. 46 and K. 406 (twice each), and K. 174 (once). The same contingency conditions prevailed as to the chamber pieces with winds: the Oboe Quartet K. 370 (once), the Horn Quintet K. 407 (four times), the Clarinet Quintet K. 581 (five times). Mention should also be made of the great Trio–Divertimento K. 564, done once at a charity concert.

Sergei Prokofiev's *Overture on Hebrew Themes* was done once. But Maurice Ravel had a strong presence: though his *Introduction and Allegro* appeared only twice, his Quartet, still near the top of the Pro Arte's top favorites, registered forty-five performances. Albert Roussel's Quartet appeared twelve times.

Franz Schubert remained a strong focus. Four of his quartets were given a total of forty-nine performances: D. 93 twice, D. 703 thrice, but D. 810 (the famous "Death and the Maiden") thirty-six times, and D. 887 eight times. The Quintet D. 956 is documented only twice. Robert Schumann's representation was small, if impressive: op. 42, nos. 2

(twice), and 3 (seventeen times); the Piano Quintet was given seven times. Bedřich Smetana's Quartet no. 1 still held a place (four times), while Verdi's Quartet was reduced (twice). Hugo Wolf's *Italian Serenade* is reported only once.

Even allowing for the ballooning presence of Beethoven, as well as of Haydn, the repertoire spread for the Quatuor Pro Arte's last eight years still seems impressive today. At the risk of seeming to run a vulgar competition, we might just tally up the statistics for the full history of the group (1912—40) as to their most favorite or most frequently performed works. The uncontested champion, if we may use the term, was Debussy's Quartet, performed at least 174 times! Trailing, but still mightily impressive, was Ravel's Quartet (117 times). Further down the scale came the Franck Quartet at sixty-eight reported performances, and Schubert's D. 810 (*Tod und das Mädchen*) fifty-two. Borodin's Second Quartet received forty-nine performances, and there were thirty-five of Dvořák's opus 96 ("American") Quartet. The strongest Haydn showing was op. 54, no. 2, at 27 performances; that for Mozart was K. 428 at thirty-five; while Beethoven's op. 74 was a clear winner at thirty-five. So many other works were played, of course, but they placed much lower in our "sweepstakes."

## Recording Activity

The Quatuor Pro Arte was not the first or the only quartet to make recordings on wax masters in the early years of the new electrical process, but they were certainly among the most prolific and, indeed, one of the most significant. The quality of these recordings is the more remarkable in that they were generally made "on the fly" during stops in London, crammed in amid concert performances, with little time to rehearse before "takes." Of course, for the most part, the group knew well the literature they recorded, so they could play with confidence—spontaneity blended with experience—virtually on the spur of the moment.

The commercial recordings that the Quatuor Pro Arte made for HMV and Victor during the years 1931–38 are, of course, the enduring heritage of the early ensemble's performing work. These recordings have lovingly been kept alive through decades of transference to successive playing media (from 78 rpm shellac discs, through 33 1/3 vinyl LP records, to compact discs). They allow later generations, who never encountered the group in "live" performance, to hear what they sounded like. And they are more than just "historic recordings," for in general they offer music making that is still artistically satisfying today.

Progress in recording technology has accustomed us to a wide range of sound in recordings, and tempts us to hear earlier ones perhaps as "primitive." Indeed, listening to the Pro Arte recordings, especially the earliest, one might find them thin-sounding at the top and sometimes deficient in the bass registers. Yet the ear is able to adjust quickly to some of these qualities, and, as the group's recording activities progressed, the sound qualities quickly improved, often with quite full-bodied results, so there is no sense our ears are being cheated.

Through the recordings, we are able to recognize the artistry that won these Belgian players so much acclaim from critics and admirers, including the praise of contemporaneous composers whose works they premiered and championed. All these composers are unstinting in their assertions that the Quatuor Pro Arte was one of the finest quartets of their time, if not the finest. There are, of course, little hints of what we might identify as a dated playing style. Onnou, whose clear and floating playing comes through so strongly in the recordings, was inclined to use a very delicate and expressive portamento, or "sliding," by his time a passing tradition. From his training, he avoided excessive vibrato, preferring what we might call a shimmering sound. And when he "shimmered," his colleagues shimmered with him, emphasizing the absolute unanimity of their playing.

As disciples of the Belgian School of string playing, our foursome was committed to total clarity of texture, utter precision, and absolute fidelity to the scores they played. These qualities could, to be sure, bring a certain objectivity to their playing, and there is only rather rare evidence of their succumbing to unbridled enthusiasm or impassioned power. Rather, there is an elegance, a deftness that maintains balance and tries to let the notes speak for themselves. Subsequent recordings of works they recorded may offer more individually idiomatic satisfaction, but there is never anything less than responsible artistry in their performing. Serious immersion in their recordings cannot fail to make that clear.

∾  ∾  ∾

It is a curious fact that the Quatuor Pro Arte's undertaking of recording activities, and their impact, have received so little notice in literature on the medium. Histories of the early recording industry have either ignored their studio work, or referred to it fleetingly, only in passing. Even Fred Gaisberg, the man responsible for making it happen, never refers to it at all in his autobiography, where (as with so many others) attention is focused on big-name solo performers and conductors, ignoring ensembles such as the Pro Arte or Busch Quartets.

Yet, as represented at first by the Haydn Quartet Society releases (and augmented by what followed), the discographic establishment of the Pro Arte was an important step in the recording of chamber music. The Pro Arte was by no means the first string quartet to record commercially, nor the only one. The Léner Quartet was the outstanding early pioneer. The Virtuoso Quartet of London made a number of recordings (including at least three disc premieres) for HMV in 1924–25. The original Budapest Quartet was also already on the scene, and continued to be for many decades. The Busch Quartet was to create recordings of enduring power and value. The Pro Arte appeared on the scene in midst of all this, playing a strong yet unbalanced role.

Their entry into recordings was, as observed, by way of Gaisberg's Haydn project. Of the eighty-three quartets Haydn has left to us (as reckoned in the Hoboken catalogue), the Pro Arte was able to record twenty-seven, plus two that were long accepted as Haydn's but since have been recognized as by another composer (apparently Roman Hoffstetter). This was an area of chamber literature that had only slowly won recording attention, so that the Pro Arte's series served significantly to advance Haydn's standing. This came to pass despite the fact that our foursome was able to record barely one-third of the full eighty-three. Of course, had not the war and the quartet's disruption broken off the recording work, more presumably would have been added.

In fact, the Pro Arte Haydn recordings set the standards for some time and provided the models for Haydn performance. In the decades since, other quartets have developed a wider range of approaches to these works, while several have even produced fully integral recordings of all eighty-three of the quartets, often opus by opus. With their inculcation in clarity, precision, and deftness, the Pro Arte could capture well Haydn's qualities of exploration, imagination, and humor. That omniscient chamber music discographer Tully Potter has expressed some disappointment with the Pro Arte's recordings of Haydn's later quartets: he finds them generally "lightweight," not bringing out the composer's growing seriousness of feeling and deepening of textures. Nevertheless, these Haydn recordings still offer rewards in listening.

The Pro Arte were able to record for HMV/Victor a total of fifty-two works. Of those, twenty-nine were part of the Haydn project, leaving fewer than half (twenty-three) to represent "the others." This imbalance reflected Gaisberg's desire to advance the Haydn series; he was slow to allow the quartet to stray from that path. The first opportunities were often provided when partners of some reputation could join them in quintets. Expanding further depended upon assessments of what music was marketable for the public of the day.

Given the quartet's increasing concert performances of Beethoven Quartet cycles, it is curious that the Pro Arte was allowed to record so little of that literature. This may have resulted from Gaisberg's judgements about their Beethoven playing, or, more likely, from his efforts to record Beethoven exclusively with the Busch Quartet. Whether or not Gaisberg intended to record a full Beethoven cycle with the Busch, he recorded only nine of the quartets with that group in the years 1932–39. Correspondingly, Gaisberg strictly reserved Haydn for the Pro Arte, never allowing the Busch Quartet to record any of their Haydn.

And so it was that the Pro Arte managed to record a Beethoven Quartet, the op. 59, no. 2, in the group's *very last* session (December 16, 1938). (Ironically, that was the very quartet whose recording by the Busch Quartet was lost at the time, though it got located and released decades later.) It displays the group's clarity and precision, in a reading more of classical restraint than of assertiveness—a kind of lightened strength. We must guess if such qualities informed all of the Pro Arte's Beethoven playing, but we miss here the kind of drier intensity that the Busch Quartet brought to their Beethoven.

Yet an irony remains. Though the quartets of Beethoven became a large portion of the Pro Arte's performing repertoire, the group was able to record very few of them, and very little of the rest of the literature with which they were so active. On the other hand, the quartets of Haydn, which were not such a large proportion of the group's performing repertoire, constitute a commanding block of what it did record.

To be sure, there need be no reservations about the one venture the Pro Arte was allowed into the quartets of Bartók. This was a composer with whom they developed an early affinity. He himself admired their performances, and dedicated the Fourth Quartet to them. The group's Brussels manager, Gaston Verhuyck, had even thought of arranging a complete concert cycle of the Bartók Quartets, as a performance pendant to the Pro Arte's Beethoven cycles. That would have set an example to a great many other quartets, then and since (including a later Pro Arte configuration), and the one recording they did make suggests what the full six works might have become in their hands. That was the First Quartet: while they do not reflect empathy with the Hungarian folk idioms on which the composer drew, they project with their beautiful clarity the process of Bartók's harmonic language, avoiding unrelenting vehemence in the interests of cumulative power.

Among the composers the Pro Arte was most suited to record were those of the French school with which they became so closely connected, giving their quartets, in some cases, their recording premieres, and fully idiomatic ones at that. The Franck Quartet is a long and often brooding work that demands prolonged dedication, which can be recognized in the Pro Arte recording. It offers a sonorous balancing of darkness and light, density and transparency. (We can hear in the third movement some handsomely representative work from cellist Maas.) The scherzo posed one of the worst problems the group faced with the relentless limitations of 78-rpm side lengths: the Pro Arte found that, to fit the complete movement onto one side they had to speed up their usual tempo to make the movement almost a minute shorter, for an accommodation of 4:50" on a crowded side.

The Pro Arte's treatment of their all-time favorite work, the Debussy Quartet, is captured in a highly satisfying recording. It is true that the 1933 sound is, by today's standards, rather pinched, but not a serious handicap to the musical results. The first two movements are remarkably passionate, the third a stimulating balance of serenity and intensity, the fourth an ardent summing up.

Likewise, Fauré's Quartet is allowed an uncluttered presentation: the middle movement of this triptych is deeply expressive without affectations, amid the flowing pace of the framing movements—all providing a fine illustration of the shared shimmering the players had perfected.

The Ravel Quartet is less perfumed than other ensembles have made it, and more pungent. The Pro Arte's elegant understatement is matched with vibrance and vivacity, a combination just right for this work.

If there was a composer for whom the Pro Arte's clarity and elegance was particularly suited, it would be Mozart. Somehow, the mercurial but multilayered character of Mozart's style fitted their own spirit beautifully, and brought out degrees of richness and vitality beyond what they might display for other composers.

Of Mozart's string quartets, only one (K. 428) was recorded by our ensemble. That performance has a dash and vibrancy that can only make us regret that they did not have the opportunity to record more of them. A reference exists to their starting another one, identified only as in D major, but left unfinished and apparently abandoned. In K. 428, Onnou's incisive leadership is strongly conveyed, and that shimmering ensemble quality is particularly affecting in the slow movement.

The Pro Arte was fortunate in having the cooperation of Alfred Hobday, who took the second viola part in three of the string quintets (K. 515, 516, 593). These are suave, rich recordings that, at least as to interpretations, can compete with just about any subsequent treatments of them on discs. In the third movement of K. 515, the first violin and first viola have a virtual duet, with the other three players in the background, so one can hear the playful and delightful interaction of Onnou and Prévost against each other. And this is followed in the fourth movement by some unusually bold displays of unleashed energy.

One of the best of the Pro Arte's recording partnership with Artur Schnabel was their recording of Mozart's Piano Quartet no. 1 (K. 478). The quartet's refinement and the pianist's sturdy command of Classical and early Romantic style produced a probing and highly stimulating rendition. At the other extreme was a recording of Mozart's popular serenade *Eine kleine Nachtmusik* (K. 525), not easily heard today, since it was never reissued by Victor, either on LP or CD.

That same fate, by the way, befell another of their recordings, in this case a work that the Pro Arte frequently played in concerts: the transcription of Antonio Vivaldi's Concerto in A Major, op. 3, no. 5. Victor, as owner of this recording, has never given it a revival on LP or CD.

(For a discussion of the mythic recording venture with Benny Goodman and the Mozart Clarinet Quintet, see appendix A.)

A somewhat similar victim of Victor's seclusive policies affects a novel recording of Franz Schubert's Trio for Violin, Cello, and Piano, D. 898, made by Onnou and Maas with Karl Ulrich Schnabel (Artur's son), a straightforward but attractive account. Likewise a recording of Schubert's "Trout" Quintet, with Artur Schnabel and Claude Hobday, Alfred's brother, is regarded as something of a "classic." The Pro Arte never recorded any of Schubert's quartets, save for the finale of the early D-flat Quartet (D. 87), a vivacious if unrepresentative example. They did, however, do the String Quintet in C (D. 956), with Anthony Pini as the added cellist. Schubert seemed to bring out our players' appreciation for melodic beauty, and their rendition of this work shows well their response to that dimension: the second movement is most eloquent, and the main body of the Scherzo is presented with unusually fine lilt. Still, their approach overall is rather light and nostalgic, but sometimes stiff and even somewhat superficial, not probing very deeply into the emotions of the composer's farewell to chamber music and to life.

Onnou is supposed to have disliked the music of Johannes Brahms, but the Pro Arte came to play his compositions quite steadily. Of his chamber works, though, they recorded only two—neither of them quartets, but rather works that involved them with other players. Among their earliest non-Haydn recordings, made in 1932, is the Piano Quartet no. 1, op. 25, with Artur Rubinstein, and the String Sextet no. 1, op. 18, with violist Alfred Hobday and cellist Anthony Pini as the added players. The Piano Quartet shows neither the pianist nor the quartet as fully comfortable with the Brahmsian idiom. Rubinstein would later record the work again, by which time he was in full command of the composer's style. But the quartet, though they play vigorously, are prevented by their polished elegance from committing fully to the robust sound that Brahms requires. As for the Sextet, its warm elements can work well for the Pro Arte players, but there is rather too much sweetness and gentleness to capture all of the Brahmsian dimensions.

The quartet recorded two other works with Artur Schnabel in 1934, among the early non-Haydn works they were allowed to capture. Both are works of prime if divergent Romantic content, and they have sensibly been paired in CD revival. For Schumann's Piano Quintet, Schnabel provided an anchor of cosmopolitan style. In Dvořák's Piano Quintet, however, despite all their energy, neither Schnabel nor the Belgians seem quite able to capture the idiomatic qualities of Slavic richness and dancelike rhythms. Still, there are appealing moments of prominence for Prévost in the third movement and Maas in the fourth.

The lack of an idiomatically Slavic feeling is also present in the Pro Arte recording of Borodin's Quartet no. 2, a repertoire favorite of theirs. The third movement is almost a cello vehicle, and Maas' playing is notable and memorable there. In general this recording has a sweet and gentle expressiveness suited to those who respond to that approach. The only other music by a Slavic composer is a mere one of the *Five Novelettes* (op. 16, no. 5) by Alexander Glazunov that they enjoyed playing. But it is a simple piece of pseudo-"exotic" trivia, done simply as a record filler.

Aside from Bartók, the only other twentieth-century composer the Pro Arte was able to record was Ernest Bloch, via his Piano Quintet no. 1. This was made possible through friendship with Alfredo Casella, who took the piano part. His Italianate feeling for lyricism, helps the quartet strike a balance with the score's brusque, even aggressive qualities, to make a still-memorable disc debut for this work.

❧   ❧   ❧

In all the foregoing enumeration, of course, we are confronted with the fact that the Quatuor Pro Arte never had the opportunity to record literature that they championed by composers important and close to them. Only one Bartók Quartet. We have no Milhaud whatsoever. No Honegger, no Hindemith, no Martinů, no Casella. No Roussel or Tansman. None of the Belgian composers—so many now of little name recognition—to whom they felt committed. One could go on and on with such a list. But it must be remembered that the Pro Arte had only seven years within which to build a legacy of recordings. Other groups, notably the Budapest Quartet, but even the Busch, had a far more extended span of time—decades—for their recording activity.

What matters is that, incomplete as it became, this skewed legacy is still our direct, listenable link with what was one of the greatest string quartets of their day, and of all chamber music history. Their recurrent revivals on discs through changing formats has been encouraging. Yet, as the marketing of recorded sound is now evolving—marketed electronically rather that through the tangible, physical objects of discs—new questions must be raised about how that legacy may continue to survive. Cultural leaders should take note and give thought.

# 3

# THE BROSA YEARS

# (1940–44)

## What's in a Name?

There is an old joke, told in many forms, but perhaps best embodied in the one placing it at George Washington's estate, Mount
Vernon. The story has it that visitors there were shown an axe and were
told by their guide that this was the original axe with which young
George chopped down the cherry tree. The visitors observed that the
axe looked quite fresh and new. Well, explained the guide, you had
to understand that it had been given three new heads and five new
handles over the years. But it was still the same axe!

Applying this story to the Pro Arte Quartet situation reflects some
mixed truths, amid mixed questions. Many commentators (especially
European) consider the Pro Arte Quartet to have come to an end with
the death of Alphonse Onnou in 1940, and the American continuation
of it to be spurious or irrelevant. Both in membership and in character,
they had lost their Belgian identity, and were no longer the Quatuor
Pro Arte of Brussels that the musical world had known for two decades.

It is true that membership and character would change. But such
circumstances were hardly unique or isolated. Many long-lived groups,
most notably the Budapest Quartet, went through exactly the same
changes, but they were not considered extinct when their initial configuration came to an end. The introduction of one or more new members into a quartet does, of course, involve tests of assimilation and
adjustment, but these have been carried out successfully in so many

cases, and none of them have given grounds for denying the reality of their continuities—with the Pro Arte or other quartets.

One concert reviewer made a pointed comparison of the Pro Arte with certain creatures in nature—starfish and such that are able to reproduce lost members and thus continue uninterrupted life.

In what continuity-deniers would have as their "last" year, one personnel change had already been carried out: Warwick Evans, a non-Belgian, was substituted for the absent Robert Maas (though, it was presumed, temporarily). The dying Onnou was replaced by Antonio Brosa. A Spaniard by birth, Brosa was an early violin prodigy. He studied in Brussels with Mathieu Crickboom (whose quartet had given the premiere of Debussy's Quartet). Brosa also caught the attention of Mrs. Coolidge, who came to consider him her favorite violinist after Onnou. Since Brosa had a genuine experience of Belgian training, he had a palpable relationship with that stylistic tradition. The Belgian connections were directly maintained by the continuing presence of the second violinist and the violist, who remained as members: Halleux for three years, to be replaced by another Belgian, Albert Rahier; Prevost for seven years. Through those years, however, there was a rapidly revolving door for new cellists, as Maas's hoped-for return never happened.

Such tumult, of course, meant not only the constant strain of ensemble adjustment to new personalities, but also an uncertainty as to what character the transitioning group should develop, national or otherwise. That strain was reflected in a recurrent saga of reassessing the very name of the quartet.

At first, Mrs. Coolidge, in agreement with the dying Onnou, had supported the continued use of the Pro Arte name for the transitioning ensemble, though she later vacillated, for a while preferring the designation of the "University of Wisconsin Quartet." That raised the hackles of Prevost, who insisted on retaining the Pro Arte name, as had been desired by Onnou. This provoked Mrs. Coolidge to burst out, "Onnou is dead. Onnou was the Pro Arte Quartet, not you." So Prevost reported later, and this certainly fueled tensions between the violist and the patroness. The episode also suggested how much Mrs. Coolidge's devotion to the Pro Arte Quartet depended upon her strong relationship with Onnou, and explains some of her subsequent fluctuations.

Nor was the matter entirely subject to her initiatives. Along the path ahead, two successive first violinists, each of whom had previously led quartets under their own names—a tradition among many quartets, if one that Onnou himself had rejected—wanted to impose their names on the Madison group, of which they became leaders. As will be seen, these efforts were rejected.

A fundamental factor in the continuation of the Pro Arte name was the group's new home, the University of Wisconsin (then essentially identified with and at Madison). As the financing commitment to the ensemble moved from annual renewals to a permanent arrangement, the university sought to guarantee its rights to the group's name. It was a prestigious name. Both President Dykstra and Music School director Bricken appreciated the distinction it would bring to the university. They also recognized that they were creating a new precedent, by securing the residence, and the identification, of an established string quartet with an American institution of higher learning. This remarkable precedent was soon recognized by commentators around the country, and imitated widely thereafter, with important results for musical life in the United States. Dykstra and Bricken could well have looked back on that as an extraordinary achievement in itself.

From the very first negotiations with Onnou, it was understood that the group would now appear under the name of the "Pro Arte Quartet of the University of Wisconsin–Madison," especially if and when they performed outside the state. This insistence on such nomenclature continued with the formal consolidation of the group's permanent place in the university's School of Music. But resentments smoldered over the years for at least one former member of the original quartet. In June of 1945 (two years after his departure), the former second violinist, Halleux, sent a memorandum to the quartet's former manager, the Belgian Gaston Verhuyck, expressing his strong disapproval over the handling of the Pro Arte name:

> You know that I had abandoned Germain [Prevost], who continued the so-called Pro Arte Quartet at Madison. Many foreigners had already participated in it. It would take too long to describe all the details that have followed my departure. But, to sum up, I can tell you this: that after the death of Alphonse [Onnou] and the absence of Robert [Maas], I have considered the quartet as no longer in existence, at least for the time being, until a logical new organization could be established. Furthermore, Brosa, who left a year after me, wanted to claim prerogatives that were unacceptable to me, a member of the Pro Arte from the beginning. As was his custom, having a marked inclination towards the foreigners, Germain had become much less sociable toward me. He continued to play with another

first violin who is now Kolisch and who has apparently fashioned the Pro Arte according to his own style. I do not know what will be the outcome of that deplorable situation.

The matter of the name was brought up in 1947, partly because of the departure from the quartet of the last of the original members, Prevost, but also in the wake of the efforts by Brosa and then Rudolf Kolisch, to impose their names on the quartet, and the further concern that other ensembles might feel free to take the prestigious Pro Arte name for themselves. In response to a request from Professor Leland Coon, then director of the School of Music, Professor Charles Bunn of the university's Law School wrote a letter of July 23, 1947, which covered an elaborate memorandum on the university's legal rights to the name. These two documents are preserved in the university's archives, and are reproduced in the annex sections of Van Malderen's study.

In his memorandum Bunn reviewed the history of the Belgian group and attempted to define what laws applied to their continuing identity. He observes that each of the original members, in departing the Brussels group, retained his own reputation but "their share of a *group* reputation they necessarily left behind when they retired." And, he notes, for seven years, "Pro Arte has been used to identify a continuous group of changing membership, connected with the university," with full understanding and acceptance by concert and radio listeners: "It follows that the Wisconsin group, and no one else, and the University as the group's sponsor and employer, are entitled to be billed and to perform as Pro Arte Quartet or Pro Arte Quartet of the University of Wisconsin. In case of controversy and resulting litigation, the Court should enjoin anyone else from making use of the name for either audience-concerts or radio broadcasts." Bunn did leave a small loophole, though one never to be used:

> If the artists who make up the quartet should leave the University together, they would necessarily take their reputations with them. If they desired to continue elsewhere as a group, and to call themselves Pro Arte Quartet, I think they would have the right to do so, and the University would have to find some other names for any group it might sponsor. But of course the retiring Quartet would have to drop the University designation from its name.

Finally, Bunn notes that the Brussels group made recordings rightfully identified under the Pro Arte name. Should the group affiliated with the university make recordings, they should see to it that a distinction is made between the old and the new ensembles by clearly noting the members' names.

All this was not, of course, a legal ruling. But it laid out what would be the University of Wisconsin's grounds for claiming and exercising rights to the Pro Arte name. It is true that, in the course of the years, two or more European ensembles took the name of Pro Arte, if without any claim of link to the Brussels tradition. The university did nothing about that, and there have been no legal disputes about its exercise of the Pro Arte Quartet name.

Yet this was not entirely the end of the matter. In 1988, after serving since 1974 as second violinist in the Pro Arte Quartet, Martha Francis Blum was to retire from performing. By then she had already been making preparations to write an account of the quartet's entire history over seventy-five years. To this end, she made contact with families and descendants of the original Belgian members. Among these was Mme Roberte Lamury-Maas, the elder daughter of the cellist Robert Maas. On September 2, 1987, Mme Lamury-Maas wrote a long and bitter letter of protest to Eunice Meske, the then director of the University of Wisconsin School of Music. In it, she protested the proposed project, and denounced the idea that the group then performing in Madison had anything to do with the Quatuor Pro Arte or their name.

Her argument was the archetypical case for the Brussels-Belgians–only principle. The original four had always signed a contract together, she claims. But the original four no longer were a performing group, meaning that the Quatuor Pro Arte had ceased to exist as of 1940. Her father, detained during the war, never resigned from the group; when he finally reached the United States in 1945, it never occurred to him that the players active in Madison at the time in any way constituted the Pro Arte Quartet, nor would he have approved of that pretension. The Madison-based musicians who used the quartet's name no longer had any of their old performing and recording ties with Belgium or Europe. The current musicians in Madison were "imposters," with no right to the old quartet's name. "There is no continuity." She requested that the University of Wisconsin officials require Ms. Blum "to give up this absurd project of writing a mendacious book."

On November 30, 1987, Professor Meske wrote a response to Mme Laury-Maas, challenging those claims quite bluntly. That all four members of the Brussels group had to agree and sign contractually as a group was not true. The deathbed understanding with Onnou was that his "beloved Pro Arte" should continue. The other two Belgians agreed and supported this aim, staying on as members longer than was claimed. As to the lack of any resignation by her father, the cellist position was kept open for years in the hopes that he would rejoin; his choice, upon reaching the United States, to not rejoin the group in Madison, was in itself a resignation: "I am sorry that your recollections cause you to be so unhappy about the continued history of the quartet. We see this continuation as a great tribute to those who initially formed it. The history will continue, with or without your cooperation by sharing your knowledge of the early years."

By the time of the celebration of the Pro Arte Quartet's centennial in 2012, this controversy over "continuation" has quite faded. The dreadful destructiveness of World War II had brought to an end several of the great prewar string quartets, notably those led by Adolf Busch and Rudolf Kolisch. The Pro Arte was unique in this company. Their survival and adoption in the United States, as a "lineal descendant" in their direct line, is now recognized on both sides of the Atlantic.

๑ ๑ ๑

The illness and death of Onnou, the leader and, indeed, the soul of the Quatuor Pro Arte, left the other two Belgians at loose ends—and at a time when the families of each were still stranded in Europe by the war.

Nevertheless, as Onnou lay dying, serious discussions were being made. When Mrs. Coolidge arrived in Madison in late October 1940, she and Onnou, together with Halleux and Prevost, discussed the future. Onnou's strong wish was that the Pro Arte should continue, even if without him. This poignantly echoes his assertion in 1918, denying the adoption of his own name for the new quartet: "Because I can die and the group must go on." In 1940, that would mean the continuation of Evans as cellist given the current unavailability of Maas, who was still expected to rejoin soon. Above all, it meant, the designation of a new first violinist. Onnou himself felt that Halleux did not have the leadership strength to assume that job. (Halleux later believed that Prevost had undercut him, and resentment over that lasted a while.) Bricken suggested his own brother, a professional violinist, but when he came to be auditioned by the two Belgians he proved totally inadequate. Bricken was peeved, especially at Prevost for the latter's strong opposition to his kinsman, and relations between the two were somewhat strained for a while thereafter. Prevost by now had formed a strong relationship with Dykstra, and felt secure in that.

For the new first violinist, Mrs. Coolidge herself suggested the Spanish-born, Brussels-trained Antonio Brosa, who had led a quartet in England (which included Anthony Pini) to which she had given support. Brosa was at that time in Boston. On the strength of her confidence in him, he was not required to audition but was invited unconditionally, and in early November, he accepted. Almost immediately, Mrs. Coolidge wrote to Brosa: "How heavy a cloud of sadness is hanging over all when I think of dear Alphonse, but I feel that it also will be a comfort to him to feel that his beloved quartet will not be obliged to stop its career on his account." Later that month, on November 26, 1940, just after Onnou's death, Mrs. Coolidge wrote gratefully to Brosa: "I cannot tell you how fortunate I feel to have found you, Toni, to carry on the work of the Pro Arte. In doing this I feel that we are all working with Alphonse and that the inspiration which we derived from him did not die when he left us."

Through all this, performance activities had to be developed. Even before Onnou's death, while negotiations with Brosa were being completed, on November 3, 1940, Halleux, Prevost, and Evans joined Gunnar Johansen and faculty bassist Bernard Stepner, under the billing of "The Pro Arte Quartet Ensemble," in a program of piano quartets by Mozart and Brahms, plus Schubert's "Trout" Quintet. Preparations for that had been tense, as Evans reported to Mrs. Coolidge:

> Alphonse is getting weaker . . . it is very difficult to keep our minds on our work. Rehearsals are both difficult and depressing. Laurent and Germain want everything to be played exactly as Onnou would have played it. I have tried to point out that this is not now realistic. When I came into the Pro Arte I did not like or even think correct the way they played Brahms, but I was glad and happy to fit in as I wanted to give my best to the group. Now it is time for them to do the same. Brosa's an excellent violinist, but quartets are another thing.

Once Brosa arrived, intense rehearsals began. On December 1, 1940, the group, now reconstituted under his leadership, gave their first Madison concert, performing quartets of Haydn (op. 54, no. 6) and Beethoven (op. 59, no. 3), plus the Debussy Quartet. Three days after this concert, Bricken wrote to Mrs. Coolidge, describing it as a "really first-ranked performance."

I have seen many people since the performance, as well as at the performance, and not yet have I found a single dissenting opinion as to
the superb quality of the playing. Frankly, I was amazed that Brosa
and the men in the quartet themselves could have adjusted themselves to each other in so short a time as to produce a performance
of this quality.

On December 8 and 16, the quartet joined with other faculty and
students, under Bricken's direction, to do the complete series of Bach's
*Brandenburg Concertos.* (In between, on December 15, Brosa played the
Sibelius Violin Concerto, a favorite vehicle of his, with the Madison
Symphony Orchestra.) On December 12, meanwhile, Bricken wrote
further to Mrs. Coolidge, giving an enthusiastic account of how the
quartet members were working well and cordially with each other, and
with strong commitment to the ensemble's continuity.

For all that, the newly configured quartet had to adjust to very
new realities. They were no longer, as in the Brussels years, a touring
ensemble of international acclaim, with a sideline in recording. They
were now a house ensemble, settled in teaching duties, with travel as a
very secondary role. Word had begun to spread in the American musical world about this, and a notable acknowledgment of the unique
step was printed in the journal *The Violin* for January–February 1941:
"Such an arrangement is believed without precedent in American colleges—that a famous string quartet should join the faculty as teachers,
performers, and general all-rounded musical models for the campus,
state, and nation. But that's the way it has worked out, and Madison
hopes that it will long continue" (pp. 157–58).

In fact, it was travel that soon publicized the new arrangement. At
the beginning of 1941, the group made their first out-of-state appearances. On January 15, at the University of Chicago, they participated in
a Concert for Relief of Belgian Refugees in Britain, playing the same
program as their one in Madison on December 1. Two days later, January 17, they appeared at Northwestern College in Watertown (WI),
with the same program, except for the substitution of the Brahms
Piano Quintet, with Johansen, for the Debussy. While in the area, they
went to the homes of two of the financiers of the Madison residence,
Joseph E. Davies (in Watertown) and George I. Haight (in Chicago),
playing the Haydn, Beethoven, and Brahms works.

Then, fulfilling plans that Bricken had made with Mrs. Coolidge,
the new Pro Arte journeyed to Washington, DC, for a series of eight
concerts (January 23, 25, 27, 29, 31, February 3, 5, 8) in the Coolidge

Auditorium of the Library of Congress, devoted to a massive survey of Johannes Brahms' chamber music, twenty-three works in all. With them went a number of colleagues from the University of Wisconsin music faculty: pianist Johansen, violist Harold Klatz, clarinetist Gustave Langenus, and hornist Wendell Hoss, plus cellist Lysbeth Le Fèvre. (The participation of violist Harold Klatz is clearly documented, and is thus specified in the printed programs. But the point has been curiously challenged by Bernard Milofsky. In a recorded interview, he recalled that Evans had invited him, then a young violist, to play second viola in the quintets and sextets. Milofsky further recalled that the music was new to him and gave him technical difficulties, while the whole experience sorely tried him emotionally. Those recollections seem questionable, however—unless clear evidence can be found that Klatz withdrew at the last minute.) Critics, curious about the new Pro Arte basic configuration, were divided in their reactions. Paul Hume rated the Brahms performances as "coarse, their style showing a lack of cohesiveness, and their sound grating." It would seem that Evans's rehearsal misgivings were justified.

The quartet returned to Madison for a series of Mozart concerts, on February 10 and 18, March 10 and 24. At the one on February 18 occurred a curious incident in which President Dykstra approached the box office to buy a ticket (then priced at fifty cents). The flustered student attendant assured him that he did not have to pay, but Dykstra insistently put down a dollar bill and asked for his change. In the midst of all that, the quartet was among the groups performing at the university's annual Founder's Day event on February 12.

There had been plans for further touring, but it is not clear that they were carried out, given the muddled state of the documentation. In mid-February the group gave two events in Wausau, which were reported enthusiastically by Bricken as proof for the idea of taking music around the state of Wisconsin. There seem to have been concerts in Cleveland and New York in late February and into March. Now, however, a wave of uncertainties developed. After the Brahms series, the period of residence agreed upon in the contract that Onnou had signed had run out. Dykstra and Bricken had been working successfully to find donors for the financing of a second year of residence. Meanwhile, the support that Mrs. Coolidge had provided for concerts in diverse locations was drying up. In 1938 she had created a Pro Arte–Coolidge Trust Fund, with Onnou as administrator. With his death, however, she had dissolved that agency of financing, though for a while her broader backing continued under the aegis of the Coolidge Foundation.

Of particular importance, there were deepening tensions among the players, for all of Bricken's rosy optimism. In anguish over the situation of their families, Halleux and Prevost became restless early on. Already regarding Brosa and Evans as "outsiders," they communicated to Mrs. Coolidge the request that she find positions for themselves in American orchestras. On December 8, 1940, she considered their requests but warned that remaining in the quartet would give them a securely permanent and prestigious situation at the University of Wisconsin.

Given the hostility of the two Belgians—who were not above feuding between themselves—Mrs. Coolidge tried to give "the outsiders" more congenial alternative work. At her request, the faculty pianist Gunnar Johansen brought Brosa and Evans with him into what was called the University Trio, which undertook their own concertizing. This only further outraged the Belgians. Their attitudes and behavior, repeatedly described as "childish," in turn angered Mrs. Coolidge, who resented being caught in the middle of all the controversy. The diplomatic Bricken did what he could smooth things over.

The continuing efforts to bring Maas from Belgium to reclaim his position stumbled along ineffectually. Evans was uncertain about his supposedly temporary status, and weary of the players' discord. He began to talk of leaving the quartet, and there were feelers sent out to possible substitutes. Among those contacted was Frank Miller (later to become principal cellist of the Chicago Symphony), who was interested but not free. Eventually, Victor Gottlieb was secured for the autumn. In the interim, Evans was persuaded to stay on through the summer, partly with the guarantee of continued work with the University Trio. By May, however, the two Belgians wrote to Mrs. Coolidge saying they would resign from the quartet if the trio were to be continued in the summer. On May 13, 1941, the exasperated lady, in a letter to Bricken, expressed her frustrations:

> As a matter of course you will understand that I could not allow the two Belgians to tell me what I should do in the summer with the two Londoners as well as Mr. Johansen. . . .
>
> . . . [Their objections to the Trio are] what I consider an entirely unwarranted attitude on the part of the two Belgians, whose very

existence as members of the Pro Arte Quartet has been prolonged by what Evans and Brosa have done for them.

> . . . I think you will understand too when I claim the same freedom for control of my summer affairs and cannot promise to adjust my plans to the dictates of two members of the Pro Arte Quartet.

Along the way, the Belgians were somewhat cowed, and agreed to accept what they had to—though tensions continued over such issues as opening or closing a window during rehearsals.

Bricken was still faced with charting a course for the coming season (1941–42), in cooperation with Mrs. Coolidge. Writing to him from Los Angeles on June 3, 1941, she expressed her exasperation and her drastic impulses:

> I have seen the letters which you wrote to Warwick and to Tony Brosa and have heard from them. As for myself, and for the recent developments of the quartet situation, needless to tell you that it is egregious to me to see so fine an organization disrupted by such childish and unreasonable behavior on the part of the two [Belgians], for whose benefit all this effort has been made.

> After hearing from both sides of the question, it seems to me that the disagreement is so fundamental that there is almost no chance of any permanent achievement together, and as my sympathy is entirely against the two Belgians. I am writing to say to you that I have lost my interest in trying to further their welfare.

> This does not trouble me as much as it would if I did not know that you have made them a wonderful offer, quite sufficient to guarantee their living, and that they are therefore not dependent upon what I might do for them in the summer. I shall probably transfer any appropriations which I might have made for them either to the University Trio or to some other quartet. Although I realize it is not my responsibility, I feel it is only fair to tell you, as I have done so many times before, that I am unwilling to promise anything to the Pro Arte Quartet beyond what they are already engaged to do for me in July.

> At the risk of seeming to meddle with your plans, may I suggest that it seems to me quite possible for the University of Wisconsin to go on with its splendid project under the leadership and name of Antonio Brosa, who could form and control a quartet of equally fine players? I am not writing this at his suggestion, although I told him that I would take the liberty of doing so.

In the meantime, I shall offer nothing further to Halleux or Prevost, feeling that I can give whatever cooperation and assistance I can afford to those who much more clearly deserve it. I am writing thus to you only from a feeling that it is fair for me to inform you. I do hope that the failure of the Belgians to act honorably and gratefully will not result in a complete collapse of your splendid Wisconsin project, as I shall endeavor to prevent it from doing so for my California plans, such as they may be, for next year.

Dear Carl, please forgive me for I have overstepped the limits of tactfulness, but I feel more comfortable to have written you this letter, and at any rate I want you to accept again concern for my constant friendship and cooperation.

This flare-up occurred, in fact, during the quartet's participation in a round of activities in California. These involved repetitions of the Brahms cycles presented earlier in Washington. One of these was given in May at Stanford University in Palo Alto, another at the State University in San José. And the cycle was repeated yet again in August back at Stanford. In between them, Mrs. Coolidge gave a party on July 4, and a cordial atmosphere seems to have been maintained.

Two communications of this period suggest the uncertainties. Still in California, Mrs. Coolidge wrote to Bricken on July 11, 1941: "After a long talk with Germain this morning I made it quite clear to him that if the internal disruptions in the quartet cannot be settled by the members themselves perhaps the thing to do is for the dissident members to resign." Yet, the very same day, Brosa wrote to Halleux assuring him that his family would soon arrive, adding, "I feel that there is enough of the great spirit about this group that will keep it together in spite of everything everywhere."

It was thus as a small dose of relief that, on July 22, Halleux's family reached Madison after a tortuous escape from Europe, via Cuba. In the correspondence between Mrs. Coolidge and Bricken, he apparently gave no comment on her idea of renaming the quartet. On August 2 she reaffirmed her thinking:

I have been very much shaken in regard to my feelings for the Pro Arte, for I felt that the two Belgians, for whom we had all made such tremendous efforts, were responding in a jealous and unreasonable way, which made it almost impossible to do anything for them, and I am therefore holding in abeyance any plans which I may wish to make for them in the future. It is a consolation to me to know that they have a contract with you which is adequate for the support of them and their families. I most assuredly hope that Maas will arrive and that the Pro Arte Quartet may once again contribute to the furtherance of the highest chamber music.

Bricken offered reassurances on August 7:

> I am sure it will interest you to know that the firm stand I took last spring in regard to the rather uncertain attitude of the members of the quartet worked wonders.
>
> It was at that time more than a mere gesture, so I felt that something definite had to be said in order to pull the members together or disband them. I can now tell you that the attitude of the Belgians is exceedingly fine and I feel that they not only are more willing to do their part and anything asked of them, but are now extremely grateful for anything that is done for them. I hope that you have begun to see this same tendency, and that I will encourage you to feel comfortable about them again.

In four successive concerts (September 15–18, 1941), the University Trio (Brosa, Evans, Johansen) performed a comprehensive survey of Beethoven's trios at the University of Southern California, Los Angeles (UCLA). And, indeed, though no longer a member of the Pro Arte, Evans would join the other two as the University Trio for a Beethoven program at the Library of Congress, sponsored by the Coolidge Foundation, on August 15, 1942.

In the meantime, the quartet's second season of residence in Madison was launched with a new cellist, since the membership of Evans ended with the completion of the last Brahms cycle in August. The second of the "temporary" replacements for Maas was Victor Gottlieb. A product of the Curtis School, he had recently served for a year with the Philadelphia Orchestra, and then for six years in the Coolidge Quartet, in which capacity he had encountered the Pro Arte members. With all the best credentials, he was accepted for a transfer now into the Pro Arte. This meant another adjustment to a new performing personality, but he was a "pro among pros" and the assimilation seemed to work.

Gottlieb apparently made his debut in a concert the Pro Arte gave in Madison on October 15, 1941. Reported as attending that concert was no less than Benjamin Britten, the young expatriate English composer who, after the failure of his opera *Paul Bunyan* the previous spring, was reaching disillusionment with his alternate life in the United States. A further PAQ concert was given in Madison on

November 9, and in December there were two concerts devoted to another series of Bach's *Brandenburg Concertos*. Amid all that, the quartet took up some travels, visiting Iowa State University and the Tennessee Educational Association in Nashville, and otherwise taking up the duties of touring around Wisconsin, with stops at Milwaukee, Portage, Mount Carroll College, and Beloit College.

After another Madison concert (January 9, 1942), the quartet was able to undertake a tour around the country, stopping mostly at educational institutions in California (Pasadena, Stockton), Utah (Cedar City, Provo), South Dakota (Vermillion), Iowa (Cedar Falls), Kansas (Winfield), Wisconsin (Milwaukee), Missouri (Fulton), North Carolina (Chapel Hill), and Connecticut (Middletown), through the rest of January. They were back in Madison for a concert on February 4. Then, at Bricken's prompting, the Pro Arte participated in cycles of quartets by prominent American composers. Framing the venture were a "Two-Day American Quartet Festival" (February 15, March 8) in Madison, under Coolidge Foundation support; and then another two-day "Festival of American Music" (April 20, 21) also in Madison. There are reports that, in between, the quartet took this same repertoire in a series of seven concerts within five days (March 15–19) around Wisconsin, Minnesota, and Illinois (Menomonie, Mankato, Rockford, Appleton, Sweet Briar, Superior, Duluth). But reports place other concerts, in Madison and beyond, at dates some of which contradict the information about that touring American series. (On one of the contested dates, March 15, Halleux was reported as playing the Beethoven Violin Concerto with the University of Wisconsin Symphony Orchestra.)

A concert in Madison on May 4, 1942, marked the final performance of Victor Gottlieb as a member of the quartet. Here we reach another way station in the saga of Maas's absence, as well as the latest demonstration of the disruption brought to the Pro Arte by World Wars. The previous December 7 (1941), it will be recalled, witnessed the Japanese bombing of Pearl Harbor and the immediate direct involvement of the United States in war. The tortuous negotiations that Dykstra and Bricken had conducted before then—including a scheme to move Maas out of Europe via Japan—had proven fruitless. The new American status as a combatant shut down formal dealings with German-dominated Europe, so that Maas was left trapped in Belgium for the duration. (The same was true, of course, for Prevost's family.)

But the coming of war introduced yet another factor—military draft. The induction of Gottlieb in the spring naturally required his departure from the quartet. He was to serve through the war, but then he initiated what would be a recurrent pattern for Pro Arte alumni, resettling in California and even working in Hollywood's film industry, so that he could be near his wife, the violinist Eunice Shapiro (herself already in California). In 1946, he joined the RKO studio orchestra. From that base, together with his wife, he organized the American Art Quartet, in which he was cellist until his death in 1963.

The latest vacancy in the Pro Arte cellist's chair was quickly filled. Chicago-born George Sopkin had been a precocious student of Emmanuel Feuermann. At the age of barely fifteen years, he was hired by Frederick Stock, conductor of the Chicago Symphony, to serve in that ensemble, which he did between 1929 and 1941. Though the University Trio was revived for their Brahms concert in Washington in August, the quartet itself had a summer hiatus, while Sopkin was brought into the fold. When a new contract between the university and the quartet was signed on October 1, 1942, his name was there.

Moreover, the university had secured new donations and grants that guaranteed the quartet their third year of residence in Madison. The new contract set forth extensions of previous terms:

1.  There would be fixed salaries for the players.
2.  Twenty-five concerts would be expected.
3.  For concerts in Wisconsin outside Madison, transportation, lodging, and meals would be financed by the university.
4.  Concerts given under the Coolidge Foundation sponsorship would be separate from University of Wisconsin duties and funding.
5.  The ensemble's official name was again defined as the Pro Arte Quartet of the University of Wisconsin.
6.  Each player would work with a maximum of four students, plus coaching of the orchestra's string section.
7.  Weekly participation in the music-in-performance course (Music 9) would be expected.
8.  All concert publicity would be at the university's expense.
9.  This contract would be renewed automatically unless written cancellation were given by either party by January 1, 1943.

Though the upheavals were not thereby ended, it was understood that the quartet would still continue.

For the season of 1942–43, the outward picture was one of conventional operations, with Sopkin integrated into the ensemble. There were a number of concerts in Madison, mostly in the Memorial Union Theater. A notable amount of time was given to benefits concerts under the auspices of the Coolidge Foundation. These were offered in Madison (December 6, 9, 16), on behalf of Belgian soldiers who had taken refuge in England. The quartet repeated these efforts, with the same repertoire, first in Madison again (February 28, 1943) and then in two concerts in New York in the spring (March 22, April 4). On April 5 the *New York Times* published an ecstatic review by Oscar Thompson, who proclaimed: "The Pro Arte Quartet has become one of the best ensembles of its kind. . . . Beethoven [op. 131] which ended the evening literally transported the public from Town Hall to the Sistine Chapel." Virgil Thomson, critic for the *New York Herald Tribune*, was likewise very enthusiastic. Unfortunately, no records survive of any concerts given around the state of Wisconsin for this season. It was rounded out by participation in three concerts of the first May Music Festival (May 3, 8, 9).

Behind the scenes, however, tensions were seething anew as further crises arose. Feeling ever more disaffected with the situation in Madison, the two Belgians renewed their inquiries for orchestral positions they might secure in cities around the United States. By the spring of 1943, Halleux was reaching the decision to resign. In despair, Prevost wrote to Mrs. Coolidge on March 9:

> Despite all my efforts to prolong the tradition, the Pro Arte is going to go under. Laurent is abandoning me, despite the support that I have given him, these last two years, when I came to see you in Los Angeles about the Evans affair. I have written widely (to Los Angeles, to Boston, to New York and Chicago) so as to obtain a job in an orchestra. Generally, the answers have been negative. No vacancies exist in viola chairs. My only remaining possibility is you, Madam, and I ask if, as possible, you might not be able to recommend me to one or another of the chamber music organizations that have been deprived of a violist as a result of the Draft. Our contract expires at the end of this year's May.

Her response of March 16 was not encouraging, but she did make at least one effort on Prevost's behalf, approaching the Chicago Symphony management and pointing out the very important role that her father had played in its history. Then, at the New York concert for Belgian relief on March 22, Prevost was able to make contact with an old friend, Désiré Defauw, now about to become conductor of the Chicago Symphony. Discussion of Prevost's job-hunting obviously arose, and two days later the violist wrote again to Mrs. Coolidge to report this and to express confidence in the effectiveness that her endorsement would bring. Nothing came of that, however. On April 6 Mrs. Coolidge informed Prevost that her appeals on his behalf to the Pittsburgh and Indianapolis orchestras had been in vain: the budget strains of the war years were proving grave obstacles. In his later recollections, Prevost portrayed her actions as meant to push him out of the quartet; only by raising his fee demands did he put off offers by Fritz Reiner and Fabien Sevitzky to hire him. In actuality, on April 8, Prevost wrote to Mrs. Coolidge, acknowledging the hopelessness of his efforts, and added the consolation: "Brosa, Sopkin, and I still have a gleam of hope of being able to continue."

On April 1, 1943, the *Wisconsin State Journal* reported that "the dissolution of the Pro Arte Quartet, one of the best ensembles of its kind, seems inevitable" if needed financing for it could not be secured. Dykstra was in hot pursuit of more donations, but on April 7 Bricken gave assurances to Brosa that the university was committed to retaining the quartet on a permanent basis.

The concert of May 9 was to be the last appearance of Halleux with the quartet. When it was announced at the end of June that the university had the funding necessary, Halleux hesitated about signing his contract. In his long-standing frictions with Brosa, Halleux had become exercised over efforts to designate Brosa as the quartet's "director," which he found disrespectful to the memory of Onnou. He also seems to have been frustrated by Brosa's conservative programming, which pulled back from the new music the old Pro Arte had always supported. Already in California, Halleux had an exchange of letters with Bricken in July in which they argued over competing designations for Brosa as "leader" or "director." Preaching the need for a "spirit of the quartet," Halleux also demanded not only a restriction in Brosa's pretentions but also his own freedom from duties that summer. Those conditions denied, Halleux decided definitively he could no longer continue. Already in April, Warwick Evans had proposed to Halleux that he join his New London String Quartet, in which Evans was cellist and no less than William Primrose was violist. Halleux accepted the offer and in later July played with this group in Palo Alto and Berkeley. In a letter he wrote to Mrs. Coolidge on July 28, he affirmed that this playing matched the best he had enjoyed with the old Pro Arte.

In Hollywood, he worked in the MGM studios, and played in several ensembles (the Roth and Hungarian Quartets, playing viola); and he served in the Los Angeles Philharmonic. He returned to Belgium in the early 1960s, and played with the Belgian National Orchestra, until a heart condition brought death in 1963.

Replacing Halleux was managed smoothly and sensibly. His successor was to be another Belgian—and, ironically, one older than Halleux. This was Albert Rahier, born in 1895. He had a lively career as both violinist and theater conductor. It happened that he was touring the United States at the beginning of 1940 as part of Belgian piano quartet. When he heard of the death of his admired compatriot, Onnou, he was among the first to send condolences to the latter's widow. Now an expatriate himself, he was serving at such institutions as Mills College and Colorado College. He had a background of performing at times with the Pro Arte, so he was a logical choice for membership now. He was a sensible, careful, and utterly reliable musician, and was admired for binging a new tone of stability to the group. He arrived in Madison in September of 1943 and immediately took up his duties in such Madison concerts of which we have reports.

As if all this had not been enough trouble, the old cello problem returned. During the course of 1943, the draft status of George Sopkin was under review, and a source of concern. The decision finally came in a telegram of induction on November 15, 1943, and his resignation had to be accepted. Sopkin continued some musical activities during his military service. Then, following the example of Gottlieb, he became in 1946 one of the creators of the Fine Arts Quartet. Founded in Chicago, in 1963 that ensemble took up residence at the University of Wisconsin–Milwaukee, after the Madison model. Sopkin served in that until his death in 2008.

Even while Sopkin's draft situation was still uncertain, negotiations were under way for his replacement. Born and trained in Vienna, Ernst Friedlander had emigrated to the United States in 1937 and was serving in the Indianapolis Orchestra when the job offer in Madison was made. Friedlander arrived in the autumn. Just when he was integrated into the quartet is not clear. After discussions the previous year, a course that Bricken had devised and lectured in, "Quartets of Mozart and Haydn" (Music 9a), and for which the Pro Arte played examples, was announced for the 1943–44 season. This was to be broadcast over the university station, WHA, each Thursday afternoon, and to begin on September 30. In the advance announcement of the series, Friedlander is listed as the cellist. On the other hand, Sopkin was scheduled to play a sonata recital with Johansen on October 14, and perhaps did so. On October 30, the Pro Arte gave a concert with the cooperation of violist Beatrice Hagen and cellist Arnold Kvam, apparently to play a string sextet (Brahms?), but whether Sopkin or Friedlander was the regular cellist is not clear. On November 28, almost two weeks after Sopkin's induction notice arrived, the quartet played a concert in which the cellist must certainly have been Friedlander.

The introduction of Friedlander into the quartet marked another and a final landmark in the quartet's cello saga. The new member was given a long-term contract, rather than a temporary one conditional on the return of Robert Maas. This step clearly signaled the university's abandonment of efforts to bring him to rejoin his Belgian colleagues in the Pro Arte.

⌘  ⌘  ⌘

The struggles to bring Maas to the United States and back to Pro Arte membership, as we have seen, had gone on for four years, since the 1939 arrival of the quartet in the United States. Dykstra and Bricken had worked all their contacts in Washington and in diplomatic circles to bring Maas out of Belgium. Such efforts had proven futile through 1941, but with the entry of the United States as a combatant in World War II, the task became impossible. Endless schemes were devised, including one to bring him out by way of Japan, but without avail. One of the finest quartet musicians of his time, Maas was doomed to sit out the war in futility, doing some theater work but mainly playing in cafés in German-occupied Belgium.

Only in 1945, when the war was ended, did Maas manage to travel to the United States. With Prevost as the sole Belgian survivor, the Pro Arte was no longer the ensemble he had known and loved. And the pattern of filling his chair with "temporary" replacements pending his eventual reintegration had ended in 1943. Under the circumstances, Bricken could promise him no position with the University of Wisconsin Music School. For a while Maas functioned as a freelance musician, playing cycles of Bach's cello suites in various venues, but also working to find a place for his distinguished talents as a quartet cellist. According to Gunnar Johansen, another wealthy patron, Mrs. William Andrews Clark (née Anna Eugenia La Chapelle), another wealthy musical patroness, asked Maas if he would prefer to go back to Madison or to form a new

quartet. He chose the latter. Mrs. Coolidge had meanwhile sounded out
the violinist Henri Temianka about *his* forming a quartet, promising it a
Beethoven cycle at the Library of Congress under her patronage. Temianka and Maas met and, with the support of Mrs. Clark, projected a new
ensemble, for which the other two members were recruited: violinist
Gustave Rosseels and violist Robert Courte.

Mrs. Clark further backed the project by purchasing—for a
reported quarter-million dollars—a complete set of four Stradivari
instruments, all of which had belonged to Niccolò Paganini. On that
basis, the new group took the name of the Paganini Quartet. It first
appeared in June of 1946. The ensemble quickly acquired great distinction. They even followed some of the footsteps of the old Pro
Arte. They were playing a concert at Mills College in Oakland on July
7, 1948, when, during the intermission, Maas suddenly collapsed and
died of a heart attack. By poignant irony, the concert was being given
as a memorial to Alphonse Onnou. The Paganini Quartet went on
without Maas until their dissolution in 1966.

Maas was tall and charming, a bit of a rover in his range of interests. He also seems to have a touch of pranksterism about him that
could have rivaled that of Prevost. Long before he joined the QPA, in
his earliest years, Maas played in a summer orchestra that worked at
a resort at the seashore of Ostend. Temianka reports that the young
Maas decided as a joke to steal onstage before a concert and unscrew
the bass drum from its supporting stand, at the top of the stage risers. When during the concert it was struck for the first time, it began
rolling down the risers with growing momentum, almost hitting the
conductor, to be stopped only offstage by audience members. Now,
Prevost would have envied that one!

≼ઙ  ≼ઙ  ≼ઙ

The arrival of a fellow Belgian, the stalwart Albert Rahier, was some
comfort to Prevost, though the potential stability brought by Friedlander symbolized the lost hope of recovering Maas. Some of the violist's grievances he could resolve for himself. It has been established
that the members of the quartet could and should give solo recitals,
but Bricken withheld this opportunity from Prevost because the viola
literature was scanty and, as he put it, "not interesting." In his recollections, Prevost tells us that, out of pique, he promptly wrote to his
old friend, the composer Darius Milhaud, sending him a check for
$400 (big money back then) as a commission for a piece for him. The

response came an amazing five days later, in the form of a set of *Quatre Visages*, op. 238, for viola and piano. In his recollections, Prevost seems to place all of this in or around 1940, but the work was composed in 1943, and Prevost gave it its premiere performance, with Gunnar Johansen, in a concert in Madison on January 9, 1944. It was an immediate success, enhancing Prevost's faculty standing. He and Milhaud moved quickly to extend this success. The composer created in 1944 a pair of Sonatas for Viola and Piano for Prevost. The first of these (op. 240) he performed in a recital with Johansen on April 9, in a program linked to the second May Music Festival. The Second Sonata, op. 244, he premiered in Madison on August 2, in a concert that as a whole was titled "In Memorium Alphonse Onnou." For this performance, he was joined at the piano by the famous Nadia Boulanger.

The involvement of Boulanger with Madison is, in fact, part of another strand in the tangled tensions of the quartet at the time. In 1943, this famous teacher and conductor was in exile from Paris during the war. She was staying in California at the time, with her close friend Igor Stravinsky. She also had a good friend at Edgewood College in Madison, Sister Edward Blackwell of the Dominican Order of Sinsinawa, through whom she brought Stravinsky there. The latter had invited Brosa to play a work of his, and Brosa assisted in organizing a Stravinsky concert on January 23, 1944—a highly successful event that drew an audience of about 600 Madisonians, according to reports. In the course of their contacts, according to Prevost's recollections, Brosa slandered Prevost to Stravinsky, saying that the violist could no longer play, and that there were efforts afoot to get Prevost out of Madison and the quartet. Though Stravinsky and Prevost had some amiable contacts, the composer conveyed this picture to Boulanger, on their way back to Hollywood.

As the story continues, Boulanger returned to Madison and Edgewood College in the summer of 1944. She made a point of asking Prevost to take her to Onnou's grave in Madison's Forest Hills Cemetery. When he did this, he asked her if they might do some playing together. She put him off rather coldly, but she immediately telephoned him to apologize and to arrange a musical meeting the next day. As soon as they played a bit, Boulanger was delighted to find that Stravinsky's reports of his incompetence were false. An immediate rapport was established, and she was interested in Milhaud's Viola Sonata no. 2—just composed (in four days) that summer and newly in Prevost's hands. It was agreed that a concert should be organized at Edgewood college in Onnou's memory, on August 2. Its program included a piece by Nadia Boulanger's gifted but prematurely deceased sister Lili, and the world premiere of Milhaud's Viola Sonata no. 2. The sum total was a great popular success, and the concert had to be repeated (on August 4), Prevost recalled.

And there is an epilogue to this episode. When, later in 1944, Prevost asked Stravinsky to compose a piece for him in memory of Onnou, the composer not only responded, but declined the fee he was offered, by way of apology for having accepted Brosa's slander. The result was the *Élégie* for unaccompanied viola (or violin), which Prevost was to premiere at the Library of Congress on January 26, 1945.

But a far more tumultuous story was to emerge in the 1943–44 season. Brosa must have become weary of all the bickering within the quartet, especially over his own feuding with Prevost, who had his personal reservations about the Spaniard's violin playing. It was also said that Brosa's wife was not happy in Madison. Above all, Brosa wanted to direct his career toward more of a balance with chamber music and solo performance. To that end, he had been in contact with Smith College in Massachusetts, resulting in an offer of a post there as professor of violin. On August 27, 1943, Brosa wrote to Bricken informing him of the receipt of this offer. Without yet making his decision, Brosa made a very pointed observation that, with the departures of Halleux and Sopkin, "the Pro Arte Quartet was as good as dead at the very time of Onnou's death and can't possibly operate under that appellation, which no longer gives me any satisfaction."

And thereby Brosa fired the opening shot in the latest battle over the group's name, raised almost as if to make it a bargaining chip in his negotiations. Mrs. Coolidge was brought into the fray, and on January 18, 1944, she wrote her approval for adopting the name of the Brosa Quartet. But, with victory in Madison at hand, Brosa changed his mind. On February 5, 1944, Bricken wrote to Mrs. Coolidge to inform her that

> Mr. Brosa has decided in his own conscience that it is better for him to seek his future outside the quartet. In this I think he is right. And, as much as I hate to see our good friend leave us, I have had to admit in my heart that his decision is probably the right one. This means, of course, that we will have to get another first-rate first violinist for the quartet. . . .
>
> I am glad to tell you that the administration is firmly behind this whole idea, which certainly encourages me, as you can well understand.

Could she, Bricken asks, suggest any candidates for the position? On February 13, Mrs. Coolidge replied that she had also heard directly of the decision from "Tony" himself:

> I suppose that I must grow to feel that his decision to leave you is a well-considered one and a wise one. But I must confess that I was much disappointed to think of his leaving all the opportunities which I understood had been offered to him and that the chance of reviving the first-class Brosa Quartet has probably been lost or at least delayed. I am so sorry that you have so much difficulty and admire your indomitable courage in fostering the best chamber music at your university. However, I do not feel able to suggest anyone to replace Mr. Brosa and should not care to take the responsibility of advising such a step, because I feel entirely ignorant of the present quartet conditions at Madison, and do not even know the names of any of the members except Prevost.

Bricken's response, on February 21, renewed his regrets about Brosa's decision: "I can assure you that, as far as I'm concerned, he leaves us with an established record both as a musician and as a gentleman. I shall always be fond of Tony. You can well believe I shall miss him enormously."

Meanwhile, on February 18 and 22, Bricken made at least one effort in his quest, offering the position to the violinist Alexander Schneider, then in the process of ending his first period of service with the Budapest Quartet. Schneider would have made a distinguished replacement, but he rejected the offer.

In point of fact, though, Mrs. Coolidge could have had a perfect candidate for the vacancy, whether or not she would actually become involved in any of the ongoing negotiations. Rudolf Kolisch had already, on February 4, 1944, written to her. An old friend and earlier beneficiary of her support, he wanted to resume contact with her. (Had he heard of the impending vacancy in Madison?) He described his reduced situation. He had now separated from his wife Josie (Josefa, Josephine), previously his manager. His quartet had been disbanded. (He had actually had a nervous breakdown, though he did not mention that.) He was surviving by playing in what jobs he could find in ensembles and pit orchestras in New York, and even doing some writing. Mrs. Coolidge replied—on February 13, the very day she had replied to Bricken, expressing her detachment from Madison. She expressed admiration to Kolisch for his "indomitable courage and spirit," and hoped that he would join her "for an hour or two of playing together." Did they meet, and, if so, just what did they discuss?

Whether or not with any prompting from Mrs. Coolidge, Bricken had come into direct contact with Kolisch himself. On March 22 Bricken wrote to Kolisch, describing the position at the university and soliciting his interest. The most important of Kolisch's responses was in a letter of March 21:

> As I told you in my telegram, your proposition interests me enor- mously. The Pro-Arte [*sic*] Quartet has always been the one which I have admired and to which I have felt kindred in spirit because of its devotion to music and its artistic seriousness. To help continue the traditions of this ensemble is a task which tempts me very much. This particular set-up, which you rightly call the unique situation of the Pro-Arte Quartet [i.e., the university affiliation], seems to be the one opportunity amidst a world of commercialized music-business to develop an ensemble according to the standards to which I have always adhered. I join you in the belief that this quartet can and will be the first in this country at least as to artistic importance. If the nec- essary relationship between its members is established, the principle "Pro Arte" will really be carried to victory as against that "Pro Negate" all around.

Kolisch visited Madison in March of 1944. He received ready approval, with particularly strong support from Prevost, who felt that the great Austrian musician's identification with contemporary music would restore the Pro Arte to their old commitments. Mrs. Coolidge also gave her endorsement. On June 11, Kolisch was given his offi- cial appointment as a member of the Pro Arte—by now "Associates in Music" without tenure—as of the autumn.

Information is scanty on the quartet's activities up until then. In their last months with Brosa, the quartet kept both ensemble and recital engagements at the university (such as in the second May Music Festival), along with marginal commitments. On May 7, 1944, for example, Prevost was soloist with the Madison Civic Symphony, playing a fake "Handel" viola concerto and an "Air for Viola and Orchestra" by Milhaud.

Brosa departed Madison after the spring of 1944. He had served what would prove the briefest term as first violinist in the Pro Arte's history, presiding over a period of transition and tumult that he could not fully control. Tall and handsome, he was charming, with almost a movie-star air. He was liked and admired personally as a "gentleman" who "got along with everybody." He even had a sense of humor. At one recital he gave with pianist Leo Steffens (apparently on February 27, 1944), Brosa was wearing a borrowed tuxedo whose trousers split, requiring him to hold them up for his bows—amid much good-humored laughter. But he also had some pretensions. In contrast to his successor, Kolisch, Rahier characterized Brosa as "dapper, a showman, not enough of a quartet player, very snooty, and looked like a Spanish marquis."

An outstanding musician, in fact, Brosa had a distinguished musical record, both before and after his service with the Pro Arte. His credits as a virtuoso soloist included his world-premiere performance of Benjamin Britten's Violin Concerto in 1940, with other concerto achievements beyond. He would eventually resettle in England where he taught in the Royal College of Music. He died in 1979.

If the departure of Brosa marked the end of one rather messy era for the Pro Arte and ushered in an impressive new one under Kolisch, there was one other departure of this same moment that brought a definitive sense of closure. That was the withdrawal of Carl Bricken from his position as director of the University of Wisconsin's School of Music. An accomplished conductor in his own right (and maestro all along of the UW Symphony Orchestra), he found a new opportunity opening to him. On March 3, 1944, he wrote to Mrs. Coolidge asking of her a letter of recommendation for him as applicant for the conductorship of the Seattle Symphony. It must have helped, and on March 15 he wrote to her reporting that he had been offered, and had accepted, the post in which he would succeed no less than the great expatriate British conductor, Sir Thomas Beecham. Bricken would continue a long career as performer and as composer until his death in 1971.

At the time of his departure, President Dykstra wrote in praise of Bricken's achievement in making the University of Wisconsin "a really unique center of musical study and appreciation."

> We in Madison who believe in the power and influences of great music are deeply affected by Carl Bricken's decision to leave, even though we recognize the distinction that has come to him.

> . . . He has developed a fine student orchestra and has given the campus and state a wonderful program of great music. The effect of this development upon the student body has been tonic, exhilarating, and, I believe, lasting. This emphasis upon the educational and

cultural values of music must become a tradition. We cannot afford to lose it.

Carl Bricken's role in the Pro Arte's history should not be underestimated. It deserves to be put beside that of Elizabeth Sprague Coolidge. If she had been the midwife the Quatuor Pro Arte's emergence to international status and acclaim, he had been the fairy godfather of the Pro Arte Quartet's relocation and redefinition in Madison. His goals continued to be pursued by his successors there, but his imprint had been decisive.

As if Bricken's departure were not enough of a loss to the Pro Arte, in the following year, 1945, President Clarence Dykstra himself left the University of Wisconsin to preside over the University of California in Los Angeles (UCLA). Within little more than a year, then, the two most important sponsors of the quartet in Madison, their most devoted advocates, had left the scene where so much uncertainty lingered.

## Repertoire

To establish a clear record of the Pro Arte's repertoire during the Brosa years is even more difficult than for the preceding decades. The documentation is terribly fragmentary. Few programs were preserved. Many concerts were not reported, and even among those that were, the works played are not specified. This is true for concerts both within Wisconsin and beyond. It does seem likely that we can get a rough idea of the music that constituted the quartet's effective repertoire, but the numbers of performances of each that we have documented are pitifully short of the actualities that are now lost.

Certainly the character of the repertoire under Brosa was quite conservative and "mainstream." Gone altogether are any representations of the contemporary Belgian composers to whom the old Brussels group had been committed. The French literature so beloved of that ensemble was now drastically reduced—Debussy's Quartet appearing only six times, Ravel's a mere two, and Fauré's Piano Quartet op. 15 only once. Of "modern" composers, one notes single performances documented for Bartók's Quartet no. 5, for Bloch's Piano Quintet, for Martinů's Quartet Concerto, and for a piano-quartet arrangement of Milhaud's *Création du monde* (once each).

To be sure, Dmitri Shostakovich first appears in Pro Arte annals with his Quartet no. 1, reported as being played at least eight times. The truncated festivals of American music yielded performances of two works by Henry T. Burleigh, and quartets by Ernst Bacon, Carl Bricken, Lewis Lockwood, Daniel Gregory Mason, Douglas Moore, Walter Piston, Quincy Porter, and Randall Thompson (one or two times each), none of which entered the quartet's working repertoire thereafter.

Just as an imbalance was given to the Belgian group's last decade through their repeated Beethoven Quartet cycles, so too was there a heavy counterweight provided by the music of Brahms for the Brosa period. Through arrangements made with the Coolidge Foundation, the Pro Arte participated in four cycles in which virtually all of Brahms' chamber works (a total of twenty-three works in all) were played, of which twelve involved the quartet and four the University Trio. The cycle curiously omitted the Third Piano Quartet, op. 60, but the Pro Arte did perform that at least twice in their regular concerts. Some four of the works the quartet seem not to have performed beyond the cycles, but others appeared recurrently in the regular concerts: the op. 51 no. 2 Quartet and the two string quintets at least one further time, the Piano Quintet op. 34 some five more times, the op. 51 no. 1 Quartet seven times more, the op. 26 Second Piano Quartet ten times, and the op. 25 First Piano Quartet no less than sixteen times. (There are also two reported performances of unidentified string sextets.). These constitute eighty-nine performances in the total Brosa-era dossier.

Another unbalancing factor was the quartet's participation in Bricken's two-semester course (Music 9a/b), "Quartets of Haydn and Mozart" and "Quartets of Mozart and Beethoven." The classroom performances were also broadcast every Thursday afternoon by the university's station, WHA—an organization that itself played a vital role in disseminating the university's knowledge and their concerts around the state. For the Pro Arte contributions, there survives the schedule just for the season of 1943–44, which yields accurate but, nevertheless, only representative figures. Of the Haydn quartets, a total of nineteen were offered, one or two taken from each of the published opus sets. Of the Mozart quartets, only four were presented, plus one string quintet. Of Beethoven's, the complete opus 18 and the complete opus 59 were gone through, plus opera 95, 133, and 135, for a total of twelve.

To those may be added the reported concert performances. For Haydn, there were sixteen, three done once, three more done twice, with op. 64 no. 6 reaching three appearances and op. 20 no. 2 four. For Mozart, ten more concert performances were reported: one each of K. 465 and K. 598, and of an unidentified string quintet, with K. 458 being given thrice and K. 387 four times. For Beethoven, op. 59, no. 2 and opus 95 were performed only once each; opera 18 no. 2, 18 no. 5, and 135 twice each; while op. 59 no. 3 was given five performances, and opus 131 all of nine, for an impressive total of twenty-three reported performances.

Otherwise, the quartet's working repertoire was—aside from participation in two more cycles of Bach's *Brandenburg Concertos*—altogether traditional and "mainstream," if meager. Dvořák's "American" Quartet, op. 96, made a strong showing in at least eight performances. Borodin's Second Quartet received five. Schubert Quartets D. 703, D. 810, and D. 887 were performed once each, and the "Forelle" Quintet twice. From Schumann, the op. 41. no. 3 Quartet was given only once, the Piano Quintet twice. Wolf's *Italian Serenade* was given at least once.

Putting the faulty data together, we may posit 124 public concerts reported, plus the twenty-eight sessions of the Music 9 course, containing a rough total of 223 performed works—all within Brosa's four-year reign.

## Recording Activity

The quartet's Brosa period corresponded with a phase of dramatic change in the recording medium. The triumph of magnetic tape as the working vehicle of recording accelerated a rapid expansion of the technology of sound recording. The culmination of this was the introduction in the late 1940s of the vinyl "long-playing record" (LP). With all that came much change in the organizations of recording companies, plus a considerable expansion of circulation to an enlarged audience—one with improved finances amid growing postwar prosperity.

As the world of music recording went through growing changes, the opportunities for performers were in considerable transition. The Quatuor Pro Arte made their last recordings for EMI/HMV in 1938. The group was too much on the move to stop in London to do any more in 1939. The latter year saw the retirement of Fred Gaisberg from the firm. In the years just before and long after World War II, the dominant repertoire personality in the company was Walter Legge. His preoccupations were with opera and lieder, and with great stars—Elizabeth Schwarzkopf (his wife) among them, plus conductors like Arturo Toscanini and Wilhelm Furtwängler, and the revitalized Otto Klemperer. Legge showed little interest in chamber music.

For his part, Brosa—juggling solo and chamber performing—seems to have had no interest of his own in making recordings. There appears to have been no effort made to revive dealings with EMI/HMV. Haydn quartets did figure heavily in the Brosa-period concert repertoire, but no attempt seems to have been made to resume the Haydn recording series that was broken off in quite unfinished state in 1938. Though the group did travel outside Madison during those years, that was entirely within the United States, never in Europe, London, or otherwise, so their access to important recording facilities was restricted. To be sure, with all of their personnel changes, potential recording companies might have hesitated to take on the group. But it does seem that no thought was given to reviving the Pro Arte's widespread reputation through record circulation. Moreover, Bricken must have concentrated his concerns on maintaining the fractious quartet's security in Madison, above any other priorities.

The absence of any commercial recording activity would be a recurrent risk for the Pro Arte in the following decades, and the Brosa years set an ominous lesson for the future in those terms.

All of which is to say that, for this chapter, there are no activities to report in this final section—at least in terms of public, commercial releases. Some recordings of the Brosa-led quartet do survive, however, in archival discs and tapes, which are listed in appendix E, part 2.

# 4

# THE KOLISCH YEARS

# (1944–67)

## Personalities and Style

Rudolf Kolisch (1896–1978) was one of the most important musicians of the twentieth century. The kind of career to which he committed himself has somewhat obscured that fact for the general consciousness. Scandalously, he has yet to be given a full-scale biography—the writing of which would be a major task. During his lifetime, he discouraged the idea, saying that he was "too busy" for such a thing.

Kolisch was born in the small Austrian town of Klamm am Semmering, son of a prominent physician (whom some claim as the modern definer of diabetes). In his sophisticated bourgeois family, his talents were recognized early. At age six he began musical studies, primarily on the violin, but also on piano, and eventually in conducting and composing. At age seven he suffered an accidental crushing by a door, which cost him the first joint of his left hand's middle finger. This damage did not deter young Kolisch, who became a "southpaw," learning to play the violin with reversed hands—right hand fingering and left hand bowing. He had a Stradivarius violin reconditioned to serve the bowing requirements, with the order of the strings reversed, running from left to right as e″–a′–d′–g in place of the usual g–d′–a′–e″.

This practice was not totally unprecedented among professional violinists, but it would affect his own playing as well as his work as leader of a string quartet. A common seating pattern for such an ensemble would spread the players by range—first violin, second violin, viola,

cello—from right to left in an arc. The Brussels group had modified
this pattern so that the cello was in the rear right, and the viola front
right. The practice Kolisch used, with some variants, was usually, from
right to left, second violin-viola-cello-first violin. If all this looked a bit
odd, it had the virtue of having *every* instrument facing out to the audience, instead of one on the right turned inward—thereby particularly
enhancing the projection of the often understated viola.

It may be added that Kolisch also pursued piano studies, and
though he did not use this instrument normally in public, there were
documented instances when he did so—as we shall see below.

Meanwhile, the young musician had a narrow escape from disaster
at age nineteen during World War I. He had enlisted in the Austrian
army and, as a lieutenant, he was ordered to the Italian front and "certain death." But two comrades rescued him and, using a spurious diagnosis of appendicitis, smuggled him by military ambulance to Vienna,
where influential contacts guaranteed his safety thereafter.

Kolisch's studies at Vienna's Academy of Music involved work
toward a doctoral degree, with a planned thesis on Schubert that was
never finished. Studies also included work, beginning in 1919, with
Arnold Schoenberg, who was emerging as the leader of what has come
to be called the Second Viennese School of musical literature, identified with atonal or serial composition. Kolisch soon became the composer's assistant in the preparation of concerts meant to present new
works. A strong affinity, both personal and artistic, developed between
the two. Young Kolisch would become the foremost apostle of that new
idiom, while Schoenberg would marry Kolisch's sister Gertrud in 1924.
In 1920–21, Kolisch made appearances as both conductor and violinist.
As their relationship deepened, Schoenberg persuaded Kolisch that
he should give up plans to be a composer or conductor and instead
create a performing group dedicated to advancing the new music.

In 1922 Kolisch formed what was first called the Vienna String
Quartet. In 1928 they changed their name to the more conventional
Kolisch Quartet, with finally defined membership. A hallmark of the
Kolisch Quartet was the memorization of scores for both rehearsal and
performance. This was an evolutionary decision, not one imposed by
Kolisch himself. Its origins were at a musical celebration by Kolisch's
group for Schoenberg's fifty-third birthday (September 13, 1927).
After they played his First Quartet and the new Third, the composer
asked for more music. They had brought no new scores with them, and
Schoenberg teased them about needing the printed music. The players

realized that they had been using the finale of Beethoven's op. 59, no. 3, for intensified study, and so they could run through that from memory, and, in fact the rest of that full work. The results excited Schoenberg, who advised them to play everything from memory. Kolisch and his colleagues decided to follow this advice. Their rehearsals proved to be intense sessions, working from full scores and not parts. Their efforts aimed not only at memorization, but at coming to grips with what Kolisch understood as the interior characters and meanings of the music, learning the "nonnormative" contents. All this was a part of the highly disciplined ethos that Kolisch established as leader.

In the course of a decade, Kolisch and his players mastered some sixty works to the extent that they could perform them by heart. (Another account claims a final total of 118 quartets.) This practice allowed them to dispense with music stands, sit closer together, and increase their reliance on eye contact. It could also make performances somewhat strained, but it was undoubtedly impressive. Their practice set an example that some subsequent ensembles emulated (e.g., Smetana Quartet, Quartetto Italiano). A later student, Rose Mary Harbison, reports that, at one concert in Nice, the quartet came out and simply asked the audience, "What would you like to hear?"

The Kolisch Quartet performed widely, in over three hundred cities around Europe. Their repertoire was built considerably around the music of the Second Viennese School, balanced by a more traditional literature, mainly Austro-German, with room for music by Bartók. In 1934 they began making some recordings for the English Columbia company. In that same year, Kolisch married the pianist Josefa Rosanska, and she appeared with him on these early recordings. In 1935, given conditions in Germany and Austria, Kolisch decided to follow Schoenberg's example of the previous year and transfer his and his quartet's residence to the United States, though they continued some performing in Europe. In that year they appeared in a Coolidge Festival in Washington DC, marking their first recognition by the great patroness. (As their friendship grew, Kolisch, too, would meet with her to play duets.) The Kolisch Quartet toured the United States and South America in 1936–37 under the Hurok management. In 1937, to inaugurate the New Friends of Music organization in New York, the quartet presented a Beethoven Quartet cycle. Kolisch himself is reported as playing with Alphonse Onnou at Black Mountain College Summer Festival in 1938. There were various concert appearances, often featuring premieres of new works (by Schoenberg and Bartók).

Kolisch became an American citizen in 1940. In that year, at a meeting of the American Musicological Society, he delivered a controversial paper, published then in the *Musical Quarterly* (vol. 29, 1943), entitled "Tempo and Character in Beethoven's Music." In this, Kolisch advocated strict attention to the composer's tempo markings, cataloguing them in relation to meters and other features. This effort by Kolisch to codify Beethoven's meanings and expressions in systematic order became a cornerstone of his own intensely analytical techniques, and ironclad ideas of time progression. When he sent a copy of this study to Mrs. Coolidge, she replied (January 7, 1944) with thanks but with doubts that she could understand it.

Given difficulties during the war years—especially the comparatively limited market in the United States for chamber music—and with internal tensions growing, Kolisch found he had to disband his quartet, though he did make some lurching efforts at reviving the group between 1939 and 1942. Taking what work he could, he did some teaching at the New School for Social Research in New York, where he also conducted important American premieres of works by Stravinsky and Bartók. On March 19, and May 22, 1944, in a concert organized for the American League of Composers, Kolisch led a quartet including his new wife, Lorna Manfred-Freedman, and a promising violist named Bernard Milofsky, in works by Bartók. Well known to Mrs. Coolidge and Prevost, by the time of those last concerts he was the logical and soon-confirmed successor to Brosa as the Pro Arte's new first violinist.

❧   ❧   ❧

With Kolisch now at the helm, the Pro Arte made a preliminary debut in a ceremony on October 30, 1944, in honor of Mrs. Coolidge's eightieth birthday. The group played Mozart's Quartet K. 575, but with the tune of "Happy Birthday to You" grafted into it in Kolisch's own arrangement. There was, in fact, nothing new about this gesture. In 1939, with his own quartet, he had played this arrangement in honor of Mrs. Coolidge's seventy-fifth birthday.

The quartet settled down to serious business on November 11, 1944, with their first full concert, repeated the next day. This was the first step in which the new leader and the continuing members could take each other's measure: two Austrians, with two Belgians between them, and only one of the Belgians a Pro Arte member of the original

Brussels configuration. Kolisch himself, after the first performance on the 11th, wrote to Mrs. Coolidge to report on the new picture. He described his very busy schedule, from the very moment of his arrival in Madison: rehearsals, playing and commenting in the music course, coaching the orchestra, giving individual lessons.

> But the fact of being able to rehearse twice daily with the quartet makes me happy, and more so the results, which were very apparent today when we played Schubert and Beethoven in our first concert at the University, the big hall here. I can truly say I have a real quartet again.
>
> The enthusiasm and devotion of Germain [Prevost] are really touching. The cellist, Friedlander, is a very pleasant surprise in that he is an excellent instrumentalist and can be developed into a quartet player of the first rank. The second violin, Rahier, is also a very fine and reliable player, and all that has to be done is to open him up a little, which I succeeded already to do to some extent.
>
> It is most gratifying to experience how they enjoyed the terrific strain of our most intensive work. During the eight weeks since my arrival, we have studied eight classic and four contemporary works. That makes me think of old times.
>
> Very soon we have to leave for a tour through Wisconsin, where we will play thirteen concerts and, besides that, we have several concerts outside the state before we leave for our tour in January. The University of Wisconsin lends or sells us to other universities and colleges, among others the University of Illinois in Chicago, where we plan a Schoenberg program.
>
> In the remaining time, so little time, we have to prepare all the work we play in Washington and the rest of our tour, and I have scheduled rehearsals for every day; I might say every hour. Malipiero's quartet we have already studied and performed, and that makes it impossible to study another in its place, but we will gladly prepare it for another occasion.

Kolisch's early backer, Prevost, was euphoric in his parallel report to Mrs. Coolidge at about the same time, in November—even while himself raising anew an old bugaboo:

> The quartet continues its work with an unprecedented discipline, a courage, and enthusiasm. We want to recover our old reputation and we are getting there. I have suggested to Rudolf the change of Pro Arte to Kolisch Quartet. With an artist of his stature, it is entirely

natural. But at the present moment it would perhaps be dangerous to effect that transformation *vis-à-vis* the university, and we will wait some months.

Prevost went on to suggest that, when they are next in Washington, he and Kolisch might play Mozart's Trio K. 498 with her, if she did not mind. The offer was generous, because her hearing was nearly destroyed by this time, and musicians who came to play with her must have had an awful time doing so.

As for that old issue of renaming the quartet, Mrs. Coolidge herself seems to have become aware of its latest revival. Prevost himself wrote to her on February 19, indicating his intent to proceed carefully in his effort to rename the quartet for Kolisch. In a letter of February 26, 1945, she wrote to Bricken—apparently still involved with the Pro Arte even while now in Seattle—that the name was not important now. "Still, I shall be glad if you arrange to take Kolisch's name, leaving the Pro Arte as an almost sacred memory of the past 30 years." The matter was raised in December 1945 when an instructor at the University of Illinois was provoked by a Pro Arte concert there to protest the "usurpation" of the old Brussels group's name, a protest that was shrugged off by the concert's managers. In the outcome, no serious move was made to rename the quartet at this time.

For their first season (1944–45), around-the-state touring seems to have been limited to appearances in Wisconsin Rapids (November 22), Port Edwards (November 27), and Nicolet (November 29). The quartet gave concerts in Illinois, and participated in a Schoenberg festival in December 1944. As part of this, the quartet was supposed to be part of the premiere of the composer's *Ode to Napoleon* on December 8, but the event was apparently cancelled. Presumably the Pro Arte's first performance of a Schoenberg quartet (the Third) with Kolisch was given in a concert at the University of Chicago on December 13, along with music of Prokofiev and Stravinsky. Mozart, Prokofiev, and Schubert were in a program at the University of Illinois in Champaign on December 19.

The year 1944 brought the initiation of an arrangement to record performances on glass discs made at station WHA, to be played throughout the United States by the Mutual Radio Network. This arrangement would last for the next five years. It thereby brought some wide national recognition to the group that one grateful but slightly confused listener (a student at the South Dakota School of Mines and Technology) described as the "Pro-Artic Quartet."

Early 1945 saw the launching of a very busy round of Pro Arte activities—better documented now. Many concerts were given outside Wisconsin, above all on the East Coast, and at first in the Baltimore–Washington area. The Schoenberg Third Quartet was featured in Baltimore on January 18, paired with the long-deferred *Rispetti e Strambotti* of Malipiero, but that was absent through much of what followed. In New York on January 21, for a Mozart viola quintet, Bernard Milofsky was brought in. At a special concert on January 26 at the Library of Congress's Coolidge Auditorium, Prevost gave the world premiere of the *Élégie* that Stravinsky had composed "*à l'intention de Germain Prevost pour être jouée à la mémoire de Alphonse Onnou.*" The performance was followed by a tribute to Onnou delivered by Mrs. Coolidge herself. This premiere launched a long procession of performances of the piece at every opportunity in Pro Arte concerts thereafter. Moreover, on February 7, in New York, Prevost played it privately for the composer himself.

The concerts in New York prompted interest as to how the quartet was sounding under their new management. Writing for the *New York Herald Tribune*, Olin Downes gave a very positive evaluation:

> The Pro Arte Quartet, under the leadership of Rudolf Kolisch, has gone Viennese. And it has exchanged the Gallic style of execution for the Central European without any loss of excellence. It has acquired in the process three new artists, Germain Prevost, the viola, being the only member left of the group that one knew in other times. At present it is another Kolisch quartet (one has already known several). And, like all the Kolisch quartets, it is a delight to hear. Its sound is light and clear, its rhythm easy-going and animated, the execution in general lively and warm and friendly and wholly lacking in upstageness. There is nothing academic here and nothing vulgar. Mr. Kolisch has a way of avoiding both the lugubrious and violent in quartet playing that is most welcome. Always the work of this organization was distinguished and beautiful. It is still so, though Gallic serenity has now been replaced by a Viennese warmth.

While in Washington, on February 2, 1945, the quartet visited the home of Mrs. Coolidge, performing for her the Bartók Fifth Quartet but also joining her in playing a Brahms piano quartet. At a private home concert on February 5 in Newark, New Jersey, they were joined by two former members of the old Kolisch Quartet. From home base in Madison, the Pro Arte carried out their spring tour around the state (Milwaukee–Downer College, Whitewater, Beloit, Richland Center, Eau Claire, Ashland, etc.). Both together and individually, the quartet members participated in the third May Music Festival in Madison, rounding things out for the spring by an appearance in Detroit. In a concert reported for May, Kolisch's wife Lorna was noted as playing a work of Douglas Moore with Johansen. The Pro Arte revived in late summer to give four concerts at Chicago's Ravinia Festival (August 14, 16, 18, 19), rounded out then by a Madison performance (August 29).

Meanwhile, threats of personnel changes had been stirred up in late winter. Prevost, who was trying to pursue the idea of renaming the quartet for Kolisch, had misgivings about the leader's ideas regarding some changes. On February 15, 1945, Prevost wrote to Nadia Boulanger about the university's renewal of the quartet's standing. He added:

> But I foresee very unhappily for much later some serious complications with Kolisch. He wants to give the position of second violin to his wife. Rahier is certainly somewhat insufficient for a group that hopes to reach a high standard but for me this change would be unfortunate. The wife, Jewish to the bone, has an impossible character and I really sympathize with my friend [Rahier]. Here we have had a long discussion about a very amicable plan. But I suspect that he will not give up and this will undoubtedly be the inevitable fracture at the season's end.

As it happened, such a dangerous scheme would not be pressed forward at this time, though the issue of Lorna Kolisch's possible admission to the quartet would return. (And we might remember that soon after, on October 2, 1945, Robert Maas would arrive in the United States, where he would, with the cordial support of Mrs. Coolidge, move on to help found the new Paganini Quartet.)

Information is again skimpy for the first half of the Pro Arte's 1945–46 season, but Kolisch initiated a series of performances of individual Beethoven quartets, on into the spring. A concert in Los Angeles on January 9, 1945 (Schubert, Schoenberg, Beethoven), prompted these critical comments published the next day in the *Los Angeles Daily News*:

> It may be a purely subjective reaction which makes me regard last night's playing as lacking in depth. Execution was flawless, and the surface had a silken finish, but it seemed that little more than the surface was presented. I would have traded much of the exquisite tone and precision for half the wallop I get by listening to a much rougher reading by, say, the Busch players. The Pro Arte delivery was beautiful, faultless and disembodied. In short, it lacked guts.

Ten days later another critic wrote of the same concert: "Here was lovely music [Schubert's D. 804] delightfully played. True, there appeared to be some disbalance in volume among the players, but not of sufficient importance to be of serious bother. One had the feeling that the first violin was being covered by the other players." More of the review demonstrated what Kolisch was up against in championing the music of Schoenberg. The critic deplored

> the almost painful experience of listening to this music more than once. But if this quartet [No. 3] is a fair sample of contemporary music then surely, music has gone far beyond the ken of this writer or there is something wrong with the music. The piece is one long incoherent mass of ugliness and, try as we would, we simply could make nothing more or less out of it.

Concerts in New York included an appearance at Town Hall, participating on Schubert's Octet (D. 803), and, as joined by the eminent Schoenberg specialist, pianist Eduard Steuermann, the Brahms Piano Quartet, op. 26. In Madison, on March 14, 1946, three members of the quartet joined the UW Symphony Orchestra, under its new conductor, Richard Church, as soloists in two works: Kolisch and Prevost in Mozart's *Sinfonia concertante* K. 364; Kolisch and Friedlander in Brahms' Double Concerto. The quartet made appearances in the fourth May Music Festival—with composer Ernst Krenek as a guest performer. A concert at the University of Chicago on May 20 included two major works by Schoenberg: the Quartet no. 3, and the sextet *Verklärte Nacht*—the latter with Lorna Kolisch on viola and cellist Arnold Kvam joining. A local critic allowed himself some comparison in his evaluation: "[The quartet] improved its ensemble considerably since it last played the Schoenberg [Quartet no. 3] on December 13, 1944, . . . but the sextet on the other hand evidently posed problems which were not entirely solved in rehearsal."

On May 21, 1946, Prevost wrote excitedly to Mrs. Coolidge to inform her that he had become an American citizen, that his daughter, Antoinette, was soon to arrive, and that his younger daughter, Germaine, would soon follow—a source of great joy after six years of separation. (Prevost's wife also made the crossing during this time.) He was relieved to see his proper family at last, ending the quartet players' wartime separations. Only on their arrival did Prevost hear the full story of what the three women had been doing during the war. He had already learned that they had established a safe house for downed

Allied airmen, when the British parents of one soldier they had saved wrote to Prevost to thank him and assure him of his own family's safety. When the women arrived, Prevost could receive the full account of their bravery and courage at great risk to themselves. Welcome as the reunion now was, Mrs. Prevost was in terrible health, and she found the Madison climate unsuitable. She soon moved west, and the Prevosts were to be separated then for some twenty years.

The 1946–47 season saw Kolisch still programming individual Beethoven quartets on a regular basis. A performance at the Cleveland Museum of Art on October 11 elicited a highly favorable reaction from the distinguished musician and local critic, Arthur Loesser: "This group is one of the leading string quartets now in America." The quartet gave a concert on October 20 at Princeton University, as part of celebrations of that institution's bicentennial. Their autumn tour is not documented. The semester was ended with a concert in Omaha, Nebraska, on December 3. In the second semester, the quartet gave five concerts in Madison, in most of which individual Beethoven quartets continued to be explored. The spring tour around the state was crowded with over a dozen stops (Appleton, Neenah, Oshkosh, Marshfield, Rhinelander, Clintonville, Luck, Fairchild, Augusta, Eau Claire, Bloomington, La Crosse, Platteville, Milwaukee) spread over March 9–26. Further concerts were given around Wisconsin, mostly in colleges and schools (Milton, Whitewater, Mayville, West Bend, Fond du Lac, Plymouth, Oshkosh, Ripon, Beloit, Green Bay, and several in the Milwaukee area) through most of April and into May.

Out-of-state engagements were rare. But in January appearances were made in Pittsburgh and then New York. An ISCM concert at Hunter College, NYC, on January 25, that included the Schoenberg Third Quartet, drew a frequently quoted review from Virgil Thompson of the *New York Herald Tribune:*

> The Pro Arte concert was crowded with as high a concentration of the brighter young and of distinguished musical personalities as your reporter has encountered this season. Execution was perfect, applause massive. Their music is a delight to hear, its sound bright and clear, its rhythms easy-going and animated. The chief delight of the evening was a work called Five Movements for String Quartet by Anton Webern.

Other out-of-state appearances were at Baylor University, in Waco, TX, in February and then on May 11 at the South Western Composer's Festival in Tulsa, Oklahoma, which constituted the season's conclusion.

The year 1947 also marked the end of membership in the quartet for the last one of the original Brussels foursome who had remained past Onnou's death.

≼ ≼ ≼

Germain Prevost—no longer "Prévost" now that he was settled in America—was surely the most colorful of all the musicians who played in the Pro Arte Quartet. Of generally sunny disposition, he was the group's jester and jokester, with a great sense of humor. Not only his colleagues but many of his students have testified to his geniality, and generosity with his time. (One dissenting report, however, perhaps from Rahier, designated him "a nasty little guy.") He also developed a love for unusual gadgets, especially for fast automobiles, which helped adjust him to American ways.

For all his Americanization, however, Prevost never fully lost his accent in speaking English, which he described as "a language less than ideal." Bernard Milofsky, his eventual successor, had much contact with him and recalled one occasion when Prevost invited him for a "meal check." Milofsky was baffled by this for (he said) five minutes, until he recognized that the invitation was for a "milk shake." Prevost was also a passionate angler who enjoyed regular fishing in Lake Mendota. On one occasion, having caught a large fish in the morning, he decided to preserve it for lunch later on. He was then staying at the University Club, in a room without refrigeration. So he put the fish in a bowl under the tap, which he turned on, assuming it ran cold water; but he mistakenly turned on the hot water, and by the time he returned the fish was no longer fit for consumption.

One may speculate about the reasons for his decision to retire from the quartet—at age fifty-six, after some thirty-five years of service in, or involvement with, the Pro Arte. Rose Mary Harbison suggests a disillusionment with Kolisch and reports his blowing up at a rehearsal and shouting "I've had it with your Schoenberg!" Dorothy Bricken claimed that Prevost, at the point of his retirement, marched into Kolisch's office and abruptly resigned. One may be suspicious of such stories. In a later interview, Prevost reminisced: "The reason I left was that the [Belgian] style was changed, the spirit was dead."

Prevost did later express regret for his decision to become an American citizen, because thereby he unknowingly forfeited his large Belgian army pension. "I think it was a mistake . . . I lost everything

I owned, millions . . . . I had a full house, beautiful house in Brussels. I lost everything. My wife became ill, but never complain [*sic*]." Maas once quipped that "Prevost wanted to stay in Belgium to protect his wine cellar." But Prevost himself pointed out what must have been the ultimate factor in his leaving the Pro Arte. As already noted, his wife, in ill health, found the Wisconsin climate difficult to bear, while his daughter Antoinette had such respiratory problems that she was advised to go to a warmer clime. They had already moved to California, and so Germain decided to follow and rejoin them. They settled eventually in Eagle Rock, a suburb of Los Angeles.

Still in excellent health himself, and by no means finished with an active career, Prevost followed the trail of Halleux, joining him in the studio orchestra of Hollywood's Metro-Goldwin-Mayer, serving in that for fifteen years. Along the way, in 1949, he appeared with the New Art String Quartet of California (April 11). In that same year, he played with the Israel Baker Piano Quartet, which included the versatile pianist André Previn (October 9); and, still further (November 23), he reunited with his old colleague Victor Gottlieb in a concert with the American Art Quartet. Prevost and Previn became very good friends, joining for concerts a number of times. Prevost served in the San Francisco Symphony Orchestra under Enrique Jorda, during 1952–53 season, rejoining it later, in 1960–63. He was invited in 1956 to become the violist of the Quartet of Budapest, which in 1959 gave a concert at Mills College: the program included the new Sextet op. 365 by Milhaud, commissioned by Prevost. He served as first violist of the Oakland Orchestra until 1969, when his eyesight began failing at age seventy-eight.

Prevost became a familiar figure around the San Francisco area, where he settled in his last years. He gave interviews to local papers. As he aged, his memory remained sharp, if not always totally accurate. In 1979 (March 19–25) the Pro Arte was in residence in Vancouver, British Columbia, to participate in celebrations in honor of the Canadian composer, Harry Adaskin, who happened to be an old friend and colleague of Prevost. Using the opportunity, Cathy Paulu, wife of the Pro Arte's then-leader, Norman Paulu, brought Prevost up from San Francisco to Vancouver, where the CBC filmed an encounter of them all. Prevost proved extremely lively and voluble. And the fullest consolidation of his recollections came in 1981 when, during a visit to San Francisco, the Paulus sat Prevost down with a microphone and tape recorder for a long interview with him—for all its gaps and weak points, an essential source for the quartet's history.

Over the years, meanwhile, when the latter-day quartet was in San Francisco, the PAQ musicians would make a point of visiting him, and playing for him, even as deterioration of his hearing was joined by increasing blindness. He eventually lost the power of speech, due to a stroke, and could communicate only through his daughter, Antoinette. There are stories of the players sitting in a circle with him in the center, so as to hear as best he could. At least once he requested a Brahms quartet. Participants in these events tell of tears coming to his eyes. One wonders if his memory allowed him to recall his own participation, as a member of Quatuor Pro Arte, in a parallel tribute in 1933 at the bedside of the dying Georges Charbonneaux (see above, p. 43).

Germain Prevost died in 1987 at the age of ninety-six. At this writing, the current PAQ violist, Sally Chisholm, holds a five-year professorship named, at her suggestion, in Prevost's honor.

&#x266C; &#x266C; &#x266C;

The season of 1947–48 began the membership in the quartet of violist Bernard Milofsky. Born in Baltimore in 1917, he began his studies there at the Peabody Conservatory, continuing at the Curtis Institute and George Washington University. A *Wunderkind* from the start, he was a soloist with the National Symphony at age twelve. First trained on the violin, from age fourteen he played in dance orchestras as a paid musician. A teacher pointed out that there was more need and opportunity for violists, and so Milofsky took up that instrument, remaining accomplished on both. But it was on the viola that he acquired a formidable reputation. No less than the highly regarded violist Walter Trampler was quoted as calling Milofsky "the best violist in America." He was active in the New York area, where he played in various orchestras—in one under Leopold Stokowski. In 1947, he made a highly successful solo debut at New York's Town Hall.

Milofsky meanwhile came to the attention of Kolisch, who used him at times in the last days of his quartet. They became friends, and particularly enjoyed playing chess together. Kolisch had called upon Milofsky as a supplemental player at least once—in a New York concert on January 21, 1946—as already noted. Thus, the Pro Arte players already had some familiarity with him. In Prevost's waning days, Kolisch had Milofsky once more take on the second viola part for a Mozart quintet, on April 26, in a concert at Green Bay. It might be guessed that this was part of an audition and screening test for the soon-to-be-vacant viola chair. At any rate, Milofsky was the new occupant when the 1947–48 season began.

In the first semester, there were relatively few out-of-state engagements (Cleveland, Princeton, Omaha), while the quartet undertook eleven stops in the Wisconsin autumn tour (Stevens Point, Medford, Wausau, Algoma, Kewanee, Marinette, Menasha, Prairie du Chien, Viroqua, La Crosse, and Milwaukee), employing the same repeated program for all but the last stop. In the spring semester, there were outside engagements (Tucson, AZ; Chapel Hill, SC; Brunswick, ME; Pittsburgh; Chicago; and Cedar Falls, IA), plus stops in Milwaukee. For the spring tour, thirteen stops in eleven towns (Ripon, Marksman, Sheboygan, Fond du Lac, Monroe, Milton, Whitewater, Milwaukee (three stops), Racine, Watertown, and Beloit), with varied programs.

The large framework of the season, however, was a grand Schubert Festival that ran at intervals from October 26, 1947, through May 30, 1948. This involved a total of seven concerts, devoted entirely to the composer's chamber works: sixteen different pieces, performed by the quartet and other faculty members. There were also non-Festival appearances in Madison. Schubert works were woven into many of the various concerts throughout the season.

One interesting feature was the appearance of Kolisch performing not as violinist but as pianist. From childhood, Kolisch had adjusted his fiddling because of his left-hand finger accident. But the accident involved difficulties that he was somehow—through his own determination—able to accommodate in his piano playing. He virtually never appeared as a pianist in public, but at least on three documented occasions, he did. Once, in the 1944 Black Mountain College Summer Festival, he accompanied one Lotte Leonard in a program of Schubert songs. Then, at the climax of the Schubert Festival in Madison, he accompanied one Maximilian Schmetler in the entire *Winterreise* song cycle, no mean feat. And, finally, he was accompanist to Helene Stratman-Thomas and the University of Wisconsin Women's Chorus in Schubert's *Ständchen* (D. 921). Apparently he would only move to the keyboard for Schubert. Later on, we will encounter three more instances of Kolisch playing piano, in February of 1957.

Notice should be made also of Helene Stratman-Thomas, soon to add her married name of Blotz. She was a distinguished ethnomusicologist (specializing in Wisconsin folksongs), a member of the voice faculty and choral director, as well as the manager for the Pro Arte. In the last capacity, she proved an efficient business partner, bringing a better order to the Pro Arte's affairs.

Reports for the autumn of 1948 list a performance in Milwaukee (November 10) in which Schoenberg's First Quartet was brought into Kolisch's Pro Arte repertoire for the first time. Engagements in Madison (September 7, October 17, November 14, December 5), as well as an outing to Pittsburgh, showed a concentration on at least two of Beethoven's opus 59 quartets. But the clever mixing of consistency with variety in choosing programs is shown in the autumn tour schedule (October 18–31), in which three distinct menus were interspersed: one used once (Superior), another used three times (Green Bay, Ashland, Ladysmith), and another used eight times (Menasha, Marinette, Antigo, Wausau, Spooner, Cumberland, Chippewa Falls, Marshfield)—all programs, with whatever variables, built around one major work, Schubert's D. 810 Quartet (*Der Tod und das Mädchen*).

In the second semester of 1948–49, Schoenberg's Second Quartet (with faculty soprano Bettina Bjorksten) was added to the repertoire, and more attention was given throughout many concerts to Haydn's opus 76. Out-of-state engagements seem to have been limited to Pittsburgh and New York, in January. Six concerts in Madison included one (May 18) in festival celebrations held for the University of Wisconsin's centennial. There were several stops in Milwaukee, within and beyond the spring tour of April 18—May 2 (La Crosse, Beloit, Evansville, Sinsinawa, Monroe, Fond du Lac, Sheboygan, Racine, Watertown, Fort Atkinson, Kenosha). In many of those programs, Beethoven's opus 74 figured frequently, but also Schubert's Quartet D. 887. The season was extended into July with a reported concert given at Frank Lloyd Wright's home in Spring Green.

The concert of January 20, 1949, devoted to Schubert's D. 887 Quartet and Schoenberg's First Quartet, elicited this evaluation the next day from a critic for the *New York Herald Tribune:*

> Quite apart from the technical excellence of the playing—as individuals and together—there is an interpretative strength and brilliance in this group that does wonders with tension, clarity of detail and the extended formal periods of these works.

> There were one or two slips of intonation in the Schubert, but such small discrepancies were drowned amid the greater unity, and the whole interpretative concept, its tonal degrees—with whole phrases,

passages, displayed within a whisper or in terms of dynamic and arresting linear brilliance—made an imposing performance. . . .

Kolisch brings, as he always did, a strength, grace, and distinction to quartet playing that is as admirable as it is rare.

The first semester of the 1949–50 season seems to have involved no out-of-state appearances, but there were four in Madison and two in Milwaukee. Otherwise, there was a busy autumn tour, October 16–29 (Fenimore, Boscobel, De Pere, Appleton, Port Edwards, Cliftonville Medford, Wausau, Oconto, Marinette, Stevens Point, Menasha). The concert programs were a grab bag of varieties and repetitions, but with Brahms's opus. 51, no. 2 Quartet figuring prominently.

Amid all this outward activity, a crisis was brewing in the university's administrative halls. Begun by a letter to the local journal, the *Capital Times*, rumors began circulating that the university might not reengage the quartet as a resident ensemble. Public opinion was aroused over this, and petitions opposing this step began to circulate, on into November. One of the leaders was a young undergraduate named John Patrick Hunter, who was in subsequent years to become a writer, music critic, and editor of that same newspaper. It was pointed out that the University of Wisconsin had set an example for establishing artists and musicians "in residence" at an institution of higher education, a practice that was being taken up even then by other institutions. And the pattern of the University of Wisconsin's allowing the Pro Arte only year-to-year renewals was condemned as scandalous. Finally, in December 1949, just before Christmas, President E. B. Fred recommended the reappointment of the quartet members at least for 1950–51, if still without faculty status. Though issues in this matter still smoldered, at least the immediate future was guaranteed.

The spring semester of 1950 brought the first full burst of Kolisch's championing of Schoenberg with the Pro Arte—which was launched after he was temporarily afflicted by pleurisy. In New York, there were two concerts, each of which drew comments from the *Herald Tribune*. In the first, on January 15, 1950, Mozart provided a curtain-raiser to Schoenberg's Quartet no. 2, with Patricia Neway as their soprano soloist. This prompted one of the paper's critics ("FDP") to observe the next day: "[The players] gave an impressively revealing interpretation marked by pervasive clarity and praiseworthy quality of tone, fineness of shading in dynamics and instrumental hues. Miss Neway was in good voice in a well phrased performance of the score." The concert on January 16, joining Schoenberg's String Trio, op. 45, with Beethoven's op. 95 and Schubert's D. 810, was evaluated by another of the paper's critics ("TGH"): "The Pro Arte has marked fineness as an ensemble, though occasionally an over-refinement inhibits breadth and vigor. In the Beethoven number there were slight exaggerations at the expense of formal definition."

But the quartet was in New York for even more serious business. Now on a contract with the small label, Dial Records, the group undertook four taping sessions. The first three were held in the station WOR studios, January 20, 24, 27; the last in Carnegie Recital Hall, February 2. The purpose was to record Schoenberg's Quartet no. 3, along with works by Webern and Berg. It is said that at least one member of the new Juilliard String Quartet—who were later to make highly esteemed recordings of all the Schoenberg quartets—attended the studio sessions, eager to learn from Kolisch. Eventually, the ghost of an old issue arose to haunt again: on April. 21, 1950, Leland Coon, director of the University of Wisconsin Music School, wrote to the Dial Records company to remind and insist that the ensemble was not to be identified as the "Kolisch Quartet," but as the Pro Arte.

Having returned to Madison for the spring semester of 1950, the quartet caught up, on February 4, with a program that had been canceled and carried over from January. They then launched a "Schoenberg Series" that would consist of five concerts offered at intervals in Madison (February 20, 27, March 13, 20, 27). In all, the works covered were the four Quartets; the "Hanging Gardens" song cycle with Bjorksten; excerpts from *Pierrot Lunaire* (with Blotz); various piano pieces; Kolisch's own arrangement of the Violin Concerto (for violin and piano); the *Ode to Napoleon*; and the String Trio. There were three other concerts in Madison that were not part of the series, and four in Milwaukee. There seem to have been no other concerts beyond Wisconsin, but there was the usual spring tour of the state, in thirteen stops over ten days (April 14–27: Beloit, Kenosha, Whitewater, Milwaukee, Racine, Sheboygan, Manitowoc, Green Bay, Oshkosh, Ripon). The programs were drawn from a rotating repertoire of Haydn's opus 76, no. 1, Mozart's K. 428, Beethoven's opus 59 no. 2, Smetana's no. 1 in E minor, and Ravel's Quartet. Schoenberg was studiously avoided in all those appearances. Finally, the quartet participated in the University of Wyoming Center for the Arts's Workshop II, at Laramie (June 19—July 21), contributing four concerts (June 22, July 5, 11, 18). For those, Schoenberg's Quartet no. 1, Berg's *Lyric Suite*, and Webern's Five Movements were mixed with works of Haydn, Mozart, Beethoven, Schubert, Reger, and Bartók.

It was clear, by this time, that Kolisch had established Madison as the new center of sponsorship in the United States for the works of Schoenberg, and of the entire Second Viennese school in general. This made Kolisch himself the country's foremost spokesman and apostle for the atonal movement—all this at a time when the university's long-term policies on the quartet's status were still somewhat unsettled.

The 1950–51 season began with the kind of low-intensity public activity that was becoming the norm by now for autumn semesters. Only three concerts are documented in Madison (October 8, November 5, December 3) and one in Milwaukee (November 21). Those framed the usual autumn state tour: fourteen concerts within October 9–23, in ten locations (Superior, Cashton, La Crosse, Tomah, Eau Claire, Wausau, Oconto, Marinette, Menasha, Green Bay). The programs were a constantly varying mix of Austro-German literature (with the single exception of Debussy's Quartet), emphasizing Beethoven's quartets, but with recurrence of Schubert's D. 887.

The first half of 1951, however, was far more busy. For one thing, it had become university policy that the quartet's off-campus appearances (aside from the tours) should be in the second semester. Only six such are reported, for Chicago (twice), Rockford, Illinois; Mount Vernon, Iowa; Fort Wayne, Indiana (at a Music Educators National Conference, April 8); and Salt Lake City (in May, National Federation of Music Clubs, of which Kolisch had been chairman of chamber music since 1947). Returning from that, Kolisch brought composer Roger Sessions, with whom Kolisch had developed strong artistic and personal ties. Indeed, in the all-Sessions program they presented in Madison on May 28, the Pro Arte gave the apparent premiere of Sessions's new Quartet no. 2, which he had dedicated to Lorna and Rudolf Kolisch. In Madison, through the semester, there were five other concerts. In Milwaukee there were three appearances, outside of the spring tour. The latter (April 13–29) involved seventeen presentations at twelve venues (Mineral Point, Platteville, Sinsinawa, Milwaukee [six times], Watertown, Baraboo, Kenosha, Racine, Sheboygan, Manitowoc, Plymouth, Waukesha). The repertoire was again greatly mixed, but was mostly Austro-German, with Beethoven again predominant.

Critical comments on at least two of the concerts are worth quoting here. One, written by "M.N.G." for the *Rockford Morning Star* on

March 14, 1951 (after the concert the previous day), gives a sunny picture of the quartet players at their work:

> Rudolf Kolisch, the quartet's left-handed first violin, who played with a dash and a fire that are sometimes pretty breathtaking; Albert Rahier, second violin, whose beautifully smooth tone provides the perfect complement to the pyrotechnics of the first fiddle; Bernard Milofsky, who manages to look strangely calm and placid, even when his rich-toned viola is producing music that is anything but placid; and Ernst Friedlander, whose cello, with its perfect sonorities, is an extremely important part of the ensemble—these are the musicians of the Pro Arte.

On the other hand, a critic for the *Milwaukee Journal*, a day after the March 20 concert at the city's Athenaeum (offering Mozart's K. 464, Milhaud's Quartet no. 8, and Schubert's D. 887), was notably negative, complaining of a "profusion of rasping, scraping, and just plain bad tone production, especially in the violin and viola passages." (Such differing reactions may, of course, reveal more about the critics than about what is being criticized.)

We have some figures for the work loads of the Pro Arte players about this time. As supplied by Helene Stratman-Thomas Blotz (May 13, 1949), the schedule for 1948–49 had called for preparing thirty-three programs for WHA broadcasts and transcription, September through May; the group rehearsed fifty-two different works, in sessions averaging thirty hours per week, beyond individual practice; each taught a prescribed number of students for a prescribed number of hours per week. Far more explicit are the terms laid out for the 1951–52 season. For each player each semester, there would be thirty-five hours per week for concert preparations, plus one hour per week preparing for the fall-spring tours. For the autumn, there would be six concerts, five string clinics, four Madison concerts, three Milwaukee concerts; for the spring semester, there would be fourteen concerts, five in Madison, three in Milwaukee, and one in Iowa. As for private instruction, in the fall semester Kolisch would have a total of six-and-a-half hours per week; in the spring eight-and-a-half hours per week, each covering two private students, four ensemble students, two research students, and various numbers of students to be prepared for courses in which they would participate. The others would have lesser and varying responsibilities. Rahier would have eleven participational students for one-and-a-half hours per week in the fall, three-and-a-half hours per week for one private student and eight for participators in the spring. Milofsky would have one-and-a-half hours per week in the fall for participational students in the fall, while in the spring two-and-a-half hours per week for one private student and for participators. Friedlander would have five-and-a-half hours per week of teaching, with four private students and eight for course participators in the fall, and three hours per week for two private students in the spring.

It all sounds complicated and regimented in such calculations, which surely were regularly adjusted along the way. But such stipulated duties do indicate the importance of teaching in the players' role within an ensemble in residence, duties that at least Kolisch and Milofsky in particular found very satisfying. On the other hand, the projected schedule makes no mention of solo recitals the quartet members would be giving, which they did continue to do.

The actual concert schedule for 1951–52, as documented, generally bore out the above calculations. In the fall semester, there were three (perhaps four) events in Madison, and at least two in Milwaukee, without extra-Wisconsin appearances. There were five "string clinics," and a total of eight—not six—concerts (Rice Lake, Amery, New Richmond, Colfax, Wisconsin Rapids, Oconto, Marinette, and Green Bay) in the state tour. In the spring the quartet played four concerts on the Madison campus, plus another off-campus; three in Milwaukee beyond five stops there on the tour (April 15–27: Milton, Beloit, Lake Mills, Racine, Lake Geneva, Monroe, Kenosha, Ripon, Fond du Lac). On February 7, Kolisch brought the Pro Arte to Washington's Library of Congress, under the auspices of the Whittall Foundation, for a memorial concert in honor of Schoenberg, recently deceased (July 13, 1951). One item in that program was the composer's youthful String Quartet in D of 1897. After its long neglect, Kolisch and his team were able to give it a belated world premiere in this performance, which was also recorded and later issued on disc. At the other end of the season, the quartet again participated in the Fourth Annual Program in the Creative Arts at the University of Wyoming in Laramie (June 9–July 11), playing five concerts.

Throughout the 1951–52 season, there was again a heavy emphasis on Beethoven quartets in the varied programming. Mention might be made, though, of a recital Milofsky gave on May 26, in whose program were two works commissioned by Prevost and utterly identified with him: the Stravinsky *Élégie* in honor of Onnou, and the *Quatre Visages* of

Milhaud—offered, one suspects, as a generous tribute by the violist to his predecessor.

In late summer 1952, Rahier gave the Pro Arte an unintentional jolt. He was on vacation in Belgium, visiting his daughter, and had written a postcard from there on August 26. But he was afflicted by an onset of migraines, which may have been the source of a stroke he suffered. On September 9 he sent a telegram to Helene Blotz reporting his sudden indisposition. His convalescence, in Belgium, would extend for six months and, accordingly, would pose a challenge to the ensemble for the 1952–53 season. The diminished quartet soldiered onward, with a diet mostly of trios and quartets or quintets with faculty substitutes—which still allowed for a lot of Beethoven. In the autumn, at least four concerts were given in Madison, three in Milwaukee, plus a tour (October 21–29) to at least seven places around the state (Spooner, Cumberland, Osceola, Barron, Milltown, Amery, Ashland). In the spring of 1953, there were six Madison concerts and three Milwaukee concerts outside the tour; the latter (April 9–23) were offered at eleven other locations (Manitowoc, Sheboygan, Watertown, Oshkosh, Berlin, Ripon, Racine, Kenosha, Lake Geneva, Janesville, Beloit). Rahier was able to be return to Madison in time for the two closing concerts there (May 6, 10). No concerts are documented anywhere outside Wisconsin for that entire season.

∽ ∽ ∽

An appropriate pause may be made here to reflect on the concert tours around the state of Wisconsin. These had existed before the Kolisch era, but they are particularly well-documented for those years. They were expected of the quartet when Kolisch took over their leadership, and he appears to have accepted that part of his (and his colleagues') obligations with approval. Kolisch throughout his career made strong statements about educating the public, and especially about encouraging amateur music making—something familiar to him in Europe but not strongly developed in the United States. His ideals and idealism about music may be gathered from this promotional statement he himself promulgated:

> When people make an effort to understand it, they often find contact with it. You can get real happiness, not just fun, from listening

to chamber music, whether written by the old masters or by modern composers.

The overwhelming majority of musically interested people are unable to play and must therefore enjoy music through listening. The two main sources of music distribution in this country, the record and the radio, are not fully adequate instruments for bringing the listener into the right contact with serious music. Only an actual performance on the highest artistic level can convey the full meaning of a great work of musical art.

The performance of great works of art in the home by non-professional players for their own enjoyment not only brings music into the home but through this practice children at the most impressionable stage of their mental development are subconsciously conditioned to this kind of music and thus develop into true music lovers.

It is essential that music be performed no matter in what form or degree of perfection.

The state-tour performances were booked by Helene Blotz, who sent out promotional circulars and notices around Wisconsin. The local host organization paid a flat fee, while the Madison authorities paid for travel and lodging. Concerts were to be without charge to the audience. Many were in public venues, but perhaps the bulk were either in University of Wisconsin Centers, or in high schools or colleges. Statistics compiled by Blotz claim a total of one hundred concerts given for the years 1942–54: eighty at Milwaukee, thirteen at Beloit, eight at La Crosse, seven at Racine, six each at Watertown, Kenosha, Oshkosh, Appleton, Sheboygan, Superior, Wausau, and Whitewater, four each at Cliftonville, Green Bay, Platteville, and Menasha. Blotz added the comment: "Although chamber music may once have been considered appropriate only for larger communities, it has been our experience that small Wisconsin towns have become as enthusiastic as Milwaukee and Madison about the Pro Arte Quartet."

Such an assertion is put into relief by the variegated responses and comments made by sponsors and listeners in sites around the state and just beyond, mostly as compiled by Blotz herself.

March 17, 1946, Mineral Point. A comment on that concert, which was "hard to sit through," made by a local agent when booking a concert for April 12, 1951, one that was eventually canceled.

June 24, 1946, University of Minnesota. A review the next day in the *Minnesota Morning Tribune*: "Here the perfect compatibility of instruments and performers was fascinatingly evident."

February 11, 1947, Wisconsin Rapids High School. When offered a concert, A. A. Ritchay replied: "Not interested—would not accept them as a gift."

October 14, 1949, Chippewa Falls. Ben M. Meyer writes: "The attendance at our last program was only mediocre. However, I have received many comments and can still hear people make very favorable remarks regarding their concert work. I will state that I believe their concerts could be made more interesting for the general public if they could have a varied program consisting of classical music as well as music of a lighter nature."

October 17, 1949, Plymouth. W. Henry Ellerbusch wrote: "While a string quartet obviously does not have mass appeal, the concert here on the campus was very well received, surprisingly so since we do very little of that sort of thing here and our students generally have not experienced much music of that type. I would like to have them back here on the campus again, whenever it will be possible. Wisconsin U and the state possess a tremendous cultural opportunity in this organization, and I personally would never forgive the parties responsible were the quartet to leave."

October 9–13, Superior State Technical College. Report of February 1, 1951, on a series of five concerts the previous autumn: "The Pro Arte Quartet can come again—and again. The group left an indelible imprint on those who heard them as to how string instruments should sound and how teamwork in music—as well as in other endeavors—brings results." Five string groups were formed as a result. Faculty member Professor William Keller wrote: "To have the privilege of hearing such a magnificent series of performances by such superb artists has done more to stimulate an appreciation of fine music in our community than we have been able to accomplish through our efforts of the past eighteen years."

October 16, 1950, Tomah. The audience was "satisfied but not enthusiastic"; a return is suggested, but "not too soon." "Felt the program [Haydn, Beethoven op. 59] a little heavy, perhaps might have changes. A 'so-so' audience. Room filled."

October 17, 1950, Eau Claire State Technical College. W. R. Davies
reports on the deep and lasting impact made by the quartet:
"They have given us the finest in chamber music, and have
made a real contribution throughout Wisconsin. I realize that
some will say that their programs have been above the average
listener, but, even so, we need just that on occasion."

April 26, 1951, Manitowoc. Roy F. Valitchka wrote the next day in
the *Two Rivers Reporter*. "This aggregation of musicians, which
has been playing together for years, the new member—Bernard Milofsky—since 1947, performed with the sureness of the
veterans they are. . . . Being like minded musicians and taking
cues from their leader, the result is an ensemble that moves
with freedom and plays with tonal depth and brilliance."

February 12, 1952. A letter from a Monroe businessman (men's and
boys' clothing) and amateur musician: "I fully well know that
the men of the quartet don't like to play down to an audience,
but speaking from years of past experience in touring college
towns and smaller towns, I have found that when we played the
little towns smaller things instead of the straight quartets on a
program, we were always received better by our audiences. Your
average crowd don't understand a deep program. So if they
could lighten it up a little in the middle, I think it would go over
better. Might be worth considering for other smaller places too.
I know that the men of the quartet will not agree at all with this
kind of thinking, as they are looking at it from the highest standards of the business. Your every day kind of person is not educated to the classical tradition that these men consider part of
their every day life. Enough of this rabbeting [*sic*], but I believe
that you will yourself admit I have a point."

March 20, 1953. Marie Rank Baldi wrote in the *Glendale Town Times*:
"These men, I am told, work all day at their art as people in
other forms of endeavor work at their desks, a full eight-hour
day. Their teamwork is near-perfection." (Then a detailed
account of Kolisch's "left-handed playing" and violin.)

October 12, 1953. A report on concert at Stout Institute, Menomonie: "A few were delighted, but it was *too much* over the
heads of too many."

The foregoing reflect, of course, the wide range of audience tastes
and understanding—from people at schools with some musical

perspective to people in small towns with limited cultural experience. These expressions show the challenges and the obstacles, but also the rewards, of the university Outreach Program's efforts to broaden the artistic perspectives of the statewide public through the Pro Arte Quartet.

      ✌   ✌   ✌

In the summer of 1953, Kolisch made his first return to Germany since his departure from Europe. The visit lasted from July to early September. It was made at the invitation of the American High Command in postwar Germany—though Kolisch undertook the travel to and from Germany at his own expense. Taking with him pianist Allen Willman, he toured and played at twenty locales of the America House, designed as cultural centers. He took a break in early August to visit the ISCM program in Darmstadt, which had become a leading center of avant-garde music in Germany. There he taught and performed. He was delighted to find that the war years and aftermath had not obliterated the memory of him and his reputation. In a letter of August 15, 1953, written from Kiel to Helene Blotz, he reported that he was "in a state of constant delight." "My return to Europe was that of a prodigal son," he claimed, describing how he had reveled in meeting old friends, and observing the revival and renewal of German culture, tastes, and vitality. He gladly reported there on his own efforts in America to promote Schubert and Schoenberg. Along the way, he did radio broadcasts in Basel, Salzburg, Innsbruck, Vienna, Baden-Baden, Stuttgart, Munich, Frankfurt, Hamburg, Paris, and London.

    Kolisch returned to Madison for a 1953–54 quartet season that was, for the most part, unexceptional. In the autumn there were three concerts in Madison and two in Milwaukee, but none outside of the state. The fall tour (October 12–25) involved eleven stops in as many towns or cities (Menomonie, Chatek, Philips, Spooner, Port Edwards, Stevens Point, Marinette, Sturgeon Bay, Oconto, Green Bay, Appleton), most with repetitions of two set programs. The novel aspect of the spring semester was a Krenek Festival (March 14–16) in Madison, with the composer himself present and participating. (Kolisch and Ernst Krenek had close professional ties, and on such foundations the composer made frequent visits to Madison.) But again, the Pro Arte made no appearances outside Wisconsin. Three concerts (beside the Krenek one) were given in Madison, and two in Milwaukee, but the latter offered five sites for the spring tour (April 20–May 3) with eight other places represented (Elkhorn, Milton, Whitewater, Monroe, Darlington, Kenosha, Lake Geneva, Racine). A curiosity of these tour concerts was that, in four of them, the programs included Samuel Barber's Quartet op. 11—the very quartet that the Belgian Pro Arte had premiered and then totally dropped (see above, p. 49), now seemingly given a second chance after this interval.

∾ ∾ ∾

One event, occurring in the autumn semester of 1953 could easily be overlooked, at this point in the Pro Arte Quartet's progress, but it deserves mention here. This was the death, on November 4, 1953, of Elizabeth Sprague Coolidge. Her vital role in the history of the quartet has already been outlined, and need not be reviewed. Much of her support had been tied to the enormous friendship and affection she had felt for Alphonse Onnou. With his death, her interest in the Pro Arte did not entirely cease, but it was weakened and strained by the turmoil of the Brosa era. For several years, she turned much more of her energy and sponsorship to her Coolidge Quartet. She had other musicians to favor, and she continued her commissioning of new works.

Except for some contacts with Prevost, Mrs. Coolidge dropped out of personal interest in the Pro Arte. After her visit to the dying Onnou, she never saw any of the quartet members again, save perhaps for Prevost. She regarded Kolisch with respect and some degree of friendship, but never with the warmth she devoted to Onnou. Ironically, one of her last involvements with Kolisch echoed one of her first. In April of 1936, Mrs. Coolidge had received a letter from one of Kolisch's sisters, Maria Seligman Kolisch, who, abandoned by her husband, asked if the great patroness could offer her assistance in finding a position in the medical profession. Mrs. Coolidge replied sympathetically but negatively. Fifteen years later, she received an appeal from the pianist Josefa Rosanska Kolisch, Rudolf's divorced wife. Josefa was in a difficult situation, and hoped to pursue her own artistic future, but hoped for some financial assistance. On May 2, 1951, Mrs. Coolidge wrote in exactly parallel fashion, expressing sympathy but regretting that she could provide no monetary help.

Such is not the most inspiring note on which to trace the departure from the scene of this truly remarkable woman and extraordinary patroness. But then, her death seems not to have caused a ripple back in Madison, from which Bricken and Dykstra and other familiars were long gone. No acknowledgment or memorial gestures on her behalf were reported there.

∽  ∽  ∽

The season of 1954–55 brought new stresses. At the outset, it was defined by the planned absence of Rudolf Kolisch himself. On the basis of his recent experiences in Germany, he had applied for a year's leave of absence, to return to Darmstadt, and this had been granted in April 1954. Some rumors began flying, and there was a "published report" that Kolisch would leave the Pro Arte permanently and Brosa be brought back to replace him. The report was roundly denied, and the three remaining members once again settled down to a year of sonatas, trios, quartets, and quintets with faculty colleagues joining in. For the first semester, we have reports of only four Madison concerts and two in Milwaukee. No autumn tour was reported. The spring semester was little different. There exists, to be sure, mention of a quartet concert given by the Pro Arte on January 20 in New York, but without indication of who might have played first violin. Other than that, there were five Madison concerts and four in Milwaukee. (In one of these venues, in March, Rahier, Milofsky, and Johansen were reported, in a witty typo, to have played Beethoven's "Assduke Trio.") A limited tour was made (April 24–27) of four cities (Sheboygan, Racine, Kenosha, and Milwaukee) with the same program for each. The New York appearance aside, there were no engagements outside Wisconsin for the season.

A new personnel crisis arose with regard to cellist Friedlander. He had entertained some solo ambitions of his own. On November 9, 1947, for example, he had made a New York debut that won much acclaim. With his pianist wife, Marie, he had done some sonata playing in the spring concerts of 1955. That summer, beginning on June 6, 1955, the two Friedlanders undertook an extended tour of Australia and New Zealand. They gave a total of twenty-five recitals and ten radio concerts. Such was the praise and warm response accorded them that they wanted to extend their stay beyond the summer, and they formally requested that Ernst be allowed to delay rejoining the quartet until later in the autumn. This was vetoed by the new Music School director, Samuel T. Burns. When Friedlander made it clear that he would extend his tour "down under" anyway, he was promptly fired, and in his turn he resigned. The Friedlanders made their new home in Sydney, where Ernst joined the local symphony orchestra as principal cellist that winter, and did solo performances. Eventually, he would return to the United States to play in the Chicago Symphony for a year, then teach at the University of Oklahoma for another year, before moving to Canada and playing in the Vancouver Symphony until his death in 1966.

As all of this was going on, Kolisch was finishing out his year at Darmstadt. It was a satisfying experience, at least as he reported it in a letter of January 21, 1955, written to director Burns in Madison. The experience's one setback was an auto accident "just at Christmas time," when "a truck drove into us and crushed us against a lamppost." Fortunately, both Kolisch and his wife escaped virtually unscathed, but their car, a prized new Volkswagen, was totally destroyed. Despite this loss, they had been fortunate in housing arrangements and found everyone friendly. As for his duties at Darmstadt, at least in the first half of the year Kolisch was able to conduct a master class with nine students of diverse backgrounds. He was also able to fulfill a long-standing dream by offering "a course in the theory and practice of musical interpretation, which establishes performance as an independent discipline, detached from instrumental instruction. This course is obligatory for all the students of the Academy." He added that he had not done as much performing as he had hoped, but that he expected to catch up with that in the months ahead, both for radio stations, and in a new round of visits to America House locations. These intentions appear to have been carried out, while Kolisch continued to pursue the teaching he so loved.

Such was his success that, during this year abroad, Kolisch regularly faced proposals for him to return to a European residence. To this he made firm reply: "My home is Madison, it is the first home I have had in more than thirty years, so there is no question of my ever accepting anything permanent in Europe."

It was not clear how much Kolisch was aware, or kept aware, about the troubles over the Pro Arte's cello chair, and about the efforts to refill it. But he must have taken some satisfaction (if not played some role) in the expulsion of Friedlander. There had been mounting tensions between them of late. For some time, Kolisch had regarded him a "an intellectual lightweight." Worse, Kolisch—who came from the Austrian elite—regarded his fellow countryman as socially inferior, someone who came from a poor family, a "lower-class" person upon whom he could look down. Other comments about Friedlander claimed that he "never lost his 'grubbing' for money," and that he "rubbed many the wrong way." Dorothy Bricken recalled him quite bluntly as "a jerk." She had found him "very difficult to work with," recalling occasions when he would play recitals at the Memorial Union Theater, his wife accompanying on the piano. On one occasion he had forgotten his "rock stop," the gadget used to prevent his cello peg from slipping. According to Mrs. Bricken, Friedlander ordered a stage technician named Claude to provide the solution:

> Well, he [Friedlander] said, you know just take a bit and dig a hole in the front of it, in the wood, and I can just put my cello right there. And Claude, who by that time had just had it with Friedlander anyway, because we had a lot of these episodes, he just said no he was not going to do that, period. So we had words. I don't remember how we resolved it finally, but we didn't dig a hole in the stage, I know that. . . We had a backstage name for him. We called him Ferdinand. This was about the period of Ferdinand the Bull on the [radio]. And he was the only one that I ever had any problems with.

Perhaps Kolisch was not alone in welcoming the cellist's departure, especially in view of his more compatible replacement.

As of September 1955, of course, the Pro Arte was suddenly in need of a new cellist. With great dispatch, the young Chicago-born Lowell Creitz was engaged. He came with varied experience,—in chamber music, in orchestral playing, and even participation in the United States Marine Band. He arrived for a relatively modest 1955–56 season, marked by only one bump. The first semester was again the limited one, with Creitz working his way into it gradually: some four performances in Madison and two in Milwaukee. The Madison concert of November 18 was billed as a "Dohnányi Festival" and consisted solely of that composer's music. No state tour was reported, and the only venture outside Wisconsin was to Chicago for two concerts, one a memorial performance in honor of the old patron, George I. Haight. The second semester was to be devoted to a Mozart Series, and that composer's music provided virtually all the fare. It started out well enough with two concerts each in Madison and Milwaukee. But then Kolisch was obliged to undergo surgery. His recovery kept him out of action until May, when he returned for a Madison concert on the 20th. Apparently plans had been made for this absence: the players returned to the alternative programming formula of trios, etc., with participation by other faculty. After two more Madison performances and one more in Milwaukee, a spring tour was made (April 22–30) to six venues (Lake Geneva, Racine, Beloit, Kenosha, Stevens Point, plus Milwaukee thrice) in eight days, using throughout the same program.

Absences in this past season and the next would dilute the foursome's intensive involvement. Nevertheless, for some months Kolisch had a reconfigured and relatively tension-free ensemble with which to work. Of that, a memo of February 1956, by one Paul Marcus, survives as a verbal snapshot.

> In one of their exhaustive rehearsals—the perfection sought by the string ensemble makes almost any other human activity seem slovenly—he [Kolisch] stands in a clear position of leadership. Milofsky is the gadfly of the group, likely to challenge the others on a musical, historical, or any other convenient basis. Rahier is quiet, intent; Creitz, having joined the group so recently, is reserved, yet firm in his opinions; Kolisch is the maestro and authority to whom the others defer to such an extent that if they have a difference of opinion they usually express it in the form of a question.

That picture was quickly dissolved, unfortunately, as one more personnel crisis arose.

At some point by 1956, Bernard Milofsky was diagnosed with multiple sclerosis—the same terrible disease that would, years later, cruelly destroy the career and take the life of the cellist Jacqueline du Pré. The condition had apparently been developing for some years, though for a while without direct effect on his playing. The situation was later recalled by his friend, Professor James Crow:

> The disease progressed in a maddening way, not gradually, but in spurts. There were periods of weeks or months in which his playing was as great as ever. Then there would be a sharp deterioration and his playing would suffer in small ways noticeable to the musical *cognoscenti.* The situation was nerve-wracking, not only for himself, but for the other quartet members, who never knew what to expect. Nor did he. And I suspect that such uncertainties exacerbated the deepening personal differences within the group.

With recognition that his career would end prematurely, Milofsky began taking courses at the university, so that he might complete a degree. Eventually, he included writing courses in his studies, and his ambition grew to write a novel. (The results of that ambition are discussed in appendix B below.)

Milofsky had been valued by his colleagues, with whom he got along well. Dorothy Bricken described him as one of these "nice, nice people" who were "wonderful to work with." "Milofsky was sometimes a little edgy and I think this was probably partly due to his illness." Rahier described him as "a good player, but he had a moody character. . . strongly built, but he had a sickly temperament."

The situation of his health became too serious for the Music School to ignore. There are some areas of uncertainties about who applied what pressures for him to leave the quartet. Fingers have been pointed at Kolisch, but the two men seem to have preserved good relations, and exchanged correspondence thereafter. Whatever the details, it was decided that Milofsky be given a year of "leave" for 1956–57, allowing him to retain his salary in order to fit certain budgetary specifications. The ensuing year must have been tragically confusing for him. One terribly poignant picture of that condition is revealed in a small report in a local newspaper, the *Capital Times*, on May 2, 1957. On that date, Milofsky was brought to court on charges of traffic violations. Before the judge, Milofsky admitted that "he was in such an upset state of mind because of his health and his efforts to find a new position," and conceded that "perhaps I shouldn't be driving at all." The judge deferred sentence when Milofsky agreed "not to drive for thirty days."

That episode seems to illustrate Milofsky's anguish. Fortunately for him, he had a resilient wife, Ruth, a talented artist as well as a person of enormous strength and resourcefulness. She returned to university studies, acquiring a Master's degree in fine arts. She obtained a position at the University of Wisconsin–Milwaukee and eventually became a professor specializing in metal sculpture. She was also active in children's art and in social causes. At age forty, meanwhile, Milofsky did serve one season (1957–58) in the viola section of the San Francisco Symphony, but then he ended his playing career. By that time, when he was dependent on Ruth's support, she, Bernard, and their two sons, moved to Milwaukee. There, now wheelchair-ridden, Milofsky himself was able to do some teaching, coaching members of the Milwaukee Youth Symphony. He communicated the pride he took in his best students in correspondence with Kolisch. Otherwise, Milofsky entertained himself playing chess and reading, while working on his novel.

Ruth Milofsky died in May 1982. Bernard moved to Lewisburg, PA, where his elder son, Carl, was a professor of physics at Bucknell University. He died in a nursing home in Lewisburg, in May 1993, at age seventy-six.

◅ఄ  ◅ఄ  ◅ఄ

For the 1956–57 season, with Milofsky "on leave," the Pro Arte was once again a trio (or the "Pro Arte Ensemble," as one posting had it), the repertoire reduced again to the alternative literature, with the participation of faculty colleagues. The autumn semester was a limited one: three Madison concerts, two in Milwaukee, and an appearance at St. Norbert's College in De Pere. No tour, and no outside concerts. In the spring, there were six Madison concerts, three in Milwaukee. An appearance on February 13 at the Music Teachers National Convention in Chicago was balanced by a presentation at the National Federation of Music Clubs in Columbus, WI, which opened the spring tour (April 26–May 8 or 15), taking in seven cities (Columbus, Juneau, St. Paul, MN, Mineral Point, Racine, Milwaukee, and Lake Geneva). But two variations in personnel appearances marked this semester. At three concerts, given in as many different sites, in February, Kolisch was identified as playing piano, to accompany Creitz in Webern's *Three Little Pieces*, op. 11. And, on two occasions (April 22, 30), Lorna Kolisch filled in on viola for two different string trios (Schoenberg's opus 45 and Webern's opus 20).

Meanwhile, there was a search made for a violist to take Milofsky's place. This time, prospects already familiar to the surviving players were relied upon. In fact, a possible replacement was at hand in the person of Lorna Kolisch. She had long wanted to be taken into the quartet, but there were misgivings, especially on her husband's part, as to her qualifications. "The tensions were unbearable for Rudy," Creitz recalled. In desperation, Lorna had actually taken a job at the local Oscar Mayer company, chopping bacon to earn money. She had given up the violin and was working instead on the viola: her appearances on that instrument during April may have been an effort to press her candidacy.

Further hindering Lorna's candidacy, however, was the university's strict rule of anti-nepotism, by which a spouse of someone already in employ in a given division could not be hired in the same division. Accordingly, following the rules, already on February 15,

1957, the position was advertised. The job description is an interesting document in itself. Any candidate should be a man (no women welcome yet) between twenty-five and thirty-five years of age, with good English and an American education. He must be an expert musician, able to play from full score, with knowledge of the literature from Haydn to Webern. He must be interested in having good students, though he would be likely to have ones with variable abilities, to which he must adapt. He might give additional solo recitals, as he wished, and the schedule would be that blocked out in the 1951–52 general contract. To his base salary ($5,000 in the preinflationary money of the day) there might be some increases; an eight-week summer season might be possible; there would be limits to outside concertizing for extra income. Promising applicants would come to Madison for a two-day audition, plus some trial rehearsals with the quartet.

The outcome was the selection of Richard Blum. A native of Chicago, "like Creitz," Blum had, during service in the army, played in military ensembles that toured Germany in various orchestral and chamber groupings. He had then served as principal violist successively in the Dallas and San Antonio Symphonies. A skilled and reliable musician, he was to prove one of the longest-serving players in the Pro Arte's history. Above all, Kolisch, who was confident in the experienced second violinist Rahier, now had on the lower parts two young newcomers who were malleable and eager to take guidance from the leader.

Thus fortified, Kolisch launched a bold new season for 1957–58. It began modestly in Madison with a concert on October 13 in which Blum made his debut by playing a reduction, with Leo Steffens on piano, in Henri Casadesus's fake "Handel Viola Concerto." But the prime business of the entire season was an intermittent Beethoven Series. Kolisch had for some time been building, piecemeal, a confident repertoire of the Beethoven quartets. Only after thirteen years was he ready to present a comprehensive counterpart to the Beethoven cycles that had become a staple of the old Belgian group's activities. The series in this case was not presented as a tight entity over five or six successive days, but rather spread out through the season, in a total of seven concerts in Madison (November 10, December 6 and 15, January 19, February 16, March 23, April 20). These were followed by supplemental samplings, begun at the Ohio Music Club in Dayton (April 22), followed by all-Beethoven programs in a truncated tour (April 28–June

3) of seven stops (four in Milwaukee, two at Madison's Wisconsin Center, one in Racine). The series came to an illustrious end with a performance of the opus 131 at Frank Lloyd Wright's estate, Taliesin on June 8, 1958, as part of a celebration sponsored by the State Department of the architect's eighty-ninth (and last) birthday.

For at least the initial Beethoven concerts, Kolisch was able to use a procedure to which he had long looked forward: projecting the pages of the score onto a screen as a work progressed, so the audience could follow the textual and sonic dimensions of the music simultaneously. He had made one experiment with this in one of his first concerts in Madison, in November of 1944. Now (1957) he could attempt it on the comprehensive scope of the Beethoven series. But the results were mixed, and many in the audience found the combination of visual and aural elements too distracting, one from the other. Apparently, this procedure was discontinued early in the series.

Reports of the 1958–59 season tell of concerts focused upon various celebrations or themes, at first in Madison. One was presented on September 28 as a tribute to the University of Wisconsin's eminent art historian, musicologist, and composer, Oskar Hagen, including a composition of his written for and dedicated to Kolisch. Two concerts (October 19, November 16) launched a pendant to the previous season's Beethoven festivities, a Haydn–Schubert–Webern Series, devoted to works by all three Viennese composers. But, through the spring semester, the three-composer format was extended in three Madison concerts (February 8, March 8, April 19) and one in Milwaukee (February 14). (In the last Madison performance, cellist Phillip Blum assisted.) Thereafter, the three-composer format (with some infusions of Beethoven) went "on the road" in the state tour (April 23—May 18) of nine stops (five in Milwaukee, two in La Crosse, one each in Platteville and Ashland). A further extension of this format was carried into the summer of 1959 (July 10–26), with a residence arranged for the month in California. During that appearances were made in San Francisco and Berkeley: at least six in all, and one of them on television.

The San Francisco performances drew the following reflections from Alexander Fried for the *San Francisco Examiner* (August 4):

> As a matter of comparison, the earlier Pro Arte Quartet had a French finesse combined with peculiar vividness, daring, and robustness, which at best were marvelous. It had its rough moments, too.

Fastidiousness and lyrical grace are special traits of the current Pro
Arte. Its four musicians interlace their roles with beautiful quality and
balance.

Its tonal impact was intimate, rather than powerful. Hence there
was some loss of profundity in Beethoven's majestic slow "Cavatina"
movement (in op. 130), and of excitement in his passionate "Great
Fugue" (op. 133). Yet there was distinguished mood in the concert
as a whole.

The 1959–60 season opened in Madison with a concert on September 21 devoted to Krenek's opus 84 Quartet, followed by two concerts (October 1, 4) in which other faculty members joined the quartet
players in Schubert's expansive Octet (D. 803), and by a pair of programs at the Wisconsin Center (October 24, 25) devoted to music of
Webern and Krenek (op. 84). But then, on the model provided in the
previous season, Kolisch undertook another project spread over the
full season: a Mozart–Schoenberg Series, a sequence of five programs,
shared between Madison (November 8, December 6, February 14,
March 13, April 10) and Milwaukee (November 10, December 8, February 16, March 15, April 12). Faculty soprano Bettina Bjorksten again
sang in the performances of the Quartet no. 2. Portions of those programs, mixed in with music by the other Austrians, Haydn, Beethoven,
Schubert, and Webern, constituted eight concerts (April 21–May 13)
in six locations (La Crosse, Sheboygan, Wisconsin Rapids, Ripon,
Milton, and Superior thrice) that made up the spring state tour. And
again there was the further extension in a summer residence at Berkeley CA (July 15–26, four concerts).

By 1959, the quartet players were designated as full faculty members of the School of Music, with tenure or tenure-track status. This
was certainly a landmark in the Pro Arte's Madison history. Nevertheless, there were some misgivings among the players about agreeing,
out of fear that more constraints might be imposed as a result. But
acceptance was made, partly as a gesture of support to Rahier. He was
contemplating retirement, and for him the new arrangement guaranteed more generous terms of departure.

The summer also involved a project to make a series of recordings
for university use. This involved the farewell to Rahier. In the spring
of 1960 he had definitely decided to retire. He was sixty-five, and was
troubled by oncoming glaucoma. "Kolisch tried to convince me to
continue some more and I accepted this summer to record for the

university Schönberg's quartets and Webern's Five Pieces. It was done in a new hall. It was hot outside." Dorothy Bricken, however, recalls that his final resignation was abrupt. Rahier moved back to Belgium in 1963. There he made up for a receding musical career with intensified activity in painting, and became a widely admired artist. Martha Blum would recall visiting him in 1977 and finding that his playing still showed wonderful strength. He generously donated his violin to the University of Wisconsin School of Music—where, according to Creitz, it was not well treated. Rahier left some charming memoirs of his experiences. He survived twenty-three years after his retirement from the Pro Arte, dying in 1983.

In this latest personnel change, the Pro Arte was again a trio, while a replacement for second violin was sought during the first semester of 1960–61. The repertoire was made up mostly of string trios, with occasional recourse to the piano quartets of Brahms (opp. 26, 60). There were four concerts in Madison, and one in Milwaukee. Otherwise the semester seems to have consisted only of an autumn state tour of eight concerts (at Ashland, Spooner, Cumberland, Osceola, Barron, Milltown, Avery, and Hurley).

By the second semester, in 1961, the Pro Arte was a quartet again, with the addition of Rahier's successor as second violinist. Having come around to full support for her, Kolisch had argued anew for the appointment of his wife, Lorna, and he was particularly frustrated by the policy ban that blocked her once again. The new second violinist was, instead, Robert Basso. Yet another Chicago native, he had orchestral experience, notably with a CBS orchestra in Chicago, as had Creitz before him. With Basso joining, the quartet played a reduced but typical round of concerts: only four in Madison (various venues), none in Milwaukee; a five-stop state tour (Thorpe, Eau Claire, River Falls, La Crosse, and Milton) playing essentially the same program. Outside the state were two appearances—in Oxford, Ohio, and Chicago.

In just that spring semester, strains that had been building up for some time began to bubble to the surface in unavoidable disruption. Basso, Rahier later observed, "was an excellent violinist but he had a hard time with Kolisch's authoritarian way and [eventually] resigned." The recurrent changes in personnel, despite the professional excellence of the newcomers, had made stable collegiality difficult. The departure of Rahier, with his calm temperament and gracious manner, proved a particular loss this time. Basso hardly represented a replacement for that presence.

Rahier himself had faced mounting frictions with Kolisch. Rahier regarded Kolisch as "rather pedantic and a dictator." Kolisch has been characterized as "a health nut," and one display of this came in his ham-handed defense of Rahier, who apparently did not use deodorant. The other players wanted to open the window during rehearsals, but Kolisch would not have it, observing that "no one ever died of stink." Beyond that, Kolisch had fallen under the influence of Wilhelm Reich, by whom he had been analyzed in his New York days. Kolisch had become fascinated by Reich's creation, an "orgone box," which was supposed to "concentrate aerial energy of the universe" for those who occupied it. This was a construction of plywood and metal, the size of a telephone booth, that supposedly stored a healing and enlivening force. At least for a while, Kolisch went so far as to insist that all the players and their spouses use this contraption. There were demurrals: Milofsky held back, and his wife Ruth flatly refused to have any part in it.

Though Kolisch was a polite and soft-spoken individual, he could be aloof and superior in his manner. His penchant for constant analysis affected his playing. Prevost recalled: "I love Kolisch, because he has exact knowledge, very good knowledge. He was not a tremendous violinist, but he was all the time listening. I said, 'Rudolf, don't listen, play.'" He was not interested in beautiful sound, he was "not an emotional violinist," bypassing expressive features. He "was a very noisy player, and he never allowed 'tone' to be important." Rosemary Harbison believed that the modification of his violin, to accommodate his reverse-hand playing, actually weakened the instrument's structure and sound. His colleagues came to find his intonation often uncertain and difficult to match. Rahier summed up the ensemble strains by saying that he and the others could "not play in the cracks any more." There were recurrent discomforts over Kolisch's insistence on rehearsing from scores. Moreover, his paramount fascination with analyzing music brought him so far as to want more rehearsals and fewer performances—even speculating that they might just abandon concerts altogether and simply make their radio broadcasts.

Accordingly, Kolisch began to appear less and less in the quartet's concerts. A clue was given in a program on July 5, 1961, when the other three players joined with Leo Steffens in what was identified as the "UW Piano Quartet." Kolisch was absent through the first semester of the 1961–62 season, when the "Piano Quartet" played a few concerts almost entirely in Madison. That situation prevailed into the next

semester, in four concerts through February, but Kolisch was back as
leader of the Pro Arte for four concerts (one on television) in Madison. It was, however, the Piano Quartet, with some faculty colleagues,
that went on a highly segmented spring tour, without Kolisch. The tour
consisted of eleven stops (La Crosse, New Richmond, Thorpe, Manitowoc, Milton, Stevens Point, Sinsinawa, Whitewater, Racine, Wausau,
and Kenosha), plus two at Frank Lloyd Wright's office complex Wingspread, scattered over the course of the full semester. To this was added
a summer season (July 10–August 21), involving the Piano Quartet in
three television performances for WHA, two public concerts in Madison, and one in Eagle River.

Kolisch was, again, totally absent in the autumn of 1962, when
the Piano Quartet (with colleagues) presented two public concerts in
Madison and two television appearances for WHA, spiced by one concert elsewhere (Glenwood City). The same situation prevailed in the
spring semester of 1963. In a concert including the *Brandenburg Concerto* no. 3, on February 3 (or 10), Basso and his wife played violins, and
Blum and his wife (Martha Francis) played violas. The Piano Quartet
did another WHA-TV performance and four Madison concerts (one of
them a program of sonatas). The group reduced the state tour to only
four stops (Green Bay, Manitowoc, Wausau, and Kenosha), plus one
out-of-state venture to Wilmington, Delaware. Two of the three string
players also appeared in Beethoven's Triple Concerto with the University Orchestra (March 24).

In sum, by the 1962–63 season, Kolisch no longer actively performed with his Pro Arte ensemble.

◈  ◈  ◈

It is clear that, within the course of his two decades of residence in
Madison, Rudolf Kolisch had become disillusioned with his situation.
He had begun with high hopes and idealistic ambitions. Even as late
as April 16, 1954, before holding formal faculty status and still an "artist in residence," he had expressed personal satisfaction with that situation: "It is an excellent arrangement. It takes me out of the 'music
business' so that one has time to work quietly, unhampered by requirements of competition.'" He clearly was glad to have put aside the life of
a freelance musician, or quartet leader, on the open market.

Along the way, however, he seems to have turned sour on his colleagues, on round-the-state touring, on the University of Wisconsin

Music School. On January 20, 1963, in a round of letters exchanged with his former violist, Bernard Milofsky, he poured out his bitterness.

> Needless to say, I share your disgust with the school of music and with [director] Burns in particular. I have done just as you advised me to do. I shall never play a concert with these people again. Of course, that, as you can imagine, is easier said than done as the "Proart" is a sacred cow in this cow state—although only a handful of people really care about it—and I am right now fighting out these conflicts.

He added a further jab: "These music education people do not understand music itself."

Four musicians who knew and worked with Kolisch have given some hints as to what motivated him, and eventually alienated him. Russell Sherman, who was in his youth when he first met Kolisch, later worked with him as a colleague at the New England Conservatory. He found Kolisch courteous and patient, ever willing to initiate and maintain a serious conversation. But, Sherman says,

> nothing could contrast more with his personal charm and flexibility than the fiery discipline which Kolisch brought to his work. . . . But all this did not mean that Kolisch sought just a literal rendering of the text. It was simply that his comprehensive knowledge and structural imagination were so profound as to be able to classify each musical element according to both the given notational factors and the implied expressive image of the composer's realm.

Sherman also insists that Kolisch resisted "sentimentality and show."

Walter Gray had been a sympathetic and admiring faculty colleague at the University of Wisconsin Music School. He remembered Kolisch as "a basic leftist of European intelligentsia," with early liberal-progressive political leanings. A sensitive person, Kolisch had particularly strong feelings about what he considered to be wrong, whether in general or as done to him. He was a "provocative" person, because he "believed" so strongly—"he knew what worked." Though he tried to avoid it, "it was impossible for him not to step on people's toes." Gray continued: "He possibly introduced more great music [in Madison], but the campus didn't really know who he was. He was a very important name in Europe, but developed a melding of Viennese and Midwestern hucksterism. Rudy didn't have the ability to adjust into 'patronage' needs." As a musician, Gray reports, Kolisch was "not interested in beauty of sound, only in musical ideas. He wanted to deny the natural music, say things with pontifical authority. Parts of his philoso-phies grew out of the excesses of the time." Gray recalls that he loved to experiment. "He would do anything once." Many of his ideas were never realized. He had wanted to try to "play late Beethoven as if it were Schoenberg."

Puzzling, though, is Kolisch's attitude toward making records. Like many other musicians, he regarded a recording as an inferior alterna-tive to a live performance—one "had to have the live performance for an ultimate statement," Gray says. It is true that he did make record-ings with his earlier Viennese quartet, in the 78-rpm format, includ-ing a complete cycle of the Schoenberg quartets. The postwar years brought a transfer to metallic tape and the long-playing record, which would have allowed him to make new and updated recordings of his repertoire. He did just a little of that (including only one Schoenberg quartet). But, Gray says, Kolisch "didn't understand new recording techniques." He did not record a new Schoenberg cycle because "he had done Schoenberg" once, and that was enough. He recognized that recordings could serve to promulgate music, but he was convinced that only live performances would serve the cause fully.

Pro Arte cellist Lowell Creitz recalled that working with Kolisch was "the greatest musical experience of my life." Kolisch was both a musi-cian and a true intellectual. Rehearsals and even performances were made with the players using scores, not parts. Rehearsals were turned into exercises in joint study of each work "from scratch." Concentration was placed on chordal balances, then on analyses of motives, tracing their uses first within and then across movements, so as to understand total structure. Sound was based on "languages," i.e., structures. Kolisch devised metronomic charts for Beethoven's works. Nevertheless, the ultimate concerns were expression, intonation, and sound. Kolisch's approach was in contrast to the German sense of structuralism and allied with the Russian model of giving the performers freedom.

Norman Paulu, Kolisch's successor as first violinist, retrospec-tively admired one legacy his predecessor left behind: "playing cham-ber music like chamber music." He noted that Kolisch had never performed professionally in an orchestra, and could therefore avoid temptations to give some chamber works, especially those of Brahms, some degree of orchestral sonority. Thus, the Pro Arte's Brahms con-tinued to be "lean and lucid."

Other testimony has come from Rose Mary Harbison, the violin-ist who first encountered Kolisch when she pursued undergraduate studies at the University of Wisconsin Music School. Her training was with Rahier, but she was deeply impressed by Kolisch's work in the Music 9 course. She found him the "most powerful, distinctly ambitious musician on the faculty." She later did more direct work with him, especially in his post-Madison years at the New England Conservatory of Music, where he had been invited by Gunther Schuller to serve as head of the Chamber Music Department. and where he developed an ensemble of his own. Not always compatible with other faculty members there, she recalled, Kolisch welcomed ideals "against the grain," ones he felt bound "to accomplish as a musician." For him, progress equaled innovation, as in his Vienna world. In this direction, he offered "real value to young professionals." He was a "formidable personality," yet "gentle, considerate, very careful with words, said little, but was exceedingly perceptive." "The best performance is one you read with your eyes," he said, but he wanted to move "far ahead of the normal performance world," seeking "engagement that went past the page"—a tall order for a string quartet.

To his mind, "the performer becomes the composer." Thus, "performing is as difficult as composing." Harbison recalls a performance of Schubert's Octet at the New England Conservatory that was "greatly admired and greatly controversial." "A catalyst for change causes explosions." It and his work were boycotted by other faculty members there. Kolisch made heavy demands, with "his incredible insistence on reaching a certain level." He required use of tempered tuning. His teaching "represented a path for performing far more challenging than was normally available, a combination of both tradition and change."

∝ ∝ ∝

Kolisch's withdrawal from the Pro Arte posed an administrative dilemma. Observations that the Pro Arte had "disbanded" are not quite correct. The quartet was still "on the books," and Kolisch was still in theory their leader, even if he no longer played as part of the group. Therefore, it was not possible to create a new faculty position to replace him in the leader's chair. He was still a tenured professor, and chose now—and for the next four years—to give his attention to teaching, which he greatly loved, and to solo engagements in Europe and around the United States.

The Pro Arte Quartet was thus, for the time, carried on by the University of Wisconsin Piano Quartet. Their 1963–64 season was entirely played in Madison, with two public concerts there and two WHA-TV tapings, plus five state tour stops (Oshkosh, Racine, New Holstein, Kenosha, Menasha), spread out in schedule. In parallel, Kolisch himself offered a three-part Beethoven Sonata Series in Madison (October 21, November 10, December 18) with pianist Gunnar Johansen. Kolisch does not appear in reported concerts for the spring semester of 1964, though he did make a European tour in the summer. Meanwhile, the Piano Quartet maintained steady activities with five Madison concerts, three WHA-TV tapings, and seven stops around the state, at intervals (DePere, Green Bay twice, Platteville, Manitowoc, Wausau twice, Milton), plus outside appearances in Philadelphia and Texas Western College. The last of those (May 17) also announced the latest personnel change. Seeing no serious future for himself in Madison, Basso had chosen to resign. His replacement—in trial if not officially—in that Texas concert was Won-Mo Kim, as the new violinist.

Kim took his place in the University of Wisconsin Piano Quartet, which he would hold for the next three years, beginning with the 1964–65 season. In the fall semester there were five Madison appearances, one WHA-TV taping, and three state-tour stops in October (Green Bay, New Holstein, Sheboygan). For his part, Kolisch gave a recital in Copenhagen with Danish pianist Bengt Johanssen (October 28), and performed the Schoenberg Violin Concerto in Berlin (November 10) with another noteworthy champion of that composer's music, René Leibowitz. For the spring semester in 1965, there were four Madison appearances, with dispersed visits to eight state sites (Beaver Dam, Union, Kenosha twice, Wausau, Marinette, Milwaukee, and Williams Bay). Back in Madison, Kolisch joined with Johansen for a two-part Sonata Series, sampling Austrian literature from three centuries (February 12, April 5).

That the University of Wisconsin Piano Quartet was by no means an inferior substitute for the full Pro Arte is suggested, early on in their touring. On February 9, 1965, after a concert in Wausau, a local critic (Lucia Swanson of the *Wausau Record-Herald*) wrote: "Once again, these musicians (Kim, Blum, Creitz, Steffens) proved that each possesses technical virtuosity and brilliance, and, more important, that in ensemble they play with empathy, blending the four instruments into a musically unified whole. The end result was a balance and rapport at all times, showing the acute musicality and sensitivity on the part of each of the four."

The two levels of operation were similar for 1965–56, with Kolisch alone and with the quartet without him. In the fall semester, the Piano Quartet performed once in Madison but six times around the state (Beaver Dam, Union, Green Bay, Kenosha, Sheboygan, Manitowoc). Kolisch, who was on leave for most of the semester, played a concert in Zurich (September 21), with Leibowitz again conducting: the Beethoven Violin Concerto (with the violinist's own cadenzas) and Schoenberg's violin *Phantasy* (the piano part as orchestrated by the conductor). Returned to Madison, Kolisch launched another Sonata Series with Johansen, the first concert of which (December 5) was followed by three more in the spring (January 16, February 20, May 1), supplemented by a Schubert program (May 9) done in collaboration with resident Austrian pianist Paul Badura-Skoda. For their part, the Piano Quartet offered in the spring semester three Madison concerts, two WHA-TV tapings, and five concerts around the state (at Racine, Milwaukee, La Crosse, Antigo, and Wausau).

That pattern had a final run in the 1966–67 season. The Piano Quartet gave four Madison concerts and one in Milwaukee. The spring semester was, however much busier; the Piano Quartet made their final appearances—three in Madison and six around the state (La Crosse, Sheboygan, Milwaukee, Appleton, Racine, and Wausau).

Far more ambitious, however, was what Kolisch designed as his farewell gestures to Madison and the University of Wisconsin. In July 1967 he would celebrate his seventy-first birthday. Following both the rules and his choice, he would retire as of that date. Altogether independently of his old Pro Arte connections, he organized three events devoted to the music of his great mentor, Schoenberg, and the other two members of the Second Viennese School (Berg, Webern). The first program (March 12) was entirely devoted to Schoenberg: some piano pieces, the violin *Phantasy*, played by Kolisch with Johansen, and some vocal and choral pieces conducted by Leibowitz, who was at that time in residence at the Music School. The second concert (April 16), was devoted to Schoenberg's epochal *Pierrot Lunaire*, given alternatively in English translation and the original German, as sung respectively by Arcenia Moser and Bettina Bjorksten, with Kolisch himself alternatively on violin and viola, as joined by a number of other (non–Pro Arte) faculty colleagues. The final concert (May 7) brought together all three of the twelve-tone masters: Berg's *Kammerkonzert*, conducted by Leibowitz; Webern's Concerto for Nine Instruments, and Schoenberg's Violin

Concerto (this time played by Kolisch with a piano reduction of the orchestral part as arranged and played by Leibowitz).

With that Viennese "last hurrah," Kolisch made his departure. He would move to Boston and continue his passionate efforts. Successively at Harvard and Brandeis Universities, he would run Schoenberg series. Above all, he would join the faculty of the New England Conservatory, as already noted, in his capacity as artist-in-residence and chairman of the chamber music program, in which he pursued his much-cherished teaching and coaching of string players and ensembles. He died in 1978, in his home in Watertown, Massachusetts.

Kolisch's memory persisted in Wisconsin long after his departure and his death. His former student in Boston, Rose Mary Harbison, together with her husband, John Harbison, had developed an annual summer concert series, the Token Creek Chamber Music Festival, on their estate in a small town not far from Madison. Cherishing her teacher's legacy, she organized two successive seasons—in 1995 (August 27, August 29, September 3), and in 1996 (August 25, August 28, September 1)—both titled "Three Concerts honoring Franz Schubert and Rudolf Kolisch." Though the programs of vocal and instrumental music were diverse, Schubert's music was a strong and recurrent element in them, and works by Berg and Webern (though not Schoenberg) were also given attention. It may be noted, however, that of all the Pro Arte members at that time, only one (Parry Karp) was among the participants.

In Madison, meanwhile, Kolisch's departure opened up a path to Pro Arte renewal, to which the University and the School of Music were sincerely committed. With his faculty position vacated, it was at last possible to consider engaging a new first violinist. Adding urgency to that need was the fact that Won-Mo Kim was also departing the faculty, which meant that both violin chairs could be refilled. The search for the new leader, in particular, had been under way for some months. In early December of 1966, the candidate Norman Paulu was in Madison for informal auditions. By the summer of 1967 both Paulu and the other prospect, Thomas Moore, joined with Blum and Creitz for a series of rehearsal sessions (July 10–29) that included five of the Beethoven quartets and others by Roger Sessions, Maurice Ravel, Lukas Foss, Paul Hindemith, Anton Webern, and Béla Bartók. In the fall of 1967, therefore, a totally renewed and rejuvenated Pro Arte Quartet was back in action.

That autumn would initiate a vastly different era for the quartet. It would follow what had been the most provocative and turbulent period in the ensemble's history—a period in which they became among the leading champions of both traditional and avant-garde music in the United States, thanks to the passions and personality of the remarkable musician who was Rudolf Kolisch.

## Repertoire

The twenty-three years of the Pro Arte's Kolisch era are far better documented than the four years of the Brosa phase. This is partly the result of Kolisch's own files, which were quite voluminous. For the earlier years of his leadership, the diligence of Helene Blotz preserved a great deal of information. Kolisch himself saved many programs and other material. Above all, the log book kept by cellist Lowell Creitz is priceless for the years from 1955 onward. There are gaps: some concerts are reported without listings of the programs, especially for the state tours. Accordingly, the information presented, if much fuller than before, is still defective, so that number tallies are, at best, only minimal and hardly definitive.

In the survey that follows, some arbitrary decisions have been made. As before, the registry includes not only string quartets but also the range of supplemental literature—trios, quintets, etc.—that often involved performing colleagues. Such a range is particularly appropriate here, not only because of the separate work of the Piano Quartet, but because the Pro Arte Quartet itself suffered so many absences and shifts of personnel, forcing alternatives to strict quartet works. On the other hand, for better or worse, generally avoided here are solo sonatas and duos that are really peripheral to the string quartet literature. As always, the concerts considered are those given before a public. Not considered are performances done for radio or, later, television transcription. Also lacking are the performances for the Music 9 course, which were teaching events, not public ones; and hardly any of their programs survive anyway. Finally, consideration is given to the Pro Arte repertoire while the group was led by Kolisch himself. Considered separately is the repertoire of the University of Wisconsin Piano Quartet as a surrogate ensemble with their own distinct distinct six years (1961–67). Likewise listed are Kolisch's

Madison performances totally apart from the Pro Arte, although his appearances elsewhere are not noted.

Depending on one's calculations, the Kolisch era lasted almost (or functionally) as long as that of the Onnou years. The repertoire of the latter did not exclusively reflect the Belgian leader's preferences, but the Kolisch period is a far more distinct product of that leader's personality and motivations. Indeed, it might be worthwhile for a study to be made—though one not attempted here—of the evolution of Kolisch's repertoire with the Pro Arte. Bypassing the indistinct lines of the short-lived Brosa years, Kolisch certainly did, of course, shift the repertoire from Franco-Belgian emphases to Austro-German ones. But the way he developed his repertoire demonstrates his careful preparation of individual works, bit by bit working them into active performance. Such a pattern is not unnatural for a quartet, but Kolisch offers some unusually strong displays of such strategic planning—even allowing for the disruptions and hindrances of personnel gaps, and of eventually overwhelming tensions within the group. Indeed, there is little literature on how individual quartet ensembles have nurtured their repertoires over time. That we have a fairly clear picture of Kolisch's efforts in his Pro Arte days would add much interest to a serious analysis of his activities.

It is not surprising that Kolisch brought a new emphasis to the composers of the Second Viennese School, if not as drastic a shift as might have been expected. Schoenberg in particular commanded his loyalty. Yet, of the quartets, the early one in D was given only once, No. 4 was performed only four times, no. 2 five times, no. 1 eleven times, while no. 3, at seventeen performances, was a clear favorite. The composer's String Trio received fourteen presentations; but *Verklärte Nacht* and the *Ode to Napoleon* were given only twice each, the Chamber Symphony and a version of the Violin Concerto only once each. Thus, Schoenberg was accorded a total of a relatively moderate fifty-two performances.

Alban Berg's music was addressed even more sparingly. His String Quartet received nine performances, and the *Lyric Suite* only ten. Anton Webern's music, however, fared a little better. His *Five Movements* (op. 5) appeared twenty-four times, the String Trio (op. 20) six times, the Bagatelles (op. 9) seven times, and the Piano Quintet (1907) only three.

Among other "modern" composers, Bartók was rather underrepresented. Of his quartets, no. 5 was favored with fifteen performances, but, eventually, no. 1 received seven and no. 6 six, while no. 3 had only one. Stravinsky was treated a little better, with fifteen performances of his *Three Pieces* and eleven of his Concertino. Krenek's Seventh Quartet was accorded eleven performances, his Fifth only one, his Theme and Variations three, and a trio five. Hindemith was represented only by his Third Quartet, in seven performances. Dohnányi, whose music Kolisch had long scorned, eventually received three performances for his opus 33 Quartet and one for his Piano Quintet. Prokofiev's Quartet no. 1 was given nine performances. Ernst Bloch's Quartet no. 2 was played only twice. And Ernst Toch's String Trio was given three performances. Malipiero appeared only three times.

Not surprisingly, Kolisch completed the Pro Arte's dismissal of Belgian composers, and sharply limited the work of French ones. The more recent specimens, to be sure, were given only the most passing treatments: two reported performances each for Fauré's opus 50 Quartet and for Honegger's Second Quartet, though Milhaud's Quartet no. 8 received three performances, and no. 9 nine. There were only three performances of Franck's Piano Quintet and two of Chausson's Piano Quartet. But attention to the single quartets of two major French composers shifted back and forth between that of Debussy (thirty-two performances) and Ravel (twenty-five), with the latter's Piano Trio ventured eight times.

It may be expected that the overwhelming proportion of Kolisch's repertoire was Austro-German. Curiously, though, the founding father of that literature, Joseph Haydn, received a rather patchy representation, in scattered appearances in this Pro Arte's concerts. Most of the published opus collections were drawn upon, if in irregular fashion. Of opus 20, only no. 4 (a dozen times); of opus 33, no. 2 (once), no. 5 (thrice), and no. 3 (eight times); of opus 50, only no. 6 (five times); of opus 54, no, 3 only once but no. 2 eight times; of opus 55, just no. 2 (twice); of opus 64, only no. 5, but seventeen times. It was only opus 76 that received complete exploration: no. 6 a mere once, no. 5 three times, no. 3 five times, no. 4 six times, and no. 2 seven times; but no. 1 a whopping twenty-two times. These reported performances total one hundred and three in all. To these may be added a single Trio (op. 75), done once.

With Mozart, Kolisch was somewhat more generous. Of the string quartets: K. 370 (once), K. 387 (six times), K. 421 (18), K. 428 (nine), K. 464 (four), K. 478 (twelve), K. 493 (three), K. 575 (twenty), K. 589 and K. 590 (twelve times each), K. 595 (twice). In all, a total of ninety-nine quartet performances. The Prelude and Fugue for quartet, K.

546, twice. Of the string quintets: K. 593 and K. 416, once each, K. 515, K. 516, K. 614, twice each. Of the Piano Quartets: K. 458, twenty-two times, K. 465, twenty-three times. Of quartets and quintets with wind instruments: Flute Quartet K. 285 (twice), the Oboe Quartet, K. 370 (once), the Horn Quintet, K. 407 (thrice), the Clarinet Quintet, K. 581 (twice). Of the piano trios: K. 496, eleven times, K. 502, once. The Clarinet Trio K. 498, once. Of the great String Trio/Divertimento in E-flat, K. 498, twice. All for a full total of one hundred and ninety Mozart performances.

The major recipient of Kolisch's Pro Arte attention, however, was Beethoven. Though he only mounted a single cycle of the complete quartets, Kolisch was careful to work them steadily into the active repertoire and repeat them regularly thereafter. From the outset, he dipped into the opus 18 quartets unevenly: no. 5, thrice, no. 2, four times, no. 6 six times, no. 4 seven times, and no. 1 nine times; but no. 3 achieved twenty performances. Kolisch was slow to move into the late quartets, and sparingly once he did: seven performances each for opus 127 and opus 132, ten each for opus 131 and opus 133, twelve for opus 135, and fourteen for opus 130. On the other hand, from the beginning and onward, Kolisch seemed to relish the middle-period quartets: opus 74 was given fourteen performances, opus 95 thirty-five performances. Above all, the opus 59 set was favored: no. 3 eighteen times, no. 1 twenty-five times, and no. 2 a lavish fifty-five times. The Beethoven quartets were thus given, in total, a reported 213 performances. Of the string trios, the Serenade, op. 8, was given fifteen times; of the opus 9 set, no. 1 received nine performances, no. 3 three. Of the piano trios, the three of the opus 1 set were given one performance each; the two of opus 70 received one and two performances, respectively; the opus 97 appeared three times. The opus 25 Serenade for flute, violin, and viola, was given once. In full total, 250 Beethoven performances.

Kolisch definitely felt a strong affinity for the music of Schubert. Among the string quartets, he clearly preferred D. 112 (fourteen times) over D. 173 (once); but, of the last works, he gave the D. 703 *Quartettsatz* twelve hearings, while playing the D. 804 twenty times and the D. 810 a full 465 times, the D. 887 following with thirty performances. That totals 123 string quartet performances. Kolisch managed the "Trout" Quintet three times, and the D. 956 Quintet six times. Of the piano trios, eight times for D. 898, and five times for D. 920, and four times for the String Trio D. 471. The Octet D. 803 was included three times. Schubert performances thus total 152.

1. Drawing ca. 1920 (B. Petrović): Onnou, Prévost, Quinet, Halleux. Courtesy of the Tully Potter Collection.

2. 1922: Maas, Halleux, Onnou, Prévost, inscribed December 13, 1926. Courtesy of the Tully Potter Collection.

Unless otherwise indicated, photographs are reproduced courtesy of the University of Wisconsin–Madison, Mills Music Library.

3. 1928: Onnou, Maas, Prévost, Halleux.

4. 1939: Onnou, Halleux, Maas, Prévost.

5. Paul Collaer. Courtesy of the Tully Potter Collection.

6. Elizabeth Sprague Coolidge: charcoal sketch by John Singer Sargent. Courtesy of the Library of Congress.

7. Elizabeth Sprague Coolidge and her "Boys."

8. 1940: Onnou, Halleux, Evans, Prévost.

9. November 22, 1940: Onnou's casket carried from St. Paul's University Chapel, Madison. Photograph courtesy of Anne Van Malderen.

10. 1940: Brosa, Halleux, Prevost, Evans.

11. 1941: Brosa, Halleux, Prevost, Gottlieb; same as above but with Gottlieb's face superimposed on Evans's.

12. Ca. 1942: Brosa, Halleux, Sopkin. Prevost.

13. 1943: Rahier, Friedlander, Prevost, Brosa (*seated*).

14. 1944: Rahier, Friedlander, Prevost, Kolisch (*seated*).

15. Ca. 1955: Rahier, Milofsky. Friedlander, Kolisch.

16. 1958: Rahier, R. Blum, Creitz, Kolisch.

17. Ca. 1960: "Pro Arte Piano Quartet": Basso, R. Blum, Leo Steffens, Creitz.

18. 1967–73: Paulu, Moore, Creitz, R. Blum.

19. May 1974, Buenos Aires, Argentina: Creitz, McLeod, (US Cultural Attaché), R. Blum, Paulu.

20. 1974: Paulu, M. Blum, Creitz, R. Blum.

21. 1976–88: Paulu, M. Blum, Karp, R. Blum.

22. 1976–88: R. Blum, M. Blum, Karp, Paulu.

23. 1976–88: Picnic with R. Blum, Paulu, M. Blum, Karp.

24. 1988–91: Paulu, R. Blum, Kim, Karp.

25. 1991–95: Karp, Chisholm, Paulu, Kim.

26. 1995: Chisholm, Perry, Beia, Karp.

27. May 2011: Perry, Beia, Chisholm, Karp. Photograph by Rick Langer.

28. May 23, 2014: Beia, Perry, Chisholm, Karp, at Onnou's birthplace, Dollhain, Belgium. Photograph by Alain Boucourt.

29. April 2012: Grave of Alphonse Onnou, Forest Hill Cemetery, Madison Wisconsin. Photograph by Robert Graebner.

The appearances of Schumann's music were somewhat modest, by comparison. Of the opus 41 string quartets, no. 2 was given only twice, but no. 3 appeared eleven times and no. 1 fourteen. The Piano Quintet was given ten times; of the piano trios, opus 63 once, opus 80 and opus 110 twice each. Schumann's total is thus forty-two performances.

The attention to Brahms, however, was more stalwart and diverse. Of the string quartets, op. 51, no. 1 received eight performances, but op. 51, no. 2 an impressive twenty-five; and opus 67 received nine, for a total of forty-two quartet readings. The Piano Quartets were treated extensively: seven times for opus 25, eighteen times for opus 26, and fifteen for opus 60; thirty-nine performances in all. The Piano Quintet op. 34, was presented four times, and the Clarinet Quintet op. 115, once. The Clarinet Trio op. 114, was given twice; the Horn Trio op. 40, once. Of the piano trios, opus 8 was played twice, opus 87 and opus 101 thrice each. Brahms performances thus totaled ninety-seven.

For whatever reason, Mendelssohn was addressed marginally, with only two performances of his Trio op. 49. Among other "marginals," Bruckner understandably received only two appearances for his String Quintet. Hugo Wolf's *Italian Serenade* was played nine times. Max Reger was given the limited favor with one performance each of a string quartet and piano quartet, and four for string trios.

Among other nineteenth-century composers, the Czech Smetana was served with five performances of his Quartet no. 1. Dvořák figured significantly: of his string quartets, the ever-popular op. 96 was played twenty-two times; op. 106, eight times; The Piano Quintet received three performances, and the Trio, op. 90, two. On the other hand, the exploration of the Quartet by the Italian Verdi, in two performances early on, was then abandoned. An earlier Italian, Boccherini, was given two performances of a trio.

Kolisch's Pro Arte was, as in the Belgian phases, rather ambivalent about taking on works by American composers. Indeed, violist Bernard Milofsky complained about this in a letter to a colleague written on May 12, 1952, eight years into the Kolisch era: "We practically never play contemporary American works (the only exceptions have been Roger Sessions, Piston and [William] Schuman, the last two I must tell you between ourselves, with resistance), we could not justify the inclusion of this quartet, thereby bypassing the whole crowd of Roy Harris, Aaron Copland, etc., etc., etc." In point of fact, Kolisch did make some fair gestures into this literature. We have noticed his venture, in a pair of performances, into the Barber Quartet that the Belgian Pro Arte

had premiered so unhappily; a venture not then continued. Among
other major Americans: Copland's Piano Quartet was performed once;
Walter Piston's Third Quartet was given four times; Schuman's own
Third Quartet was played once; but Roger Sessions was represented
eleven times. Among more obscure Americans, Béla Rozsa appeared
once, as did Felix Borowski (his Third Quartet). Cecil Burleigh, Carl
Eppert, and Oskar Hagen—all Wisconsin-identified figures—were
granted two performances each. A total, then, of only twenty-seven
American performances.

All of these reported data add up to a total of 1,225 works, performed within a total of 580 concerts by the Kolisch-led Pro Arte
Quartet.

❧  ❧  ❧

Reckoned separately is the repertoire of the University of Wisconsin
Piano Quartet, which functioned for six years (1961–67) as the bridge
between Kolisch's withdrawal from playing with the full Pro Arte and
the complete revival of the quartet.

In that period, the Austro-German dimension still bulks large, if
not as overwhelmingly as for the quartet. Haydn, to be sure, is minimally represented, by three trio performances. But Mozart's representations took a commanding lead. The two Piano Quartets were each
given fifteen performances, one of the Flute Quartets four, the Clarinet
Trio six, and the String Trio–Divertimento K. 563 and the Violin–Viola
Duo K. 424 six each. A string Divertimento, K. 439b, and a Prelude
and Fugue received one each. The total of Mozart performances in the
Piano Quartet era was thus fifty-four.

Beethoven was a slightly less dominant figure in this arena. His
string trios appear most frequently. The opus 3 was played once; of the
string trios of op. 9, no. 1 was played three times, no. 2 six, and no. 3
five; the String Serenade op. 8 was played five times; the Piano Trio op.
11 once, the clarinet version of it twice; but the Piano Quartet op. 16
was given eleven performances. The group participated in a performance of the Septet, and members also played as soloists in the Triple
Concerto. The sum for Beethoven was thirty-seven.

The other German Romantics were in reduced presence.
Schubert's Piano Trio D. 898 was given twice, and the Quintet D. 956
only once. An unidentified trio by Schumann was played once, but
his Piano Quartet, op. 47, 17 times. Brahms was better served. Of the

piano quartets, opus 26 was performed four times, opus 25 eleven times, and opus 60 thirteen times, with the Horn Trio presented four times. Reger's Trio op. 141b was played four times. And the Czech Dvořák was represented by his Piano Trio op. 87 five times.

In the French category, we note only the two piano quartets of Fauré: opus 15 twelve times, opus 45 six times; and Chausson's Piano Quartet, op. 30, seven times.

Of "moderns," we find Dohnányi's Serenade six times, plus a Trio and a Sextet once each. The *Bachiana brasileira* no. 1 of Villa-Lobos just once. Ernst Bloch's Concerto Grosso no. 1 once (in ensemble). Alfredo Casella's *Serenata* Quintet once. Hindemith's op. 34 Trio seven times and his Clarinet Quartet once. Lennox Berkeley's Horn Trio twice. Benjamin Britten's Oboe Quartet once.

Under the heading of "early" composers, we have a "Piano Quartet" by Jean-Baptiste Loeillet. A version of Handel's Concerto grosso op. 6 no. 1 once. Bach's *Brandenburg Concerto* no. 3 and four Harpsichord Concertos once each. A piano quartet of Johann Christian Bach twelve times. Two items by Boccherini totaling three performances. A Bassoon Quartet by Franz Danzi, once.

Finally, a sampling of American composers. David Diamond's Flute Quintet, Norman Dello Joio's Trio (flute, cello, piano), Howard Boatwright's Serenade, and Bernhard Heiden's Bassoon Quartet, all once each. Irving Fine's *Fantasia* for string trio, eight times, and University of Wisconsin faculty composer Robert Crane once.

In all, these constitute a total of 228 reported works played by the University of Wisconsin Piano Quartet, within a total of 118 reported concerts, during the group's six years.

ঙ ঙ ঙ

As for Kolisch's independent activity in Madison, there are fourteen documented performances. The works involved were Bach's Sonata no. 2, Mozart's Sonatas K. 304 and K. 454 (each twice), plus K. 526, all ten of Beethoven Violin Sonatas (plus op. 30 no. 2 and op. 47 an additional time each), Schubert's Sonata D. 574 (twice), a Liszt sonata arrangement, Brahms's Sonata op. 108, Debussy's Sonata, Busoni's Sonata op. 36a, Bartók's unaccompanied Sonata, Schoenberg's *Phantasy* (thrice), Ravel's Sonata, and Webern's *Four Pieces* op. 7—all (save the Bach and Bartók) with Gunnar Johansen. With René Leibowitz conducting, Kolisch participated in various piano and choral works, *Pierrot Lunaire*, and the Violin Concerto, all of Schoenberg; Berg's *Kammerkonzert*, and Webern's *Concerto for Nine Instruments*.

## Recording Activities

Rudolf Kolisch came to the Pro Arte Quartet as no stranger to recording work. His first ventures go back to 1929 in London, where he recorded more fully in 1934. Before that, he recorded in Berlin in 1931, and then in Boston in 1937. Those ventures drew upon the works of Mozart, Schubert, Schumann, and Wolf. In 1936, meanwhile, through the generosity of Hollywood filmmaker Alfred Newman, Kolisch was able to use the United Artists studies to record all of the string quartets of Schoenberg: nos. 1–3 on December 29–31, 1936, and no. 4 on January 8 or 9, 1937 (coinciding with the world premiere). These Schoenberg recordings were issued in 78-rpm sets by the Alco label. The Library of Congress made an archival recording of a Kolisch-led performance (April 14, 1940) of Schubert's Octet.

All of those recordings are of great interest for studying the career and legacy of Kolisch himself, but only in one case are they of relevance for our consideration of his recordings with the Pro Arte of Madison. In fact, the latter represent a distinct documentation of his devotion to the music of the Second Viennese School—if with only two interesting exceptions.

One such exception is Bartók's Quartet no. 5. This work was commissioned by and dedicated to Elizabeth Sprague Coolidge, and had first been performed by the Kolisch Quartet in Washington on April 5, 1935 (in a concert at the Coolidge Auditorium in which the group also gave the American premiere of Berg's *Lyric Suite*). The Pro Arte performance was given on January 26, 1945, at the outset of Kolisch's leadership with the group. It was captured as an archival recording by the Library of Congress, and not released commercially until it was included in the Music & Arts label's Kolisch commemorative CD set. Unfortunately, the recording sound is dim, dull, and somewhat murky, not easy listening today. A lot of detail is lost: Kolisch's own, quite pointed playing comes through, but most of the other parts are obscure. There is evidence of energy in the performance, but in general, this recorded document does not do justice to Kolisch's long identification with Bartók's music.

The other exception is of the same vintage: a Library of Congress archival transcription of a concert performance at the Coolidge Auditorium on February 2, 1945—made just after the aforementioned Bartók transcription. The work is Roger Sessions's Quartet no. 1, one of the few American works that Kolisch was to program with some frequency. Unlike the Bartók recording, this one did eventually achieve commercial release, in an LP issue from the New World Records label; however, it has never been reissued on compact disc.

As to making commercially marketable recordings during his Pro Arte years, Kolisch's intentions are not clear. Did he have any broad strategy for a recording program? It would appear not, though such other factors as personnel changes and career distractions may have played a part. Did he plan, at least, within a series of recordings of Berg and Webern, a comprehensive treatment of Schoenberg's quartets, to replace the earlier Alco cycle? That, too, is difficult to answer. In fact, we have only two quartets by the composer in Kolisch-led recordings, and one of them a repertoire outlier, at that.

Not reckoned among Schoenberg's numbered quartets is one in D major, written in 1897 when the composer was twenty-three. It is an apprentice work, showing vividly how deep were Schoenberg's roots in late nineteenth-century Romanticism: we hear echoes of Brahms, of course, for whom he had a life-long admiration, but also of the folksy Dvořák. This youthful experiment is rarely performed and recorded today, and Kolisch himself seems not to have included it in the Pro Arte's working repertoire, save once—in what appears to have been its world-premiere performance. That was in yet another concert at the Library of Congress, on February 7, 1952, preserved in yet another archival transcription that was not released commercially until it was included in the Music & Arts commemorative album. By 1952, the Library's recording facilities had improved, and this result is quite respectable and listenable in today's terms. The performance has a kind of happy enthusiasm to it, if with some occasional intonation problems on Kolisch's part, and a bit of blurry rushing in some of the theme-with-variations third movement.

The one among the numbered Schoenberg quartets that Kolisch rerecorded with the Pro Arte was no. 3. This is the first of the composer's quartets to employ the fully developed "atonal" technique he had perfected. Its sonorities do not bring it too far from the sound world of Brahms, but the constructional concepts are vastly different and intellectually challenging. Kolisch undertook his second recording of it on January 24, 1950. It was in the second session of a recording series that Kolisch had contracted with the small Dial Records label, which had access to the facilities of radio station WOR in New York. He seems to have sought no arrangement with any of the major, more widely distributing companies. Perhaps that was because he found more support from one of the very small and enterprising ones that had been spawned by the new era of quality magnetic-tape recording and the LP record.

With this work we have an unusual and valid opportunity for comparison, as between the 1936 recording and the 1950 one. The improvement in sound quality is immediately apparent: the ambience is more open, the textures are rendered clearly in bright and vivid (though still monophonic) sound. As to performances, the newer Pro Arte one seems precise and sharply engaged, and yet not without expressiveness and even lilt. The older recording captures a little more Viennese warmth and inflection, though the rich cello work here of Benar Heifetz is not so generously matched by Ernst Friedlander. In all, however, the Dial recording is altogether preferable as a document of Kolisch's commitment to this music, as its first champion. For the other three numbered quartets, though, we are still dependent upon the 1936 cycle.

Kolisch was also deeply involved with Alban Berg and his music, notably the *Lyric Suite*, the premiere of which the violinist and his early quartet gave in 1927. It is among the most frequently played of the Second Viennese School's works for string quartet, even though it is extremely difficult to play. In recent decades we have learned a lot about the very private emotional subtext that Berg embedded in the score, but Kolisch clearly understood that emotional depth was the real point of this atonal masterpiece. Other recordings have appeared before and since this one, but his remains an indispensable presentation. This impassioned performance was made for Dial on February 2, 1950, in lucid sound of considerable presence, even if only monophonic.

The very first of the sessions for the Dial label, on January 20, 1950, was devoted to two works by Anton Webern. The *Five Movements for String Quartet*, op. 5, marked the composer's first full commitment to atonality, but also began his goal thereafter of achieving brevity in expression. This set was the most programmed by Kolisch of all the Second Viennese School compositions for string quartet. The *Six Bagatelles for String Quartet*, op. 9, represent an ultimate in Webern's penchant for drastically compressed, epigrammatic construction. Perhaps because of their demands on both players and audience, Kolisch performed them less frequently in concerts. Both sets are still not "easy listening" for most audiences today. Kolisch's Pro Arte players invest genuine conviction in bringing them to life, managing subtle nuances in music wherein the meanings are suggested rather than stated.

Kolisch does appear in three recordings in what we might call supplemental works, all captured in his last year in Madison, while he was working on his own and quite apart from his erstwhile Pro Arte colleagues. (All three are included in the Music & Arts Kolisch commemorative set of CDs.) Of the three, two are of works by Schoenberg, in performances given during the 1966–67 farewell concerts given in that composer's honor. One is of the *Phantasie*, op. 47, for piano and violin, played with pianist Gunnar Johansen, presumably on March 12, 1966. The other is of the Violin Concerto, op. 36, with a university ensemble (the "Wisconsin Festival Orchestra") under René Leibowitz. The recordings were made by local Madison technicians, and the results are variable. That of opus 47 is serviceable, if not as clear as one might like. That of opus 36 is, quite simply, terrible: the sound is muddy and opaque, with Kolisch's playing often lost in the sludge. Though he did not give the premiere of this work or record it commercially (those two tasks were assumed by Louis Krasner), Kolisch was closely identified with the work. He deserved to have recorded it properly: that this is the only substitute documentation of his way with it is tragic.

The third of those marginal recordings was also made in Madison in that last season, some time in 1966, apparently as a private taping. In it, Kolisch draws upon his long work with Bartók, and especially with this work, the Sonata for Solo Violin. In this performance, the violinist is still a powerful and vibrant performer. He gives added value in restoring the composer's original exploitation of microtones, which the dedicatee and first exponent of the work, Yehudi Menuhin, had eliminated in his performances and in his published edition of the score. Again, this is a part of Kolisch's recorded legacy that had enduring documentary value.

While the Kolisch-led Pro Arte never made any commercial recordings of music beyond that of the Second Viennese School, a significant number of performances of "mainstream" literature are preserved from public performances and Music 9a classroom presentations and survive in the archives of the University of Wisconsin's Mills Music Library, as noted in appendix E, part 2.

The Pro Arte Piano Quartet left no recorded legacy of their work.

## 5

# THE PAULU YEARS, I

# (1967–79)

## Regrouping

With the departures of both Rudolf Kolisch and Won-Mo Kim by summer 1967, only Richard Blum and Lowell Creitz were survivors of the previous quartet configuration. The obstacle of Kolisch's withdrawal since 1962 while still a faculty member was now removed. The issue of what to do when a quartet member became disaffected but remained as a faculty member was bypassed for now—though it would arise disastrously once more in years ahead. At this point, meanwhile, the temporary façade of the "UW Piano Quartet" as a device of continuity was no longer needed. The School of Music, in a new phase of expansion of its performing faculty, was ready and willing to reinstate the Pro Arte Quartet by appointing new occupants for the two violin chairs.

The new first violinist was Norman Paulu. Born in 1929, in Cedar Rapids, Iowa, he had the famous Joseph Szigeti among his teachers. Paulu had played in the 7th Army Symphony Orchestra at the same time as had Richard Blum, so there was a personal link between them. Paulu had professional experience in both orchestral and chamber playing. He had been concertmaster of the Oklahoma City Symphony; and he would repeat that role for a few years with the Madison Symphony Orchestra. He had also been first violinist of the Lyric Quartet of Oklahoma.

The new second violinist was Thomas Moore. Born in 1938 of a musical family, he received his training at the Eastman School of

Music. His experience likewise included both orchestral and chamber playing. Early on, he had used a research grant to study the music of Schoenberg, Berg, and Webern in Vienna with Rudolf Kolisch, during one of the latter's teaching stints there—giving Moore at least an indirect connection to the Pro Arte traditions.

For the first time in their history, the Pro Arte Quartet now had a team of players all born in the United States, none of them in Europe. What that would mean in their evolution was not immediately clear, nor would it be for some time. Reacting to Kolisch's background exclusively in chamber music playing, Paulu wanted to use his orchestral experience to bring a fuller, more rounded sonority to the Pro Arte's playing. At the same time, Creitz and Blum introduced the two new players to the analytical techniques of rehearsal in which Kolisch had trained them, and these were retained.

In all, it seemed that the Pro Arte now could look forward to a vigorous rejuvenation of their traditions.

&#x264D; &#x264D; &#x264D;

The new configuration's first season (1967–68) had a skimpy opening in the autumn. Beginning a tradition of some dormitory concerts on the Madison campus, the quartet gave a reduced program in Sellery Hall on October 25 that was later performed in full on November 12. The group played at a convocation on November 16. Their only other Madison appearance was at a private concert in the Paulu home in which the distinguished Viennese violist Paul Doktor joined the group for two Mozart Quintets and, a rarity, the Bruckner Quintet. Touring stops were limited to Waukesha and Sinsinawa in November and Sheboygan in December.

The second semester (1968), however, was a very busy one, and continued on into the summer. In January, the quartet gave another short Sellery Hall concert that was given in full three days later. Then, from the beginning of February into March, the quartet made a state tour of seven sites (Beloit, Milwaukee, Platteville, Racine twice, La Crosse, Janesville, Prairie du Chien, Manitowoc). Amid these stops there were two tapings for broadcasting four concerts in Madison, followed by leaps to Boulder, Colorado, and Laramie, Wyoming. After those came more concerts around the state (Sheboygan, Racine, Green Bay, Wausau, Ladysmith), with a season finish in Madison—a women's club, and the institution French House, where Moore, Creitz, and Steffens played the Ravel Trio. But work extended into the summer with four Madison concerts (two on the UW Union Terrace), punctuated midstream (July 13) with an appearance at the Montalvo Music Festival in California.

In Paulu's first season with the quartet, a clear direction was revealed: a renewed commitment to contemporary composers, mostly American, with whom Paulu had personal contacts. Notable was Samuel Adler, who was invited to lecture in Madison and to attend the premiere of his Quartet no. 4 (March 21, 22). This quartet was then recorded by the group June 2–7, together with a quartet by Herbert Fromm. A quartet by Sessions was in the final summer concert (August 9).

We also have a critic's testimony judging the revived Pro Arte in their first season. Following the California appearance (at which works by Mozart, Ravel, and Beethoven were played), Dale Craig of the *Palo Alto Times* wrote:

> The quartet's playing was characterized by superb emotion, rich blend, technical assurance, and ensemble precision; but also by rushed tempos, mechanical rhythmic rigidity, and a certain immaturity and lack of depth. Too much of the phrasing seemed to have been carefully calculated, then rehearsed until life has been strained from the music.

> But it has to be stressed that the Pro Arte players had marvelous accord, with every ensemble detail meticulously worked out.

Perhaps in those comments we may discern the effects of attempting to digest Kolisch's analytical approach to rehearsing.

In the following season, of 1968–69, caution over possible audience resistance to programming American works limited their attention to Andrew Imbrie's Quartet no. 2, while otherwise the group showed itself still working their way into largely standard repertoire. The autumn season again began, and closed, at Sellery Hall, followed by a Music School convocation. There were five other Madison appearances, plus a taping for WHA, balanced with six concerts scattered around the state (River Falls, La Crosse, Wingspread, Kenosha, Beloit, and Baraboo).

The spring semester (1969) followed similar patterns. There were some five concerts in Madison, plus two more there of divergent character: in one (February 12), only Moore and Creitz joined Steffens for "An Evening of French Chamber Music"; in the other (April 18) the

Pro Arte combined variously with members of the Fine Arts Quartet from Milwaukee in a Mozart quintet, Schoenberg's *Verklärte Nacht,* and the Mendelssohn Octet (repeated April 20 in Milwaukee). Through the semester, too, the group made ten stops around the state (Milton, Milwaukee twice, Wingspread, Platteville, Spring Green, Marshfield, Racine, Willamette, Ashland). And appearances were managed out of state (Emporia, Kansas; Oklahoma City, Tulsa; Iola, Kansas), plus a videotaping. In Oklahoma City, Paulu was given a particular welcome by those who remembered him as concertmaster in the local orchestra. And the concert there was hailed in particular by John Acord III of the *Daily Oklahoman* for its inclusion of the one American work carried over that season, Imbrie's Quartet no. 2: "The quartet's performance of this marvelously difficult work was one of utmost perfection and the cohesive blend of the individual players was a joy to hear."

There was yet another summer season (1969). In mid-July the Pro Arte made two appearances out in California (Stockton, Saratoga) and one in Oregon (Eugene). They returned briefly to Madison for two concerts, one on the Memorial Union Terrace. Then it was back to the West Coast again for three weeks. Their activities included two concerts at the Masson Vineyards (August 2, 3) and at least one at the August Moon Festival at Krug Vineyards in the Napa Valley. But the visit's main focus was a period of study with Andrew Imbrie of his quartets at Berkeley, plus at least one performance there (August 12) and one at the Cabrillo Festival at Monterey Bay (August 24).

Amid these California appearances, we have a fresh assessment of the new Pro Arte's performing progress from Robert Commanday, writing in the *San Francisco Chronicle* on August 4, 1969: "The Pro Arte Quartet . . . is an excellently balanced, wholly professional ensemble. Its virtues are not in the direction of brilliance, rich sonority, strongly pronounced personality but rather steadiness, thoughtful, committed playing, and consummate musicality. They bear the string quartet name that is oldest from the point of continuous use . . . and they carry its tradition in the right style." This impression might be supplemented by comments written a year later by Jack Rudolph in the *Green Bay Press Gazette*: "In the Pro Arte, the music had a strong and virile vehicle of performance. The quartet, rapidly regaining the eminence it once enjoyed, performed with aggressive momentum, strong tonal balance, and the flair that only mutual confidence can engender."

In the 1969–70 season, the fall semester included four stops in various Madison locations and three around the state (La Crosse,

Wingspread, Beloit). But the highlight of the semester was the new association with Andrew Imbrie and his music, in potent combination with the opening of the university's new concert venue in the just-built Humanities Building. The locations of the School of Music had for some time been scattered through several separate buildings, and its auditorium, Music Hall (which was originally the university's library) had become inadequate. The construction of the comprehensive Humanities Building (also housing the History and the Art Education Departments) had been an artificially prolonged process, but its new auditorium, Mills Hall, was ready for dedication in November of 1969. The celebrations there included the Pro Arte performance of Imbrie's Quartets 1–3 (November 13); a guest lecture by Imbrie himself; and a concert including the premiere of his Fourth Quartet (November 17).

By now-established practice, the second semester (1970) was the busier half of the year. After a Madison concert (January 11), the group appeared twice at the Eastman School in Rochester NY (February 7–8). Thereafter, they interspersed episodes of in-state touring (Beloit thrice, La Crosse twice, Green Bay and Wingspread once each) with five public concerts in Madison (plus concerts in three campus dormitories, April 28–29), and quick ventures to colleges in Springfield, Missouri (April 7) and Marshall, Minnesota (May 16). The repertoire was heavily focused on Beethoven, but quartets of Adler and Imbrie did figure recurrently.

Again there was a summer extension. A grant allowed a week of renewed study with Andrew Imbrie (June 12–19). After a stop in Milwaukee (June 22), the Pro Arte made another stay in the west: three appearances in South Dakota in July (Rapids City twice, Black Hills), then presentations in California at the Masson Vineyards in Saratoga, at Berkeley, at the Cabrillo Festival in Aptos, and at the Krug Vineyards.

The autumn semester of 1970–71 settled down to seven concerts in Madison, plus two dormitory performances, with three state-tour stops (Manitowoc, Marinette, Milton), spiced by a jaunt to Lincoln, Nebraska. The spring semester began with a mix of five Madison concerts, and a mere three around the state (Beloit, La Crosse, Green Bay). There were trips out of the state, to Nebraska (Hastings, Lincoln); to Buffalo, New York; and in April to California (Berkeley, San Francisco) and Wyoming (Laramie), the latter proceded by two days of coaching with Arnold Elston on his quartet (April 15). In mid-May into June, however, Paulu led the quartet in the American Pro Arte's first international tour, to Brazil (Recife, Brasilia, Rio de Janeiro, São

Paulo, Curitiba, Porto Alegre) and Argentina (Buenos Aires). During this period there were protests and demonstrations in Latin America, and the State Department provided escorts to protect the musicians from any dangers. Such provisions proved unnecessary. The players and their concerts were welcomed enthusiastically by local critics. Returning home, the quartet topped off all of this with an appearance (June 20) at Lincoln's Nebraska Chamber Music Festival.

The 1971–72 year began with an autumn featuring seven Madison concerts, as against three appearances at colleges around the state (Ripon, La Crosse, Milwaukee). There were also four presentations back at Lincoln, Nebraska, which was developing an important educational program in music. A novelty, however, was a venture to Edmonton, Alberta (Canada), on October 13. That appearance provoked one of the few negative critical reactions of this time. On the day after the concert, Keith Ashwell wrote in the *Edmonton Journal*:

> It would be nice to say that an encouraging opening was complimented by the standards of musicianship that are conveyed by the name of Pro Arte. But, while the mechanics were above reproach and the working out of the music—at least in the Haydn [op. 20/4] and Debussy—for which we have our precedents—admirable, the performances were not bound over-all by great style and wisdom.

For the spring (1972) semester there were eight varied appearances in Madison, interspersed with performances around the state (Wisconsin Rapids, Manitowoc, Green Bay, Marinette, Menomonee, Appleton, Baraboo, Beloit). There was still time for a quick appearance (January 21) in Berkeley, CA, when the group made their only other commercial recording of this period.

But in the course of this spring (1972), a new personnel crisis exploded. While the group was in the midst of some touring, second violinist Thomas Moore informed his colleagues that he was withdrawing as a member of the Pro Arte Quartet.

෴ ෴ ෴

It was in a memo dated April 30, 1973, that Moore submitted his formal request to the School of Music, asking to be transferred from a 50-percent appointment in the quartet to full teaching status. He explained this "as a result of my own needs and growth both as a performer and as a teacher." He elaborated further: "In the last few years I have felt a

growing commitment and desire for teaching and in direct ratio to a
need for the time and opportunity to perform the significant literature
other than the string quartet which deserves to be played and heard."

Moore was a brilliant musician and teacher, but he did have some
personality issues. When he left the University of Wisconsin School
of Music a few years later, he pursued a productive career. He served
on the faculty of the University of Miami until 1992, while also being
concertmaster of the Florida Philharmonic. He toured widely as a
performer, but was most notable as a tireless and highly appreciated
teacher. One might even measure his decision to leave the Pro Arte
against some later expressions of feeling by Norman Paulu himself that
commitment to quartet membership was almost a full-time job in itself,
restricting the possibilities of other activities.

Nevertheless, Moore's decision was regarded as a betrayal of his
colleagues, and certainly as a destructive step. He held a specific faculty position, which he retained, and it was not feasible that an entirely
new position be suddenly created just to cover his vacant chair in the
quartet. This situation has recurred with terribly negative effects essentially down to the present, at which point the second violin chair has
been financed out of foundation resources, and carries no formal faculty status. Here beginneth the "Curse of Tom Moore."

⋙  ⋙  ⋙

Moore played with the quartet through May 1972. He seems to have
appeared with them at least once during the new season, on November 13, in an Omaha concert. Otherwise, from August into March
of the 1972–73 season, the Pro Arte turned into a trio once more,
or was joined by faculty colleagues in piano quartets for at least four
Madison concerts, plus some other collaborations. By late winter,
however, the Music School had engaged John McLeod as a substitute second violinist, so that the group could fulfill their various
commitments. Thus reconstituted, the quartet played one Madison
concert (plus another trio presentation on May 7 (for Brahms's
birthday), four state appearances (La Crosse, Ripon, Wausau, Manitowoc), as well as out-state offerings in Nebraska (Norfolk, North
Platte), one in Oklahoma City, and two separate ones (April 8, July
3) in Laramie, Wyoming.

McLeod remained as second violinist for the 1973–74 season. The
autumn season was restricted to seven concerts in Madison and only

three around the state (Stevens Point, Beloit, Platteville). The spring semester was more hectic. It opened with a three-day period of study with Seymour Shifrin on his Quartet no. 5. This was followed, over the semester, by five Madison concerts—in two of which, March 27 and March 30, the Pro Arte were joined by the Beaux Arts Trio—and five around the state (Milwaukee thrice, Ripon, Northland, Manitowoc), plus separate plunges into California (Berkeley, January 27, February 3) and Nebraska (Chadron, Scottsbluff, March 11, 13).

But the season was rounded out, spectacularly, by the Pro Arte's second tour of Latin America, from late April to early June 1974. It involved a total of sixteen concerts in eight countries: Dutch Antilles (Aruba), Brazil (Recife, Brasilia, Rio de Janeiro, Piracicaba, Campinas, Santos, Curitiba), Bolivia (Cochambamba), Paraguay (Asunción), Argentina (Tucaman, Bahia Blanca, Buenos Aires twice), Colombia (Bogotá), and San Salvador (El Salvador).

The concert in Berkeley in January prompted one review deserving notice. On the 27th of that month, Paul Hertelendy wrote in the *Oakland Tribune*:

> This group specializing in modern music is entirely American, a far cry from the all-Belgian personnel that started it back in 1912. It has commissioned numerous works and played important world premieres, including one of the Bartók string quartets. [Actually, the Pro Arte never premiered a Bartók quartet, but his Quartet no. 4 was dedicated to the group.] The group is a refreshing contrast to the romantic and Viennese sound often heard today; its emphasis is accuracy, clarity, and focus—excellent for the music of Roger Sessions and Mozart, and at least viable for Brahms, whose Quartet no. 3 served as the centerpiece of the concert.

These comments raise an interesting point: if the Pro Arte had shed "the romantic and Viennese sound," with what had they replaced that sound? Presumably, without using the word, that critic was proposing that the quartet now offered not just negation but an alternate "American" sound. And what would that be—"accuracy, clarity, and focus"? It is noteworthy that Norman Paulu has at times advocated the creation of a new "American" quartet sound, without fully specifying its qualities. In his later reflections, though, Lowell Creitz has posited that the Pro Arte shifted from Belgian and Austro-German qualities to what he called an "American compromise style, lacking Kolisch's structuralist rigor." Some degrees were maintained, then, of traditional styles, but only after shedding efforts to learn from the Kolisch approach. The issue remains unresolved.

On return from the Latin American tour in the summer of 1974, yet another crisis presented itself. McLeod's temporary membership was concluded. (He was to pursue a subsequent career at the University of Missouri where he was the second violinist of the Esterhazy Quartet until his retirement in 2006.) Moreover, the University of Wisconsin had decided to discontinue financing the Pro Arte as artists in residence; the remaining three players would simply become full-time teaching faculty. This decision could have meant the final dissolution of the quartet. But Paulu and his two colleagues would not have it so, and were determined to go on, even on their own.

Joining in this endeavor was a new second violinist, and the group's first female member: Martha Francis Blum, the wife of Richard Blum. (For a time, she played under her maiden name of Francis but soon shifted to using her marital surname.) Born in Los Angeles, she had extensive training and performing experience. Early in her career she played with the Fred Waring Orchestra. She met her husband while playing in the San Antonio and Dallas Symphonies. After moving to Madison she played variously in the Chicago Lyric Opera and Grant Park Orchestras, as well as in the Madison Symphony and the Kenosha Orchestra (as concertmaster). Active in Madison's chamber music, she was a founder of the Capitol Quartet and the Vilas Master Quartet, for the latter of which at least three concerts at campus sites are documented (May 20, October 11, 1972; March 21, 1973).

As a self-sufficient foursome, the marginalized Pro Arte protested their situation by refusing to play in campus concerts. Instead, for their formal 1974–75 season, finding rehearsal opportunities as best they could, the group played at outlying sites around the state (Manitowoc, La Crosse, Token Creek, Beloit, Platteville, Baraboo), and made one appearance in Madison at the First Unitarian Society. But there were then extensions. Between June 14 and 21, the quartet played at least four concerts in Anchorage, Alaska. Further, in July and August, the group (apparently without Martha Blum) played string trios and piano quartets in at least three in-state sites (Token Creek, Hilltop at Spring Green, each twice).

The first semester of 1975–76 was slender, with two trio concerts (one including participation in Schoenberg's *Kammersymphonie*), and a quartet program in two outlying University of Wisconsin Centers (Richland, Fox Valley). The spring semester was dominated by four performances in February and April, arranged in cooperation with the First Unitarian Society in Madison. After a stop at the Manitowoc Center (April 22), the group played at Harvard (April 26) and Princeton (May 9) Universities (with Bethany Beardslee, soprano). Returning westward, they participated (May 12–14) in making a video, "What Is a Quartet?," for National Educational Television, followed by some four concerts in June, once again at the University of Wyoming in Laramie.

In the spring of 1976, Lowell Creitz resigned as a member of the Pro Arte, after twenty-one years of service to it; though, as we shall see, he still played with them intermittently for some months thereafter. (He also took a leave of absence to study in Europe.) This paved the way for the early admission to the group of Parry Karp, a precocious young cellist, then twenty-one.

Karp was born in Lexington, KY, where his father, the distinguished pianist Howard Karp, was on the faculty of the University of Kentucky. (Howard's wife and Parry's mother, Frances, also was, and still is, a pianist of distinction.) The elder Karp moved to the faculty of the University of Illinois (1962–72). The year he relocated in Madison to join the University of Wisconsin faculty was the year that young Parry began college studies at the University of Illinois. As a student of cello, he became caught up in quartet work, studying with several former members of world-class string quartets (Hungarian, Végh). In the April of his senior year, 1976, he received a phone call from Paulu, pointing out that, with the resignation of Creitz, there was a cello opening with the Pro Arte, for which he was invited to apply. Karp remembers spending some four or five days in Madison in which he worked intensively with the other players in complete quartets (Haydn, Mozart, Beethoven, Mendelssohn, Debussy, Bartók). Karp had planned on graduate studies in New York or Los Angeles, but "it was my dream to play in a professional quartet," so he accepted the invitation to join the Pro Arte in August. To make up for his gap in graduate study, he enrolled at the University of Wisconsin School of Music in a Masters degree program, completing the degree the following August (1977).

Parry Karp's initiation into the quartet was involved with some momentous family activities. His parents, Howard and Frances, launched a tradition with a concert on September 6, 1976, their first Labor Day appearance in what would become a Karp Family Annual celebration—a tradition that has lasted down to the present writing. In that first concert (billed officially as "An Evening of 19th Century Chamber Music"), Paulu, the two Blums, and all three Karps played

Dvořák and Schumann works. And on September 18, Parry gave a recital with his parents.

Likewise, at the outset of the 1976–77 season, Paulu, Blum, and Creitz gave a string-trio concert (September 17). Parry Karp took his full place in the group for a concert at the Memorial Union Theater in Madison (Oct. 24). (He was, in fact, also now established in the quartet's appearances in the "Music in Performance" course, Music 203.) The group then went east to participate in the ISCM program at the New England Conservatory (October 27) and a Fromm Foundation gathering at Harvard University (November 1). They returned to Madison for a concert (December 7) that included the great Schubert Quintet D. 956, in which Creitz played the fifth part on the tenor violin, a rare instrument of which he had lately become a practitioner and champion.

That last concert prompted an observation by a local critic, Dave Wagner of Madison's *Capital Times:* "The cellist in both pieces [Beethoven, Schubert] was Parry Karp, whose debut with the Pro Arte was an eminently successful one, giving the ensemble an extra measure of energy. This would be only one of a number of perceptions as to the new vigor that the dynamic young player was bringing to the group.

By the spring semester in 1977, it was clear that the Pro Arte was no longer boycotting the Madison campus, supposedly as a stipulation made by young Karp as a condition for joining. Aside from appearances in the regular "Music in Performance" classes, the group made at least six appearances in its facilities. In one (February 13), they were joined by the first violinist's wife, the talented oboist Catherine Paulu, in Arthur Bliss's Oboe Quintet. She repeated that in a Pro Arte concert in Oklahoma City (February 18). On March 6, Creitz rejoined the Pro Arte, with other faculty colleagues, in performances of Mozart's *Ein musikalischer Spass* and a Beethoven Sextet, in which he played, in turn, cello and tenor violin. Karp gave his graduate recital on March 29, with his parents assisting. And on April 30 Howard Karp joined the group in Schumann's Piano Quintet. In addition to those campus appearances, the Pro Arte played once again at the First Unitarian Society, with Creitz again on tenor violin in the Schubert Quintet (May 6). It was also Creitz, on cello, who went with the quartet to the University of Wyoming at Laramie for six performances in June and early July.

At the outset of the 1977–78 season, the nascent Karp Family's Labor Day Concert was given its second round as a "Faculty Chamber Music Recital," in which the members of the Wingra Woodwind Quintet and Howard Karp joined with the Pro Arte for a varied program.

(The same program, but without the wind contributions, was repeated in Stevens Point on October 5.) In this period, too, Parry Karp gave frequent chamber concerts with one or both of his parents. The quartet made three appearances in Madison (in the last, December 7, again joined by Cathy Paulu), and one at the University of Illinois (where Parry Karp had done his undergraduate studies, this time with Howard Karp participating). In the spring semester (1978), the quartet gave three Madison performances—in the last, with faculty pianist Carroll Chilton involved. On April 13, however, the quartet appeared at Columbia University in New York, where they played Martin Boykan's Quartet no. 2, and about this time they made a recording of the work for the CRI label, their first with Karp participating. In late spring, they were back in Laramie, Wyoming, for the Western Arts Music Festival for four concerts (June 6, 8, 13 and 20).

The addition of Karp to the quartet promised to bring renewed stability and new vitality to the ensemble. But, in the course of the spring of 1978, he was offered a position at the University of British Columbia, in Vancouver, Canada. This was a serious career opportunity, given the uncertain standing of the quartet vis-à-vis the university. Karp tried to negotiate, without clear results, and he was obliged to meet the Vancouver deadline by accepting a starting appointment of one season. Meanwhile, the other quartet members were making it clear that they could no longer continue their work without a definite fiscal commitment from the university.

At this point appeared another music-loving chief administrator as hero. An amateur musician and great music-lover himself, Irving Shain had just become the University of Wisconsin–Madison's chancellor in 1977. (With the expansion of the UW into a complex of campuses by now, the title of president went to its overall executive, while the leader of the Madison campus was now designated as chancellor.) Word had begun to circulate that the Pro Arte might disappear from Madison for good, and once again a flood of newspaper alarm and citizen protests emerged to prod Shain into taking action. After a series of conferences among all concerned, it was agreed that Karp would spend just the one year (1978–79) as visiting professor in Vancouver, while Creitz would fill in for him in the cello chair for that time, at least for Madison concerts. Shain, who was in the process of developing his expansive Outreach program—in which the university's cultural resources would be made available to the widest audience—was able to conjure up the funding for the entire quartet as a continuing part of the School of Music.

On that basis, Karp departed to Vancouver for the 1978–79 season. Before leaving, Parry joined with his father to participate in the third Labor Day concert (September 4). Creitz participated in four Madison concerts, in two different WHA Radio efforts, and in visits to Cedar Rapids, Iowa, and Baltimore. For his part, while active in Vancouver performance, Karp rejoined the Pro Arte for concerts in Madison (November 8), in Baltimore (November 12), and Princeton (November 17). Reports of other concerts are not clear, but he was with the group on the east coast when they recorded the Quartet by Paul Lansky in November.

In the second semester (1979), Moore emerged from his shadows to participate, with the Pro Arte members (Paulu, two Blums, Creitz) in a Faculty Chamber Music Concert offering works of Mozart and Bach. Through the semester, Creitz served with the quartet in two Madison concerts plus two WHA events, as well as for in-state appearances at Averno, Platteville, Green Bay, and Wausau, plus Evanston, Illinois. On the other hand, in a reversal of the proverbial mountain going to Mohammed, the Pro Arte spent a week (March 19–25) in Vancouver for a residence in which Karp rejoined them. The occasion was a celebration of the important violinist and composer Harry Adaskin. Since he was an old friend of Germain Prevost, Cathy Paulu personally escorted the nearly blind violist up to Vancouver for a reunion that was notable for its uninhibited television conversation.

Karp was back in Madison for a concert (April 29) in which the quartet was joined by pianist Marylène Dosse. Karp remained with the Pro Arte for their residence (May 10–20, concerts on May 12, 18, 19) in Berkeley CA. On May 21, the *San Francisco Chronicle* published a review by Robert Commanday of the group's concert on May 18: "The oldest string quartet in continuous operation sounds in some respects as if it were one of the newest. Its priorities are rhythmic integrity, structural clarity, and expressive energy." Karp joined them again for their return appearances at the Wyoming Arts Festival in Laramie (June 12, 17, 21, 26, July 10), and for another Latin American tour of of some six weeks in the summer. In the latter, between July 15 and August 21, a documented thirteen concerts were given: in São Paulo and Florianopolis, Brazil; in Asunción, Paraguay; in Montevideo, Uruguay; in Bahía Blanca and Cordoba, Argentina; in Tegucigalpa, Honduras; in Temuco, Chile; as well as in Ecuador and Mexico.

Information on that Latin American venture allows us an unusual picture of the repertoire strategy that could be developed for a prolonged tour. The Pro Arte assembled a working pool of ten compositions, which could be rotated and remixed from concert to concert, three items to each program. An identical grouping was used for only two concerts. The ten works were: Bartók Quartet no. 4 (six times); Beethoven's op. 18, no. 2 (four times); his op. 59, no. 2 (six times); Davidovsky's Quartet no. 3 (three times); Dvořák's opus 61 (three times); Haydn's op. 20, no. 2 (three times); Mendelssohn's opus 12 (five times); Mozart's Oboe Quartet K. 370 (once); Ravel's Quartet (four times); and Webern's Bagatelles, op. 9 (four times). That is thirty-nine items over thirteen concerts. The constant reshuffling obviously had the advantage of sparing the players the debilitating strain or boredom of playing the same three works thirteen times over the course of six weeks.

At any rate, during his year in Vancouver, Karp did regularly rejoin the Pro Arte: he recalls doing some fifty concerts, including a tour of the east coast and a west-coast tour. He also remembers playing in half of the in-state appearances over the full 1978–79 year.

By this point, the summer of 1979, the replacement of Lowell Creitz by Parry Karp was definitive. Shain had arranged that quartet membership no longer counted as part of tenure, so that in the future, if a member resigned, 50-percent faculty membership was still allowed that member—thus resolving the Moore crisis. Paulu and Richard Blum were tenured faculty at 50-percent teaching time, while Karp was also taken on for faculty teaching. Martha Blum was allowed to take the second violin chair beside her husband since, by this time, the university had abandoned the nepotism rule that banned married pairs from serving in the same division; but she had no formal faculty status and was funded, eventually, from separate foundation monies, an anomalous arrangment that continues to haunt—and hamper—the quartet's relationship with the university.

Above all, however, a new Pro Arte configuration was now firmly in place, to define the next nine years as a period of congenial stability.

# Repertoire

While many data are missing or incomplete, the documentation for this period of Pro Arte history is considerably more reliable than elsewhere, thanks in particular to Lowell Creitz's personal performance log. Nevertheless, figures and totals must still be considered minimals or approximations. The quartet was in the habit of giving concerts containing selected movements from works, rather than those scores complete; generally, where the information was usable, these instances have been noted as if they were complete performances. Some quartet combinations, quintets, and small-ensemble works are included in the main listing; but most trios, piano quartets, and other works specifically used by the substitute configurations are listed separately. Performances by quartet members in solo sonatas are not listed.

The initiation of Norman Paulu's leadership marked a definite new direction in terms of repertoire. The most immediate departure was from the emphasis that Kolisch had placed on music of the Second Viennese School. The Paulu quartet came little and late to Schoenberg: of the quartets, only no. 1, quite belatedly but eventually five times; the sextet *Verklärte Nacht* appeared four times along the way, with participation in the *Kammersinfonie* only once. Berg was represented only by the early opus 3 Quartet, if eight times. Somehow, however, Anton Webern's music was much more to the group's taste: the Six Bagatelles, op. 9, were given thirteen times, and the String Quartet seven times; but the *Five Movements*, op. 5, were performed a documented twenty-four times.

The Pro Arte tradition of devotion to contemporary music was redefined under Paulu as intense commitment to new and almost totally American composers—American if not by birth, at least by career. In many cases their works were commissioned or at least premiered by the ensemble. Collegial support was given to at least two fellow faculty members in the School of Music: Les Thimmig's *Seven Profiles* was given twenty-three times, as against Hilmar Luckhardt's Third Quartet four times and the Fourth twice.

By far, the American composer most identified with, and supported by, the Paulu Pro Arte was Andrew Imbrie (1921–2007), whose four quartets were studied with the composer and appeared repeatedly in the group's programs: eleven, eighteen, four, and seventeen times, respectively. Also served by them was the important Roger Sessions (1896–1985): his First Quartet given four times, the Second fifteen, and his Quintet five times.

At least twenty-three other composers, of varying degrees of prominence, were addressed by this Pro Arte—who often worked directly these composers. Samuel Adler (b. 1928): Fourth and Fifth quartets, performed six and three times, respectively. Milton Babbitt (1916–2011): Second and Fourth Quartets, played twice and four times, respectively. Leslie Bassett (1923–2016): Sextet, once. Martin Boykan (b. 1931): Second Quartet performed thrice (and recorded). German-born Herbert Brün (1918–2000): Quartet no. 2, four times. Edward T. Cone (b. 1917): String Trio, once. Mario Davidovsky (b. 1934): Third Quartet, five times. Jacob Druckman (1928–96): *Animus II*, once. Arnold Elston (1907–71): Quartets 1–3, once, once, and twice, respectively. Lukas Foss (1922–2009): Quartet no. 1: twice. Herbert Fromm (1905–95): Quartet, eight times. Roy Harris (1898–1979): Flute Quartet, once. Czech composer Karel Husa (1921–2016): Third Quartet, three times. Leon Kirchner (1919–2009): Quartet, once. Karl Korte ((b. 1928): Quartet no. 2, five times. Paul Lansky (b. 1944): Quartet no. 2, once. Richard Meale (1932–2009): Quartet, once. Czech-born Václav Nelhýbel (1919–96): *Oratorio*, twice. Slovak composer Tadeáš Salva (1937–95): Quartet, thrice. Seymour Shifrin (1926–79): Fifth Quartet, four times. Godfrey Winham (1934–75): *The Habit of Perfection*, twice. P. T. Witt (?): Quartet no. 1, four times.

Against such specialized contemporaneous literature, the first Paulu era culled through the necessary mainstream music to build a repertoire both less broad and less deep than that developed under Kolisch. To be sure, the heavily Austro-German range that Kolisch had favored still provided a central core, if not so expansive a one.

The attention to Haydn was far less extensive and probing than under Kolisch. The first quartet taken up remained by far the most popular with Paulu's group: op. 20, no. 4 was played a total of twenty-four times; the only other one from this publication, no. 2, only twice. The next frequently turned to was op. 76, no. 1, as a lagging ten times, followed by op. 33 no. 2, nine times. As for others: op. 3 no. 5, four times; op. 50 no. 1, thrice; op. 55 no. 1, four times; op. 64 no. 5, five times; op. 74 no. 1, twice; op. 76 no. 2, twice; op. 77 no. 2, five times. The quartet version of the *Sieben letzten Worte* was done twice.

The Mozart component was narrower but more dense: of the string quartets, K. 575 was, as with the Haydn example, the outsized favorite, in a striking thirty-four performances. K. 590 was a distant follower, at eleven performances, K. 387 at eight. Of others, K. 428 was played four times K. 458 once, and K. 589 thrice. The Adagio and Fugue K. 546, twice. Of the viola quintets, only K. 515, once, and K. 593, a full ten times; the Oboe Quartet, K. 370, three times. The Adagio and Rondo (originally with glass harmonica) K. 617, once. Opportunities to join others produced one performance each of the Divertimento K. 251 and the *Musikalischer Spass*.

Progress into the Beethoven quartets was cautious and cumulative. Eventually, all were played, but there was no effort made at this point to bundle them all into a cycle. Attention, too, was concentrated on the late quartets. Opus 127 was given six times, but opus 130 sixteen times; opus 131 thirteen times; opus 132 only five times; opus 133 thirteen times; and opus 133 fourteen times. The six of opus 18, however, were presented sparingly, respectively five, three, four, six, two, and four times. Of opus 59, no. 1 was played only three times, no. 2 six, but no. 3 was preferred at eleven performances. Opus 74 received a generous eleven performances, but opus 95 only four. The Pro Arte joined with partners for the Sextet, op. 86, only once.

The works of Schubert were treated with particular scantiness. The early Quartet D. 112 was done only once. Two mature works did receive much more attention: the *Quartettsatz* D. 703 and the Quartet D. 804 each had sixteen performances, but the last two quartets were nowhere in evidence. The Andante and Rondo, D. 487 was given once, but the D. 956 was managed four times, and the Octet twice. Mendelssohn received more limited treatment with one performance of the opus 13 quartet, if four collaborative renditions of the Octet. Likewise skimpy was the representation of Schumann. Of the quartets, only op. 41, no. 3, if twelve times; the Piano Quartet, op. 47, was given once, the Piano Quintet, op. 44, twice.

Bruckner's Quintet was ventured only once. Brahms was accorded a modest but quite respectable showing: The two quartets of opus 51 achieved, respectively, a very impressive twenty and sixteen performances, though opus 67 was accorded only four. The Viola Quintet op. 111 was performed eight times. Of more contemporary composers, Dohnányi was given only one appearance with his opus 26 Piano Quintet. Stravinsky received two placings with his *Three Pieces*. Hindemith's Third Quartet, op. 22, was granted sixteen performances, but his Fourth received only two, and his Clarinet Quintet one. Of the Bartók Quartets, a patchy showing: no. 2 and no. 4 twice each, if no. 5 received thirteen performances and no. 6 got fourteen.

In the Slavic realm, Dvořák stood out, if very selectively: of the string quartets, only opus 61 and opus 105, twice each; the opus 77 Quintet once, but the opus 81 Piano Quintet six times. Tchaikovsky's sextet, *Souvenir de Florence*, was managed collaboratively once.

The once-intensive French focus dwindled significantly. Franck's Piano Quintet was given twice, while Chausson's Concerto and d'Indy's opus 24 once each. On the other hand, this period saw a tense race between the Quartets of Debussy and Ravel for most played work of this period, achieving forty and thirty-nine performances respectively.

Mention may be made of three British composers, whose works were given one performance each: Vaughan Williams's *On Wenlock Edge* song cycle, Arthur Bliss's Oboe Quintet, and Easley Blackwood's Concertino, op. 5.

Finally, there were some "early" works fitted in once in each case. Bach's *Brandenburg Concertos* nos. 1 and 2, in collaborations; a trio sonata by the Scotsman Thomas Erskine (1732–81); a Boccherini quintet; and a flute quintet by Friedrich Kuhlau.

As for the repertoire of small chamber pieces used in the concerts of reduced players, we may perceive: one from Beethoven's op. 3 Trios (thrice) and no. 1 from the op. 9 (five times); Brahms' Trio op. 8 (once) plus the Piano Quartet Op. 60 and the Piano Quintet Op. 34 (twice each); Dvořák's opus 87 Piano Quartet (once); Fauré's Piano Quartet (once); Haydn's E-flat Trio (twice); Hindemith's String Trio (once); Kirchner's Piano Trio (once); Mozart's Piano Quartets K. 478 (thrice) and K. 493 (four times), plus his Divertimento–Trio K. 563 (twice); Schoenberg's Trio (six times); Schubert's "Trout" Quintet D. 667 (once); and a Telemann Trio (once).

In sum, for this twelve-year period, we have a documented total of 141 compositions in 331 reported concert appearances.

A study of the earlier Paulu repertoire has an interest that seems particularly evident. That is the process by which a leader and his colleagues start from near scratch in building up their working repertoire. Most quartets probably go through something like this in their earlier stages—and we have seen this in the case of Kolisch's era—but it again seems quite sharply etched for the early Paulu configuration. A few initial works would be chosen, worked on, then performed repeatedly, repetitiously, almost as if to assimilate them thoroughly. Those works would continue to appear in the group's concerts along the way, while attention would move on, in the same assimilative process, to new selections. The systematic gradualness of this process is strikingly evident in these first-dozen Paulu years, reminding us of what a slow and methodical job it is for a quartet to learn not only works of music but the workings of themselves within the works.

## Recording Activities

After the Quatuor Pro Arte's prewar cultivation of the highly prominent EMI recording complex, the subsequent American phases of the quartet's history showed little initiative in resuming any such connections. The Brosa years were too brief, and too hampered by personnel changes amid war conditions, to allow anything in that direction. To be sure, some surviving groups, such as the Budapest Quartet, were able to hang on to some recording acceptance, especially in the United States, and then be ready to take advantage of the new postwar LP boom. Kolisch, who had already pursued some considerable recording work in Europe before the war, seems to have been content merely with capturing his Pro Arte presentations of Second Vienna School compositions, and little more. Accordingly, it could (and should) have fallen to the new Paulu configuration to restore the Pro Arte name to its previous discographic prestige.

That was not, however, the course pursued. Whether the result of university regulations or limitations of player initiatives, during the twelve-year period considered, the Pro Arte undertook only three recording efforts, involving four compositions. Those were all the work of American contemporary composers, and that fact apparently points up the rationale. It was in the tradition of the original Belgian group to support composers of their time—at least in concert performances, if never allowed to do so in recordings. In the Paulu era the rationale was inverted. While their concert repertoire was widely spread and comprehensive, the recording ventures they undertook were devoted exclusively to new and even avant-garde music. Also involved now, in all probability, were the initiatives of the players, especially Paulu, to exploit personal and professional contacts they had with composers of their day and world. Such a pursuit was not likely to commend them to major recording labels, eager for wide sales. It was thus to the small, specialized labels spawned by the LP blossoming that the revived Pro Arte made sparing appeal.

Notable, too, is that the works recorded in this phase of the Paulu years were almost all linked, to one degree or another, to the Second Viennese atonalist/serialist movement, which may our may not have served as a factor of limited marketability.

The first project involved the work of two German-born, American-trained composers, undertaken in June 1968 at the studios of the University of Wisconsin's radio station, WHA. The 1957 String Quartet of Herbert Fromm (1905–95) is a handsome work in a conservative, still tonal style by an accomplished craftsman. It is cast in seven sections, as an expansive set of variations, in artful but hardly pedantic counterpoint, darkly reflective but lyrical in quality.

The quartet was able to work directly with the other composer, Samuel Adler (b. 1928), who appeared in Madison to lecture at the time the players were preparing his String Quartet no. 4 (1963). In that score, Adler—who studied with Fromm—creates music of great energy, but with lyrical qualities of its own, spiced by some selected touches of atonalism. The fourth of its five movements is a kind of shared cadenza, employing aleatory techniques associated with John Cage: each of the four players is given the notes and entrance-points of their parts, but without rhythmic, dynamic, or timing specifications— these are left up to each player. Obviously, with so many possibilities allowed, no one performance of this movement could be "definitive." It is reported that, working under the composer's supervision, the players made ten separate "takes" of this movement, each one inevitably different; one was selected as the most satisfactory for this release. The playing by the Paulu–Moore–Blum–Creitz configuration is superlative, showing their confident collegiality at this early point, while the recording sound remains marvelous for its vivid detail, close miking, and precise directionalism, allowing each player to be identifiable individually. The two works were nicely paired in a single LP release.

The second recording effort was not made until January of 1972, at Hertz Hall at the University of California, Berkeley. The one work involved was the String Quartet no. 3 (1961) by Arnold Elston (1907– 71), who had recently passed away. The Pro Arte had just added this quartet, the only composition Elston published in his lifetime, to their repertoire. Though he had studied with Webern in Vienna, and approved of atonal techniques, Elston used them sparingly in his own works. Cast in three movements, this quartet balances tightly conceived harmonies with cumulative expressive power. The playing is ripe, the recording lucid. The recording was taken up and disseminated by Composers Recordings, Inc. (CRI), a nonprofit label devoted to promoting contemporary music.

It was only in April of 1978, while the quartet was in New York City for a gathering of the Composers' Guild at Columbia University, that opportunity was found to record the Quartet no. 2 (1973) of Martin Boykan (b. 1931). Again, this was a composition that the Pro Arte had recently brought into their repertoire. Though he had received training from Walter Piston and Aaron Copland, as well as from Paul Hindemith, Boykan's studies in Vienna were crucial in turning him into one of the leading American practitioners of atonality in his compositions. The Second Quartet, while organized into four movements, was conceived as a single continuity, culminating in its finale, the longest of the movements. The serial techniques are rigorously applied, though a clear sense of line and overall structure is evident. This performance shows the quartet's newest configuration of Paulu–Blum–Blum–Karp—the one that would endure for a dozen years—already capable of disciplined, even athletic ensemble playing. The recording, made by freelance engineer David Hancock, was also taken up by the CRI label.

That new configuration made another recording of parallel history. Paul Lansky, born in 1944, was a student of both Milton Babbitt and George Perle. Early on, he made a commitment to atonality. For a while, Lansky worked with Perle in the latter's ideas of "twelve-tone tonality," a variant of strict serialism, and his Quartet, composed in 1971, was a major product of that period. Though Lansky moved into further directions of his own thereafter (further studying the interrelationship of notes), he returned to this score in 1977, drastically compressing and rewriting it. In its revised form, it is cast in three movements, two shorter but related ones flanking a long and episodic core. In the composer's own words: "One way to view the overall shape of the piece is thus to think of the third movement as an image of the first as seen through the increased range of possibilities offered by the second." The performance is another strong one, given particular authenticity by the fact that the Pro Arte players worked directly with the composer, making suggestions of their own. This, too, was taken up for initial circulation by the CRI label.

These releases, CRI and otherwise, initiated the very distinctive recording legacy of the prime Paulu years.

# 6

## THE PAULU YEARS, II

## (1979–95)

### Stabilities

The relative resolution of the Pro Arte's slightly skewed status in the University of Wisconsin School of Music, the settling in of Martha Blum as Moore's eventual replacement, and the secure establishment of young Parry Karp as cellist, all prefigured in 1976, came together decisively by 1979.

Momentum was on ready display in the 1979–80 season, even with a slow start in the autumn semester. Eight reported concerts included extensive collaborations with other faculty colleagues on such works as Samuel Barber's *Dover Beach* (with soprano Ilona Kombrink); Britten's *Fantasy Quartet* (with oboist Marc Fink); and some chamber-orchestra works (Stravinsky, Varèse, Brahms) led by faculty conductor Catherine Comet. Oboist Catherine Paulu was also involved, as was her daughter, flautist Laura Paulu. Szymanowski's quartet no. 2 was the first to be adopted in the group's repertoire. In New York in November, the group also made their next recording.

The spring semester (1980) was another busy one. Another collaborative concert prefaced two more in Madison, while the group made five in-state appearances in February and March (Janesville twice, Watertown, Manitowoc, Fond du Lac). In mid-March, they spent a week in Vancouver, British Columbia, where Karp had made connections. The Pro Arte seemed to find particular favor in their latest appearances there. Writing in *The Province* on March 17, Ray Chatelin wrote: "The Pro Arte String Quartet is an ensemble of such directness, it is difficult to understand how it also manages to play with such careful attention to nuance." Reviewing the same concert, Lloyd Dykk of the *Vancouver Sun* commented specifically on the group's handling of Bartók's Third Quartet: "Threading of thought, subtilization and clarity were what made the Pro Arte's performance so engrossing, though dynamically too, I felt everything was there. What faithful musicians the Pro Arteans are, sticking scrupulously to the score while bringing the best of themselves to it." In April the group participated in the Boulder Bach Festival in Colorado (though playing Brahms). In May of 1980, the Pro Arte made their first recording for the Laurel label, taping the original version of Beethoven's Quartet op. 18, no. 1, in Mills Hall. That summer of 1980, the Pro Arte renewed their involvement in the Western Arts Festival in Laramie, Wyoming, with four concerts (June 10, 12, 17, July 8). The quartet also spent time in residence in Princeton, NJ, working with musicologist Lewis Lockwood on that score, to which he had specifically drawn Paulu's interest.

In the season of 1980–81 that followed, that Beethoven "original" appeared frequently in the quartet's programming, as did other items that the group would soon be recording for Laurel. Two Madison concerts are registered for the fall semester, plus one in which Richard Blum played the solo part in Berlioz's *Harold en Italie* with the Madison Symphony Orchestra. There was apparently also a return visit to Vancouver in October. In December, the group launched their recording series of the chamber works of Bloch for Laurel Records with sessions in December, again in Mills Hall. Scanty reports of the spring semester indicate one concert each in Fond du Lac and Milwaukee, and only four in Madison (at one of which the world premiere of Madison-born Fred Lerdahl's Quartet no. 2 was given). In the summer, however, the Pro Arte was again festival-bound. Most of the time was spent at the Rocky Ridge Music Center at Estes Park, Colorado, giving three concerts (July 5, 12, 19), but with a stop also back in Laramie for its Western Arts Festival, where they gave one concert (July 7).

The 1981–82 season was reportedly limited: one concert each in Milwaukee, Green Bay, and Stevens Point, and four in Madison, plus an appearance in Tulsa, Oklahoma. The Milwaukee concert prompted some strong comments from Lawrence B. Johnson for the *Milwaukee Sentinel*: "The Pro Arte Quartet . . . may be one of Wisconsin's most undervalued resources. Beyond individual accomplishment and an unfailing ensemble spirit, this quartet holds a distinctive edge over many of the world's most celebrated foursomes: These players understand and believe in true pianissimo. I've rare encountered such quiet eloquence." For the spring semester, we hear of one Milwaukee concert, six in Madison (including another premiere, of the Sixth Quartet of Elliot Weisgarber, dedicated to the ensemble), plus two in-state stops (Berlin, Racine), and one in Decorah in nearby Iowa. And, in late April and early May, recording sessions were renewed in Mills Hall for Laurel Records, involving more Bloch and the two Szymanowski Quartets.

Reports surviving for the 1982–83 season again indicate a scanty autumn (three Madison concerts, one each at Fond du Lac and Berlin, but one on November 5 in New York's Carnegie Recital Hall for the ISCM). That last appearance prompted Tim Page of the *New York Times* to observe: "The Pro Arte Quartet plays to win. The ensemble's work is marked by an obvious enthusiasm for the new music it programs, and the desire and ability to impart the same excitement to the audience . . . . [It] produces a tone that is homogenous, lean and expressive." The spring semester, however was augmented by a summer extension. (It also included the inauguration of a series of concerts, extending into the following autumn semester, featuring the chamber music of Brahms, or Brahms mixed with Webern, in which the Pro Arte participated variously.) There were six Madison concerts, one on June 22, dedicated to the memory of the recently deceased Albert Rahier. These were balanced by four in-state appearances (Elroy, Milwaukee, Manitowoc, Viterbo). There were also residencies in Vancouver, British Columbia (March 7–12), and Boulder, Colorado (April 6–13), augmented by a stop in Boulder City, plus a concert in Wichita Falls, Texas. Back in Madison in May, more recording sessions were held in Mills Hall for Laurel Records, capturing more Bloch and the Lerdahl quartet. The summer saw them playing three concerts in Madison, and one in Chattanooga at Tennessee's Riverbend Festival (in which Creitz, regularly a collaborator with the quartet, replaced Karp).

A somewhat fuller schedule, as reported, marked the 1983–84 season. Eight appearances in Madison were interlaced with three concerts around the state (Ashland, Washington County Center, Watertown), augmented by a jaunt to California (Twin Cities, San Francisco, Santa Cruz) in mid-November. Also, in two University of Wisconsin Symphony Orchestra concerts (October 7, 8), Paulu and Karp were the soloists in Brahms's Double Concerto. The spring season of 1984, however, opened strikingly with a tour by the Pro Arte of Portugal and Spain through the month of January, sponsored in part by the Calouste Gulbenkian Foundation of Lisbon, an active supporter of musical activities. Reported stops were made in six cities (Oporto, Lisbon, Seville, Alicante, Barcelona, and Bilbao), plus a quick digression to Cannes (January 24). Although the information on these appearances is incomplete, it may have been at this time, or in connection with this tour, that the quartet recorded music by two Portuguese composers, sponsored by the Gulbenkian Foundation and released by the Educo label.

Upon returning home, the quartet devoted the rest of the semester to five concerts in Madison and four around the state (Milwaukee, Menasha, Marinette, Richland Center); the season climaxed with another appearance in New York at the Carnegie Recital Hall (including a new collaboration with soprano Bethany Beardslee).

The 1984–85 season opened in the autumn with a confirmed reinstatement of the Labor Day concert of chamber music built around the Karps (three of them, plus two Blums), on September 3. Perhaps the stimulation of the previous winter's tour to Portugal and Spain had whetted the quartet's appetite for more such travel, for that was to be the outstanding feature of the 1984–85 opening semester. After two in-state stops (Eau Claire, Milwaukee) and one in Madison, the Pro Arte spent over two weeks in Central and South America: Mexico (Mexico City); Chile (Temuco, Valparaiso); Peru (Lima, Ariquipa); Columbia (Bogotá). Along the way, concerts were matched by workshops with local composers. On return, there was a memorial concert for the recently deceased director of the Music School, Dale Gilbert, featuring Barber's *Dover Beach* (again with Kombrink). Three other Madison concerts followed: one, on December 3, giving the premiere of a quartet by University of Wisconsin faculty member Stephen Dembski. And there were five appearances around the state (West Bend, Fond du Lac, La Crosse, Appleton, Oshkosh). One of the Madison events evoked the following comments from Bruce Murphy, in the November 16 issue of the Madison weekly, *Isthmus*:

> The quartet has been a highly successful champion of contemporary chamber music since its formation in 1912, and judging by its current incarnation it's easy to see why. The sheer sound of the ensemble is absolutely gorgeous, free of intonation problems and marked by a touch of old-world Viennese suavity that helps sell even the most astringent works. And yet the group is attuned to the distinctive rhythms and energies of American music and is easily the master of the most technically daunting contemporary works.

The spring semester (1985) opened with the first of what would eventually be six concerts in Madison. That first concert (January 20) included the Brahms Piano Quintet, op. 34, with Howard Karp as pianist—and that is the only clue to the possible dating (otherwise totally obscure and forgotten) for the Pro Arte's first recording under the auspices of the University of Wisconsin's School of Music. (The quartet, with a different pianist, played the work again on January 25.) The latter days of January were spent in California, with concerts reported in San Francisco (twice), and Santa Cruz. It was one of those that drew some interesting comments on the dynamics of the ensemble, as posed by Robert Commanday in the *San Francisco Chronicle* of January 28:

> The string quartet with the long-play record was in town last weekend, performing as though it would never quit. This was the Pro Arte Quartet, founded in 1912, and thereby, history's oldest. Personnel have changed, obviously, but like planaria, starfish, and certain other creatures, it replaces—as skillfully but rather more quickly than those—a member lost, strayed, stolen, retired, or whatever.

> In short, unlike most other quartets, this is not the first violinist's group, not one dominated by his personality and musical idiosyncrasies, not as subject to his ups and downs. That may be partial explanation of the longevity.

> As evident again in its performance . . . the Pro Arte style is less style than a quality, integrity. The playing is neither hyper-active and keyed up, nor ultra-sonorous and romantic, nor anything else so fixed in profile, but rather what the piece on the music stands at the moment wants it to be.

Rather a different picture from that of Kolisch days, then. On the next day, January 29, the *San Francisco Chronicle* carried the same critic's appreciation of a particular work in the group's programming: "The Pro Arte String Quartet, longtime exponents of [Andrew] Imbrie's music, gave a fabulously finished performance of his String Quartet no. 4 (1969). The group originally commissioned it, and with their superlative musicianship and ensemble, made a convincing case that it is a magnificent work." The second semester (1985) included at least one in-state stop (Hartford Union High School), plus six Madison appearances (one with Kombrink joining again, for Respighi's *Il tramonto*). Room was found for another ISCM appearance at Carnegie

Recital Hall in New York (May 2). In June the quartet was again in Laramie for the Western Arts festival (one concert on June 11).

The first semester of 1985–86 was launched by the "Annual Opener" (or ultimately "Karp Family") chamber-music concert on Labor Day (September 2). This was followed by nine appearances around the state (Ashland, Eau Claire, La Crosse, Monroe, Portage, Columbus, Milwaukee, Menasha, Fond du Lac), with three more concerts in Madison. This semester saw the first tentative ventures into Shostakovich's quartets. Also, in a concert for "American Music Week" (November 9), the group made their next reported revival of the Barber Quartet that had been avoided by Pro Arte configurations since the unhappy premiere by the Brussels players in 1936. For the second semester, we have reports of five concerts in Madison, with two in-state events (Ripon, Baraboo). In February, however, the quartet appeared on University of California campuses (Berkeley, Santa Cruz) for at least two concerts (February 15, 16). In May the Pro Arte also made their latest Bloch recording, in Mills Hall, for Laurel Records.

The Pro Arte could preen themselves in their selection as among the finalists in the first Arturo Toscanini Artistic Achievement competition that spring. A different kind of prominence was involved in the quartet's participation, during June 2–14, in what was announced as a "First" Contemporary String Quartet Symposium and Festival in Madison. (In point of fact, there never was any further such event.) The background to, and substance of this event is discussed in appendix C.

The 1986–87 season was somewhat more conventional. For the autumn semester, following the Labor Day concert (noted as the eleventh) on September 1, there were five more Madison concerts and five around the state (Ashland, Rice Lake, La Crosse, Milwaukee twice). In December (16–17) the Pro Arte recorded Karol Rathaus's Quartet no. 5 for release by the CRI label. The spring semester did, however, mark the Paulu-led group's belated venture into territory that had been the Elysian Fields of the old Brussels ensemble: the Beethoven quartets. Mixing them with some of the quintets, this Pro Arte spread out a survey that would run over three semesters, in seven concerts (January 30, February 22, April 4, September 19, November 7, 1987; January 30, April 9, 1988). Meanwhile, the quartet delivered one other Madison event and six in-state concerts (Oshkosh, Baraboo twice, Platteville, Menasha, Sturgeon Bay), largely carrying over their Beethoven selections. On February 24, they performed at no less than the Grammy Awards in Los Angeles and reportedly participated in the University of Colorado Bach Festival in Boulder. A visit to Asheville, NC (May 9) yielded the spring semester to another recording session in June, in Laurel Records' own studios in Los Angeles—in a break from Bloch, taping the Quartets nos. 1 and 2 of Miklós Rózsa, with the composer himself present. In early summer, the quartet was at the Houston Lyric Art Festival for two concerts (June 14, 18).

Following the Annual Opening Concert (September 1), the Pro Arte's Madison concerts in 1987–88 were mostly devoted to the Beethoven series, certainly in the autumn semester, with two exceptions. There were appearances at Carroll College (September 20) and Phoenix, Arizona (Sept. 25); later, at in-state sites (Milwaukee, Menasha, La Crosse) and a concert in the Coolidge Auditorium in Washington, DC (November 13). But the highlight of the semester was a long-planned visit to Czechoslovakia in early October. This had been arranged through the efforts of Slovak composer Tadeáš Salva, who had developed a friendship with Paulu. The activities included performances in Košice, Bratislava (in its twenty-third annual festival), and Brno (in its twenty-second annual festival), all in Slovak or Moravian regions. Accompanying Paulu was his family, including his daughter, flautist Laura Ellen, who appeared in two concerts, and would join the quartet at other times. Sadly, Catherine Paulu soon entered a struggle with cancer that was, among other things, an enormous emotional strain on Norman through this time.

The second semester (1988) finished the Beethoven series, with five other Madison concerts, plus two in-state concerts (Ashland, Janesville). One noteworthy event was the Pro Arte's participation in a concert by the Madison Symphony Orchestra, of which Paulu was the concertmaster. He led his group in the world-premiere performance of Gunther Schuller's new Concerto for String Quartet and Orchestra (a sister-work to Martinů's work of the same rare type). There were also far-flung appearances. One was scheduled in San Francisco for March 20, with a program that was to include a piece by Tison Street for oboe and string quartet, with Catherine Paulu to play the added part. But Cathy, Paulu's beloved wife, died the previous month, and apparently the concert was canceled; uncertain, too, was the fate of another in Washington, DC, for April 17. The quartet also participated in a concert on April 13 held to honor the arrival of the new chancellor, Donna Shalala. Though the precise date is totally obscure and forgotten, it was some time by or before the end of the 1988 spring season that the Pro Arte was authorized by the Music School to make their first recording under University auspices: of the Brahms Piano Quintet, op. 34, with Howard Karp.

✑   ✑   ✑

June of 1988 marked the departure from the quartet of Martha Francis Blum, and with that the end of the dozen years of a stable membership under Paulu. Among her motives was her determination to shift to research and writing, specifically with regard to the history of the Pro Arte Quartet. The looming fiftieth anniversary (in 1990) of the ensemble's settlement in Madison was a stimulus, and Martha Blum, with the encouragement and support of the Music School's director, Eunice Meske, undertook to write the Pro Arte's history. Grants and funding were arranged to support studies in Madison, journeys to Belgium and around the United States, plus archival investigation and interviews. (In one, she played for the aged Prevost in California.) Her work was extensive and impressive, with the goal of producing a full-length book on the quartet's history. All the work never coalesced completely, and was boiled down eventually into the first half of a publication that celebrated the quartet's fiftieth anniversary in Madison and the twenty-fifth anniversary of the Wingra Woodwind Quintet.

✑   ✑   ✑

After a search, a new occupant of the second-violin chair—again, as artist-in residence, not a full faculty member—was found in the person of Jae-Kyung Kim. Born in Korea, Kim studied at Peabody Conservatory in Baltimore, and had already begun to win recognition in activities around the country. Her integration into the ensemble seems to have been smooth, though the reports of her first season (1988–89) give only five concerts for the autumn—three in Madison, one in Fond du Lac, and one in Ithaca, NY. An impression of her new presence was noted in a review of the first concert (Oct. 23) the following day by Carmen Elsner of *The Wisconsin State Journal:* "And Sunday night, also in Mills Hall, Jae Kim, second violinist with the Pro Arte Quartet, did very well . . . . She doesn't stand out—she fits in, except in lines where she played solo, and solo parts were in just about every movement of the three works in the program [Haydn, Janáček, Smetana]." As a random observation, Kim's succession to Martha Blum meant not only a second female membership in the Pro Arte, but a kind of confirmation of the second violin chair as a female one—by circumstance, if not intention. Kim's own successor, as will be seen, would be a woman.

The spring semester (1989) was launched with a concert in Fairbanks, Alaska (January 6). Six Madison concerts have been reported (including three at the Elvehjem Museum), and six around the state (Verona, Platteville, Marshfield, Boscobel, Manitowoc, Ashland). There were also appearances in Berkeley, California (February 5) and New York, at Weill Recital Hall, as part of the "Washington Square Contemporary Music Society" event. On May 19 there was an appearance in Asheville, North Carolina. The Washington Square concert prompted some mixed reaction from *New York Times* critic John Rockwell on May 7: "On the basis of Wednesday's concert, this is a first-rate quartet that doesn't quite attain the technical polish and interpretative profile of its top international competition. Still, it serves composers well, and on Wednesday it had some interesting composers to serve [Janáček, Imbrie, Diesendruck]."

The 1989–90 season was a full one. In the autumn semester, following the fourteenth Annual Labor Day Concert (September 4), there were eight Madison concerts, plus a Blum family recital (four members); and seven in-state appearances (Janesville, Middleton twice, Fond du Lac, Portage, Minocqua, Oshkosh). In further outreach, there was a concert in Detroit (October 22), and early December was spent in California, where concerts were given in Berkeley, San Francisco, and Los Angeles. While in the last city, the quartet also made their last recording sessions of the Bloch works for Laurel Records, this time in the Bing Auditorium of the Los Angeles County Museum. In the spring semester (1990), four concerts are reported for Madison, and four around the state (Wauwatosa, Sheboygan, De Pere, Wausau), plus one in Oklahoma City (February 25).

To open the 1990–91 season, the fifteenth Annual Labor Day Concert (September 3) now offered no fewer than four Karp family members (Howard and Frances, with sons Christopher and Parry). The quartet seems to have made a brief trip to San Francisco (September 7?). But the first of five concerts in Madison was designated as launching a celebration of the Pro Arte's fiftieth anniversary of residence at the University of Wisconsin. Three in-state concerts were given (Oshkosh, Fond du Lac, Monroe), but also out-of-state appearances were made in Philadelphia, Cambridge, Washington, DC, and New York. In the final Madison concert, the Pro Arte played the Martinů Quartet Concerto with the University of Wisconsin Symphony Orchestra. In the

spring semester (1991), five Madison concerts (plus some supplemental participations) were balanced by three in-state appearances (Prairie
du Chien, Milwaukee, Ripon), and a venture to Houston, Texas (June
9). On August 8, the group appeared at the Sandpoint Festival in Spokane, Washington, in a performance of the Schuller Quartet Concerto
written for them.

The October 5 concert, launching the fiftieth anniversary season,
also involved some experimentation with the players' seating, as commented upon by reviewer Steve Groak in the *Wisconsin State Journal,*
printed three days later:

> For the last several years, the Pro Arte Quartet has consistently played
> with a potent blend of passion, clarity, and understanding.
>
> Sounding a bit rough and ready, however, it has never been a par-
> ticularly beautiful sounding quartet—until Friday night at UW–Mad-
> ison's Mills Concert Hall during a recital which kicks off a tour to
> include several major East Coast venues. . . .
>
> It is hard to know how much a change in seating arrangement caused
> the quartet's larger, richer, more finely balanced sound.
>
> Violist Richard Blum and second violinist Jae Kim switched places.
> Blum now sits with his instrument projecting out toward the audi-
> ence. That is a big help, since Blum, who plays beautifully, does not
> have a particularly big sound. His greater presence created a more
> seamless mix between the fiddles on top and the cello on the bottom.
>
> Surprisingly, Kim's presence seemed more noticeable, too. Perhaps
> she gets to play out more now that her instrument is projecting away
> from the audience.
>
> The other noticeable difference in the quartet's sound was a more
> subtle control by cellist Parry Karp, who has had a lot to do with the
> quartet's exciting performances of the last few years. Gone was his
> occasional tendency to overpower the rest of the group.
>
> The new beauty of sound did not come at a cost to the exciting, argu-
> mentative quality of the quartet's playing. These qualities paid off
> in a challenging program, which opened daringly with Webern and
> Charles Ives [followed by Bloch and Ravel].

Whatever the values of that experiment, troubles may be inferred
at the other end of the season. The concert in Houston (June 9, 1991)

produced seriously mixed reservations from two local critics. Writing two days later in the *Houston Chronicle*, Charles Ward was unhappy with the results in Bloch's *Two Pieces* and the Sibelius Quartet. "The Pro Arte gave them vigorous, if scrappy interpretations." While he admitted that the group "played both works with an ease and confidence that conveyed the spirit of the music well," he went on to say that "the members' ensemble work was not always clean and precise—sometimes they made Bloch's harmonies seem too dissonant—but the spirit was engaging and convincing." Ward was even more critical of the third work in the program, Dvořák's op. 97 Quintet, in which Lawrence Wheeler was guest violist:

> Again the playing was spirited and stylistically apt. Again, too, the execution was just slightly askew.

> . . . In the piece, Dvořák played extensively with the notes that define whether a piece is in a major or minor key. In general, Wheeler and the Pro Arte players had just enough trouble with the intonation to leave a listener doubting whether they were playing the music as written or having trouble getting it correct.

And, on this same concert, Carl Cunningham in the *Houston Post* focused on one particular player:

> The Pro Arte String Quartet left mixed impressions . . . .

> Basically, the problem centered around the variable performance of the quartet's first violinist, Norman Paulu. Too often Paulu's playing was not technically tidy and his intonation didn't zero in on the center of the pitch.

> Thus, the main melodic lines didn't have the silvery tonal sheen one would expect and there were fuzzy edges in the ensemble much of the time.

Cunningham went on to put Paulu at fault for difficulties in all three works on the program.

One cranky critic might be written off, but two of them together suggest, at the least, that this June 9 concert was certainly a problematic one.

For all those ups and downs, a serious change was to come. That 1990–91 season proved to be the final one for violist Richard Blum. He had served in the Pro Arte from 1957 to 1991, a total of thirty-four years—the longest time of service in the group thus far. His departure removed from the quartet the last connection with the era of Rudolf Kolisch. Blum's replacement was the third woman to join the quartet, Sally Chisholm. After studying philosophy at the University of Oklahoma, she had trained as violist at Indiana University, one of her teachers being Samuel Rhodes. She was for a time first violist in the Midland-Odessa Symphony in Texas. She was also a founding member, for sixteen years, of the Thouvenal Quartet (also Texas-based), which performed on NBC's *Today Show*, toured China and Tibet, and won first prize in an international quartet competition; they also co-commissioned quartets by Milton Babbitt, Elliott Carter, and Mel Powell.

Chisholm's first season (1991–92) with the Pro Arte began with the sixteenth Annual Labor Day program (September 2), with four Karps joined by violist Katrin Talbot (Parry's wife) in Brahms's op. 25 Piano Quartet. This program was dedicated to the memory of Gunnar Johansen, who had died the previous May 5. For the Pro Arte itself, the season began auspiciously with a Madison concert on October 4. Two days later, the *Wisconsin State Journal* printed a review by Steve Groark that assessed the ensemble's new dynamics.

> The Pro Arte Quartet, whose latest version played a Dvořák Quartet with breathtaking excitement Friday night, seems to be weathering its latest change well. . . .
>
> When second violinist Jae-Kyung [Kim] joined the group three years ago, her presence was most notable for the lack of change it made in an already fine-sounding ensemble of international reputation.
>
> Violist Sally Chisholm's debut, replacing veteran Richard Blum, an excellent chamber musician, was a little more dramatic.
>
> The quartet's sound in Mills Concert Hall was noticeably bigger and darker. Balances among the four voices were even better, with inner lines more clearly articulated, than in the past.
>
> . . . The seeming reckless abandon—actually well-controlled—with which they went after Dvořák's "American" Quartet in F-major, op. 96, is not new for the Pro Arte, but seemed to have a bit more edge to it.
>
> One concert is too early to tell, but Chisholm's entrance into the quartet may turn out to be as dramatic as cellist Parry Karp's was in

1976, which at a stroke transformed the Pro Arte to a group with double its former passionate intensity level. . . .

At Friday's performance, the outer movements of the Dvořák got lively, dancing, singing treatment. They even had an ineffable "swing" to them, as if the quartet were playing slightly off the beat the way jazz musicians do.

The group's sound became brighter, even harsher at times in the Beethoven [op. 59:1]. It was appropriate for Beethoven's more rigorous, argumentative composition.

Their performance of Mozart's "Hoffmeister" Quartet in D Major, K. 499, showcased their new sound, somewhat at the expense of Mozart's music, which could have used more bite in places. The sound was exquisite, burnished, rich, but was a bit too rounded, especially in the last movement, where rhythmic excitement was smoothed over.

Similar perceptions greeted a concert on October 11, in a review by Charles McCardell in the *Washington Post* days later:

With a history that stretches back nearly 80 years and a residency at the University of Wisconsin since 1940, the Pro Arte Quartet has a tradition going for it and, one would expect, old-school values regarding musicianship. Yet the overall impression left Friday night at the Kennedy Center's Terrace Theater was of a high-spirited group unafraid to wear their hearts on their sleeves.

In hindsight, one perceived a foursome scarcely able to curb its enthusiasm.

Further critical reactions continued in this vein. Reviewing in the *Janesville [WI] Gazette* of November 25 an all-Dvořák concert the previous evening, Ted Kinnaman wrote of the group's "beauty of tone and phrasing":

The Pro Arte's playing here was well-nigh as flawless as in the earlier quartet. Only on one or two occasions, in soft passages in which the first violin carried the solo, were the accompanying instruments a bit loud for the solo.

It should be noted that the violist Sally Chisholm is new with the quartet this year, and her full-burnished tone blends well and complements the already rich sonority of the ensemble.

It is gratifying to note that while over time the personnel of the Pro Arte Quartet has inevitably changed, the high quality of the playing has not.

All these reactions played out against the autumn semester of 1991, for which are reported six concerts in Madison, three around the state (Sheboygan, Fond du Lac, Janesville), and the one in Washington, DC. On November 3, the quartet joined Howard Karp in Franck's Piano Quintet, in another concert in memory of Gunnar Johansen. In December, in Mills Hall, the quartet made their first recording of music by Tamar Diesendruck, which was also their first work for the Centaur label. Reports for the spring semester of 1992, however, are even more scanty: two concerts in Madison, and one in Milwaukee. But there was a brief jaunt to Germany for concerts in Stuttgart (March 22) and in Mainz (March 29).

The appearance in Mainz did, however, prompt a pungent European assessment of the Pro Arte. The *Allegemeine Zeitung, Mainz* of March 30 carried these comments by W.-E. Lewinski:

> After the first eight measures one knew that, in the latest matinee of the Mainz Municipal Theater, one of the greatest American string quartets was to be heard, favored in the choicely sensitive, highest cultivated sound, characterized by a brilliant playing technique as much as by imaginatively creative power. Each of the four string players has his own profile, but the interaction is so perfect that it achieves a fascinating unity. . .
>
> . . . Also noteworthy, how here young and ever-young musicians found a clear unanimity, how provocatively they knew how to design a program.

Complimenting those comments were the reactions on March 31 of Frani Kuhl for the *Mainz Rheinzeitung*:

> . . . The unfortunately rather sparse but enthusiastic audience thanked the Pro Arte Quartet . . . [for] a technically as well as interpretationally brilliant performance.
>
> Wherein are the special qualities of the four American musicians? Constantly sharp contours between one another, now and then almost brittle sound production on one hand, constantly well-plumbed balances—like the wonderfully played middle parts in the second movement of the Haydn quartet. And. on the other

hand, in the sound-shaping that the quartet controls to almost orchestral scope.

The autumn semester of 1992 opened with the seventeenth Annual Labor Day Concert (September 1), the quartet joining Howard Karp in Piano Quartets of Mozart and Fauré. (The two Blums were back, in a collegial presentation with violinist Tyrone Greive and Parry Karp, on October 24.) In all, there were five Madison concerts, one each in Oshkosh and Pardeeville, an appearance at a location in Illinois (November 13), and another in Houston TX. That last one (November 17) again provoked the rather snide reactions of two local critics, who decried both the program selections and the performances. Writing two days after the concert for the *Houston Chronicle*, Charles Ward opined that the Pro Arte "showed no change in its lackluster playing." He again drew his aim on a favored target.

> In previous Houston engagements, the Pro Arte has shown an interest in lesser-known chamber works.
>
> Unfortunately, the group was totally preoccupied by them Tuesday in Rice's Alice Pratt Brown Hall . . . [in works for guitar and strings by Malcolm Arnold and Mario Castelnuovo-Tedesco].
>
> . . . At a length of almost 56 minutes, the performance seemed interminable. Bloch's work [Quartet no. 1] was intermittently interesting, but it required an ensemble with both inspiration and total technical control to sell it.
>
> Instead, the Pro Arte members virtually duplicated their performance of Bloch's music a year ago: vigorous and scrappy.
>
> Listeners could admire the group's luminous sound in some sections, but they had to shift uneasily at the technical lapses, particularly from Norman Paulu.

Ward further deplored "the sense of ennui that permeated the evening."

The spring semester of 1993 is reported as containing four Madison concerts and four in-state appearances (Wauwatosa, Kenosha, Milwaukee, Fond du Lac). In early May, the quartet recorded Imbrie's Fourth Quartet for the Gunmar label (an operation run by Gunther Schuller), in Mills Hall. The concert programs of this semester were particularly marked, however, by the recurrent appearances of quartets by Shostakovich, which would actually presage a major project of the next season. The summer of 1993 was marked by touring abroad: a concert (June 22) at the Schloss Ebnet, Freiburg im Breisgau, Germany; then two (July 9, 10) in North Norfolk, England (followed on July 11 by a program of Bach solo violin works given by Paulu); then back to Germany for an appearance (July 14) at the Rheingau Music Festival.

During the autumn semester of 1993, one curious enterprise was taken up: connections with music schools in Japan. In a quick journey, the Pro Arte appeared in the Otaru International Music Festival in Hokkaido, for two concerts. They played a program of their own on October 6. The next day they did two performances of the Dvořák Piano Quintet, op. 81, with two different young Japanese pianists (Kazuko Nakagawa and Satsuki Shibano). This venture would be renewed in later years only in the Perry era (2002, 2004). And, for the moment, such activity was completely overshadowed by the final grand project of the Paulu years.

Unlike predecessors in leading the Pro Arte, Paulu had not been a strong proponent of composer-focused cycles. He did, he said, like to do "something big" every five years. His commitment to the chamber music of Ernest Bloch was embodied in regular performances of those works, and their recording, but not in any organized unity. He and his players had participated in a comprehensive series in 1983 that was devoted to the chamber music of Brahms. And he had finally conceded a series of the Beethoven Quartets and Quintets in 1987–88. But he had been slow to come to the music of Dmitri Shostakovich. At first, he accepted the long stereotype of the composer as merely a Stalinist hack. Gradually, however, Paulu came to appreciate the depths and power of Shostakovich's creativity. Occasionally, at intervals, Shostakovich quartets would intermittently be programmed, culminating in a determined commitment of which the 1993 spring concerts gave the first acknowledgment.

Indeed, virtually the entire 1993–94 season was given over to the fifteen string quartets of Shostakovich. The core of the series was five concerts presented in Madison through the season (September 25, November 21, February 4, March 6, April 15), while spillover programming of the repertoire was present in appearances around the state (Oshkosh, Sturgeon Bay, New Glarus, Beloit). As the quartet began preparations for the cycle, they drew upon a distinguished visitor, Rostislav Dubinsky, former first violinist of the old Borodin Quartet, who had been close collaborators with Shostakovich. Dubinsky and pianist Luba Edina joined with the Pro Arte in a concert on February 17 that consisted of violin sonatas, with the conclusion of Tchaikovsky's sextet, *Souvenir de Florence.*

The intense Shostakovich series was an event of national stature. Above all, it was a crowning achievement for Norman Paulu, in whose honor a "tribute concert" was offered in the old Music Hall on May 21, 1994. (Mills Hall was, through summer and autumn 1994 closed for renovations.) The Shostakovich series as a whole was followed by the local Madison critics. Reacting to the September 25 concert, Jess Anderson wrote in *Isthmus* that

> in all three works [Quartets 2, 7, 12] the Pro Arte seemed to reach and remain at the apex of quality playing. Doubtless they were moved and inspired by the majesty of the undertaking.
>
> I think this opens a new era for the Pro Arte, which for the first time in years has emerged as a solid, unified, seamlessly joined ensemble of four first-rate musicians playing with a single voice and a single vision. Nothing less would carry them through the daunting tasks they face.

Writing for the *Capital Times* after the November 21 concert (Quartets 11, 4, 5), Kevin Lynch added: "These four superb players conveyed the original tragedy of self-beaten Russians and what they might share of each other's hopes. These are things that the Pro Arte is helping Americans to know and understand for a new political era. This is more than a rarely performed cycle of 15 quartets. This is great, historic music making." On the concert of February 4 (Quartets 14, 8, 4), Jess Anderson wrote for *Isthmus* that

> . . . again complete togetherness of the players rounded out a unique performance.
>
> For the first time, I started to have separation anxiety about the Pro Arte, for first violinist Norman Paulu's retirement looms ever closer, and even under the most favorable scenarios it will be a little while until we can hope to have this kind of concentrated excellence again. Well, one of the great joys of music is its very transitoriness. We can all look forward to hearing great works again.

Anderson expressed powerful retrospective feelings in reporting on the emotional final concert of April 15 (Quartets 1, 10, 15):

With two stark white candles affixed to each of the four music stands and the stage lights turned way down, the Quartet No. 15 in E-flat major [*sic*], Op. 144 summed up not only the universe of Shostakovich's quartet writing, but also the career of the Pro Arte's leader, Norman Paulu, who is retiring at the end of the semester. . . . If one expected to be overwhelmed, that's exactly what took place. After the last note had evaporated, there was a silence of several seconds before the first applause began. Perhaps it was a combination of being drained emotionally, of regretting that something miraculous had at last reached its conclusion, and of extricating oneself from the somber seriousness of the music.

When it finally came, the applause was thunderous, unremitting through five or six bows, and at that not half the tribute the Pro Arte deserves for achieving a great cultural landmark.

Backstage, Paulu was exhausted, ashen and subdued, for together with his colleagues, he had clearly given all it was in his power to give.

The Shostakovich cycle was clearly the crown to Paulu's long and distinguished career as leader of the Pro Arte. And the group gave a special "Tribute concert" in his honor on May 21, 1994. (There is also an unconfirmed report that the quartet appeared in the Freiburg Music Festival, joining the St. Petersburg Quartet in part of the Mendelssohn Octet and the Freiburg Baroque Orchestra in the Bach *Brandenburg* Concerto no. 2.)

Paulu's reported retirement was in fact deferred for a year, due to a delay in the establishment of his successor, and despite his undergoing open-heart surgery in the summer. So, what was to be his actual last season with the quartet (1994–95) saw his valiant return for four Madison concerts, and one in Wausau, in the autumn semester. In the last of the Madison appearances (December 3), the Pro Arte was joined by the visiting Emerson Quartet in Mendelssohn's Octet (December 3). (The following day, be it noted, Chisholm played the solo part in Berlioz' *Harold en Italie* with the UW Symphony Orchestra.) The spring semester (1995) began with a Madison concert (January 21) marking the reopening of the refurbished Mills Hall. Another campus concert in Madison, on February 14, involved the Shostakovich Quartet no. 8, in a commemoration of the fiftieth anniversary of the firebombing of Dresden in World War II. (It also marked the forty-fifth anniversary of the opening of the new Union Theater.) After another concert in Mills Hall (February 26), two more in Madison (March 18, April 12) involved the quartet's players in a presentation of Bach's *Brandenburg Concertos* by faculty ensembles. A single out-of-state venture is reported for New York in the Washington Square Contemporary Music Society event (March 21), which allowed Paulu a final gesture of support to composers of his time (Samuel Adler, Ruth Crawford Seeger, Jeff Hayes, George Perle). And his apparent farewell to recording came on April 13 with a session in Mills Hall for Diesendruck's Second Quartet, while his last performance with the PAQ was in a University of Wisconsin concert in Mills Hall on April 22, 1995.

Paulu therewith entered his comfortable retirement in Colorado, which he still enjoys at this writing. As it happened, Jae-Kyung Kim also chose to withdraw from the quartet, to pursue career and personal opportunities elsewhere. Suddenly, then, by the spring of 1995, the Pro Arte had to sustain a fifty-percent shift in personnel, something that had not occurred since 1967 when Paulu himself had first arrived. Yet another considerable redefinition of the ensemble now lay ahead.

## Repertoire

The defective and spotty documentation of Pro Arte concerts is a plague to be suffered in all phases of the quartet's history, but it is again serious in the second Paulu phase. Program preservation was grossly uneven. The departure of Lowell Creitz meant the end of his thorough personal log as a source, though quite extensive program files collected by his cello successor, Parry Karp, provide much continuity. For all that, though we often do have reports of concert dates and appearances, they often come without any indication of the works played in the programs. Once again, therefore, it is true that all figures offered for numbers of concerts, and especially for the performances of works, may be regarded as minimums, somewhat short of the realities that can no longer be confidently reconstructed. However defective, though, the figures offered give us valid ideas about the quartet's performing range.

For the sixteen seasons under consideration here, we continue to observe the devotion of the Paulu configuration to American composers. A few, of course, represent established old-timers: Charles Martin Loeffler's Quintet (twice); Charles Ives's two quartets (once each); George Gershwin's *Lullaby* (twice); Aaron Copland's *Two Pieces* (five times); Samuel Barber's Quartet (four times) and his *Dover Beach* (thrice). But it was the players' contemporaries who interested them, even if performances of their works were not very numerous. (Items marked * were also recorded.) The following are reported as receiving attention: Samuel Adler (b. 1928), Quartet no. 8 (twice), and Piano Quintet (once); Milton Babbitt (1916–2011), Quartet no. 2 (once); Leslie Bassett (1923–2016), Sextet (thrice); Ruth Crawford Seeger (1901–53), Quartet (thrice); Mario Davidovsky (b. 1934), Quartet 3 (twice); Stephen Dembski (b. 1949), Quartet (once); Tamar Diesendruck (b. 1926), Quartet no. 1* (thrice), Quartet no. 2* (once); George Edwards (b. 1943), Quartet no. 2 (twice); Robert Evett (1922–75), Piano Quintet (once); John Harbison (b. 1938), Piano Quintet (once); Andrew Imbrie (b. 1921), Quartets no. 4* (twice) and 5 (nine times); Paul Lansky (b. 1944), Quartet (once); Fred Lerdahl (b. 1943), Quartet no. 2 (four times); Richard Meryl, *Golden Phoenix* (once); Morango, *Almost a Tango* (once); David Noon (b. 1946), Quartet no. 2 (six times); Leo Ornstein (1893–2002), Quartet no. 2 (twice), George Perle (1915–2009), Quartets no. 8 and no. 9 (once each); Daniel Perlongo (b. 1942), Quartet no. 2 (twice); Vincent Persichetti (1915–87), Piano Quintet (once); Charles Porter (?-?), Quartet (three times); Mel Powell (1923–98), Quartet (thrice); Karol Rathaus (1895–1954), Quartet no. 5* (twice); Miklós Rózsa (1907–95), Quartet no. 2* (twice); Tison Street (b. 1943), Adagio (thrice); Lloyd Ultan (1929–98), Quartet no. 2 (once); Elliot Weisgarber (1919–2001), Quartet no. 6 (thrice); Ramon Zupko (b. 1932), *Noosphere* (once). In addition, the Pro Arte participated in the world premiere of Gunther Schuller's Concerto for String Quartet and Orchestra in 1988.

Also to be noted are some Iberian and Latin American composers: Mexican-American Mario Castelnuovo-Tedesco (1895–1968), Guitar Quintet (twice); Portuguese Luis de Freitas Branco (1890–1955), Quartet* (twice) and Quintet (once); Argentine Alberto Ginastera (1916–83), Piano Quintets (once); Mexican Mario Lavista (b. 1943), *Diachronia* (once).

Two composers stand apart, the one for connection with recording activities (Bloch), the other for a major concert series (Shostakovich). The music of Ernest Bloch holds overlapping positions in the "mainstream" and "modernist" categories. Interwoven with the recordings made of them, the virtually complete chamber works involving the string quartet were also programmed in concerts: the Quartets* nos. 1 (eight times), 2 (thrice), 3 (once), 4 (seven times), 5 (six times); shorter pieces,* *In the Mountains* (thrice), *Night* (six times), *Passages* (twice), *Prelude* (four times), *Two Pieces* (thirteen times); Piano Quintets* nos. 1 (four times) and 2 (once).

The string quartets of Shostakovich found their way into the repertoire at first only slowly and very selectively, but then in a burst within and around the full series: nos. 1 (thrice), 2 (twice), 3 (thrice), 4, 5, and 6 (once each), 7 (eleven times), 8 (thirteen times), 9 (once), 10 (twice), 11 and 12 (thrice each), 13 (five times), 14 (twice), 15 (thrice); the Piano Quintet (once).

Of other "modernists" we note the Bartók Quartets, nos. 1 and 2 (twice each), 3 (seventeen times), 4 (thirteen times), 5 (four times) and 6 (thrice), plus the early Piano Quintet (twice). Among the Viennese atonalists: Schoenberg's Quartets were represented by nos. 1 (four times) and 2 (once), as well as by *Verklärte Nacht* (twice). Berg's *Lyric Suite* was favored ten times, his opus 3 quartet twice. Webern was well-represented: his *Langsamer Satz* (20 times), the *Five Movements* (four times), the opus 9 *Bagatelles* (nineteen times), and the opus 28 Quartet (five times). Of Szymanowski's two quartets,* no. 1 appeared thrice, no. 2 eight times. Stravinsky's *Three Pieces* turned up only once; likewise Martinů's Quartet Concerto; also Benjamin Britten's *Fantasy* Quartet (twice) and Malcolm Arnold's *Serenade* op. 50 (once).

The bread-and-butter "mainstream" concert literature was headed, as always, by the Austro-German category. Some fifteen quartets by Haydn were presented. The most popular by far were two from opus 20: nos. 2 (seventeen times) and 4 (twelve times). Otherwise: of opus 33, no. 2 (six times), of opus 50, nos. 1 (once) and 6 four times); of opus 55, no. 1 (once); of opus 64, nos. 4 (once) and 5 (twice); of opus 71, nos. 1 (thrice) and 2 (once); of opus 74, no. 2 (once); of opus 76, no. 2 (once), 4 (thrice), no. 5 (once); of opus 77, no. 1 (thrice).

Seventeen compositions represented Mozart. Of the string quartets: K. 387 (seven times), K. 421 (five times), K. 428 (four times), K. 458 and K. 575 (twice each), K. 464 and K. 465 (once each), K. 499 (twice), K. 589 (twice), and K. 590 (four times); the Adagio and Fugue K. 546 (five times), one of the Flute Quartets (thrice), the Oboe Quartet K. 370 (once), the Piano Quartet K. 478 (once), the String Quintets, K. 515 (thrice) and K. 516 (twice); the Clarinet Quintet (twice).

Attention to Beethoven was boosted by the 1987 series, which offered all seventeen of the quartets, but which presented them individually quite frequently. In all: of opus 18, by far no. 1,* (twenty-eight times) mostly in the "original version" that the group also recorded; for the rest of opus 18, no. 2 (eight times), no. 3

four times, no. 4 thrice, nos. 5 and 6 three three time each; of opus
59: no. 1 seven times, nos. 2 and 3 twelve times each; opus 74 five
times, opus 95 five; of the Late Quartets, opus 127 (eighteen times),
opus 135 (fifteen times), and opus 132 (twelve times) were clear
favorites; followed by opus 131 (eight times), opus 130 (four times).
Also the Fugue, opus 133 (seven times); but the Quintets opus 4
(once), opus 4 (once), opus 29 (thrice), opus 104 (once). As odd-
ments were Trio opus 9, no. 3, and a quartet arranged from the
Piano Sonata opus 14 (once each).

Schubert was scantily served: the Quartets D. 112 and D. 804 once
each, D. 810 twice, though the Quartet D. 887 ten times, and the Quintet D. 956 five times, plus the Trio no. 1, D. 898 (twice). Mendelssohn's
music fared much better. Of the quartets: opus 12 (seven times),
opus 13 (eight times), opus 44, nos. 1 and 2 (twice each), no. 3 (eight
times), opus 81 (thirteen times); the Quintet opus 18 (six times), the
Sextet opus 110 (once), the Octet (twice).

Schumann was treated more sparingly: of the opus 41 Quartets,
no. 1 nine times, no. 2 twice, no. 3 five times; the Piano Quintet opus
44 thrice. Attention to Brahms was wider but still somewhat shallow: of
the string quartets, opus 51, no. 1 (five times), no. 2 (ten times), and
opus 67 (eight times); of the piano quartets, opus 25 (thrice), opus
26 (twice), opus 60 (thrice); the Piano Quintet op. 34 (nine times),
the string quintets opus 88 (twice), opus 111 (five times); the Clarinet Quintet (five times), the two Sextets (twice and once respectively).
Bruckner was represented only by the quintet Intermezzo (once). Wolf
by his *Italian Serenade* (four times).

As for Slavic and Central European composers, Dvořák naturally
was given ample attention: the quartets opus 51 (seven times), opus
61 (four times), opus 96 (eight times), opus 105 (five times) and opus
106 (thrice); also the *Cypresses* and the two Waltzes (once each); the
String Quintet op. 97 (four times), and the Piano Quintet, op. 81
(five times). Smetana's Quartet no. 1 was given five times; Janáček's
two quartets were given four and five times respectively. The Slovak
Tadeáš Salva (1937–95) appeared via a set of Variations (twice) and his
Quartet no. 3 (thrice). The Piano Quintet by the Pole Ignacy Friedman (1882–1948) was given twice. Tchaikovsky was represented only
by the Sextet *Souvenir de Florence* (once), Borodin by his Quartet no. 2
(twice), and Rachmaninoff by a *Romance* (twice). Dohnányi received
reasonable attention: his Quartet op. 33 (once), his Piano Quintet
(three times), his Serenade op. 10 (once); another Hungarian, György

Kurtág was represented once. We might also slip in the Finnish master Sibelius, with his one Quartet (seven times).

Debussy's Quartet was reduced to four performances, but Ravel's was accorded a considerable twenty-five. Franck's Piano Quintet and Fauré's Piano Quartet no. 1 each appeared thrice; Chausson's Piano Quartet op. 3 and his Concerto were each peformed once. Italians were represented only by the Verdi Quartet (twice), Puccini's *Crisantemi* (thrice), and Respighi's *Il tramonto* (once). And Arriaga upheld the honor of Spain with his Quartet no. 1 (twice).

Of Englishmen, we find only Elgar, with his Piano Quintet; Vaughan Williams, with his *On Wenlock Edge*, John Ireland with his Sextet (all once each); and Arthur Bliss with his Oboe Quintet (twice).

Alone among "early" masters, we find Purcell's Pavane and Chaconne, plus two cycles of Bach's *Brandenburg Concertos*. Boccherini rated only a Guitar Quintet (once), and Jan Vanhal was represented by a single quartet (once).

Our final figures give us a minimum of 233 compositions, performed in at least 300 concerts, in the sixteen-season period considered.

## Recording Activity

On November 15, 1983, Heuwell Tircuit wrote in the *San Francisco Chronicle*: "The Pro Arte Quartet played an interesting, wonderfully balanced program [Webern, Beethoven, Bloch, Brahms] with a high level of class Sunday [November 13] at San Francisco State. It left me wondering why this sterling group, in residence at the University of Wisconsin, does not have the international recognition it deserves as one of the great quartets of our time." The critic's bafflement might have been countered with a question: When and where have you seen any recordings by the Pro Arte on sale?

Such would not be an idle question. In a period when the record market was booming, and when a new generation of string quartets were vying for attention, dissemination of their work and worth was most immediately possible by means of attracting the interest of major and widely distributed record labels. Tours helped, but were single-shot events that could not be bolstered by the repeated listening that recordings allowed. Certainly, for the original Quatuor Pro Arte, Mrs. Coolidge's promotion first brought the group to international attention. But it was the ensemble's recordings that bolstered, expanded, confirmed, and crowned the Brussels Pro Arte Quartet's reputation as one of the greatest groups of their kind in their time—and even thereafter. In the latter half of the twentieth century and since, the successive configurations of the Pro Arte followed no such pattern.

Though committed in their concerts to the composers and music of their time (and of their homeland, as well), the Brussels group was allowed to record virtually none of that literature. With hardly any exceptions, their recorded repertoire was built, as we have seen, on the "mainstream" repertoire, as stretched only sparingly into the twentieth century. With Paulu's later Pro Arte, the recording approach was exactly the reverse, as we have already observed. The "mainstream" repertoire was essential for concert purposes. But, with two exceptions, such literature was avoided in recordings. With an undeniable nobility of purpose, the Paulu Pro Arte chose to use the recording medium as an extension of their promotion of contemporary composers, mostly American. That would, again, limit the appeal of their work to major record labels, interested in wide public interest and extensive sales. By contrast the Fine Arts Quartet, resident at the University of Wisconsin–Milwaukee—and including a former Pro Arte member, George Sopkin—achieved considerable success, distribution, and national recognition by recording "mainstream" literature, even for a relatively small label.

Fortunately for the ensemble's purposes, they early established dealings with a small California label, one of the many that the LP medium had spawned. Owned and operated by the enlightened Herschel Burke Gilbert, Laurel Records, based first in Los Angeles and then in Berkeley, was committed to progressive repertoire choices and the highest quality of sound engineering. And, in fairness, Laurel's releases did circulate to a fair extent, winning very enthusiastic approval from critics in many cases.

Ironically, the first collaboration with Laurel resulted from the Pro Arte's exploration (together with musicologist Lewis Lockwood) of "original-version" Beethoven—in this case of the opus 18, no. 1. Paulu was apparently impressed with the Laurel label's quality and negotiated this recording venture. The recording (May 1980), one of a series made in the quartet's home base of Mills Hall, employed the talents of the School of Music's engineer, James Stuht. The performance is vibrant and well nuanced, and recording sound is very vivid. The LP album included a leaflet analyzing some of the differences between the original and the published version of the score. As the only recording ever made of this "original" version, and a document of its kind, the fact that the LP edition is now obsolete and was never replaced with a CD reissue is a sad loss.

The success of this recording prompted Paulu and Gilbert to propose an ambitious series, the chamber music of Ernst Bloch that included string quartets, a major contribution to the literature by a highly individual and important composer. The project was begun in the spring of 1981, at which time it promised to be the first complete recorded cycle of the Bloch string quartets—until, midstream, the distinction was stolen by the Portland Quartet, which raced forward and achieved the premiere complete cycle for itself. But the Pro Arte's recording of the Quartet no. 1 was a disc premiere all of its own. Composed in 1916, this work lasts some fifty-six minutes, a sprawling bleak work that the composer has insisted was an embodiment of his agonized feelings during World War I. It was plainly influenced by Beethoven's late quartets, and requires patience from both players and listeners. But it is a powerful work, and the Pro Arte played it repeatedly and devotedly in their concerts.

The following spring, the Pro Arte and Laurel again met in Mills Hall (with Stuht) to record the Quartet no. 2, plus some of the composer's brief pieces for string quartet. The second quartet, composed in 1945, again caught Bloch responding to a world war, the Second in this case; this time his response was one of great agitation, embodied in tight counterpoint that climaxes in the longest movement, a powerful passacaglia-and-fugue finale. It was not until May of 1986, after a lot of intervening activity, that the Pro Arte resumed the Bloch Quartets with Laurel, this time at the latter's studios in Los Angeles. The results were the Third and Fourth Quartets. And it was after another interval, in December of 1989, that the Pro Arte completed the cycle with the Quartet no. 5. By that time, Martha Blum had been replaced by Jae-Kyung Kim, and the venue was the Bing Auditorium in the Los Angeles County Museum.

The last three quartets, composed respectively in 1952, 1954, and 1956, show the composer in his final years as still experimental, but also more reflective and even playful, and committed to a neoclassical working within traditional forms and tonality. As always, the quartet members show intense commitment in their playing, and the recordings remain of the finest quality.

Along the way, the Pro Arte recorded a number of short pieces for string quartet, ranging from serious to nostalgic, composed by Bloch at various times. But two major works were added to the series: his two quintets for piano and strings. These come from poles in his life. No. 1, an assertive and highly praised work was composed in 1923, when Bloch was still working out his feelings in the aftermath of World War I, but it is also among his first works in the idiom of "neoclassicism" to which he became increasingly and recurrently devoted over the years. No. 2 is one of his last works, written in 1957, reflecting the composer's defiant efforts to come to terms with his declining health. In both of these (recorded disparately in 1989 and 1992), the Pro Arte was joined by Howard Karp as pianist; and for no. 1, Martha Blum was replaced by Kim.

The Piano Quintet no. 1 presents an unusual opportunity, because it is the only work in which we can compare the performance of the original Brussels ensemble with that of a later configuration. The Quatuor Pro Arte recorded it in 1933, the Paulu ensemble fifty-six years later. The 1933 recording was the disc premiere of the work. The pianist was the distinguished composer Alfredo Casella, who contributed his penchant for Italianate lyrical feeling in a mix with the Belgians' feeling of elegant restraint, though there is genuine intensity throughout. The 1989 recording displays an even greater intensity of emotion, and a cleaner distinction of moods and color. The differences in recording technology over a half-century really play their role, too. The 1933 sonics are somewhat dark, reducing the piano too much to the background, and emphasizing Onnou's bright playing at the expense of slightly muffling the other players. By contrast, the 1989 sound allows for leaner, more clarified overall sound and better balances.

The first two quartets and the Second Quintet were recorded for LP release, and then brought out on CD in a scrambling of Laurel reissues, involving the subsequent CD recordings that completed the series. These reissuings may be traced in the appendix E discography. (All these Bloch recordings are still to be had on direct order from the surviving Laurel Records company.) But in the reissue stampede, one work, not by Bloch, was omitted, and has effectively been lost. This is Fred Lerdahl's Quartet no. 2, which was recorded in the same 1983 sessions that captured Bloch's Second Quintet. Lerdahl (b. 1943), who began as an atonalist, has become both a composer and a theorist of rhythmic and textural contrasts, with special use of variational techniques. His Quartet no. 2 is cast in two parts, each of which is an arc encompassing contrasting gestures and ideas. It is a compressed score, and its difficulties in performance are admitted by the composer in his expressions of admiration and gratitude for how the Pro Arte players realized and even helped define the music.

Woven through the Bloch project were a number of other recordings. One was for the Laurel label itself, undertaken in May 1982 in Mills Hall, at the time the Pro Arte made their second Bloch recording (Quartet no. 2). This was of Szymanowski's two quartets. These two became recurrent items in the group's concert programming, and there is no better description of the Pro Arte's rendering of them than in Roy Gunther's concert review of November 16, five years later: "Karol Szymanowski's Second String Quartet opened the program. The ensemble's admirable attention to detail and precise coordination produced sounds of shimmering beauty and a perfect blend of romantic pathos and folk-derived rhythmic vigor." On the record, the performances are certainly intense, and the sound is dazzlingly vivid. This Szymanowski recording was one of those that Laurel issued on LP but never reissued on CD. There have been recordings made of the two works by other groups, but it is a pity that the Pro Arte's admirably competitive ones are no longer available.

Two more recordings seem to be of this time, though the utterly sloppy information about their recording dates contrasts with Laurel's far more conscientious documentation. One is a release made for the very small Educo label of California. It was apparently part of a series devoted to Portuguese chamber music, sponsored by the Gulbenkian Foundation of Lisbon—and possibly of the same time as the quartet's visit to Portugal in 1984. The LP disc (no CD, so gone forever) contains the String Quartet (1911) of Luis de Freitas Branco (1890–1955), and the Piano Quintet (1952) of Armando José Fernandes (1906–83), with Howard Karp as pianist. The two works are well crafted, with evidence of French influences: of Debussy for Freitas Branco, and of Ravel for Fernandes. The playing sounds a little sluggish at times, and the sound is rather muffled and low-grade stereo. No data whatsoever are given about the place and date of recording, much less about the music.

Another undocumented curiosity marks the first recording made of the Pro Arte specifically by and for the University of Wisconsin School of Music. The Pro Arte played the Brahms Piano Quintet op. 34 with Howard Karp on a number of reported occasions, notably 1981 and 1985. It may have been in the latter year that this recording was made, presumably in Mills Hall (with Stuht as engineer). Suffice it to say that the performance is handsomely mellow, if moderate in pacing and a little understated in feeling. This recording is noteworthy in that, together with that of Beethoven's op. 18 no. 1, it represents the only straying by the Paulu configurations away from contemporary Americans into the "mainstream" literature in their disc releases.

A word should be said, however, about the phenomenon of the Music School's recordings. Despite the wishes of Chancellor Wiley to produce recordings, there was actually no mechanism of any kind to finance and distribute these. They could be seen as vanity releases for internal circulation rather than for any wide commercial marketing. But there were no specified monies to create such recordings. Neither in the School of Music itself nor in the university as a whole was there any coherent recording program for the Pro Arte or other faculty performers. Administrative confusion, inconsistencies, contradictions, and downright hostilities were constant obstacles. This Brahms release, and others, appeared only in LP format, without any CD reissue, serving no broad promotional purposes for the Pro Arte. Not only were no recording data supplied, but there is not even a release number given to the album (as was the working pattern in all these ventures). Such negligence may have been due partly to a negative attitude of the players toward recording "mainstream" literature, but largely to the barriers erected by the School of Music itself. Viewed in these terms, the residence of the Pro Arte in Madison, a godsend in many ways, was a terrible impediment to the group's achievement of the national and international attention they deserved.

Five more recordings remain from this time period. In December of 1986, the Pro Arte held sessions in Mills Hall to record the String Quartet no. 5, op. 72 (1927) of the European-American composer Karol Rathaus (1895–1954). This three-movement work reflects the composer's eclectic mix of minimized atonality with contrapuntal skill and a rhythmic vitality derived from his Polish background. The performance and sound are exemplary; the recording was joined with those of other chamber and vocal works of his and issued by the CRI label.

In June of 1987, the quartet had their annual spring recording sessions at the Laurel studios in Los Angeles to record music of a composer linked with that city through his work with Hollywood movie scores. Miklós Rózsa, however, diligently expressed the "other" side of his musical personality in "serious" composition. Of the three works of his then recorded, his Quartet no. 1, op. 22 (1950), blends late- or post-Romantic backgrounds with intricately crafted textures and Hungarian-derived rhythmic flair. The Quartet no. 2, op. 38, from thirty-one years later, suggests some crossover from his film composing in a more dramatic spirit, with strong thematic content. The third work recorded was his then-new *Rhapsody for Cello and Piano*, in its disc debut, as played by Parry and Howard Karp. These performances are strong ones, and were given particular authority by the composer's own presence as they were made.

The final Bloch recording (Quartet no. 5) in December of 1989 marked the end of the Pro Arte's activities with the Laurel label. Its remaining three ventures were undertaken with the personnel shift from Martha Blum to Jae-Kyung Kim in the second violin chair. And they involved other record companies. For the small but plucky Centaur label, the Pro Arte recorded their work with the avant-garde, postmodern composer Tamar Diesendruck (b. 1946). Her writing in the 1940s was caught up with the imagery of the musical scene as a confusion of "stuff" and the "babble of Babel." To evoke all that, she created eclectic collages that toss about suggestions, evocations, and even parodies of a vast range of musical elements, even creating imitations of such composers as Beethoven, Mendelssohn, and Stravinsky. All that is embodied in her two string quartets. The first (1988), called *Such Stuff,* is a vast explosion of a work cast in four movements (the second being designated as "In Homage to Stravinsky"). It was commissioned by the Serge Koussevitzky Foundation. The Pro Arte gave its 1989 premiere in New York, and then recorded it in Mills Hall in December of 1991. The Quartet no. 2, titled *Babel Dreams*, was composed in 1992, as part of a cumulative concept for a full-evening's assemblage of her music to be called *Theater of the Ear*—which was not given a complete performance until 1999. Meanwhile, the Pro Arte recorded the Second Quartet, cast in two movements, in April 1995, at the very end of Paulu's membership in the group. The two quartets were released together by Centaur in 1999, and no. 2 was reissued in 2009 as part of the *Theater of the Ear* assemblage. Without any bases for comparison, it is difficult to assess the Pro Arte's success in a precise rendering of chaos, but their renditions certainly constitute a high-water mark in the ensemble's devotion to the latest in contemporary music.

A quotable reaction to Diesendruck's music is to be found in a review of a concert performance by the Pro Arte (if by the Perry configuration to come) of her Quartet no. 2 at Harvard University on April 30, 1999. On May 2, Susan Larsen wrote in the *Boston Sunday*

*Globe*: "The second movement offers healing, says Diesendruck. Healing turns out to be a contrapuntal episode of such shameless prettiness it would make Samuel Barber blush. The Pro Arte plays so sensationally together, yet each with a vibrant individual voice, that you were taken in."

It was between the Diesendruck recordings that the Pro Arte finally documented on discs their long involvement with Andrew Imbrie (1921–2007) and his string quartets. The Pro Arte played all of them through the Paulu years. Both the Fourth and Fifth Quartets (1969 and 1987, respectively) were composed for the Pro Arte (the latter with the support of the University of Wisconsin's Brittingham Family Foundation, through the agency of Chancellor Shain.) In sessions at Mills Hall in April 1993 (Stuht again as engineer), the ensemble recorded both of them, as well as a long (over sixteen minutes) *Impromptu* for Violin and Piano, played by Paulu and Howard Karp. The three works were released on Gunther Schuller's small GM (Gunmar) Recordings label. Both quartets are cast in three movements, and reflect Imbrie's preoccupation with motivic and harmonic transformation processes, carried through contrasting moods. They display influences of Bartók and especially of Imbrie's principal teacher, Roger Sessions.

## 7

# THE PERRY YEARS

# (1995–Present)

## Redefinitions

The current phase of the Pro Arte Quartet's history began with another major personnel transformation, with both the violin chairs occupied by new players. They came with close prior associations: they had been, respectively, concertmaster and principal second violin of the same orchestra, the Wichita Symphony.

Both before and since his joining the Pro Arte, David Perry was building a career of national dimensions as one of America's finest violinists of our time. He acquired a particular reputation for precision of playing and absolute accuracy of intonation—one colleague quipped that Perry "has never visited the spaces between the notes." He studied at Juilliard with Dorothy DeLay, won notable prizes, and pursued a lively career as an ensemble leader, with only marginal activities as a soloist. He became concertmaster of several orchestras, including that at the Aspen Festival, and he was active with the Orpheus Chamber Orchestra. While in Wichita he was first violinist of the local Fairmont Quartet, and also taught on the faculty of Wichita State University.

Born in Reno, Nevada, Suzanne Beia was something of a childhood prodigy. She served as concertmaster for several orchestras, not only in her native city but in others around the country. She has also worked in chamber ensembles, notably the Sedgwick String Quartet in Wichita. Because of her limited academic record, she was not given full faculty status, but instead has fifty-percent status at the University of Wisconsin for performing and coaching as an artist in residence—a status that all members of the quartet hold for half of their budgetary positions. One feature that was established at the outset of the Perry years—and at his insistence—is that performance activities were to be suspended during the summer months. The few summer ventures that were undertaken represent exceptions that prove the rule. In effect, the Pro Arte has become an ensemble for the academic year only. (Perry is active at Aspen, Colorado; both he and Chisholm also perform at Door County's Midsummer Music, while she has also become involved with other summer festivals, notably the famous one at Marlboro, VT; Beia plays with summer groups in Madison, while Karp has involvements in Colorado and Hawaii.) Generally speaking, too, the quartet members now spend a good deal of their time in individual activities, apart from commitment to the group—far more so than was the case with previous PAQ configurations, in which the players were more completely dedicated to the ensemble's work.

*❧  ❧  ❧*

The first season of the new configuration—1995–96—as surviving reports indicate, was a modest one. In the autumn semester, there were six Madison concerts (one at the First Unitarian Society), and at least three around the state (Spring Green, Eau Claire, Baraboo). Writing the next day of the first concert (September 29), reviewer Ron Wiecki for the *Wisconsin State Journal* reacted optimistically: "This was an auspicious beginning for the new ensemble and assured that it will in a short time rival the ensemble and rapport that the quartet's members had achieved by the end of last year's concert season." In the second semester (1996), there were seven Madison concerts. In one of them (April 12), Chisholm's husband, Eugene Purdue, took the second violin part, as the quartet joined with the Wingra Wind Quintet for Schubert's Octet. And in the last (May 4), the live performance of Ralph Shapey's Quartet no. 9 was recorded by the School of Music. (The Shapey work was one of six commissioned by the School of Music in honor of its centennial, each work destined for one of the school's different performing ensembles. The premiere performances of those works made the 1995–96 season a "year of premieres.") There were also five concerts around the state (Racine, Wauwatosa, Mukwonago, Kenosha twice), plus one in St. Paul, Minnesota. The Shapey work aside, the repertoire was solidly mainstream. There had been talk of an invitation to the quartet to perform at the White House in Washington, in connection with the centennial celebration of the University of Wisconsin School of Music, but apparently nothing came of the idea.

That programming picture was slightly modified in the 1996–97 season. The Pro Arte participated in the twenty-first Annual Opening Concert on Labor Day (September 2), and gave eight more Madison Concerts. (With a Music School ensemble, Perry and Beia were soloists in a new Double Concerto by Kathleen Hoover.) Two in-state concerts are reported (Minoqua, Fond du Lac). The Perry group made their first visit to New York, to participate in the Washington Square Contemporary Music Society's event in Merkin Hall. Their concert for that (October 3) included three modern works, the Shapey Quartet among them. This drew the wry review opening by Steven L. Rusenhaus for the journal *The Music Connoisseur:*

> The report of the death of the string quartet as both a compositional and performance medium, to paraphrase Mark Twain, has been greatly exaggerated, if the number of fine performing foursomes in the concert halls or the fascinating new works being written for them are indications. The Pro Arte Quartet's recent concert at Merkin offered still further proof of that. . . .
>
> To end a concert of 20th century works with music by a Romantic is an unexpected but shrewd bit of programming. (Most "mainstream" concerts do the opposite, sticking a new work between two warhorses to keep the audience in its collective seat.) Mendelssohn's *String Quartet in E Minor* (Op. 44, #2) came across like a sorbet after a three course meal—refreshing.

The second semester (1997) was launched with the boldness of confidence. The Pro Arte Quartet was a participant in a six-concert multi-ensemble cycle of the Beethoven Quartets. The prestigious Emerson Quartet contributed two concerts at the Memorial Union Theater in the autumn of 1996, the Pro Arte did two in their turn (February 7, 8), and the Orion Quartet gave their two in April. It was no mean feat for Perry & Co. to put themselves in direct comparison with two of the most admired American string quartets. Writing for *Isthmus* on February 14, Jess Anderson glowed with pride:

> In two concerts devoted to Beethoven's string quartets, the Pro Arte Quartet achieved an amazing level of subtlety, concentration and intensity at the Wisconsin Union Theater last weekend. Though

not flawless—great performances seldom are—the UW ensemble reached the very highest standard, both in the overall expressivity of the music and in the fine details of individual sections. . . .

At the end of the second program the capacity audience stood up to signal its heart-felt appreciation for the Pro Arte's accomplishments. And rightly so, I thought, for the group had to my ears surpassed even the Emerson Quartet, which kicked off the Union Theater's year-long cycle of Beethoven quartets last fall.

Behind all that lurked a cruel irony. The Emerson and Orion Quartets were engaged by the Wisconsin Memorial Union Theater at the usual guest rates—something between $5,000 and $8,000 each. By contrast, the "pay" for the PAQ players was a pair of complimentary tickets for each of them, allowing free entrance to any events in the theater's season. Was the Pro Arte Quartet being flagrantly denied parity with their visiting colleagues, or just treated as merely fulfilling obligations as part of the "Wisconsin Idea"?

The rest of the spring semester was represented by seven more Madison concerts, and four in-state appearances (Wauwatosa, Wausau, Stevens Point, West Bend). But there were also ventures to Chicago (January), San Francisco (March), and Las Cruces, New Mexico (June).

The 1997–98 season was a somewhat more settled one. For the autumn, five Madison concerts were reported, two in-state concerts (Fond du Lac, West Bend), and a visit to Roosevelt University in Chicago. One of the Madison concerts (November 1) was offered in honor of James Crow, a distinguished faculty geneticist, amateur violist, and generous patron. He himself played the added viola part in the Bruckner Intermezzo. But the occasion was also a memorial tribute to the recently deceased (May 1993) Bernard Milofsky, Crow's teacher and friend. Offered was a piece for viola and piano entitled *Requiescat* by George Tsontakis, commissioned by James and Ann Crow with Milofsky's son David, as played by Sally Chisholm. In the spring semester (1998) there were seven Pro Arte concerts in Madison, and four in-state ones (Ripon, Watertown, Wauwatosa, Dodgeville), plus visits to San Diego, CA and Oak Park, IL.

Reports for 1998–99 suggest modest activity in the first semester: six appearances around the state (Platteville, Ripon, Brookfield, West Bend, Oregon, Fond du Lac) and eight concerts in Madison, plus participation in a Chicago event. The first of the Madison appearances

(September 24) prompted Jess Anderson to comment in the *Isthmus* (October 2) on the quartet's progress: "The Pro Arte's ensemble is remarkable. The players have coalesced their four strong musical personalities into a single instrument now, putting their performances at the level of true mastery." But the last two of those Madison concerts involved a tight but quite daunting enterprise: the complete quartets of Bartók in one day (November 21): the odd-numbered ones in an afternoon program and the even-numbered ones in the evening, with a lecture in between, by a visiting scholar. For the spring semester (1999) reports indicate six Madison appearances, and three in-state ones (River Falls, Janesville, Three Lakes), plus one in Cloquet, Minnesota, one in Palm Beach, Florida, and one at Harvard University. In one of the Madison concerts (February 24) the Pro Arte joined with the Fairmont String Quartet in another round with Mendelssohn's Octet. The Harvard appearance involved participation in a Tamar Diesendruck event.

The autumn semester of 1999–2000 saw nine Madison concerts (many involving collaborations with faculty colleagues and others (Eugene Purdue, Leanne League). The in-state appearances were limited to two (West Bend, Platteville), with a concert also at Oklahoma City University. For the spring semester are reported only five Madison appearances and five in-state (Racine, Wauwatosa, Fond du Lac, Milwaukee, New Richmond), with another late-spring venture to San Diego.

For the 2000–2001 season, the quartet members were particularly active individually. But they joined in six Madison concerts, with only two in-state appearances (West Bend, Platteville). In the last days of December 2000, at Purchase Conservatory of Music in Purchase, New York, they made a rare commercial recording, for Albany Records, of quintets by Roger Sessions and Samuel Rhodes, plus a quartet by Walter Mays. In the spring, we hear of six Madison concerts and three in-state appearances (Racine, Wauwatosa, Janesville). But over April 30–May 1 they launched their first round of recordings for the UW School of Music, two Dvořák Quartets, at Green Bay's Weidner Center, Green Bay.

Subsequent seasons followed parallel patterns, though with surprising digressions in evidence. For the first semester of the 2001–2 season, eight concerts are reported for Madison (plus one in which the Pro Arte joined the Wisconsin Chamber Orchestra in works of Elgar and Mozart), and four around the state (Marshfield,

Northland College, Manitowoc, Beloit). A Madison concert on October 20 garnered these praises from Jess Anderson in *Isthmus* (October 26): "When one reaches the level of the UW's Pro Arte Quartet, comparisons fall by the wayside, and one is left with the deep satisfaction that perhaps only musical miracles can produce. . . . I don't recall ever hearing a more unified, revealing quartet recital than this one." The spring semester (2002) began conventionally: five Madison concerts are reported, and seven around the state (Appleton, Wauwatosa, Platteville twice, Green Bay, Fond du Lac, West Bend). Perry played the Beethoven Violin Concerto with the University of Wisconsin Chamber Orchestra (February 23). In the last two Madison events, faculty colleagues joined: Ilona Kombrinck in Respighi's *Il Tramonto* and Christopher Taylor in the Brahms Quintet, op. 34. It had been established early in the Perry years that the quartet would not be operational in the summer months, so as to give the players opportunities for individual activities. That convention would be breached from time to time, but never more strikingly than for the first time in 2002.

Reviving a venture first made in 1993, the Pro Arte undertook the first of two visits they would make under Perry to Japan. The quartet gave four concerts in three cities, on July 4 (Kyoto), July 5 (Nagoya), July 8 and 9 (Tokyo). The programs in each case offered the Haydn op. 76, no. 5 and the Mendelssohn opus 13, and each time with a local pianist joining them for the Brahms Piano Quintet op. 34 (successively: Hivoko Mukunoki, Emi Naitoh, Mitsue Sawada, and Hirokazu Goto), plus the Brahms Clarinet Quintet opus 115 (with Toshia Hojo) in the first concert. To top off all that, the quartet then visited Washington state to give four concerts there. Two were in Leavenworth (Icicle Creek Chamber Music Festival: July 27, 28), in which the Kairos Quartet joined them in the Mendelssohn Octet; and two more were at the Bellingham Festival (July 30, 31).

The 2002–3 season was more modest. In the autumn semester, there were five concerts in Madison (one as part of a memorial for the Twin Towers disaster of 9/11), one in-state (Portage), one in New York (Washington Square Contemporary Music Festival), and one in Chicago in December. In the spring, there were three in Madison, six around the state (Manitowoc, Wauwatosa, Dodgeville, West Bend, Wisconsin Rapids, Ephraim). A lone summer event was a concert (July 18) at Lake Forest Academy in Illinois.

Activity increased in 2003–4: nine Madison concerts, three around the state (Ripon, Stoughton, Green Bay—the last jointly with the

University of Wisconsin's Wingra Wind Quintet), plus an appearance at Notre Dame University, in the autumn. For the spring, four concerts in Madison, five in-state ones (Wauwatosa, Pewaukee, Fond du Lac, West Bend, Manitowoc), and a performance at UC–San Diego in La Jolla, CA. But then the quartet made their second summer visit to schools in Japan (Nagoya, July 8; Hakata, July 10; Tokyo, July 11 and 12; Chiba, July 13), their programs including collaborations with local players (successively, Emi Naitoh, Yuri Nakayama, Maki Watanabe, Yuriko Urat, with Makiko Seki and Atsuka Mihara on the final date), in piano quintets by Dvořák, Brahms, and Schumann.

In 2004–5, the picture was more staid. In the autumn, six concerts in Madison, and three around the state (Stoughton twice, Manitowoc). In October (15) there was a visit to Kennesaw State University in Georgia. But in December, sessions were held at Mills Hall for the next School of Music recording, of quartet music by Mendelssohn. In the spring, only two full concerts in Madison and four in-state concerts (Pewaukie, Three Lakes, Menomonie, West Bend), plus recording sessions (with faculty oboist Mark Fink) in mid-May. The concert at the Reiter Center in Three Lakes (February 1) drew this grateful and quite extensive appraisal from a local critic, Ligia Vascan, in the *Vilas City News-Review*:

The Pro Arte performed such a strong repertoire [Haydn, Berg, Mendelssohn], which challenges every musician and the audience as well.

They didn't adjust the repertoire in order to be "successfully accepted" by the general audience, which the Milwaukee Symphony Orchestra has done, performing only Pop concerts here.

As serious and respected musicians, Pro Arte brought a repertoire which stretched some minds in order to understand and accept some of their music.

The Pro Arte Quartet seems to be an outstanding ensemble from many points of view.

First of all, they are four extraordinary musicians, each of them with remarkable backgrounds (soloists, concertmasters and great pedagogues) who together form a perfect unit, an indestructible whole.

They gained a very special color of the sound which can be accomplished after years of practice together. What impressed me very deeply was their expressiveness with a large palette of dynamics and agogic effects.

They feel each other and control each moment of music, having in their attention their individual parts as well as the ensemble music.

These wonderful musicians are blessed with all the qualities of real artists. They prove a deep understanding of music and then recreate it taking care of the composer's style and demands, but filtered through their own musicality.

These special qualities place them among the best artists of our time.

Here we come once again to long-standing issues of concern about how much "serious" music could the "provincial" audience tolerate. The matter was hinted at again when another local critic waxed enthusiastic about a concert on October 1, 2005: "The program was both accessible and stretching for our audience." Generally, one draws the impression that the long years of in-state touring by the Pro Arte contributed greatly to educating and sensitizing both audiences and observers.

In the first semester of the 2005–6 season, four Madison concerts are reported, with two in-state appearances (Northern Lakes, Monroe), plus a concert in October at Kennesaw State University, in Atlanta, Georgia. Again, late December brought more recording sessions for the School of Music releases: a completion of Marc Fink's material; and the commercial recording of music by Brian Fennelly for Albany Records. The second semester opened with the first of the celebrations that would dot the year for the 250th anniversary of Mozart's birth. There are reports of seven Madison concerts and five around the state (Pewaukee, Wauwatosa, Racine, West Bend, Ephraim), augmented by out-of-state appearances at Luther College in Decorah, Iowa, and Ellensburg, Washington.

The opening event of the 2006–7 season was the annual Labor Day starter (September 4), now openly labeled the "Thirtieth Karp Family Concert." By this time it was able to field four Karp musicians, in-law Katrin Talbot, and two thespian granddaughters, in music written quite explicitly for them by Joel Hoffman. There were six Madison concerts—one (September) a centennial tribute to Gunnar Johansen (1906–91)—and three around the state (Menasha, Manitowoc, Whitewater). There was also another visit (October) to Kennesaw State University. The tally for the spring semester, following a January appearance in London, Ontario, is merely three Madison appearances, but concerts in five state venues (Platteville, Appleton, West Bend, Ephraim, Pewaukee). The Madison events included involvements in a series of "Brahms Celebrations"—it being his turn after Mozart, apparently. In a pair of these (March 24, 25), the quartet was joined by visitors, violist Samuel Rhodes and cellist Bonnie Hampton, in the composer's two Sextets.

The stop in Appleton, however, allows the opportunity to take note of the fact that many of the appearances around the state were devoted to training clinics with students, arranged at local high schools. Testimonials survive as to the appreciation and benefits resulting from such events. On the one in Appleton, on February 1, 2007, one of the North High School officials reported: "The Pro Arte played beautifully with passion and great expression. The piece they did with the students went very well and will be a great memory for the students." A year later (February 11, 2008), a staff member at the La Crosse Central High School testified: "The members of the quartet were outstanding as both performers and clinicians. My quartet students came back today with a new pair of eyes for rehearsing. The quartet members were both kind and encouraging. I would do this again at the drop of a hat."

Since the 1970s, the Pro Arte Quartet operated for their noncampus activities under the Arts Outreach program, at the time a part of the School of Music, but intended as a function of the "Wisconsin Idea" vision. (The program was later relocated under the Arts Consortium scheme, which soon evolved into the current Arts Institute. Along the way, there were differences about the status of the PAQ activities vis-à-vis the other faculty performing ensembles.) As it happened, for the first semester of 2007–8, the Arts Outreach offices granted the quartet a sabbatical leave. The ensemble did ultimately make an appearance in Prairie du Sac by early December of 2007, and only three Madison concerts are reported otherwise for the first semester, and one in-state (Prairie du Sac). But, in October the Pro Arte made their first jaunt to Europe as part of the group's sabbatical grant. That arrangement, however, did not directly include Beia, given her status as a nonfaculty member. She did, nevertheless, make some appearances with them in Italy. Stops are reported in Italy (Lucca, Florence, Urbino).

After the group's return for the second semester (2008), there were seven Madison concerts, and an equal number around the state (Milwaukee, Edgerton, La Crosse, West Bend, Ashland, Marinette,

Ephraim), plus a concert in Evanston, Illinois. The programs for many
of these concerts were sprinkled with examples of Boccherini quartets
gleaned from their sabbatical. The concert in Ephraim in May drew
from Door County journalist and connoisseur Erik Erickson a particularly penetrating assessment of the ensemble's standing, in his *Penin-
sula Pulse*:

> When the Pro Arte Quartet came to the Ephraim Moravian Church
> on May 16, it gave us both its best playing to date and a fresh, beau-
> tifully conceived program [Mendelssohn, Dvořák, Beethoven]. This
> ensemble has an illustrious history extending many decades past.
> Its present incarnation may be the finest ever, an exciting blend of
> impetuosity and mature musicianship. Nothing these artists under-
> take is ever routine; they find ways to breathe a new aspect into their
> work—and that affords new unexpected rewards.

> We must begin with the astonishing leader—David Perry, a violinist
> known to every colleague as one of the outright best among today's
> fiddlers. A silken tone, fiery facility and consummate musicianship
> are absorbed by all who work with him. Fortunately, his associates
> have obviously profited from his gifts and the results have been spar-
> kling. Second violinist Suzanne Beia has become ever more subtle,
> ever more technically accomplished. Violist Sally Chisholm is miracu-
> lous—lush, exquisite in tone (from her Amati/Guarneri hybrid).
> Her musicianship is commanding and her detailing a wonder. Cellist
> Parry Karp has sharpened his art, now vibrating faster and fitting in
> with his associates more compellingly.

The 2008–9 season is credited with seven Madison appearances
and five in-state concerts (Minoqua, Marinette, Richland Center, Fond
du Lac, Monroe), with one venture (December 9) in Cincinnati, Ohio.
In December, the Pro Arte participated in activities at the Cincinnati College Conservatory of Music, giving a concert on December 8
that offered quartets of Mozart, Bartók, and Schubert. For the spring
semester (2009), we are told of four Madison concerts, and five around
the state (Racine, West Bend, Middleton, Waukesha, Ephraim).

For the first semester of 2009–10, we have reports of six Madison
concerts and one in Ashland. The spring semester was more busy: fifteen Madison concerts, six around the state (Wauwatosa, Ripon, Prairie du Sac, Baraboo, West Bend, Ephraim), followed by one exception
to the summer-off practice, in an appearance at the Fairbanks Summer Arts Festival in Alaska (July 21). Standing out, however, was the
first venture to New York City, to reassert their status in that important

venue: Carnegie Hall's Weill Recital Hall (May 12, 2010). The quartet had not appeared in New York City since March of 1995, in the final months of the last Paulu configuration. Now, this event was to serve as the kickoff for a landmark step in the quartet's history. Starting with an absent-minded awareness that the Pro Arte would be soon reaching the century mark of their existence, snowballing schemes turned into an official Centennial Celebration. The Wisconsin Foundation marked the occasion by sponsoring a University of Wisconsin alumni reception before the New York concert.

Unfortunately, the reception for the quartet was rather backhanded and even ungracious. Writing in the *New York Times* of May 15, critic Steve Smith began his review: "For a musical ensemble with a famous name, legacy is a double-edged sword. On the one hand, a storied name can grab attention. On the other, an illustrious history can be burdensome when it sets up expectations that are difficult to live up to. The Pro Arte Quartet, which performed at Weill Hall on Wednesday evening, is presumably acquainted with both sides of the issue." The reviewer then devoted the bulk of his space to a summary of the quartet's long history, down to that moment.

> If the ensemble's name created grand expectations, the reality was more modest: a respectable concert of worthwhile pieces played for a small but receptive audience chiefly composed of university alumni and friends, to judge from the name tags most of the audience members wore. You were struck by the group's sound during an opening account of Haydn's Quartet in C (op. 74, no. 1): Mr. Perry, effusive and bright; Mr. Karp, magnanimous and rich; Ms. Beia and Ms. Chisholm blending warmly between them.

> One aspect of the quartet's legacy, its vital advocacy for contemporary American composers, went unheralded here. Yet there was a strand of heritage in its claim to Zemlinsky's Quartet no. 2; both Zemlinsky and the violinist Rudolf Kolisch, who led the Pro Arte Quartet from 1944 to 1967, were related by marriage to Schoenberg. In its heaving contours, intense chromaticism and psychological agitation, the music also seemed kin to early Schoenberg. The players embraced it with a convincing authority and beauty.

> An account of Dvořák's Quartet in E flat (op. 51) lacked the precision and refinement that the Emerson String Quartet brought to the piece at Alice Tully Hall on Sunday. But in its flexibility and congeniality, the Pro Arte performance struck closer to the work's sentimental core.

As an evaluation of the Pro Arte at the brink of their centennial celebration, then, the foregoing perhaps reflects the group's inadequate
promotion (especially via recordings) in order to command something
of the broad respect they deserve.

For a low-power 2010–11, the fall semester saw six Madison concerts, four around the state (Fond du Lac, Ephraim, Eau Claire, Ladysmith), plus one in London, Ontario. At the first Madison concert
(September 25), two of the works (Mozart, Schumann) were recorded
by the School of Music. For the spring semester, we hear of three Madison concerts, and one in-state appearance (Stoughton).

The 2011–12 season had a conventional beginning in their fall
semester: four Madison concerts (one at the opening of the Wisconsin
Science Festival) and four in-state appearances (Three Lakes, Ashland,
Ephraim, Platteville); and in the spring semester there were two independent concerts in Madison, four in-state (Rhinelander, Janesville,
Fond du Lac, Ephraim), and six out-state appearances (two in Washington State, one in Rolla, Missouri, one in Kansas City, and two at Mountain Lake, Florida). One of the Madison concerts (January 15) was titled
"A Celebration of the Life of [the recently deceased] Jim Crow."

But high drama crept in with the full-scale autumn launching of
the celebration of the Pro Arte Quartet's centennial. The extended
and complicated sequence of activities was coordinated skillfully by
Sarah Schaffer, the quartet's agent for out-of-state performances from
2005. There were various sideline events, including exhibits in several university buildings and a lavish exhibition at the Dane County
Regional Airport (March 1–September 3, 2012), at whose opening
the quartet played. But two major undertakings were the highlights of
the celebrations, which stretched as far as the 2013–14 seasons. One
of these ventures would not find fulfillment until the spring of 2014,
but the other began in the 2011–12 season: a series of six commissions
given to various composers. Most of these commissions were financed
by the university's School of Music, though major support was provided in two cases by local benefactors: Stanley and Shirley Inhorn plus
John and Carol Palmer for William Bolcolm, Robert W. and Linda M.
Graebner for John Harbison.

These works were premiered in ten widely spread concerts but in
clusters of interlocking programs. Most (3) were offered in Mills Hall,
but one was given in the Memorial Union Theater, while four were
offered at the Chazen Museum's Sunday broadcast-concerts, and even
the Music in Performance course was drawn (twice) into the recurrent

exposures of the new works. The concert at the Union Theater (March 24) constituted an appropriate full-circle connection: the Belgian group had made their first Madison appearance in 1939 as part of the festivities attending the *opening* of that hall; now, marking the hall's own seventy-fifth anniversary, they joined in celebrating the PAQ's own centennial. Each premiere concert was surrounded with related events, notably guest lectures.

The first event was on October 22 and 23: Walter Mays's Quartet 2 had its premiere, with other music on the program (as became the working pattern). Two lectures were also given by music historian Joseph Horowitz. On November 19 came the premiere of Paul Schoenfield's *Three Rhapsodies* for piano quintet (with Brian Hsu as pianist), with lectures by broadcaster Bill McGlaughlin. Energy was spared for a separate Madison concert (December 6), and sessions were held (December 11–12) in Mills Hall to record the Mays and Schoenfield works for Albany Records.

In the spring semester the quartet continued the commission premieres. William Bolcom's Piano Quintet no. 2 had its turn on March 24 (at the Memorial Union Theater) and 25, with Christopher Taylor as pianist, plus lectures by *New York Times* critic Anthony Tommasini. The premiere concerts were planned so that each included works with some appropriateness to the new work: the Quartet no. 7 of Milhaud, dedicated to the QPA's long association with the composer, was chosen for several, with particular aptness in Bolcom's case, since he had studied with the French composer. On April 21 and 22, John Harbison's Quartet no. 5 was premiered, with lectures by British discographer Tully Potter. Among other features of these events of April 2013, a small group of participants (including Van Malderen, Potter, and this author) gathered at the grave of Alphonse Onnou in Forest Hill Cemetery, where Sally Chisholm played the *Élégie* for solo viola that Germain Prevost had commissioned from Stravinsky in memory of Onnou. In May, sessions were held in Mills Hall to record for Albany Records the Schoenfield and Harbison quartets. Two remaining commission premieres (and recordings) would come later.

Meanwhile, a small drama was played out in February 2012 in Florida. Paul and Carol Collins were long-time and generous financial contributors to the School of Music. (Among other things, they contributed to endowing the professorship of David Perry.) Unable to attend the festivities in Madison, they arranged for the Pro Arte to perform for them and invited guests at their estate in Lake Wales, Florida.

Three of the quartet members arrived there individually to find that Beia had been detained in Madison due to a health emergency. The immediate reaction was to pull back to the trio solution, and on February 20 the threesome performed in a program that included the Dohnányi Trio, a movement of Schubert's Piano Trio no. 1 (D. 898), and a few other items. Out of deference to their generous hosts, they took the exceptional step of inviting a few local musicians to join them. Their program of February 21 included the Haydn op. 54, no. 2, Webern's *Langsamer Satz*, and Shostakovich's Quartet no. 4, along with movements from quartets by Barber, Franck, and Mozart.

In August, 2012, the quartet again ventured into summer activities. Through Perry's long contacts with the annual festivals at Aspen, Colorado, it was arranged that the Pro Arte would participate in teaching and concerts. Harbison was also involved that year, and had just produced his *Finale, Presto*. (This was his contribution to a set of commissions to contemporary composers to "respond" to an unfinished work by a great master, designed as a completion of Haydn's Quartet op. 103.) So, in a concert of August 15, the Pro Arte performed that piece, together with the new Quartet no. 5 by Harbison, along with music by Bloch, Barber (his opus 11), and Schubert (the C-Major Quintet, D. 956).

There was a recess in the celebrations for the 2012–13 season, though the already-premiered commissions were occasionally worked into the group's concerts. Seven Madison concerts are documented for the autumn semester, plus one at Grinnell College. In the spring, there were five Madison appearances, two in-state ones (Brookfield, Ephraim) and forays to Kansas City, Columbia, and St. Louis, all in Missouri. Then the ensemble initiated what became a series of dinner-concerts at the University Club, including one on February 14 titled "Valentine's Dinner with the Pro Arte Quartet." Two other Madison concerts were given, one (April 10) with violist Nobuko Imai as guest.

The first semester of the 2013–14 season was generally conventional: seven concerts in Madison, and five in-state (Sturgeon Bay, Egg Harbor, UW–Sheboygan, Fond du Lac, Frederick). One Madison concert was given (September 30) at the Wisconsin Public Television studios in honor of the centennial; excerpts of this were included in a video documentary on the quartet.

In the spring of 2014, some routines continued: three independent appearances in Madison, two in-state (Fitchburg, Ephraim). But the centennial celebrations were renewed with flair—if after one in-state concert (Prairie du Sac). Preparations for the fifth commissioned work, planned for premiere in November of 2016 had been delayed by a health crisis in the Karp family that autumn. But Benoît Mernier's String Quartet no. 3 was finally performed, first in a "pre-premiere" at Prairie du Sac, but then officially on March 1 at Mills Hall. The quartet took time for two local concerts (April 17, May 5) before packing their bags for the second major undertaking of the centennial celebration: a tour of Belgium.

Between them, Sarah Schaffer and the original Brussels group's historian, Anne Van Malderen, had arranged a "return to roots" for the Pro Arte. The passage by air was marred by a comedy of almost disastrous scope as a result of the then-pesky issue of ivory. In February of 2012, the US Fish and Wildlife Agency had placed draconian restrictions on the transportation of ivory objects, under the requirements of CITES (Convention on International Trade in Endangered Species). The goal was to strike at the horrifying slaughter of elephants and the profiteering traffic in the tusks. Now, the quartet's instruments do contain small bits of ivory in their construction—Sally Chisholm's viola has beautiful ivory edging decoration known as purfling. But these instruments were made generations, even centuries, before this new crisis. That such long-past use of ivory pieces should hinder the transportation of stringed instruments was quite far-fetched. The quartet learned of the ban in May, the month of the celebration. Special permits—effectively, passports for the instruments themselves—would take 60–90 days to acquire. With the help of Wisconsin Senator Tammy Baldwin, these documents were obtained just in the nick of time.

Upon arrival at the Brussels airport, the players found that the security officials there had never encountered this situation before and did not know what to do. As a result, at least Chisholm and Karp were detained for the first day of the visit. This threatened the quartet's ability to rehearse for their concert the next evening. Schaffer besieged the American Consulate, while Van Malderen contacted a Belgian cabinet minister. Between them they finally secured the release of the two in time. Rehearsals had to be held the following day in the hotel bar, for lack of better facilities. But the quartet members did begin their experiences in meeting descendants and relatives of the original Quatuor Pro Arte members.

The initial concerts of the tour were in Brussels (May 22, 23). The first of these was organized by Michel Arthur Prévost, a grandnephew of the founding violist, Germain Prévost. Their performance began with Chisholm playing Stravinsky's Élégie, commissioned by Prevost in memory of Onnou, but otherwise it replicated the 1938 program celebrating the original quartet's twenty-fifth anniversary. A grandson of the original cellist, Robert Maas, himself a cellist, attended the concert with his granddaughter. It had been expected that the King of Belgium himself would also attend, but this plan ran into the rules of the election then in progress, rules requiring the sequestration of the royal family for a period around voting day. In his place he was represented by an advisor, Hubert Rosin, who also accepted gifts of photographic and documentary materials for the Royal Library. That institution was the site of the second concert: the program included Bartók's Quartet no. 1, in tribute to the large collection of that composer's manuscripts held by the library.

The following day (May 24), the players went by train to Dolhain, Limburg, Alphonse Onnou's birthplace. Met by paparazzi at the station, they were treated to a "typical" Belgian lunch and then given a tour of the historic district. There was a municipal ceremony in which the mayor presented the quartet with the city's seal, followed by a reception with cognac and chocolates. This was followed by a parade. The band, with members ranging in age from seven to ninety, played "The Star-Spangled Banner" during the unveiling of a plaque to mark Onnou's house. Then a trip to the local library, where Anne Van Malderen had mounted an elaborate exhibition of the town's history and of Onnou memorabilia. All this was capped by a concert that evening at a hall where Onnou himself would have played as a boy. Stravinsky's *Élégie* in honor of Onnou was part of the program.

Back in Brussels, May 26 was spent at the Royal Conservatory where the original QPA players had studied. This was followed by another train trip, to the final stop, the Catholic University at Louvain-la-Neuve (May 27). At both of those two concluding concerts, Mernier's new Quartet no. 3 was performed, in its Belgian premiere, with the composer in attendance. A banquet concluded a visit that had proven to be a national event for Belgians. The airport departure was managed without any instrument challenge: Karp went on to engagements in England, while the other three flew back to Madison.

The Pro Arte took up its 2014–15 season with the premiere of the final work in their Centennial Commissions series, Pierre Jalbert's *Howl* for Clarinets and String Quartet, in a concert of September 26 at the Memorial Union Theater (along with Mozart's Clarinet Quintet and a quartet by Arriaga). The commissions series was given its final seal when recording sessions were held in Mills Hall, May 15–16, 2015, for the Mernier and Jalbert works.

Because of the delays involved in premiering Jalbert's composition, the recording session in 2015 must join with the Belgian tour the previous year as the symbolic terminal points for our narrative. Of course, the life and work of the Pro Arte Quartet go on, and in that sense this book stands as premature. It is, however, meant to be the final element of the centennial celebrations.

## Repertoire (through 2015):

Whereas many earlier phases of the quartet's history have been plagued by inadequate preservation of program information, the Perry years are much better served. The notable resource is a file of programs kept by Perry himself. It is not fully complete, leaving many gaps (especially in some program contents), but it is richly comprehensive, and allows a very good picture of repertoire evolution, scope, and character. We are much better informed as to performances around the state, and as to those in the radio broadcast series "Sunday Afternoon Live at the Elvehjem"—or, after the museum's name changed, "at the Chazen." Likewise we have more information on the quartet's contributions to the "Music in Performance" course on the Madison campus, which no longer involved excerpts from large works but presented complete works. All of this fuller information allows us to see how their programs were planned in repetitive clusters, drawing upon the scores concentrated upon at the time. (Mention should be made that the Pro Arte, in their travels within and beyond the state, often augmented their concerts with master classes and coaching sessions in school situations, but those have not themselves been taken into account in our tallies.)

One point that does emerge from our tally of repertoire is that the ensemble pursued a kind of "survey" approach. Despite the reduced emphasis upon some composers, the character of the repertoire has thus been more broad, if perhaps more shallow, than even that of the Paulu years. The range of selections covered has been notably wide, but with only a varied number of performances given almost all choices, with hardly any of what might be called "favorite" works accorded unusual repetition.

The great preoccupation of the Pro Arte's Paulu years had been promoting the music of contemporary composers, mostly American. Under Perry, that preoccupation has hardly been abandoned. Some nineteen contemporary composers, mostly American, may be identified among those whose music was performed. A good many of those works, too, were commissioned by the quartet, or by the School of Music, as financed by generous contributions from donors and foundations. The culmination of this was the extensive program of commissioning new works in celebration of the quartet's centennial.

To make the point, here are works of that category, in reported Pro Arte concert performances (marked with an asterisk if also recorded): Jan Bach (b. 1937), Tuba Quintet (five times); William Bolcom (b. 1938), Piano Quintet no. 2* (four times); Victoria Bond (b. 1945), *Dream of Flying* (six times); Tamar Diesendruck (b. 1946), Quartets 1* and 3 (once; twice); Brian Fennelly (b. 1937), *Airs and Interludes*, Quartet no. 3 (once; five times); John Harbison (b. 1938), Quartet no. 4 (four times), no. 5* (eight times), *Presto* (thrice); Joel Hoffmann (b. 1953), *Another Time* (thrice); Pierre Jalbert (b. 1967), *Howl* (twice); Leon Kirchner (1919–2009), Quartet no. 2 (thrice) and no. 4 (twice); Robert Kritz (b. 1928), Quintet (thrice), and songs (once); György Kurtág (b. 1926), *Aus der Ferne III* (thrice); Robert Mann (b. 1925), *Invocations*; Walter Mays (b. 1941), Quartets nos. 1 (eleven times) and 2* (thirteen times); Benoît Mernier (b. 1964), Quartet no. 3* (four times); Astor Piazzolla (1921–92) *Oblivion* (once); Samuel Rhodes (b. 1928), Quintet* (once); Paul Schoenfield (b. 1947), *Three Rhapsodies for Piano Quintet* (thrice); Roger Sessions (1896–1985), String Quintet* (twice); Ralph Shapey (1921–2002), Quartet no. 9* (six times); Randall Thompson (1899–1984), *The Wind in the Willows* (twice); George Tsontakis (b. 1951), *Requiescat* (once).

By contrast with their substantial commitment to contemporary composers, the Perry Pro Arte has retreated significantly from the Second Viennese School, of whose music the Kolisch team was a champion. In 1995–2014, only one work by Schoenberg (the Quartet no. 2) was reported (once). Only an early work by Berg, his opus 3 Quartet, was performed (thrice). The only selection by Webern— a fairly popular one—was his late-Romantic *Langsamer Satz* (fifteen times). Among other "modernists," we find Milhaud represented only by his Quartet no. 7 (thirteen times), the once-favored Bloch only by his *Prelude* (seven times) and a *Presto* (once), and Stravinsky by his *Three Pieces* (twice)—though his *Élégie* was played twice in Onnou commemorations. Attention to the Bartók quartets was quite varied: no. 1 once, no. 2 nine times, no. 3 thrice, no. 4 seven times, no. 5 six times, no. 6 six times. Kurtág appeared twice. Shostakovich was clearly now a "mainstream modernist" as well: of his quartets, no. 3 (thirteen times), no. 4 (seven times), no. 5 (eleven times), no. 7 (six times), no. 8 (twice), no. 12 (once), no. 14 (six times). Prokofiev's Quartet no. 2 tailed along with six performances. Zemlinsky, however, surged with new concentration: of his quartets, no. 1 (eight times), no. 2 (six times), no. 3 (five times), and no. 4 (seven times).

Turning to the general categories of the "standard" literature, we observe the inevitable predominance of the Austro-German tradition. Of Haydn's Quartets, reports indicate a total of twenty played variously but very repeatedly: op. 1 no. 1 (seven times); op. 20, no. 4 (twelve times), and no. 5 (once); op. 33 no. 3 (thrice); op. 42 (once); op. 50 no. 4 (three times); op. 54, no. 2 (twenty-one times), no. 3 (four times); op. 55, no. 2 (thrice), no. 5 (once); op. 64, no. 4 (thrice), no. 5 (four times), no. 6 (eleven times); op. 74, no. 1 (seven times), no. 2 (four times), no. 3 (five times); op. 76, no. 1 (twice), no. 2 (thrice), no. 3 (nine times), no. 4 (four times); no. 5 (thirteen times), no. 6 (thrice); op. 77, no. 1 (twice), no. 2 (four times); op. 103 (six times). Additionally, *Die sieben letzten Worte*, three times.

For Mozart, the picture given is of parallel scope but greater intensity. Of the quartets, K. 428 was a clear standout at twenty-one reported performances, followed by K. 589 at nineteen, and K. 387 at thirteen. Of the others: K. 171 (one), K. 387 (K.421 (seven), K. 458 (six), K. 464 (six), K. 465 (seven), K. 475 (eight), K. 499 (one), and K. 590 three). Of the string quintets, K. 406 (thrice), K. 515 (twice) K. 516 five times), K. 614 (once), and K. 593 (thrice). The Oboe Quartet was given twice, a Flute Quartet once, the Horn Quintet once, and the Clarinet Quintet six times; the Adagio and Fugue K. 546 nine times, the Divertimento K. 136 twice, and the Adagio from the Divertimento K. 287 twice.

As for Beethoven, the opus 18 Quartets were reportedly prominent: no. 1 five times, no. 2 eleven times, no. 3 twelve times, no. 4 four times, no. 5 once, and no. 6 four times. The three of op. 59 were reported thirteen, four, and four times, respectively. Opus 74 was given eight times, opus 95 four. Of the late quartets, opus 130 was a favorite at fourteen times, with opus 133 at nine. Opus 127 appears once, opus 131 four times, opus 132 eight, and opus 135 seven.

With Schubert, this ensemble was more venturesome in exploring early quartets: D. 87 four times, D. 112 thrice, D. 173 twice, and D. 353

thrice. Showings were variably respectable for the later ones: D. 703 six times, D. 804 six times. D. 810 a robust nineteen times, and D. 887 sixteen times. The "Trout" Quintet D. 667 only twice, the Quintet D. 956 nine times; the Octet twice. Some dances, D. 89 twice; the Rondo for violin and strings, D. 438 once.

Schumann's works received comparatively modest treatment. Of the opus 41 threesome, there were three, five, and eight performances respectively. The Piano Quintet, op. 44, thrice. Mendelssohn's music was much elevated in the Perry years, however. All seven of his string quartets were represented: opus 12 (five times), opus 13 (eighteen times), the three of opus 44 (eight, twelve, and four times, respectively), opus 80 (five times) and opus 81 (nine times); plus the two String Quintets, opus 18 and opus 87 (twice each); a Fugue, op. 81 no. 4 (once), and the Octet (eight times).

Bruckner's Quintet appeared thrice. Brahms was given respectable if inconsistent place. The two opus 51 Quartets appeared fifteen times and twice respectively, the opus 67 six times. The String Quintets op. 88 and op. 111 respectively twice and thrice. The Piano Quartets were notably absent, but the Piano Quintet op. 34 appeared eleven times and the Clarinet Quintet op. 115 twice; the two Sextets thrice and five times respectively. Fritz Kreisler's A-Minor Quartet was played at least once.

Of Central European composers, Dvořák was given more than past prominence. No less than eight of his fourteen Quartets were presented: opus 9 (once), opus 34 (fourteen times), opus 51 (nine times), opus 61 (thrice), opus 80 (twice), opus 96 (seven times), opus 105 (once), opus 106 (seven times). The *Cypresses* six times; the Waltzes thrice; and the Piano Quintet op. 81 five times; an arrangement of an aria from *Rusalka* once. Smetana was represented only by his Quartet no. 1 (twice). Both of Janáček's Quartets were played (four times each). Dohnányi's Piano Quintet appeared once. Only Szymanowski's Second Quartet appeared (thrice). Tchaikovsky's three Quartets earned two, six, and four performances, respectively. Glazunov's *Novelettes* still survived, in four performances. Ignacy Friedman's Piano Quintet was given once.

Scandinavia had unconventional representing in Grieg's Quartet (four times) and in the now-respectable Sibelius Quartet (twice).

The French category sustained the oddest changes. Franck's String Quartet appeared eighteen times, his Piano Quintet only once. Debussy, long one of the leading composers in Pro Arte repertoires, was represented only four times, by reports, while his near rival, Ravel, was represented by his Quartet thirteen times. Outrider Germaine Tailleferre placed well with her Quartet (eight times).

Italian literature could now be amplified by Boccherini. As a result of the Pro Arte's study of the composer's music during their sabbatical in Lucca, seventeen performances of five of his quartets were given: op. 2 no. 1 (three times), op. 13 no. 5 (once), op. 32 no. 4 (five times), op. 39 (four times), op. 58 no. 2 (four times). Verdi barely held his place with one performance of his Quartet. Puccini's *Crisantemi* was given three appearances, while Respighi's *Il Tramonto* survived in one.

A rare Spanish representation was given with Arriaga's Quartet no., 2 (thrice).

British composers were represented by Frank Bridge's Piano Quintet (once), the *Phantasy Quintet* of Vaughan Williams (thrice), Elizabeth Maconchy's Quartet no. 10 (twice), and the *Phantasy Quartet* of Benjamin Britten (twice), as well as the latter's Quartet no. 2 (once). A straggling American was Samuel Barber, whose Quartet op. 11, was given its due at last in all of eight performances, augmented by one of his "Dover Beach" settings.

The only appearance of "early" music was left to an adaptation of Vivaldi's "Winter" Concerto, op. 8 no. 1 (once).

(It is perhaps worth mentioning that in quintet performances the PAQ could draw upon the talents of such distinguished collaborators as Leon Fleisher, Samuel Rhodes, Nobuko Imai, and Bonnie Hampton—a measure of how much the ensemble is respected by professional colleagues.)

From the figures available, we therefore reckon an impressive total of three hundred and thirty-two concert performances within 1995–2014, containing an estimated 193 compositions.

# Recording Activity

The recordings made by the Pro Arte in the years 1995–2015 fall into two categories: those (unnumbered) made for limited distribution by the University of Wisconsin School of Music, and those made for commercial sale by Albany Records. We shall consider them in that sequence of groupings—which, as it happens, has us beginning with music commissioned for one centennial celebration and ending with commissions for another centennial.

To celebrate its one-hundredth anniversary in 1995, the School of Music commissioned original works by six composers with varying levels of connection with the School, the University, or Wisconsin in general: John Harbison, Daron Hagen, Davit Ott, Joan Tower, Libby Larsen, and Ralph Shapey. The resulting six works received their premieres in concert at Mills Hall during the academic year 1995–96. Those concert performances were recorded "live" by the ever-reliable engineer James Stuht and were gathered together in a two-CD set issued by the School. To those six, a seventh work was added, a commission to Thea Musgrave in honor of the 150th anniversary of the founding of the University of Wisconsin itself, first performed in 1999. Each of the seven works was written for and performed by a different School of Music faculty group.

The Pro Arte Quartet participated in performing the String Quartet no. 9 by Ralph Shapey (1921–2002). A highly individualistic musical personality, Shapey liked casting unconventional, even provocative material in traditional forms. This quartet is cast in four movements, all growing out of variations posed in the first. The ensemble matched tightness of composition with tightness of performance, in strong sound.

The next three releases, made in 2001–5 for the School of Music, marked a sharp departure from the prior attention given to contemporary music, and a reversion to that first venture of the Paulu years with the Brahms Piano Quintet. Made more than three years apart, the first two of the three were each devoted to a composer of high "mainstream" status: Antonin Dvořák and Felix Mendelssohn.

The Dvořák release was made not in Madison but at the Weidner Center studios in Green Bay in the spring of 2001. Offering two of the composer's string quartets, one in D Minor, op. 34, the other in E-flat, op. 51, the release betokened the emerging emphasis placed in the Perry years on Dvořák's total quartet output, and especially on the ones before the final three; these two, indeed, were to be played most frequently in concerts by the Pro Arte. The two works date from the composer's first winning of recognition. That was thanks in no small measure to the group's championing of Brahms, whose strong influence can be perceived in these scores. These affectionate performances testify to the clear enjoyment the Pro Arte took in these lovely works, though it must be said that the ultimate kind of gutsy Slavic sound somewhat eludes them.

The Mendelssohn disc results from sessions held at Mills Hall on the Madison campus in the spring of 2004. Once again it involves a composer to whom the Perry Pro Arte devoted attention amplified over that of prior years. Three works are presented: the Quartet no. 2 in A Minor, op. 13; the Fugue in E, op. 81, no. 4; and the Quartet in D, op. 44, no. 1. Each work represents a stage in the composer's compositional evolution, giving the program a kind of unity as a survey. The Pro Arte demonstrates their perception of a "classical" Mendelssohn, rather refined and circumspect, even in the brief displays of the composer's "elfin" character. The result is very enjoyable listening, but gives perhaps less than full justice to Mendelssohn's underestimated strength. Still, the bright clarity of the recording sound is a good match with the composer's ebullient spirit.

The last of the formal recordings by the School of Music was a celebration not only of the Pro Arte but of a frequent faculty colleague and collaborator, the superlative oboist Marc Fink. The four compositions involved were meant to be a bundle, displaying Fink's varied tastes and skills. The quartet (whether in full, reduced, or augmented) joins in with perfect collegiality. Of the four works, the most novel is a Divertimento in C, op. 9 (of 1823) for oboe and quartet, by Bernhard Henrik Crusell (1775–1838), digesting three quasi-movemnts into a single one: light and indeed "diverting" music. Mozart's incomparable Oboe Quartet in F, K. 370, is delivered with graceful suavity. Benjamin Britten's *Phantasy*, op. 2, for oboe and string trio (1932) is a work of episodic restlessness, testing the oboe's coloristic range. John Harbison's 1977 *Snow Country* is a long and moody evocation of a dreary Wisconsin winter, subtly nuanced.

To all these may be added, as a kind of afterthought, a concert recording made in September of 2010, intended for promotional purposes rather than any circulation. In it, the Pro Arte is heard in a suave, if perhaps understated performance of Mozart's Quartet in E-flat, K. 428, and a brisk and forthright rendition of Schumann's Quartet in A, op. 41, no. 3.

For Albany, the Pro Arte made four releases in our time period. In the first of these, we find the Pro Arte again active in chamber music of important twentieth-century American composers. Roger Sessions (1896–1985) was one of the most prominent and assertive of his generation. His three-movement Quintet of 1958 embeds a spikiness and spunk within relatively traditional, and nonserial, rationales. The violist Samuel Rhodes (b. 1928) joined the Pro Arte players in that recording, as well as in his own Quintet, composed ten years later, which shows some influence of Sessions, but is a sonorous score. The three

movements are carefully structured, the longest being a finale exploit-
ing variations techniques. The Quartet for Strings (no. 1) by Walter
Mays (b. 1941), written in 1998, was composed for the Pro Arte—as
would be the case with his Quartet no. 2 to come. Of its two movements, the first is episodic and harmonically restless, the second dark
and moody. The performances are meticulous, and the ensemble's frequent collaboration with Rhodes ensures total compatibility between
his own and the Sessions score. The recording was made in December
of 2000, not in Madison but at the Purchase Conservatory of Music in
Purchase, NY.

The next involvement with Albany, five years later, was by way of
contributing to an anthology of music by Brian Fennelly (b. 1937)
assembled by the label itself. For this, the composer's String Quartet
no. 2, titled "Arias and Interludes," was recorded in December 2005, in
Madison, but with Audio for the Arts facilities. This is a clever work, in
an often pointillistic style, cast in seven interrelated movements, brack-
eted into two parts. Four of the movements are "Arias," each giving
one of the ensemble's four instruments a chance to dominate—splen-
didly so by the four Pro Arte players.

Culminating their collaboration with the Albany label, the Pro
Arte has recorded for it the six works commissioned for the Centennial Celebration of the group. The first two (Walter Mays, Paul Schoenfield) were recorded in Mills Hall in December of 2011, the next two
(William Bolcom, John Harbison) in May 2012. Those four were issued
by Albany in a two-CD set. Because of schedule delays and a number
of factors, the last two commissions were performed and recorded
slightly later: The fifth work (Benoît Mernier) and the sixth (Pierre Jalbert) were recorded in May of 2015 and have appeared in a single-disc
second volume, also from Albany.

The Quartet no. 2 by Walter Mays is titled "Dreaming Butterfly,"
inspired by an ancient Chinese philosopher's speculations. Its five
movements trace the dreamer's transformation into a butterfly—or
is it a butterfly dreaming?—following its perceptions and adventures,
which Mays treats less through sound effects than through suggestive
evocations. Schoenfield's *Three Rhapsodies for Piano Quintet* demonstrate
the composer's varied interests in popular culture and ethnic traditions. The first of its three movements elaborates on a rock 'n 'roll
song, the second adapts Hungarian structure, the third transforms certain Hassidic elements.

The versatile Bolcom had ample experience in chamber music writing, including a prior piano quintet. Highly conscious of tradition, he has seen his work as extending it, and he likes to think of his Piano Quintet no. 2 as in the line of such works by Schumann, Fauré, and especially Brahms. The character of the music is energetic and burly, in the Brahmsian sense, with demanding piano writing as a strong challenge specifically meant for Christopher Taylor. The two had enjoyed a long relationship, starting when the pianist sent some of his boyhood piano compositions to Bolcom. In his turn, Harbison has had some varied contacts with members of the Pro Arte. His Quartet no. 5 is an adventuresome work, cast as a single movement, but itself divided into ten contrasting movements of short length, some evoking classical idioms, but always looking forward in spirit.

Mernier's Quartet no. 3 was conceived as a deliberate effort to distance himself from his previous effort, the composition of an opera. He thus has sought to create "pure" music as against anything "programmatic," suggestive of narrative, personifications, or theatrics. There are nine movements, of varying lengths, some interrelated, but devoted to abstract ideas and impulses. Jalbert discovered, early on, that his emerging Quintet for Clarinet and Strings (bass clarinet in the final movement) had much in common with Allen Ginsberg's poem "Howl" in terms of construction and stylistic techniques, encouraging the composer to evoke the poem's mixtures of spiritual reflections and assertive shrieks. The second of its three movements employs chant-like lines to suggest liturgy, the clarinet in constant dialogue with the string group.

# CONCLUSION

# Retrospect and Prospects

There is a famous Chinese saying, attributed to Confucius—as are all good Chinese sayings—to the effect: It is difficult to make predictions, especially with regard to the future (Or was that Yogi Berra?). So it is with the Pro Arte Quartet.

Though many string quartets have endured for decades, frequently with changes of personnel, only one has survived for a century. From their beginning to his demise, Alphonse Onnou was determined that the Quatuor Pro Arte should not die with him, but should find continuing life through their commitment to the University of Wisconsin in Madison. Despite recurrent changes in personnel and periodic crises, that commitment has been the anchor of survival.

Such survival is by no means ended. Our story is incomplete as of this writing, for the Pro Arte Quartet remains alive and active in Madison, still adding to their history. They maintain their decades-long pattern of giving concerts regularly, both in Madison and in tours around the state of Wisconsin. They continue to make appearances around the country. They continue to seek out new works by contemporary composers, and to do their share in championing the ongoing idiom of music for string quartet. Both in contemporary and in "mainstream" quartet literature, they diligently maintain the highest standards of ensemble skills and interpretative artistry.

It must be admitted that there are uncertainties as we look to the Pro Arte's future.

The quartet's livelihood and status are at the disposal of the University of Wisconsin. At this writing, there are shadows cast at both the national and state levels. The state of Wisconsin itself is in the midst of drastic political and fiscal change, involving heavy discrimination against educational institutions. The University of Wisconsin has been subjected to significant budget cuts, and there will be much upheaval in the years to come, involving sharp prioritizing of activities. The School of Music (now renamed the Mead Witter School of Music) faces its share of such budgetary constraints, whose full impact is only beginning to be understood. To be sure, the high standards and growing reputation of the School and of its faculty, especially in the field of training young performers, will certainly be sustained as fully as possible. More to our point, the current director of the School, Susan Cook, offers optimism with regard to the Pro Arte Quartet.

"It will continue to exist," she says emphatically, expressing the opinion that the quartet's status is "pretty safe" for the outlook ahead. She anticipates more coordination of their overall activities by the Music School. Discussion is going forward of a plan to endow ultimately each chair of the ensemble, a plan mainly launched by Robert and Linda Graebner. The first of these endowments has already been arranged for violist Sally Chisholm. (She has aptly chosen to name it the "Prévost Chair.") If this plan proves feasible (meaning the acquisition of sufficient funding), it will be implemented in successive steps, until all the chairs are accommodated.

A serious obstacle to that scheme might involve the latest recurrence of the Curse of Tom Moore on the second violin position. In the artistically splendid Suzanne Beia, the quartet has a member with only half-time status and 50-percent salary. She is an artist in residence without full faculty standing; she does no teaching, though some coaching. To sustain her livelihood, she must take on performing commitments beyond those of the quartet—concertmaster positions in Madison's two professional orchestras and its opera orchestra, while feeding a robust appetite for chamber performing around the Madison area and beyond—commitments that she does, as it happens, find very satisfying. The result is that her schedule places limits on the quartet's plans for concerts, travel, and recording.

Ironically, Beia's situation has only augmented the Curse of Tom Moore, which isolated the second-violin chair. Moore's faculty position, which he detached from his quartet membership, was taken up upon his departure by violinist Tyrone Greive, who was never involved with the quartet; when Greive retired, his position of violin professor was dropped from the budget. If the School of Music were to provide the money once again to finance the second-violin chair, it is unlikely as of now that Beia, who (without a Bachelor's degree) lacks full academic credentials, could be included in the search, thus risking the loss to the Pro Arte of her talents and experience.

Cook's hope, on that count, would be that an alternate faculty position might be created that would cover Beia's situation. And it is clear, in fact, that any endowment arrangements will be a long process, over many years, so future personnel circumstances might change. But director Cook does insist that the School of Music remains committed to the Pro Arte's "second century."

The performing operations of the Pro Arte members are really fourfold: giving concerts at the University of Wisconsin in Madison; giving concerts on tour around the state (under Outreach); giving what concerts they can outside the state (in the United States and abroad), as handled by a separate agent; and fulfilling teaching duties in the School of Music. Thus against the players' performing operations must always be balanced their teaching obligations. The University of Wisconsin established the model for quartet residencies in the United States, but the original model has been bypassed by other academic institutions that host residencies of this kind. At most of these institutions, quartets are given the freedom to tour and concertize nationally and internationally, with only limited or token stops at their "home" campuses for teaching purposes. Such evolution, however, has not affected or modified the UW/PAQ connection. The academic patronage that Elizabeth Sprague Coolidge and Carl Bricken imagined proved to be the salvation of the QPA at a critical point in their history. By now, however, the connection has turned into a serious burden.

To be sure, the players continue to find their teaching functions to be valuable and satisfying amid their performing. Nevertheless, those functions require a dimension of energy commitment that is larger than that borne by most other quartets with academic affiliations. As Richard Blum once said, "It tends to drain you physically. You end up giving 100 percent to both jobs." Norman Paulu has given a positive picture of the Pro Arte as a "campus quartet": "You know, commercial string quartets are notorious for their personality problems. Professional musicians are career-centered. I think a setting like ours, however, attracts a different kind of person, one as committed to teaching and sharing as to music." Nevertheless, however, Paulu later came to feel that a quartet's involvement with a university was, to his mind, ultimately unhealthy for the musicians.

At this writing, there seem to be no immediate prospects for any of the members to depart or, more likely, to retire. But such situations are bound to come sooner or later. If and when they do, will the University and the School of Music be certain to fill the resulting gaps? Crises of this nature have occurred before, of course, in 1949 and 1978. But in each case, a favorable resolution was partly the result of strong community outcry against the dismantling of the Pro Arte Quartet. Should such a threat recur, would there be, could there be, such a community reaction once again? In the current age, when our primary and secondary educational systems have failed so dismally in teaching anything substantial about music, and in which our general public is so crushingly dominated by the vast nihilism of commercial mass culture, one may be concerned—especially as the strong role the Pro Arte has played in Wisconsin's statewide cultural life has been diminishing. The Outreach appearances around the state survive for now. But the idea, once vividly promoted, that the provision of a residence for the quartet was one of the great cultural achievements of the university, seems pale and thinning nowadays. The two final volumes of *The University of Wisconsin: A History*, by E. David Cronon and John W. Jenkins, published by the University of Wisconsin Press—vol. 3: 1925–45 (1994); vol. 4: 1945–71 (1999)—between them make a total of three cursory references to the Pro Arte Quartet, and no more. A more condensed and popularized account, *University Madison U.S.A.* by Robert E. Gard (Wisconsin House, 1970) makes absolutely no mention of the PAQ, while a great deal of attention is given to successful University of Wisconsin sports teams. It is no surprise in our time that "high culture" has low priority in public consciousness.

A most recent symbol of this situation may be cited. One of the few important media for establishing the quartet's presence in wide audience awareness has been their appearances in weekly Sunday midday broadcasts from what was the University's Elvehjem Art Museum, now renamed as the Chazen Museum, broadcasts carried statewide over Wisconsin Public Radio. Parry Karp was the original organizer of this project. To be sure, the Pro Arte was only one of a number of groups who performed in these concerts, but they were a mainstay, and informally considered the museum's "quartet in residence." Suddenly however, in May of 2014, the new director of WPR abruptly announced the cancelation of those broadcasts. Only murky reasons were given. This announcement happened to come at exactly the moment that the Pro Arte was making their historic and prestigious tour of Belgium, so that it served as a particularly brutal slap in the quartet's collective face. The WPR funding had been essential for these broadcasts. The Chazen has taken some steps on its own to revive the concerts on a monthly basis, and the PAQ has been accorded four of the eleven program slots in this new series. These concerts are at least given worldwide dissemination by live streaming. That is now limited, however, to a project of the Chazen Museum itself, no longer sustained by the state's supposedly culture-minded "public radio." In this regard, Wisconsin's "public radio" displays a diminished responsibility to its public.

The PAQ has long functioned under the university's Outreach program, which is now itself under the jurisdiction of the new Arts Institute. That organization handles all of the group's in-state appearances. But the Arts Institute has come to consider the quartet's functions as a "philanthropic" or "charity" program, perhaps to be canceled if it was not self-sustaining. For now, the Arts Institute provides a 50-percent staff person, leaving travel and promotion expenses to the performing group itself. In effect, despite the long history of the quartet's outreach as a function of the Wisconsin Idea, the university's support for PAQ has become more and more tightfisted. The quartet's out-of-state appearances are—as they long have been—in the hands of an independent manager, Sarah Schaffer's own arts management firm, Ars Nova, LLC. Given all the schedule constraints (especially with Beia's situation), however, engagements have become few and not easy to program. And Schaffer's functioning in this regard is itself under challenge from the School of Music.

Another way the quartet has had of promoting their existence and merits also now has dubious prospects. As we have seen, over the Madison years—some seven and a half decades—the Pro Arte did not follow the example of the original Brussels group in pursuing a lively program of making recordings. Recordings that were made have some specialized significance, and do represent a legacy of a more restricted time, in terms of survival and audience. Even that picture, however, seems in doubt for the future.

The players in the current Perry configuration have mixed feelings about the very idea of making recordings: indeed, they are divided two against two on the issue. Two of the players are frankly "allergic" to such activity. The argument against it is that the intense preparation required creates greater tensions and frictions beyond the normal, an unwelcome strain. Whatever the players' feelings, however, the prospects for any further recording seem quite dim. In its new budget adjustments, the School of Music has decided that it will arrange no more record releases of its own. That medium of promoting the Pro

Arte, however limited it has been, is thus eliminated. The only other recording avenue has been the Albany Records label.

In point of fact, the quartet's dealings with Albany have always been at the initiative of the ensemble, and not of the label itself. Each recording venture must be proposed and reviewed if it is to be accepted by Albany, and a subsidy must be provided the company to supplement its input. The subsidy comes from the centennial celebration budget, but Albany retains the net profits. The costs of recording and issuing a release are considerable. As examples, take the two Centennial Commissions albums. Volume 1, a two-disc set, had a final budget of $21,380, while the single-disc volume 2 ran to $17,535. In both cases, the only payments to the musicians were accorded to the guest participants—pianist Brian Hsu and clarinetist Charles Neidich. The actual members of the quartet (as well as faculty member Christopher Taylor) were presumed to be *donating* their services and received no fees whatsoever.

Under the circumstances, the prospects for further projects with the Albany label are, to say the least, highly uncertain.

And, of course, who knows how the media of recording and musical dissemination will themselves be transformed in a time of galloping technological change and fickle public fancies.

❧    ❧    ❧

Serious concerns about the future should not be allowed to overshadow celebration of the past and present. The century-long history of the Pro Arte Quartet has displayed for us the vision and energies of many people important to that history. The artistry of Alphonse Onnou, among his Belgian colleagues, generated an ensemble that reached the top ranks of music making for their time. Mrs. Elizabeth Sprague Coolidge, an absolute paragon of patronage, enabled the QPA to attract an international audience. With her help, Carl Bricken and Clarence Dykstra brought to the University of Wisconsin the gift of the Pro Arte's residence. Rudolf Kolisch made the PAQ and Madison the foremost center in the Western Hemisphere for the music of the Second Viennese School. Irving Shain brought a renewal to the quartet after a time of crisis. By their leadership, first violinists Norman Paulu and David Perry have sustained the status of the Pro Arte as a leading specimen of the American string quartet. The century of the Pro Arte Quartet is a century filled with heroes.

And then there is the miracle of the music itself. The dynamics of a functioning string quartet, at least for those who are not among their members, must seem almost metaphysical. Pondering the century-long history of a distinguished ensemble must generate a certain degree of awe. Through the successive generations of the Pro Arte Quartet, groupings of four distinct individuals have confronted works in one of music's greatest categories of expression. Somehow transcending handicaps, tensions, even animosities, they have managed to produce the miracles that are great musical performances. In the end, that is perhaps the best reason for holding onto faith in humanity.

# APPENDIX A

# Benny Goodman and the QPA

One great and rather bizarre mystery haunts the Pro Arte's recording history—that of Mozart's Clarinet Quintet K. 581, and its association with Benny Goodman. During the 1930s, that great jazz musician was developing an interest in classical music literature, with the Mozart Quintet as his first target. For their part, the Pro Arte performed the work a reported eight times over the years, at least twice with the distinguished clarinetist Louis Cahuzac.

The performance catalogue compiled by Anne Van Malderen asserts that the quartet played it twice in public with Goodman: first on July 10, 1935, at Mills College, and then on February 12, 1938. Those reports are apparently incorrect, for there is no evidence that the Pro Arte ever played the work with Goodman in public performance. But Van Malderen also reports that Goodman and the Pro Arte made an incomplete recording of it with Goodman in "early 1936," at the Abbey Road studios in London (pp. 486–87).

Now, it is clear from Van Malderen's own performance registry that such a dating is of insecure credibility. In January 1936 the Pro Arte was involved in "overlapping" Beethoven Quartet cycles in Belgium. To be sure, the quartet was in the London area in February 1936, and in one concert played this Mozart Quintet, if not with Goodman as soloist.

The literature on Goodman, however, offers conflicting information. There are no references to Goodman ever playing with the Pro Arte in public; the Van Malderen reports of such on two occasions may be regarded as quite dubious. As to the ill-fated recording session, we are given a very different picture.

According to the jazz recording producer and critic John Hammond—also violist of the Coolidge Quartet—he himself urged Goodman to investigate classical literature. (Hammond thought it would be healthy to build bridges between jazz and classical music making, an idea he later concluded was a mistake.) Goodman knew virtually nothing of classical music, and had never heard—or heard of—the Mozart Clarinet Quintet, which Hammond suggested for a start. Around the spring of 1935, Hammond pulled together three other New York string players (himself on viola), and for three weeks, once a week, they rehearsed the quintet with Goodman. They then included their results in a private concert, with over 150 invited guests, at the mansion of Hammond's mother on East 95th Street, late in 1935—the first time that Goodman played a classical work before an audience. "Naturally, I had a tough time at first adapting myself to this sort of thing . . . . but the music did appeal to me," he reflected (This story occurs in various narratives by Hammond, *John Hammond on Record*, New York: Ridge, pp. 159–61; Benny Goodman with Irving Kolodin, *The Kingdom of Swing*, New York: Ungar, 1961, pp. 166–69; James L. Collier, *Benny Goodman and the Swing Era*, New York: Oxford University Press, 1989, p. 339).

Apparently pleased with the results, Goodman decided to make a recording, and arrangements were made with Victor Records to hold a session at their Chicago studio, with no less than the Pro Arte Quartet. No date is indicated for this session, but it was said to be "about a year later" after the private performance in late 1935. It proved to be a terrible mistake. The best account is Goodman's own recollection:

> I must have been more than slightly distracted at the time, as I normally take a very serious view of a serious venture. I was on a one-nighter tour of the Middle West. The night before the recording date, my band and I were playing in Wisconsin. When the engagement was over, we piled into a bus, drove through the night and arrived in Chicago at six A.M. Four hours later I breezed into the recording studio, met the Pro Arte members for the first time, sat down, took out my clarinet with the same reed in it [a reed different from that for classical use] that I had used the night before for the "One O'Clock Jump" and bashed right into the Mozart Quintet—and right out of the studio a few bars later. After playing for maybe five minutes, I started saying to myself, "What the hell am I doing here? This is nuts. I don't know this piece." I just wasn't prepared. So I excused myself, saying, "I'm sorry, gentlemen. Thank you, but this was my mistake."

Of course, the Belgian players' English was limited, so that communication was hampered. But as Goodman later also recollected: "I just got up and walked out. You know, they were very nice guys. They just sat there and didn't do a thing to humiliate me." (Ross Firestone, *Swing, Swing, Swing: The Life and Times of Benny Goodman*, New York: Norton, 1993, pp. 243–47; Collier, p. 339; D. Russell Connor and Warren W. Hicks, *BG on the Record: A Bio-Discography of Benny Goodman*, New York: Arlington House, 1969.) But John Hammond imposed a different picture: "The string players did not treat Benny with the respect he deserved, and in the uncomfortable atmosphere he froze" (Hammond, p. 161).

The experience was salutary for Goodman. He undertook more serious study of the work. After a successful concert performance in a CBS broadcast of December 11, 1937, with the Coolidge Quartet, and a single movement also played with them on January 18, 1938, Goodman was better prepared for a second try. His recording in the New York Victor studios on April 25, 1938, with the Budapest Quartet, proved a musical and public success. And Goodman *did* actually play the Mozart Quintet at Mills College—but with the Budapest Quartet, and in August 1939.

Goodman's development of a "classical side" continued. He recorded the Mozart Quintet twice again (with the American Art Quartet in 1951 and the Boston String Quartet, 1956), adding a concert performance at Stratford, Ontario, in 1965 (broadcast by CBS). Of the Brahms Clarinet Quintet, Goodman gave only a partial performance in a CBS telecast of November 6, 1960, with the Fine Arts Quartet. Goodman would go on to record Mozart's Clarinet Concerto (1938, not released; then again in 1956), as well as the two Clarinet Concertos of Carl Maria von Weber (1967, 1968); he also did Carl Nielsen's Clarinet Concerto (1966).

In twentieth-century music, he was distinctly active. In 1938 he recorded Debussy's Rhapsody for Clarinet and Orchestra, with John Barbirolli. In 1951 he participated in Leonard Bernstein's recording for Columbia of Milhaud's *La création du monde*. Goodman was also active in promoting new works. With Joseph Szigeti, he commissioned what became Béla Bartók's *Contrasts* [originally Rhapsody] for clarinet, violin, and piano, of which he made the definitive recording, along with Szigeti and the composer, in 1940. In 1947 he also commissioned Aaron Copland's Clarinet Concerto, recording it with the composer only in 1963, for Columbia. Goodman participated in a classic recording of Stravinsky's jazz-inspired *Ebony Concerto* for Columbia (1965).

We return, for our purposes, to the dating of Goodman's abortive attempt at the Mozart Quintet, left so obscurely reported as "about a year later" after the 1935 private performance. From what is documented of the quartet's performance schedules, the group was nowhere near Chicago in late 1936. They were in Chicago, however, in February 1937, for a Beethoven Quartet cycle. Such a timing might seem feasible. We do know that the Pro Arte was in Chicago in February of 1938, but that seems too close to the recording that April with the Budapest Quartet: Goodman would have needed more time to prepare himself in between.

In fact, scraps of newspaper evidence help clarify the picture. A small notice published in the *Chicago Daily Tribune* on Thursday, April 30, 1936, reports that the Pro Arte Quartet would be Goodman's guests when he played in the Eddie Dowling broadcast review on Tuesday evening, May 5, after which they would all repair to the RCA studies to record the Mozart Quintet. Another notice, even smaller, and retrospective, appeared in the suburban *Belvedere Daily Republican* on May 20, saying that the quartet had flown from New York City for purposes of making the recording—no reference made to its failure.

Now, those reports conflict with Goodman's recollections, already quoted, that he arrived in a scramble on the morning of the recording session, held shortly thereafter. Some failure in his memory might be the explanation for that conflict. (And his memory that he was carrying over from the last—jazz—performance a reed not suited to Mozart might fit the situation of rushing from the Dowling broadcast to the Victor studios.) Searches of newspapers in the Wisconsin area provide no report of Goodman's presence or appearance in the state on May 4, 1936. On the contrary, announcement is made in the *Wisconsin State Journal* of Sunday May 3 that Goodman and his band would appear at the Orpheum Theater in Madison on Wednesday and Thursday, May 6 and 7!

At any rate, it would seem that Van Malderen was correct in her surmise about the date of the recording session, if not the venue. After all this tortuous argumentation, we can now date that unfortunate episode to Tuesday, May 5, 1936, in Chicago.

Two questions linger. In human terms, what did the Pro Arte players, instruments in hand, actually do with themselves after Goodman walked out? And were their expenses paid?

# APPENDIX B

# Two Novels

Many string quartets have had books written about them. These are, to one extent or another, factual accounts, some press agentry aside. Among the many unique things about the Pro Arte Quartet is that it is perhaps alone in being the inspiration for fictional writing, especially by one of a group's members.

## Bernard Milofsky

In the course of his career as a brilliant violist and as member of the Pro Arte String Quartet, Bernard Milofsky conceived the idea of writing fiction. He took a few courses at the University of Wisconsin in creative writing, and at some point began writing a novel. It was about the travails of a string quartet and its members, and it was given the title of *Fiddlers Four*. Milofsky continued to work on it after he left Wisconsin. He was engaged in the project in 1962 and in 1964, when he was given encouragement in letters from Rudolf Kolisch. As the work continued thereafter, Milofsky was eventually joined in some of the writing by his son David. A publication-ready manuscript was prepared, under the title first of *The Fiddlers Four* and then of *The Casa Bella Quartet*. Through a series of two agents in New York, it was submitted to more than one publisher, but was never accepted. In its final form, it remains unpublished.

In the collection of Mills Music Library at the University of Wisconsin–Madison there is a volume of 708 pages in typescript, indicated as a draft entitled *Fiddlers Four: A Novel*, heavily revised, as of 1960. This was edited and personally typed by James Crow in 1995, two years after Milofsky's death.

The history of this typescript is full of questions. It clearly represented an early form of the novel, as it was taking shape. As such, it cannot be accepted as a full representation of the novel as finally written. James Crow was a distinguished professor of genetics at the University of Wisconsin–Madison, and an amateur violist of considerable skill. He undertook some studies with Milofsky in his Madison years and the two became good friends. After Milofsky stopped playing, he bequeathed his viola to Crow, who used it lovingly for his own playing. The friendship, and contacts, continued after Milofsky moved to Pennsylvania. In 1996, three years after Milofsky's death, Crow and his wife Ann were joined by David Milofsky in commissioning a piece in memory of the deceased violist, performed on November 1, 1997.

Just how or when Crow obtained this preliminary draft of the novel is not at all clear. Perhaps it was a gift from the author to his young friend, but there is no evidence that the two ever discussed it, and Milofsky's family seem to have had no knowledge of it. When Bernard's son David Milofsky examined the typescript in the Mills Library in 2013, he professed outrage. He insisted that it did not represent the novel as finally completed, by then bearing the title of *The Casa Bella Quartet*. He has insisted that Crow, his family's former friend, had no right to prepare the version he made of a very primitive draft, totally on his own, without family permission. He also suggested that a number of people in Madison were biased in favor of Crow, to the discredit of his father, about whom inaccurate information was being disseminated.

Crow obviously did not use any of Bernard Milofsky's continued work on the novel, and that fact is a handicap to trusting it. Yet Crow undertook the toil of going through the 1960 manuscript and typing up an edited version of it as a gesture of admiration and affection for his old friend. That Crow's 1995 edition represents a preliminary effort at the novel is obvious, and it is quite understandable that David Milofsky should wish to protect his father's mature work. He has insisted that the Crow draft—"pirated" and "bowdlerized"—is quite unrepresentative of the finished and "final" draft submitted for publication. A clear examination of that issue is, however, impossible at present, since access to the latter has been emphatically denied.

All of which leaves us with the Crow version. Bernard Milofsky's novel, as he planned it, was a reflection of his experience with the Pro Arte Quartet. Its leading character, while it may have touches of self-portrait, is based in many ways on Rudolf Kolisch, though most of the actions described, especially those involving personal hostilities and violence, are very much a matter of imagination. That will emerge clearly in the following summary of the Crow draft—which is discussed simply as that draft of 1960 and, perforce, not at all a definitive or "final" version intended by the original author.

ৰ্চ  ৰ্চ  ৰ্চ

The Crow version is organized in three books, subdivided into chapters. At least in this version, the books bear the titles of "Furiant," "Deliriando," and "Le Streghe [The Witches]." The novel is cast as *The Journal of the Casa Bella Quartet* by one William Esca, who is the observer of most, if not all, of the events.

Book 1, the longest of the three, begins with an account of the young Viennese violinist and composer Marcus Otto, who falls in love with all of the three women who give a performance of his String Trio: violinist Maia von Eber, violist Andrea Dante, and cellist Olga Hallant. With them he forms a string quartet that, over the course of twenty years after a Berlin debut, becomes the world's greatest, playing from memory. Esca first encounters the quartet around 1934, when he makes a recording of them. He meets them again in 1939, by which time Esca has a lovely wife, much younger than himself, the pianist Theodora (Thede). When the quartet finds itself stranded in the Western Hemisphere, Esca is invited to become their manager, and his home in New York City (Casa Bella) becomes home for them all.

When they are to play at a wedding on September 7, 1950, violist Andrea fails to appear, and the shattering news comes of her death. Its mysterious circumstances will haunt the quartet thereafter: was it an accident? suicide? The players visit her grieving family. Unable to find a violist of equal merit, they agree to form a piano quartet, with Maia on viola and Thede on piano. There are musical and personal tensions over Thede, and she begins an affair with Otto. Plans are made for a tour, and during it strains grow: Thede's behavior is increasingly selfish and irresponsible. Limits to her playing and her memory emerge. In Newark there is participation in an exciting performance of Mozart's *Sinfonia concertante*. Oboist Frank La Presti is added to the ensemble. Just as Andrea's journal (in Italian) arrives, Esca is worried about his heart troubles, and leaves the tour to return to New York.

Book 2 opens as the tour continues: Thede takes up with Frank along the way. In Chicago, Otto and Olga prepare to solo in a performance of Brahms's Double Concerto; there are heightened tensions in rehearsals. The performance is magnificent, but Otto has a tiny memory lapse, dropping out five notes in the finale. This is devastating for him, and is followed by some physical breakdowns among the players. It comes out that Mamma Dante (Andrea's mother) is dying; Maia makes a suicide attempt; Otto is near death for a while. As the tour resumes, on a road to San Diego, a flood sweeps away their van, with all their instruments, as well as the piano technician's son—who has been Thede's latest lover. While in California, the players participate in some scrappy movie projects.

Book 3 finds Esca translating Andrea's journal; he visits the Dantes and obtains her papers. Esca's further reading of the diary reveals a number of shocks (her brother Tomasso's sexual exploitation of her, and her subsequent misery). Mamma Dante dies. Esca goes to his estate in Maine, where he finds more tormenting revelations in the journal (the failure of Andrea's affair with Otto). The quartet members arrive: Maia reports on Thede's behavior. There is a terrible rehearsal, and the journal's revelations about Andrea's death are exposed, indicating Thede's responsibility. A violent climax ensues: Otto is knocked out, and Olga is fatally stabbed in a tussle with Thede, who smashes through a window to fall to her death. The aftermath is all desolation and emptiness.

❧   ❧   ❧

Clearly, as the Crow version indicates, at least the novel's early state had only glancing relationships to the facts of the Pro Arte's situation and of Kolisch's life. Milofsky was trying out his novelist's license to let his imagination run freely, very freely. Just how much was altered in the later and final drafts of the novel, however, cannot be determined at this time.

## David Milofsky

The second son of Bernard Milofsky, born in 1946, David Milofsky is a Professor of English at Colorado State University, specializing in the teaching of writing. He was educated partly at the University of Wisconsin, and has become a active writer of both fiction (four novels) and nonfiction, as well as a journalist and broadcaster.

His second novel, *Playing from Memory*, was published in 1981 in New York by Simon and Schuster. Both his father and his mother, Ruth, were still alive at that time, and David included a note in the book as follows: "I would like to acknowledge the contributions of my father, Bernard Milofsky. Some of the musical scenes in this book are based on his unpublished novel *The Fiddler's Four* [*sic*]. I am grateful to him for his advice and support." The novel, some 270 pages long, is divided into five parts, which are subdivided into a total of forty-four chapters.

~6 ~6 ~6

The brief first chapter opens at the end of a concert by a string quartet in Chicago, when the second violinist, Ben Seidler, blacks out and falls, but quickly recovers. The quartet's first violinist, Heinz Ober, is concerned about this, in the light of similar recent incidents. It is noted that Ober is a left-handed violinist, and is a champion of Reich's orgone box.

In chapter 3 Ben is recovering, amid the anxieties of his wife, Dory. Left alone, Ben recalls his background. Despite the disapproval by his father, Moshe, of a professional musical career, Ben had trained at the Peabody and Curtis schools. At twenty-eight, while still freelancing, he was at the musicians' union hall and was sought out by Heinz Ober, who had taken over the Casa Bella Quartet "when the old guy died." Short, distinctive, arrogant, Ober had trained in Vienna, "[had] known Schönberg and was a close friend of Bartók." Ober had grilled Ben as a possible recruit, warning him of the difficulties and hard work involved, including the necessity of playing from memory: "We must have our attention free to concentrate on the music and on one another. To play as an ensemble, it is important that we know each other intimately. In any case, if you don't really know a composition, you have no business playing it in public." Ober is described as "an enigma. Avuncular one moment, imperious the next." Ben was offered membership under Ober, and promptly accepted.

Ben recalls how much learning and experience he gained under Ober: "Then there were the rehearsals. Day after day, week after week, for months, years, Ober was never satisfied. Repeatedly he stopped to criticize one player or another. At turns biting and sarcastic, he could also be sweet, wheedling, or imploring, his goal always to goad them into playing better than they knew they could." There were tours, recordings, and talk of academic tenure. Reflections ended, Ben goes to a postconcert reception.

Chapter 4 finds Ben and Dory visiting her Baptist grandfather in Kentucky, where they inspect family graves. Dory is worried about Ben's recent fall. Recollections are renewed. Ben and Dory had met in 1947 after his first season as artist-in-residence at the University of Wisconsin: the others being violist Antoine Beaulieu and cellist Ernst Richler. After lingering in Madison, Ben had traveled east to seek a wife. He was introduced to Dory, who was studying pottery. After a botched meeting in Manhattan, they drifted into a muddled courtship, culminating in a Labor Day weekend together on Long Island. There was confusion, and Ben, worried about his family situation, stopped to see them in Washington: their reactions to his love for Dory were tense. Back in Madison, Ober was cynical. Ben proposed to Dory by phone; in Washington that November, she visited Moshe's tailor shop. In December, Ben and Dory married in New York, her happiness clouded by apprehensions. Now, back in the present, in the light of the recent accident, plans for a January vacation at Wisconsin Dells are spoiled by Ben's need to see Ober's doctor.

In Chapter 5, Ben is given a diagnosis of multiple sclerosis. This explains his deteriorating vision and his difficulties in walking. Naturally, it has serious implications for the future. In agitation, Ben drives home to find Dory (now a student of the philandering teacher Sam) in her studio (which is full of images of Ben). The news is clearly frightening. Ober is noncommittal about the future. Ben visits other multiple sclerosis patients, some scary, one, the helpless Mrs. Barrow, inspiring sympathetic misery over her advanced stage.

Part 2 begins with chapters 6–8. Ill and discontented, Moshe regrets ten years of separation from Ben and his family. Despite the contempt of his wife, Sarah, Moshe resolves to go to Wisconsin, his hopes high. A surprised Ben meets his father and, from his office in Music Hall, telephones Dory, who is alarmed. Moshe joins the family, and draws out from Ben information about the latter's condition. There are tensions, partly relieved by games of checkers. Moshe develops a particular closeness to Ben's elder son, Michael. Amid Dory's worries about failed efforts to investigate Madison's Jewish community and life, Moshe proposes holding a *Shabbos* (Sabbath) service. In full devotional mode, he tries to explain it all to the boys, and the prayers go well.

Chapter 9: Dory begins a diary (May 20, 1957), after a failed childhood experience at it, this time for private thoughts that others might read. May 28, 1957: sadness over Moshe's departure. June 11, 1957: worries that she and Ben are excluding each other; concerns for her fingers in the heat. June 17, 1957: sparring with Sam; her loneliness, diminished sexuality. June 23, 1957: feelings of inadequacy as both artist and isolated mother. July 3, 1957: difficulties with Ben's condition, fears of worse; their reduced intimacy. July 18, 1957: embarrassment over a urine jar in the car's glove compartment. August 5, 1957: tensions with Sam. August 27, 1957: the situation is improved, with two teaching jobs in prospect.

Chapter 10: Ben is taking physical therapy, but has difficulty walking to a local watering hole and conducting small talk. Tensions are developing with Ober: Ben refuses to think of resigning from the quartet, but takes on some university composing work, producing an "unplayable" violin sonata; he is optimistic about future alternatives, even on the stock market. In October, Dory is anxious about how much her sons—the sporty Michael, the independent, chess-playing Charles—understand about their father's condition, which she tries to explain to Michael.

Chapter 11 pictures the professional strains on Ben, notably an eighteen-week season at the university followed by touring on the east coast, with some recording activity in New York.

> For the most part Ober's strategy was successful: under his leadership the Casa Bella had become one of the most acclaimed American string quartets. Yet even this did not satisfy Ober. Now he wanted to tour Europe and the Far East (p. 85).

> . . . In fact, Ober's long hours of practice were intended specifically to weed out any idiosyncratic tendencies his musicians might have had. Interpretation was between Ober and the composer, and the composer was usually safely dead (p. 90).

These rehearsals were relentless, totally commandeering time to achieve perfection, much to the resentment of the two old-timers, Richler and Beaulieu, who were themselves at odds with each other. Ober himself was contemptuous of the tall but lower-class Richler, while Beaulieu was strongly anti-Semitic. Both looked down upon Ben, the American Jew. But all were drawn together in scorn for their School of Music colleagues and for Wisconsin audiences. The touring was particularly stressful for Ben, eliciting his rigorous physical self-discipline. In Chicago, on their return trip, Ober compliments Ben for improved playing. In the second

half of a Chicago Symphony concert, Ben and Richler are highly competitive soloists in the Brahms Double Concerto. The performance is
brilliant, but in the finale Ben falters briefly, dropping five notes. There
are ugly recriminations with Richler afterward, but Ober remains silent
amid a swarm of audience greeters. Escaping to an alley with Ben, Ober
raises questions about the effects of the latter's disease; to prove his fit-
ness, Ben goes off running on his own.

Chapter 12: Moshe, no longer tied to work, continues travels to
California and then back east. In a brief, angry return to Washington,
he sells his shop, and separates from Sarah (who goes to Miami). In
Madison in early summer, he adopts "western" cowboy garb and buys
the two boys the same outfits. Leaving for Boston (from the much-
expanded Madison airport), he asks about Ben's health and offers to
help, perhaps to move there.

Beginning part 3, chapter 13 returns to Dory's diary. June 23,
1958: new family strains amid fears over Ben's declining confidence,
and worries about their sons. June 25, 1958: still smarting over his
Brahms slip, Ben is practicing extensively and frenetically; still, moods
are better. Ben's has improved activities with the boys: chess and din-
ing at Cuba Club with Charles, baseball in Milwaukee with Michael.
July 10, 1958: restlessness in summer heat. July 16, 1957: she and Ben
are sleeping apart, with empty sex, despite memories of their original
sensuality; she worries about the future as her youth wanes. July 17,
1958: the situation is now reversed and feelings are revived.

Chapter 14: Ben struggles up the Music Hall steps to Ober's office.
Ober has resented Ben's marriage as ending his friendship with Ben.
There is a tense discussion of pressures by the School of Music for the
ailing Ben to be dropped from the quartet. Furious at the offer of a
"sabbatical" to ease him out, Ben resigns on the spot.

Chapters 15–16 trace the deepening crisis. Ben contacts friends,
plans possible jobs. Dory is appalled at moving to Tulsa, and maybe
San Francisco afterward. His hands trembling, Ben is ready to go on
alone. Dory becomes understanding; there is an agonizing departure,
during which Ben slips on a train step. Alone and at loose ends, Dory
works at her art, now using metal. Sam belittles her work, demands
better, driving her away in fury.

Chapter 17 contains letters. November 19, 1958. Ben to Dory:
things are working out with playing in Tulsa; his concern about the
boys, and about her. Ben to Charles, playing postal chess. Ben to

Michael with baseball talk. November 23, 1958. Dory to Ben, giving assurances, if with worries about Michael.

Chapter 18: at night, with weakened vision, Dory collapses in the bathroom. The boys help her dial a doctor who brushes her off; she calls Sam, who comes to help; with dawn, her vision renews, and she yields herself to Sam.

Chapter 19 shows Ben with mounting bladder problems during his orchestral work in Tulsa, welcoming relief in his apartment. Joe, a bootlegger comes, becoming a visitor for revealing conversation but then mockery; Joe flees, leaving Ben lonely.

In chapters 20–21 the marital crisis is faced. Dory and Sam are now lovers, and he has become a family fixture with the boys. On Valentine's Day there is a conflicted discussion of the future. At the train station, Dory meets Ben, who seems the same but looks older. He is solitary, finds difficulty readjusting to Madison without the quartet. He sends Dory a note announcing his removal from the household, making cold phone-calls to the boys. Contacted, Moshe responds and visits: when Dory confesses her conduct, Moshe seeks assurances of her loyalty to Ben and promises help. Ben, meanwhile, is restless in the Belmont Hotel. Suspicious, he discovers Dory's affair. Sam has left, and cannot be confronted. Moshe comes, talking of Sarah and urging continuing marriage. Ben agrees to meet Dory. She arrives in great anxiety and doubt: she apologizes, attempts justification; they argue, but come to understand and recognize their mutual need. Ben is finished as a performer. Dory obtains a position in Milwaukee, to which they move. Sam avoids her, but she calls him for a wrenching farewell.

Beginning part 4, chapter 22 again draws on Dory's diary. October 16, 1960: now homebound, Ben reads and composes, and, though weaker, manages the cooking; the boys make new friends in new schools; Dory finds satisfaction in teaching and wins promotion. December 1, 1960: Dory now sleeps alone, and has more time of her own. January 8, 1961: the boys show new anxieties. February 16, 1961: Ben's anger (over a urine bottle, a paradox, since she is supporting him). March 22, 1961: she faces difficulties with men at school, and discrimination. April 11, 1961: reflections on health and aging. April 14, 1961: remembering a deceased radical friend, she regrets her absorption in her own struggles. May 5, 1961: Ben falls, breaking a tooth; she wishes he were more angry. June 5, 1961: the term over, she borrows a studio for the summer, where she thinks about the surrounding black population; summer liberation for her is suffering for Ben. June 10, 1961: Ben and the boys are in declining health and spirits.

Chapters 23–24: Moshe, on a forty-five-day tour of the country by rail, stops in Milwaukee, where he had gotten a nice house for Ben and his family; while Dory is on her summer work binge, Moshe spends time with the boys, and talks with Ben before leaving. Dory returns late in the evenings, angering Ben, who, bitter in his loneliness, threatens the exhausted Dory with divorce. The next day, when she returns home on time, Dory finds that Ben has gone to the Knickerbocker Hotel; she confronts him there and he seems to accept returning.

Chapter 25: Dory establishes regular evening hours; more understanding, Ben is back to work at composition. He is suddenly visited by Ober, who updates him: a certain Barry is the "new baby" in the quartet; but now, as associate professors and not artists in residence, the players find that the load of classes and committees reduces their "individuality"; Beaulieu and Richler want tenure, while Ober needs to retire, at the cost of losing his touring quartet. Ober tells Ben of Howard Jacoby's Young Musicians organization as perhaps a teaching opportunity; Ben considers this, and promises postal chess with Ober.

Chapter 26: Ben is appointed to Jacoby's group, causing excitement. In a positive meeting with Jacoby, arrangements are made for his first students to form a quartet: one student is cellist Julie Barker; but first violinist Roger Sherman is clearly the best of them; to prepare for conservatory, Roger asks for private lessons with Ben, who is first reluctant but agrees. Dory hires Lucile Plavy as housekeeper.

Chapter 27 returns to Dory's diary. March 11, 1962: she worries over Michael's isolation and hostility toward Ben. April 3, 1962: Michael is bitterly jealous of Roger, and resent's Dory's absence. April 21, 1962: worries over Charles's aloofness and lack of expression. May 16, 1962: weaker, Ben is more wheelchair-bound, a failure at sex, and anguished. June 8, 1962: Roger is now a surrogate family member, though in reduced tension with Michael's questions about his future.

Chapter 28: Ober visits, chatting up housekeeper Lucile; Ober hints that things are bad in Madison; discussion of Ben's students. Jacoby agrees on a concert for them in November: Ben works with them, on his own new pieces; they are improving, and enthusiastic. Before the concert, in a backstage wheelchair, Ben observes their warmup: Roger is intense, just as Ben had been; second violin Sally Freeman is paralyzed by terror, but Ben reassures her. Listening to the concert, he is pleased with his students' professionalism at their stage of growth. The audience is so enthusiastic that Ben is obliged to face an ovation given for him, with Ober, Dory, and Moshe sitting in the front row.

More of Dory's diary in Chapter 29. December 11, 1962: revitalized by the concert, Ben feels new excitement about music and the future; he ponders taking his student quartet on tour, in the fashion of the Casa Bella, becoming something of an Ober himself. Frustrated at hopes for tenure, Dory confronts her stagnant situation. January 4, 1963: Ben has a relapse but continues to work with his students. February 16, 1963: winter is depressing, family cohesion has waned, nostalgia is sad. February 21, 1963: Dory senses life has diminished, leaving only memories. February 24, 1963: she ponders how totally she has been shaped by men; younger women, whom she envies for their youth, esteem her as "a success in a man's world," but she finds their respect no substitute for "compassion, intimacy, love." March 1, 1963: with signs of spring, things appear not so bad; despite dismal future prospects, Dory and Ben still manage and keep trying.

Chapter 30: while Michael avoids them, Ben works intensively through the summer with Roger toward an audition for Juilliard, which is important for both of them. Jacoby arranges a solo recital for Roger, which is well received; but Ben remains doubtful through the winter. He sends Roger to work with Ober in Madison; Roger is reluctant, but returns grateful. There are arguments over how to handle the venture to New York: through a friend there, Ben monitors their audition. It is initially a cliff-hanger, then the decision is negative; an alternate training is arranged at Oberlin Conservatory. Crushed, convinced the failure was his, Ben offers his resignation to Jacoby, who reassures him and revives Ben's interest in other quartet students; but Ben feels he had relived his own youth through the now-accepting Roger.

More of Dory's diary in chapter 31. April 12, 1967: on her forty-eighth birthday, Ben prepares an elaborate and generous private celebration, greatly moving for her. April 15, 1967: Michael's mood has shifted dramatically; he makes plans at the university. May 13, 1967: relations are good with the boys—Charles tall and handsome, Michael attentive, interested in his parents' past. June 6, 1967: Michael graduates, while Dory worries about what he will become, and is afraid of his feelings. July 15, 1967: Michael has a summer job in construction, and a used car provided by Moshe; Dory is proud of his manliness. September 9, 1967: she brings Michael to Madison for study at the University, feeling loss but pride. October 2, 1967: Dory delights in the unexpected receipt of tenure. October 26, 1967: a doctor suggests that the progress of Ben's disease is arrested, but he needs therapy, and he is much reduced physically (and his beard has gone white); nevertheless, still with students, his composition, his chess, Ben has adjusted to his separation from playing; optimism prevails.

Part 5 is opened by chapter 32: Dory is reduced to serving coffee and cookies at a faculty reception for a visiting artist, with whom she converses about travel and status. Sam appears, and Dory goes out with him for drinks. He reproaches her for her failure to communicate, and she defends her choice in Ben's favor; he is lonely and dissatisfied with his success; they agree to talk again, and she leaves him to brood.

Back to Dory's journal in chapter 33: November 20, 1970: out with a cold, she worries that in her absence she is failing her students. November 22, 1970: she is finding satisfaction in yoga. November 24. 1970: reflecting on meeting Sam, she wonders if she has conveyed to him her admiration and gratitude. November 26, 1970: she makes reluctant preparations for Thanksgiving, to which Michael (now happy, more mature) will come with a girlfriend, Ricky. November 29, 1970: Dory had not liked the bourgeois and "prissy" Ricky; reflections on her not leaving Ben, a more interesting man than Sam, whom she finds in a worse state than her own. December 2, 1970: she is showing more warmth to her colleagues now. Are academics more alone than others? December 10, 1970: she is involved in committees, one on student conduct; she has mixed feelings about the new generation of young radicals. December 15, 1970: bogged down in work, she is looking forward to a family Christmas.

Chapter 34: Ben encourages the frustrated cellist, Julie Barker; reflecting on his situation, he is glad to be out of the old quartet life. Wondering how he ever managed as a player, he is still devoted to music, and regrets his isolation. Pleading illness, violinist Sally Freeman cancels a class. With the afternoon free, and Dory not on hand, Ben contemplates a cigar, but he remembers the fire he had started with one. He has no feeling in his immobile legs, though his penis is still fine. He finds he feels closer to Michael than Charles: Michael calls: they banter over his condition, and there are questions about a check; Ben appreciates his concern and attention, though is bothered by his lack of respect. He takes a cigar after all, but the match falls, a fire starts, and, failing to stop it, he grabs for the telephone.

Chapter 35: Ben is in the hospital, burned mainly on his legs, not critically. Dory visits him while he is sedated; coming the next day, she reproaches him, but with continuing affection. He is in a ward with others: a black man whose wife caught him with another woman and scalded him with boiling water, and a swollen-fisted farmer.

Chapters 36–38: Charles and Michael argue about the possible need to institutionalize Ben; Dory points out how bad most homes would be, though she is willing to consider a Jewish retirement facility. Michael insists that he quit the University of Wisconsin and his job to take care of Ben at home, even at the cost of his relationship with Ricky; as Michael drives Charles to the airport there are tensions ending in truce. With Ricky gone, Michael vacates his room in Madison. Ben is back home, with a bedsore; he and Michael banter, discuss death and funerary desires—there will be no funeral or memorial, only a family playing of his records and tapes; cremation, with his ashes on the mantel. Michael had youthful difficulties in understanding what his father did, or was, and it was Roger who had to show him. Ben is taken to the hospital with infected bedsores; he has radical hip surgery and endures a difficult recovery. Dory's visits between home and university are draining: she is miserable, while Ben feels guilt. Michael visits also. Ben dreams about those missing five notes in Brahms, and about Ober's craze for memorization, and reflects on how good a musician he had been.

Chapters 39 gives more of Dory's journal. March 5, 1971: everyone is under strain. March 8, 1971: the sense of isolation is terrible. March 12, 1971: frustration over poor communication with the insensitive Charles. March 16, 1970: Ben has mouth sores from the antibiotics; clergymen and well-wishers besiege him, while he jokes with the nurses.

Chapter 40: the spruced-up Moshe visits, replacing the exhausted Michael in attending Ben. Moshe is finished with travels and is with Sarah once more. Ben is too tired to talk.

Chapter 41 returns to the diary: March 18, 1971: with Michael and Moshe there, the house is a mess. March 20, 1971: daily rotation of visits to Ben by Lucile Plavy, Michael, and Dory. March 22, 1971: Dory remembers sitting with the dying all through her life; she pities those who die without someone close in attendance. Ben suffers, but clings to life, remembers Dory as young. March 26, 1971: as she watches courting squirrel pairs over breakfast, Dory misses Ben; she still feels left out by Ben's family, while Moshe is upset at the prospect of burying a son. March 29, 1971: Ben must be dying. The infection is worse, and more surgery may be required; his consciousness limited, he will not eat. Desperate for whatever time is left, Dory hopes to get an overnight cot.

Chapter 42: Given a room in the nurses dormitory, Dory cancels classes, and spends days with Ben reading; the doctor gives little cheer about medication. In loving conversation, Ben expresses gratitude to her for bringing him back to family life; they recollect their courting and first meeting, and reflect on doing and having so much. Ben regrets that his death means the loss of togetherness with her.

Chapter 43: Ben's funeral is held in Madison. A Reform rabbi presides, while Moshe, who shuns the non-Orthodox, sits *shiva* at home. Roger brings Ben's creation, the Seidler Quartet, from Ohio to play Schubert's *Death and the Maiden*. Ober delivers a eulogy, and the student quartet players perform one of the pieces Ben wrote for them. There is a reception at which some of Ben's recordings are played. With Jacoby, Dory greets Beaulieu and Richler, and consoles Sally. She leaves, exhausted, and Sam approaches her outside for an awkward conversation.

Chapter 44: in conclusion, Dory's diary. April 3, 1971: Dory finds it difficult to think of Ben as gone. The memories of him are imperishable, so many little things; perhaps the disease drew them closer to each other than they would have been. Alone and lonely, she has no regrets. April 11, 1971: on her fifty-second birthday, while Michael is off to see his girlfriend, and Moshe is back in Florida with Sarah, Dory sits in Ben's room, excavating it, like "an anthropologist." After twenty-three years focused on Ben, what is next? But now she knows that she can live without him.

◄ᴓ  ◄ᴓ  ◄ᴓ

David Milofsky is a skilled professional writer. His novel *Playing from Memory* is marked by variety in narrative structure and in sustaining interest. It is also very rich in detail. That fact, given its reflection on the history of the Pro Arte Quartet, justifies the full, lengthy, and careful summary of it presented above.

This novel gives us, indeed, a mirror into a phase of the quartet's life. Yet, it is inevitably a cloudy mirror. As a novelist, Milofsky has rightly used his imagination to tell a story and not to present history. In conversation, he has asserted that it is not an autobiography, nor a family history. Yet he admits that he has drawn freely on his family life, using its members as models for his characters. He even notes that he used himself as the prototype for the family's younger son, Charles, in the novel. A most notable example of his freedom is his reversal in the novel of the order of his parents' deaths: Ruth Milofsky died in 1982, eleven years before the decease of her husband, in 1993.

David Milofsky has certainly drawn upon facts and memories about the Pro Arte Quartet for his purposes, to a degree that allows him to tease the reader with hints of its actual personalities. The character of Heinz Ober is quite obviously based upon Rudolf Kolisch, whose attitudes, principles, and practices are rather closely mirrored in the novel. Milofsky confirms that his father and Kolisch remained in continuing contact after Bernard's departure from the quartet. The novel's Antoine Beaulieu, violist, and Ernst Richler, cellist, are quite clearly transformations of violinist Albert Rahier and cellist Ernst Friedlander. Milofsky does change his own father's identity as a violist to that of a violinist in the novel.

That shift of instrument points up one opportunity for comparison between Milofsky's treatment of quartet personnel and that of his father's writing, in its problematic Crow version. This regards the incident of the brief memory slip in a performance of the Brahms Double Concerto. Pro Arte players at times did solo stints in concertos, and that Brahms work was such an example. Members of the PAQ are reported as joining with orchestras in performances of it. One instance was a pair of University of Wisconsin Symphony Orchestra concerts on March 10, 1946, when Kolisch and Friedlander played the solos. That was before Bernard Milofsky joined the quartet, and, to be sure, it is not mandatory that we find an explicit factual prototype for fictional purposes. In the Crow version of Bernard's novel, his Kolisch clone, Marcus Otto, and his cellist Olga Gallant play in the performance in which Otto drops five notes in the concerto's finale. David Milofsky has his Ben Seidler play against the Friedlander clone Richler when making the mistake. Here we have the clearest case demonstrating what David admitted from the start: that he had based some incidents on what was in his father's novel. Another demonstration of that, of course, is David's carrying over the name of the Casa Bella Quartet from his father's work.

David Milofsky's novel is, above all, a portrait of a musician and his family, and mostly placed in the period after the character of Ben leaves the quartet in Madison. It gives us a picture of what life must have been like for Bernard Milofsky in the decades of his "retirement." Again, that picture must be perceived as through the veil of fiction.

It does bring to life much of what we know of Bernard's tempestuous personality. Above all, it is powerful portrayal, however fictionalized, that suggests touchingly how the factual Bernard Milofsky was able to salvage useful musical activity out of his declining health.

This novel is a kind of testimony to Bernard Milofsky's life. But it creates a complimentary portrait—one that all but "steals the show"—of Ruth Milofsky, the obvious model for the character of Dory. Ruth Milofsky was a woman of remarkable personality and strength. In her self-sacrifice and self-assertion as the support for her family, her son found the basis for Dory, who is the triumphant heroine and survivor by the time the book concludes.

On that count, David Milofsky's novel is not only of interest for the study of the Pro Arte Quartet: it is also a moving work of fiction.

# APPENDIX C

# The Contemporary
# Music Project (1984–86)

In the autumn of 1984 the University of Wisconsin Graduate School
awarded the Pro Arte a grant enabling it to solicit submissions of
chamber compositions, in line with the group's intense commitment
to new music. The scores submitted would be studied by the quartet,
and any deemed worthy of attention could be programmed for performance. A small advertisement was placed in one musical journal,
with the expectation that the response would be modest. Instead,
an eventual total of 150 submissions were made by 147 composers
(some submitting two or more compositions). A number of submissions were belated, but are reckoned among the total elicited by the
announcement.

The list of submissions is given below. It is interesting simply for
the range of composers who responded, which varies from totally
obscure musicians to composers of very considerable stature by that
time—e.g., Milton Babbitt, John Cage, Henry Cowell, George Crumb,
Ross Lee Finney, Otto Leuning, Quincy Porter, Seymour Shifrin (posthumously), Karl Weigl (also posthumously), and Charles Wuorinen,
not to mention Igor Stravinsky's son Soulima. Some composers, too,
were represented by other works in the quartet's programs. Perusal
of the names on the list reveals a number of curiosities. Noticeable is
the large number of Czech and Slovak composers who made submissions—an indication of the contacts that Paulu and his quartet had
developed with that musical world, and a harbinger of the group's
later tour there in October of 1987.

As it worked out, only two works (one each by Fred Lerdahl and
Elliot Weisgarber) can be traced in subsequent Pro Arte programs.

A capstone to the project came in June 2–14, 1986, when the quartet launched what was titled "The First Contemporary String Quartet Symposium and Festival in Madison." (In point of fact, there never was a "Second" or any other such event.) Guest participants in this gathering proved to have no relation those who had submitted scores made a year-and-a-half before. The composers involved were: Stephen Dembski (of the UW faculty), Ramon Zupko of Kalamazoo, Michigan; Thomas Oboe Lee of West Somerville, Massachusetts; Richard Moryl of Roxbury, Connecticut; John Lennon of Knoxville Tennessee; Mario Pelosi of Portland, Oregon; Daniel Perlongo of Indians, Pennsylvania, and Charles Porter of Brooklyn, New York. Also participating were two "laureate" composers, Karel Husa and Andrew Imbrie.

Here now is the list of composers and their works submitted to the 1984 solicitation, as documented in the Mills Library archives):

Adams, Daniel (b. 1956). *Transformation in Three Movements* (1979)
Alexander, Williams (b. 1927). String Quartet no. 2, "Sarum" (1940)
Babbitt, Milton (1916–2011). String Quartet no. 3 (1972)
Babbitt, Milton. String Quartet no. 4 (1976)
Barney, Uri (?). String Quartet (1976)
Bassett, Leslie (1923–2016). String Quartet no. 4 (1982)
Beerman, Burton (b. 1943). *Misogamy* (1969)
Beerman, Burton. *Four in Six*, for String Quartet (1973)
Borwick, Douglas Bruce (b. 1952). *Dialogues*, for Two Violins, Viola, and Cello
    (1970)
Boury, Robert Wade (b. 1946). String Quartet in G Major (1984)
Boykan, Martin (b. 1931). String Quartet no. 3 (1984?)
Bresnick, Martin (b. 1946). String Quartet no. 2, "Bucephalus" (1984)
Brooks, Richard (b. 1942). String Quartet (1970)
Bulow, Harry T. (b. 1951). *Densities*, for String Quartet (1981)
Burlas, Ladislav (b. 1927). *Kadencia*, for Solo Violin (1974)
Cage, John (1912–1992). *String Quartet in Four Parts* (1960)
Caltabiano, Ronald (b. 1959). String Quartet (1984)
Carl, Robert (b. 1954). *Path between Cloud and Light*, for String Quartet (1985)
Černik, Vratislav Petr (b. ?). *Punkva*, Fantasy for Solo Violin 1982)
Chihara, Paul (b. 1938). *Primavera*, for String Quartet (1979)
Con, Karel (?). *Ticha posta*, for String Quartet (1985)
Cone, Edward (1917–2004). Capriccio for String Quartet (1981)
Cowell, Henry (1897–1965). String Quartet no. 5 (1962)
Cowell, Henry. String Quartet no. 4 "United" (1966)
Cowell, Henry. *Quartet Romantic; Quartet Euphometric* (1974)
Crumb, George (b. 1929). *Black Angels* (Images 1), *Electric String Quartet* (1971)
Dahlquist, Jack (b. ?). String Quartet no. 2, in three movements (1981)
Davis, Donald Ray (b. 1957). String Quartet, 1983

Dedman, Malcolm (b. 1948). String Quartet, 1977–79
DeFotis, William (b. 1953). *Two Pieces for String Quartet* (1981)
Devátý, Antonín (b. 1903). String Quartet no. 2 (1983)
Dresher, Paul (b. 1951). *Casa vecchia* (1982)
Dubiel, Joseph (b. 1955). Clarinet Quartet in A (1981)
Eben, Petr (1929–2007). String Quartet (1985)
Elkins, Noam (c. 1966). String Quartet, op. 19 (1981)
Emmert, František (Franz Gregor?). Sonata for Violin and Piano (1981)
Enriquez, Manuel (b. ?). Quartet no. 2 (1983)
Epstein, David (1930–2002). String Quartet (1971)
Euba, Akin (b. 1935). String Quartet (1957)
Feld, Jindřich (1925–2007). String Quartet no. 5 (1982)
Felix, Václav (b. 1928). *Quartetto amoroso* (1979)
Fennelly, Brian (1937–2015). *String Quartet in Two Movements* (1971/74)
Fennelly, Brian. *Empirical Rag, Version no. 9* (1981)
Fennelly, Brian. String Quartet no. 2 (1981)
Femeyhough, Brian (b. 1943). Sonatas for String Quartet (1968)
Femeyhough, Brian. String Quartet no. 2 (1981)
Filas, Juraj (b. 1955). *Helios*, Sonata for Violin and Piano (1987)
Finney, Ross Lee (1906–1997). [Title uncertain]
Fišer, Luboš (1935–99). *Quartetto d'archi* (1984)
Fišer, Luboš. Sonata for Solo Violin (1987)
Fisher, Stephen (b. 1940). String Quartet no. 1 (1979)
Frank, Andrew (b. 1946). String Quartet no. 3 (1982)
Grahn, Ulf (b. 1942). String Quartet no. 2 (1979)
Gutchë, Gene (1907–2000). Quartette, op. 29, no. 1 (1963)
Harris, Donald (b. 1931). String Quartet (1965)
Hrusovsky, Ivan (1927–2001). *Three Three-voiced Canons for Violin and Cembalo* (1986)
Jacobi, Frederick (1891–1952). String Quartet no. 3 (1949)
Jacobi, Frederick. *String Quartet on Indian Themes* (1954?)
Jerabek, Pavel b. (?). Sonata for Violin and Piano (1969)
Jirásek, Ivo (1920–2004). String Quartet no. 2, "Ludi con tre toni" (1985)
Johnson, Roger Orville (1929–2000). Quartet no. 1 (1968)
Kalabis, Viktor (1923–2006). String Quartet no. 4, ad honorem J. S. B. (1984)
Karpman, Laura (b. 1959). String Quartet (1980)
King, John (b. 1953). String Quartet no. 3 (1981)
Koch, Frederick (b. ?). String Quartet no. 2 (1964)
Kosut, Michal (b. ?). *Pták fénix* (The Phoenix), for Violin and Piano (1976)
Kraft, Leo (1922–2014). String Quartet no. 2 (1959)
Kramer, Lawrence (b. 1946). *Cantilena*, for String Quartet (1963)
Kreutz (b. 1906). Quartet venuti (19??)
Kubička, Miroslav (b. 1951). *Quartetino* (1980)
Kučera, Václav (b. 1929). *Vedomi souvislosti*: String Quartet in Memory of Vladislav Vančura (1976)
Kurtz, Arthur Digby (b. 1929). String Quartet op. 10/11 (1963)
Kvěch, Otomar (b. 1950). String Quartet no. 4 (1980)

Leclaire, Dennis (b. 1950). String Quartet (19??)

Lefkoff, Gerald (b. 1930). String Quartet no. 2 (1983)

Lerdahl, Fred (b. 1943). String Quartet no. 2 (1980–82)

LeSiege, Annette (b. 1945). Suite no. 2, for String Quartet (1984)

Liang, David Mingyue (b. 1941). *Golden Anniversary String Quartet* (1987)

List, Andrew (b. 1956). String Quartet no. 2, in memoriam Aaron Copland (1893)

Luening, Otto (1900–96). String Quartet no. 2 (1976)

Luening, Otto. String Quartet no. 3 (1978)

Maconchy, Elizabeth (1907–94). String Quartet no. 10 (1976)

Margolis, Jerome N. (b. ?). String Quartet, 1965 (1984)

Mayuzumi, Toshirō (1929–97). *Prelude for String Quartet* (1964)

McKay, Neil (b. 1924). String Quartet no. 1 (1961)

Mead, Andrew Washburn (b. ?). String Quartet (1978)

Mojžíš, Vojtěch (b. 1949). String Quartet no. 2 (1986?)

Neikrug, Marc (b. 1946). Quartet no. 2 (1972)

Nielsen, Erik (b. 1950). *Anamnesis,* for String Quartet (Aug.–Oct. 1982)

Nobre, Marlos (b. 1939). String Quartet no. 1 (1967)

Oakes, Rodney ( b. 1937). *Movements,* for String Quartet (1893)

Očenáš, Andrej (1911–95). *Das Poem vom Herz,* op. 39, for Solo Violin (1970)

Ortiz, William (Alvarado) (b. 1947). String Quartet (1976)

Ostrander, Linda Woodaman (b. 1937). Variations and Theme for String Quartet (1958)

Owens, David (b. 1937). Quartet for Strings (1969)

Owens, David. *Divertissement* for String Quartet (1984)

Payne, Dick (b. ?). *Suite for String Quartet* (1980)

Pelosi, Mario (b. 1951). *Four Movements* for String Quartet (19??

Pelosi, Mario. *Composition for Two Stringed Instruments: A Musical Narrative for Violin and Violincello* (1985?)

Peterson, Wayne (b. 1927). *Transformations,* for String Quartet (1974)

Pizer, Elizabeth Faw Hayden (b. 1954). String Quartet, op. 52 (1981)

Podešva, Jaromir (b. 1927). *Pet kusu,* for Violin and Piano (1967)

Podprocky, Josef (b. 1944). Quartet no. 2 (1982)

Poole, Geoffrey (b. 1949). String Quartet (1983)

Porter, Quincy (1897–1966). String Quartet no. 3 (1963)

Primosch, James (b. 1956). String Quartet (1983)

Reise, Jay (b. 1950). String Quartet no. 2 (1982)

Retzel, Frank (b. 1948). *Schism I,* for String Quartet (1975)

Rhodes, Philip (b. 1940). String Trio (1974)

Rothman, Daniel B. (b. ?). *Wass Nacht an dieser Stimme? In memoriam Primo Levi* (1987)

Salemi, Paul (?). String Quartet (1979)

Salva, Tadeáš (1937–95). *Rozpravky: o zazracnych huslickach samohrajkach* (1987)

Saudek, Vojtěch (1951–2003). String Quartet (1986?)

Sawyer, Eric (b. 1962). String Quartet (1991–92) (1992)

Semiatin, Lionel (1917–2015). String Quartet no. 2: Passacaglia (1945)

Semiatin, Lionel. String Quartet no. 3 (1945)

Serebrier, José (b. 1938). *Fantasia for String Quartet* (1971)

Shifrin, Seymour (1926–79). String Quartet no. 4 (1973)

Shifrin, Seymour. String Quartet no. 3 (1974)

Silver, Sheila (b. 1946). String Quartet (1975)

Smith, Julia (b. 1911). Quartet for Strings (1968)

Standford, Patric (1939–2014). String Quartet no. 1, op. 4 (1977)

Standford, Patric. String Quartet no. 2 (1983)

Steinbert, Carolyn (b. 1956). String Quartet no. 1 (1985)

Steinke, Greg A. (b. 1942). Music for String Quartet (1974)

Stiles, Frank (b. 1942). String Quartet no. 1 (1970)

Stiles, Frank. String Quartet no. 2 (1976)

Stiles, Frank. String Quartet no. 3 (1977)

Stiles, Frank. (b. ?). String Quartet no. 4 (1978)

Stout, Alan (b. 1932). String Quartet no. 10, op. 72, no. 2 (1962)

Stravinsky, Soulima (1910–94). String Quartet (1985)

Tang, Jordan Cho-tung (b. 1948). String Quartet no. 1 (1972)

Taranto, Vernon Anthony Jr. (b. 1946). *Microfantasies*, for String Quartet (1960)

Taub, Bruce J. (b. 1948). Variations for String Quartet (1973)

Tautenhahn, Gunther (1938–2014). String Quartet no. 2 (1982)

Terni, Jiri (b. ?). Obelisk, Concert Fantasy for Violin and Piano (1983)

Wagner, Werner (1927–2002). String Quartet no. 1 (1969)

Ware, Peter (b. 1951). *Artua*, for String Quartet (1973)

Washburn, Robert (1928–2013). String Quartet (1964)

Weigl, Karl (1881–1949). String Quartet no. 8 (1949)

Weisgarber, Elliot (1919–2001). Quartet no. 6 (1980)

Wilcox, A. Gordon (b. ?). String Quartet: 1967, 1975 (1984)

Wilhoit, Frank (b. ?). Quartet in D, op. 13 (1981)

Wood, Hugh (b. 1932). String Quartet no. 3, op. 20 (1980)

Wuorinen, Charles (b. 1938). String Quartet (1970–71)

Wuorinen, Charles. String Trio (1971)

Zaimont, Judith Lang (b. 1945). *De infinitate caeleste*, for String Quartet (1970)

Zámečník, Evžen (b. 1939). *Obrazy*, for Violin, Cello, and Piano (1978)

Zeljenka, Ilja (1932–2007). *Elegia*, for solo violin (1977)

Zenkl, Michal (1955–83). String Quartet (1976)

# APPENDIX D

# Commissions, Dedications, Premieres

## Commissions by PAQ

### Quatuor Pro Arte of Brussels

The group apparently never issued commissions of its own, but frequently presented works commissioned by Elizabeth Sprague Coolidge or her Foundation.

### Pro Arte Quartet of the University of Wisconsin

With date of composition; * indicates also premiered by the PAQ, with date given; # indicates recording by PAQ.

Adler, Samuel. *String Quartet no. 5 (1969). November 11, 1970
Bolcom, William. *#Piano Quintet no. 2 (2011). March 24, 2012
Diesendruck, Tamar. *Quartet no. 3, "Dagger" (with Koussevitzky Foundation, 2005). April 22, 2006
Fennelly, Brian. *#Quartet no. 2, "Arias and Interludes" (with Koussevitzky Foundation, 2001). December 3, 2002
Harbison, John. *#String Quartet no. 5 (2011). April 1, 2012
Imbrie, Andrew. *#String Quartet no. 4(1969). November 17, 1969
———. *#String Quartet no. 5 (1987). November 8, 1987
Jalbert, Pierre. *#Howl, for clarinet and strings (2014). September 26, 2014
Lerdahl, Fred. *#String Quartet no. 2 (with NEA, 1980–82, 2010). October 22, 1982
Luckhardt, Hilmar. *String Quartet no. 4 (1970). December 3, 1971
Mays, Walter. *#Quartet no. 2, "Dreaming Butterfly" (2011). October 22, 2011
Mernier, Benoît. *#String Quartet no. 3 (with Koussevitzky Foundation, 2013. February 28, 2014
Sessions, Roger. *Quartet no. 2 (1951). May 28, 1951

Shapey, Ralph. *#String Quartet no. 9 (with School of Music, 1995) May 4, 1996

# Dedications to PAQ

## *Quatuor Pro Arte*

\* indicates also premiered by QPA

Bartók, Béla. Quartet no. 4 (1928)
Cartan, Jean. *Quartet no. 2 (1930)
Casella, Alfredo. *Concerto for String Quartet (1924)
Cowell, Henry. *Quartet no. 3, "Mosaic" (1925)
Fitelberg, Jerzy. *Quartet no. 2 (1928)
Gruenberg, Louis. *Four Indiscretions*, op. 20 (1922)
Honegger, Arthur. Quartet no. 2 (1934–35)
Houdret, Charles. Quartet (1928)
Huybrechts, Albert. *Quartet no. 2 (1927)
Jacobi, Frederick. Quartet no. 2 (1933)
Martinů, Bohuslav. *Quartet Concerto (1931)
Milhaud, Darius. *La cantate de l'enfant et de la mère* (1938) [also ded. to Collaer]
———. *Quartet no. 7 (1925)
Reichel, Bernard. *Little Quartet (Sonatine) for Strings* (1924)
Rieti, Vittorio. *Madrigal in Four Parts* (1927)
———. Quartet no. 1 (1926)
Tansman, Alexandre. Quartet no. 3 (1925)

# Pro Arte Quartet of the University of Wisconsin

\* indicates also premiered by PAQ

Davidovsky, Mario. *Quartet no. 3 (1976)
Weisgarber, Elliot. *String Quartet no. 6 (1981)

# World Premieres by PAQ

## *Quatuor Pro Arte*

With date of composition, date and place of premiere; * indicates dedicated to QPA.
Alfano, Franco. Quartet no. 1 (1918). January 16, 1924, Paris

Barber, Samuel. Quartet, op. 11 (1936). December 1, 1936, Rome

Béclard d'Harcourt-String Quartet (1930). January 7, 1933, Paris

Berkeley, Lennox. Quartet no. 1 (1935). November 20, 1935, Aberdeen

Berezowsky, Nicolas. Sextet, op. 26. April 4, 1940, Washington DC

Binet, J. String Quartet (1927). February 11, 1931, Brussels

Bliss, Arthur. Oboe Quintet (1927). October 19, 1927, Venice

Cambon, M. Quartet in F-sharp Minor (19??). March 31, 1933, Marseille

Cartan, Jean. Quartet no. 2 (1930). December 12, 1932, Paris

Casella, Alfredo. *Concerto for String Quartet (1924). February 8, 1926, Brussels

Chevreuille, Raymond. Quartet no. 1 (1930). January 12, 1932

Defauw, Désiré. Suite for Double String Quartet (19??), April 1, 1913, Brussels

Delcroix, L.. Piano Quartet, op. 1 (1903). March 1, 1913, Brussels

Dohnányi, Ernst. Piano Quintet no. 2, op. 26 (1914). December 20, 1927, Brussels

———. *Serenade*, op. 10 (1902). November 8, 1927, Oxford

Fitelberg, Jerzy. *Quartet no. 2 (1928). April 8, 1929, Geneva

Goosens, Eugene. Quartet no. 1 (1915). January 1, 1920, Brussels

———. *Phantasy Sextet*, op. 37 (1923). May 20, 1926, Antwerp

Harris, Roy. Quartet no. 2,"Three Variations on a Theme," (1933). October 22, 1933, Chicago

Honegger, Arthur. Quartet no. 1 (1917). March 22, 1923, Geneva

———. Quartet no. 3 (1937). October 22, 1937, Geneva

Houdret, C. String Quartet. May 10, 1929, Brussels

Howe, Mary. Fugue (1922). July 27, 1935, Oakland

Huybrechts, Albert. *Quartet no. 2 (1927). November 19, 1928, Brussels

Jongen, Joseph. *Deux Sérénades* for String Quartet (1918). April 10, 1913, Brussels

———. *Release*, for Piano and Strings (19??). January 30, 1920

———. Quartet no. 3 (1921). February 15, 1923, Brussels

Koechlin, Charles. Quartet no. 1 (1913). May 19, 1921, Paris

———. Quartet no. 3 (1921). November 13, 1922, Brussels

Krenek, Ernst. Quartet no. 4 (1924). October 4, 1930, Munich

Leirins, C. Piano Quintet (19??). April 1, 1913, Brussels

Levy, Ernst. Quartet no. 2 (1921). March 22, 1923, Geneva

Leyden, R. van. Cello Quintet. October 4, 1930, Munich

Martinů, Bohuslav. Quartet no. 5 (1938). June 30, 1938, Los Angeles

———. *Quartet Concerto (1931). October 10, 1932, London

Marx, Karl. Fantasie and Fugue (1929). October 18, 1930, Berlin

Milhaud, Darius. Quartet no. 6 (1922). March 13, 1923, Brussels

———. *Quartet no. 7 (1925). January 10, 1925, Brussels

———. Quartet no. 8 (1932). May 13, 1933, Asolo

———. Quartet no. 9 (1935). May 21, 1935, Paris

———. *La cantate de l'enfant et de la mère* (1938). May 18, 1938, Brussels

Ornstein. Leo. Piano Quintet, op. 92 (1927). January 12, 1928, New York

Pierné, Gabriel. Sonata da camera (1927). October 1, 1927, Venice

Pijper, Willem. Quartet no. 2 (1920). April 8, 1925, Amsterdam

Pizzetti, Ildebrando. Cantata, *Epithalamium* (1939). April 12, 1940, Washington DC
Poot, Marcel. Ballad for String Quartet and Orchestra (1937). May 5, 1938, Brussels
Prokofiev, Sergei. Quintet for Oboe, Clarinet, and Strings (1924). December 13, 1926, Brussels
Rasse, François. String Quartet (1906). April 7, 1921, Brussels
Reichl, Bernard. *Little String Quartet (Sonatine, 1924). December 1, 1924, Brussels
Rieti, Vittorio. *Madrigal in Four Parts* (1927). December 25, 1927, Brussels
Roussel, Albert. Quartet (1932). December 9, 1932, Paris
Saleski, Gdal. Suite for String Quartet (19??). June 25, 1933, Oakland
Salzedo, Carlos. *Préambule et Jeux* (1929). October 28, 1929, Geneva
Satie, Erik. "Jack-in-the-Box" (orch. Milhaud, 1926). May 3, 1926, Brussels
Schmitt, Florent. Piano Quintet, op. 51 (1908). January 1, 1914, Brussels
Smith, David Stanley. Quartet in E-flat Major (1927). October 8, 1927), Brussels
Tansman, Alexandre. Quartet no. 2 (1933). December 1, 1923, Paris
Vreuls, Victor. Quartet (1918). January 26, 1920, Brussels
Walque, J. de. Quartet. February 17, 1923, Brussels
Ysaÿe, Théophile. Piano Quintet, op 5 (1913). April 10, 1913, Brussels

## *Pro Arte Quartet of the University of Wisconsin*

With date of composition, date and place of premiere; * indicates PAQ commission; + indicates dedication to PAQ; # indicates recording by PAQ.

Adler, Samuel. *Quartet no. 5 (1969). November 11, 1970, Madison
Bolcom, William. *#Piano Quintet no. 2 (2011). March 24, 2012, Madison
Brun, Herbert. Quartet no. 2 (1957). June 8, 1978, Laramie, Wyoming.
Burleigh, Cecil. Piano Quintet, "Hymn to the Ancients (19??). May 3, 1943, Madison
Davidovsky, Mario. Quartet no. 3 (1976). April 13, 1978, New York
Diesendruck, Tamar. #Quartet no. 1, "Such Stuff" (1987). April 15, 1989, Madison
———. #Quartet no. 2, "Babel Dreams" (1992). February 24, 1993), Madison
———. *Quartet no. 3 "Dagger" (2005; with Koussevitzky Found.). April 22, 2006, Madison
Edwards, George. Quartet no. 2 (1982). May 8–17, Richland Center and New York
Fennelly, Brian. *#Quart no. 2, "Arias and Interludes" (with Koussevitzky Found.; 2001). December 3, 2002, New York
———. #Quartet no. 3 (2004). December 14, 2006, New York

Hagen, Oscar. Suite, "Wisconsin Summer." March 6, 1949, Madison

Harbison, John. *#Quartet no. 5 (2011). April 21, 2012, Madison

Imbrie, Andrew. *#Quartet no. 4 (1969). November 17, 1969, Madison

————. *#Quartet no. 5 (1987). November 8, 1987, Madison

Jalbert, Pierre. *#*Howl* for clarinet and strings (2014). September 26, 2014, Madison

Lerdahl, Fred. *Quartet no. 2 (with NEA, 1980—82, 2010). October 22, 1982, New York

Luckhardt, Hilmar. *+Quartet no. 4 (1970) December 3, 1971, Madison

Mays, Walter. *#Quartet no. 2, "Dreaming Butterfly" (2011). October 22, 1911, Madison

Mernier, Benoît. *#Quartet no. 3 (with Koussevitzky Foundation, 2013). February 28, 2014, Madison

Nelhybel, Vaclav. *Oratio I*, for Oboe and String Trio (for Catherine Paulu, 197?). June 23, 1977, Laramie Wyoming.

————. *Oratio III* (1978). December 7, 1977, Madison

Perlongo, Daniel. Quartet no. 2 (1983). December 2, 1984, Madison

Salva Tadeáš. String Quartet (1975). October 27, 1976, Boston

Schoenfield, Paul. *#Three Rhapsodies for Piano Quintet (2011). November 19, 2011), Madison

Schoenberg, Arnold. *Ode to Napoleon* (1942). Scheduled for December 8, 1944, Chicago, but apparently cancelled.

————. #String Quartet in D Major (1897). February 7, 1952, Washington, DC

Schuller, Gunther. *Concerto for String Quartet and Orchestra (1987). February 20, 1980, Madison

Sessions, Roger. *Quartet no. 2 (1951). May 28, 1951, Madison

Shifrin, Seymour. Quartet no. 5 (1972). November 15–16, 1973, Platteville and Madison

Shapey, Ralph. *#Quartet no. 9 (with School of Music, 1995). May 4, 1996, Madison

Toch, Ernst. String Trio (19??). March 1, 1953, Madison

Ultan, Lloyd. Quartet no. 2 (1980). February 14, 1981, Madison

Weisgarber, Elliot. +Quartet no. 6 (1981). February 7, 1982, Madison

# APPENDIX E

# Discography

## Commercial Recordings

*Chronological*

Quatuor Pro Arte: 1931–40

Each year and date is followed by day of the week: Sun, Mon, Tue, Wed, Thu, Fri, Sat. Original issues are all 78 rpm; matrix numbers are listed first, followed by 78-rpm issues, then LP and CD reissues. HQS = Haydn Quartet Society. All recordings were made in London and are monophonic. In addition to commercial recordings, included are several recordings that were not completed and aborted.

Personnel: Alphonse Onnou, violin; Laurent Halleux, violin; Germain Prévost, viola; Robert Maas, cello.

1931: November 30 (Mon), Queen's Small Hall, Studio D
JOSEPH HAYDN (1732–1809): Quartet in G Minor, op. 74, no. 3, "Rider" (Hob. III:74). 2B 2458–61; HMV set DB 1632–33; in HMV set HQS vol. 2, DB 1927–31; **LP**: in EMI set 2906043; **CD**: in Testament vol. I, SBT 3055; in Allegro vol. 2, 4012; in Enterprise/Strings QT 99–388, or Tactus TC 99388; in Gramofono AB 78 916.
1931: December 1 (Tue), Queen's Small Hall, Studio D
JOSEPH HAYDN (1732–1809): Quartet in C Major, op. 33, no. 3, "Bird" (Hob. III: 39). 2B 2464–67; HMV set DB 1630–31; in HMV set HQS vol. 1, DB 1628–31; **LP**: in EMI set 2906043; **CD**: in Testament vol. 2, SBT 4056; in Allegro vol. 2, CDO 4012; in Enterprise/Strings QT 99–380.
1931: December 1–2 (Tue–Wed), Queen's Small Hall, Studio D
JOSEPH HAYDN (1732–1809): Quartet in G Major, op. 77, no. 1 (Hob. III:81). 2B 2468–75; EMI set DB 1634–36; in HMV set HQS vol. 2I, DB 2159–65, or Victor set M 525; **LP**: in HMV set 2906043; **CD**: in Testament vol. 2, SBT 4056; in Enterprise/Strings QT 99–370.

1931: December 2 (Wed), Queen's Small Hall, Studio D
JOSEPH HAYDN (1732–1809): Quartet in C Major, op. 20, no. 2 (Hob.
III:32). 2B 2476–79; HMV set DB 1628–29; in HMV set HQS vol. 1, DB
1628–31; **LP:** in EMI set 2906043; **CD:** in Testament vol. 1, SBT 3055; in
Allegro vol. 1, CDO 4011; in Enterprise/Strings QT 99–386.
    [NB: Before official takes were made for the above recording, experi-
mental 33 1/3 hill-and-dale recordings were registered, and survive. It is
not known whether the players gave their permission for this documentation. The Quatuor Pro Arte are heard rehearsing the Menuetto and
Adagio of Haydn's opus 77 no. 1 and the opening Moderato of opus 20
no. 2. They speak in French but the speech sound is a little indistinct,
and the words have not yet been deciphered. It is thus known that they
could rehearse the first movement of opus 20 no. 2, but otherwise they
sightread it. It was apparently after this recording that they went to a
local pub for some healthy drinking.]
1932: October 6 (Thu), Abbey Road, Studo 3
JOSEPH HAYDN (1732–1809): Quartet in G Major, op. 54, no. 2 (Hob.
III:58). 2B 3950–53; HMV set DB 1928–29; in HMV set HQS vol. 2, BD
1632–37; **LP:** in EMI set 2906043; **CD:** in Testament vol. I, SBT 3055; in
Allegro vol. 2, CDO 4012; in Enterprise/Strings QT 99–383.
1932: October 6 (Thu), Abbey Road, Studio 3
JOSEPH HAYDN (1732–1809): Quartet in C Major op. 54, no. 1 (Hob.
III:57). 2B 3954–56; HMV set DB 1930–31; in HMV set HQS vol. 2, DB
1632–37; **LP:** in EMI set 2906043; **CD:** in Testament vol. I, SBT 3055; in
Allegro vol. 2, CDO 4012; in Enterprise/Strings QT 99–383.
1932: October 7 (Fri), Abbey Road, Studio 3
JOSEPH HAYDN (1732–1809): Quartet in D Major, op. 33, no. 6 (Hob.
III:42). 2B 3958–59; HMV set DB 1632–33; in HMV set HQS vol. 2 DB
1927–31; **LP:** in EMI set 2906043; **CD:** in Testament SBT 4056; in Allegro
vol. 1, CDO 4011; in Enterprise/Strings QT 99–374.
1932: 7 October (Fri), Abbey Road, Studio 3
JEAN SIBELIUS (1865–1957): Quartet in D Minor, op. 36. "Voces intimae": first movement. 2B 2960 [test recording, rejected and destroyed]
1932: 7, 10, 11 October (Fri, Mon, Tue), Abbey Road, Studio 3
JOHANNES BRAHMS (1833–1897): Piano Quartet no. 1 in G Minor,
op. 25, with Artur Rubinstein. 2B 3967–78; HMV set DB 1813–16, or Victor set M 234; **CD:** Enterprise/Piano Library PL 233; Biddulph LAB 027
(with Quartet no. 2, Rudolf Serkin and Busch Quartet.).
1933: February 7, 8 (Tue, Wed), Abbey Road, Studio 3
CLAUDE DEBUSSY (1862–1918): Quartet in G Minor, op. 10. 2B 6273–
79; DB 1878–81, or Victor set M 186; **CD:** in Biddulph LAB 105 (with
Ravel, Fauré Quartets).
1933: February 8 (Wed), Abbey Road, Studio 3
ALEXANDER GLAZUNOV (1865–1936): *Five Novellettes*, op. 16: 5. *Orientale.* 2B 6883 [not released].
1933: February 8 (Wed), Abbey Road, Studio 3

ERNEST BLOCH (1880–1959): Piano Quintet no. 1, with Alfredo Casella, piano. 2B 4120–27; HMV set DB 1882–85, or Victor set M 191; **CD**: in Andante set 2970 ("Quatuor Pro Arte").

1933: May 18, 27 (Thu, Thu), Abbey Road, Studio 3
CÉSAR FRANCK (1822–90): Quartet in D Major. 2B 4196–400, 4601–05, 4608; HMV set DB 2051–56, or Victor set M 259; **CD**: in Biddulph LAB 106 (with Bartók Quartet no. 1); in Andante set 2970 ("Quatuor Pro Arte," 4 CDs).
   [NB.: The Quatuor Pro Arte had to play the Scherzo half a minute faster than they were accustomed to doing, in order to get it onto one side.]

1933: May 18 (Thu), Abbey Road, Studio 3
FRANZ SCHUBERT (1797–1828): Quartet no. 10 in E-flat Major, op. posth. 125 (D. 87): 4. Finale, Allegro. 2B 4607; in HMV set DB 20[50-]56, or Victor set M 259; **CD**: in EMI CDH 63031 (with "Trout" Quintet); in Andante set 2970 ("Quatuor Pro Arte," 4 CDs).

1933: December 8 (Fri), Abbey Road, Studio 3
MAURICE RAVEL (1875–1937): Quartet in F Major. 2B 5486–93; HMV set DB 2135–38, or Victor set M 400; **CD**: in Biddulph LAB 105 (with Fauré, Debussy Quartets); in Andante set 2970 ("Quatuor Pro Arte," 4 CDs).

1933: December 8 (Fri), Abbey Road, Studio 3
ALEXANDER BORODIN (1833–87): Quartet no. 2 in D Major. 2EA 5479–85; HMV set DB 2150–53, or Victor set M 252; **CD**: in Andante set 2970 ("Quatuor Pro Arte," 4 CDs).

1933: December 11 (Mon), Abbey Road, Studio 3
JOSEPH HAYDN (1732–1809): Quartet in E–flat Major, op. 33, no. 2, "Joke" (Hob. III:38). 2B 5496–99; HMV set DB 2160–61); in HMV set HQS vol. 2I, DB 2159–65, or Victor set M 525; **LP**: in EMI set 2906043; **CD**: in Testament vol. 2, SBT 4056; in Allegro vol. 1, CDO 4011.

1933: December 11 (Mon), Abbey Road, Studio 3
ROMAN HOFFSTETTER (1742–1814), formerly attributed to Joseph Haydn (1732–1809): Quartet in F Major, op. 3, no. 5, "Serenade" (Hob. III:17). 2B 5500–01; HMV BD 2159; in EMI set HQS vol. 3, DB 2159–65, or Victor set M 525; **LP**: in EMI set 2906043; **CD**: in Testament vol. 2, SBT 4056.

1933: December 11 (Mon), Abbey Road, Studio 3
ALEXANDER GLAZUNOV (1865–1936): *5 Novelettes*, op. 16 no. 5. *Orientale.* 2EA 5502; in HMV set DB 21[50–]53, or Victor set M 252 (with Borodin Quintet); **CD**: in Andante set 2970 ("Quatuor Pro Arte," 4 CDs).

1933: December 11 (Mon), Abbey Road, Studio 3
JOSEPH HAYDN (1732–1809): Quartet in E-flat Major, op. 64, no. 6 (Hob. III:68). 2B 5503–06; HMV set DB 2162–63; in HMV set HQS vol. 3, DB 2159–65, or Victor set M 525; **LP**: in EMI set 2906043; **CD**: in Testament vol. 2 SBT 4056; in Enterprise/Strings QT 99–377.

1933: December 12 (Tue), Abbey Road, Studio 3
JOSEPH HAYDN (1732–1809): Quartet in B-flat Major, op. 71, no. 1
(Hob. III:69). 2B 5507–10; HMV set DB 2164–65; HMV set HQS vol.
3, DB 2159–65, or Victor set 525; **LP:** in EMI set 2906043; **CD:** in Testament
Vol 2, SBT 4056; in Enterprise/Strings QT 99–377.

1933: December 12 (Tue), Abbey Road, Studio 3
ANTONIO VIVALDI (1678–1741): *L'estro armonico*, op. 3: Concerto no 5
in A Major, for two violins, cello, strings, and continuo, arr. Pochon. 2B
5511–12; HMV DB 2148, or Victor 8827.

1934: January 31 (Wed), Abbey Road, Studio 3
WOLFGANG AMADEUS MOZART (1756–91): Piano Quartet no. 1 in G
Minor (K. 478), with Artur Schnabel. 2B 5583–90; HMV set DB 2155–58,
or Victor set M 251; **LP:** in Angel/EMI COLH 42 (with G-Minor Quintet);
**CD:** in EMI set CHS 7 63870 (Mozart Chamber Works, 2 CDs); in
Arabesque Z6593 (with Piano Quartet no. 2); in Iron Needle 1342.

1934: February 11 (Sun), Abbey Road, Studio 3
ANTONÍN DVOŘÁK (1844–1901): Piano Quintet in A Major, op. 81,
with Artur Schnabel, piano. 2B 6009–16; HMV set 2177–80, or Victor set
M 219; **CD:** in Arabesque Z6613 (with Schumann Quintet); in Music &
Arts CD 1196 (with Schumann Quintet).

1934: February 14 (Wed), Abbey Road, Studio 3
WOLFGANG AMADEUS MOZART (1756–91): Quintet no. 3 in C Major
(K. 515), with Alfred Hobday, viola 2. 2B 6023–29 [rejected]

1934: February 15 (Thu), Abbey Road, Studio 2
WOLFGANG AMADEUS MOZART (1756–91): Quintet no. 4 in G Minor
(K. 516), with Alfred Hobday, viola 2. 2B 6030–37: HMV set DB 6043–46
(217–76), or Victor set M 270; **LP:** in Angel/EMI COLH (with G-Minor
Quintet); **CD:** in EMI set CHS 7 63870 (Mozart Chamber Works, 2 CDs).

1934: February 15 (Thu), Abbey Road, Studio 3
WOLFGANG AMADEUS MOZART (1756–91): Quartet in D Major
(K.?). 2B 6038 [incomplete, not released]

1934: October 29 (Mon), Abbey Road, Studio 3
JOSEPH HAYDN (1732–1809): Quartet in F Minor, op. 20, no. 5 (Hob.
III:35). 2EA 477–80; HMV set DB 2398–99; in HMV set HQS vol. 4, DB
2398–404, or Victor set M 526; **LP:** in EMI set 2906043; **CD:** in Testament
vol. 1, SBT 3055; in Allegro vol. 1, CDO 4011; in Enterprise/Strings QT
99–386.

1934: October 29 (Mon), Abbey Road, Studio 3
JOSEPH HAYDN (1732–1809): Quartet in C Major, op. 76, no. 3,
"Emperor" (Hob. III:77). 2EA 481–86; HMV set BD 2402–04; in HMV set
HQS vol. 4, DB 2390–404, or Victor set M 526; **LP:** in EMI set 2906043;
**CD:** in Testament vol. 1, SBT 3055; in Allegro vol. 3, CDO 4013.

1934: October 30 (Tue), Abbey Road, Studio 3
JOSEPH HAYDN (1732–1809): Quartet in E-flat Major, op. 50, no. 3
(Hob. III:46). 2EA 487–90; HMV set DB 2400–01; in HMV set HQS vol.
4, DB 2398–404, or Victor set M 526; **LP:** in EMI set 2906043; **CD:** in Testament
vol. 1, SBT 3055.

1934: October 31 and November 2 (WE, FR), Abbey Road, Studio 3
BÉLA BARTÓK (1881–1945): Quartet no. 1, op. 7 (Sz. 40). 2EA 491–95, 497–99; HMV set DB 2397–82, or Victor set M 320; **CD**: in Biddulph LAB 106 (with Franck Quartet); in Andante set 2970 ("Quatuor Pro Arte," 4 CDs).

1934: November 2–3 (Wed, Thu), Abbey Road, Studio 3
WOLFGANG AMADEUS MOZART (1756–91): Quintet no. 3 in C Major (K. 515), with Alfred Hobday, viola 2. 2EA 500–7; HMV set DB 2383–86, or Victor set M 270; **CD**: in EMI set CHS 7 63870 (Mozart Chamber Works, 2 CDs); in Andante set 2970 ("Quatuor Pro Arte," 4 CDs).

1934: November 3, 19 (Sat, Mon), Abbey Road, Studio 3
ROBERT SCHUMANN (1810–56): Piano Quintet in E–flat Major, op. 44, with Artur Schnabel, piano. 2EA 535–42; HMV set DB 2387–90, or Victor M 267; **CD**: in Arabesque Z6613 (with Dvořák Quintet; in Andante set 2970 ("Quatuor Pro Arte," 4 CDs); in Music & Arts CD 1196 (with Dvořák Piano Quintet).

1935: March 6 (Wed), Abbey Road, Studio 3
VITTORIO RIETI (1898–1994): Quartet in F Major. OEA 1308–11; Victor 1821–22. [NB: This recording was made for and is owned by the Victor Company, not EMI.]

1935: March 6–8 (Wed, Fri), Abbey Road, Studio 3
FRANZ SCHUBERT (1797–1828): Quintet in C Major, op. posth. 163 (D. 956), with Anthony Pini, cello 2. 2EA 1305–07, 1318–24; HMV set DB 2561–65, or Victor set M 299; **CD**: in Biddulph LAB 093 (with Brahms Sextet); in Enterprise/Strings QT 99–334 (with "Trout" Quintet); in Gramofono AB 78 879 (with "Trout" Quintet); in Andante set 1990 ("Schubert: Chamber Music," 4 CDs).

1935: March 7 (Thu), Abbey Road, Studio 3
JOSEPH HAYDN (1732–1809): Quartet in F Major, op. 77, no. 2, "Lobkowitz" (H.III: 82). 2EA 1312–17; HMV set DB 2778–80; in HMV set HQS vol. 5, DB 2774–80, or Victor set M 527; **LP**: in EMI set 2906043; **CD**: in Testament vol. 1, SBT 3055; in Allegro vol. 3, CDO 4013; in Enterprise/Strings QT 99–388, or Tactus TC 99388; in Gramofono AB 78 916.

1935: March 8–9 (Fri, Sat), Abbey Road, Studio 3
JOHANNES BRAHMS (1833–97): Sextet No. 1, op. 18, with Alfred Hobday, viola 2 and Anthony Pini, cello 2. 2EA 1325–29, 1331–33; HMV set DB 2566–69, or Victor set M 296; **CD**: Biddulph LAB 93.

1935: November 16 (Sat), Abbey Road, Studio 3
FRANZ SCHUBERT (1797–1828): Piano Quintet in A Major, op. 114, "Trout" (D. 667), with Artur Schnabel, piano, Claude Hobday, double bass. 2EA 2529–38; HMV DB 2714–18, or Victor set M 312; **LP**: Angel/EMI COLH 40; **CD**: in Arabesque Z6571 (with Piano Sonata D. 959); in EMI CDH 63041 (with quartet mvt.); in Enterprise/Strings QT–99–334 (with C-Major Quintet); in Pearl set GEMM CDS 9272 ("Schnabel Plays Schubert, 2," 2 CDs); in Gramofono AB 78 879 (with C-Major Quintet); in Master Series 586; in Andante set 1990 ("Schubert: Chamber Music," 4 CDs); in Music & Arts set CD 1175 ("Schnabel: Complete Schubert Recordings," 5 CDs).

1935: November 18 (Mon), Abbey Road, Studio 3
JOSEPH HAYDN (1732–1809): Quartet in D Major, op. 20, no. 4 (H.III: 34). 2EA 2539–42; HMV set DB 2774–75; in HMV set HQS vol. 5, DB 2774–80, or Victor M 527; **LP**: in EMI set 2906043; **CD**: in Testament vol. 2, SBT 4056; in Allegro vol. 1, CDO 4011; in Enterprise/Strings QT 99–380.

1935: November 18 (Mon), Abbey Road, Studio 3
JOSEPH HAYDN (1732–1809): Quartet in F Major, op. 74, no. 2 (Hob. III:73). 2EA 2543–46; HMV set DB 2776–77; in HMV set HQS vol. V, DB 2774–80, or Victor set M 527; **LP**: in EMI set 2906043; **CD**: in Testament vol. 2, SBT 4056; in Allegro vol. 2; in Enterprise/Strings QT 99–374.

1935: November 19 (Tue), Abbey Road, Studio 3
GABRIEL FAURÉ (1845–1924): Quartet in E Minor, op. 121. 2EA 2547–54; HMV set DB 2763–65, or Victor set M 372; **CD**: in Biddulph LAB 105 (with Debussy and Ravel Quartet).

1936: November 15 (Sun), Abbey Road, Studio 3
WOLFGANG AMADEUS MOZART (1756–91): Quartet no. 16 in E-flat Major (K. 428). 2EA 3108–13; HMV set DB 2820–22, or Victor M 375; **CD**: in EMI set CHS 7 63870 (Mozart Chamber Works, 2 CDs).

1936: November 18 (Wed), Abbey Road, Studio 3
WOLFGANG AMADEUS MOZART (1756–91): Quintet No. 5 in D Major (K. 593), with Alfred Hobday, viola 2. 2EA 4456–61; HMV set DB 3090–92, or Victor set M 350; **CD**: in EMI set CHS 7 63870 (Mozart Chamber Works, 2 CDs)

1936: November 19 (Thu), Abbey Road, Studio 3
JOSEPH HAYDN (1732–1809): Quartet in A Major, op. 55, no. 1 (Hob. III:60). 2EA 4462 –65; HMV set DB 3118–19; HMV set HQS vol. 6, DB 3115–21, or Victor set M 528; **LP**: in EMI set 2906043; **CD**: in Testament vol. 2, SBT 4056; in Enterprise/Strings QT 99–377.

1936: November 19 (Thu), Abbey Road, Studio 3
JOSEPH HAYDN (1732–1809): Quartet in E Major, op. 54, no. 3 (Hob. III:59). 2EA 4466–69; HMV set DB 3116–17; in HMV set HQS vol. 6, DB 3115–21, or Victor set M 528; **LP**: in EMI set 2906043; **CD**: in Testament vol. 1, SBT 3055; in Allegro vol. 2, CDO 4012; in Enterprise/Strings QT 99–383.

1936: December 3 (Thu), Abbey Road, Studio 3
JOSEPH HAYDN (1732–1809): Quartet in G Major, op. 64, no. 4 (Hob. III:66). 2EA 4506–09; HMV set DB 3120–21; in HMV set HQS vol. 6, DB 3115–21, Victor set M 528; **LP**: in EMI set 2906043; **CD**: in Testament vol. 1, SBT 3055; in Allegro vol. 2, CDO 4012; in Enterprise/Strings QT 99–399, or Tactus TC 99388; in Gramofono AB 78 916.

1936: December 3 (Thu), Abbey Road, Studio 3
JOSEPH HAYDN (1732–1809): Quartet in C Major, op. 1, no. 6 (Hob. III:6). 2EA 4510–11; HMV set DB 3115; in HMV set HQS vol. VI, DB 3115–21, or Victor set M 528; **LP**: in EMI set 2906043; **CD**: in Testament vol. 2, SBT 4056.

1937: November 15 (Mon), Abbey Road, Studio 3
JOSEPH HAYDN (1732–1809): Quartet in D Major, op. 50, no. 6, "Frog" (Hob. III:49). 2EA 5568–71; HMV set DB 3544–45; in HMV set HQS vol. 7, DB 3543–49 or Victor set M 689; **LP**: in EMI set 2906043; **CD**: in Testament vol. 2, SBT 4056; in Allegro vol. 1, CDO 4011; in Enterprise/ Strings QT 99–380.

1937: November 15 (Mon), Abbey Road, Studio 3
JOSEPH HAYDN (1732–1809): Quartet in C Major, op. 74, no. 1 (Hob. III:72). 2EA 5572–75; HMV set DB 3548–49; in HMV set HQS vol. 7, DB 3543–49, or Victor set M 689; **LP**: in EMI set 2906043; **CD**: in Testament vol. 2, SBT 4056; in Allegro vol. 2; in Enterprise/Strings QT 99–374.

1937: November 16 (Tue), Abbey Road, Studio 3
JOSEPH HAYDN (1732–1809): Quartet in B-flat Major, op. 64, no. 3 (Hob. III:65). 2EA 5576–79; HMV set DB 3546–47; in HMV set HQS vol. 7, DB 5343–49, or Victor set M 689; **LP**: in EMI set 2906043; **CD**: in Testament vol. 1, SBT 3055; in Allegro vol. 2, CDO 4012; in Enterprise/ Strings QT 99–388, or Tactus TC 99388; in Gramofono AB 78 916.

1937: November 16 (Tue), Abbey Road, Studio 3
WOLFGANG AMADEUS MOZART (1756–81): Serenade no. 13 in G Major, "Eine kleine Nachtmusik" (K. 525), with Claude Hobday, double bass. 2EA 5580–83; HMV set DB 3381–81, or Victor set M 428. [NB: This recording was made for and is owned by Victor, not EMI.]

1937: November 16 (Tue), Abbey Road, Studio 3
ROMAN HOFFSTETTER (1742–1815), formerly attributed to Joseph Haydn (1732–1809): Quartet in B-flat Major, op. 3, no. 4 (Hob. III:16). 2EA 5584–85; HMV set DB 3543; in HMV set HQS vol. 7, DB 3543–49, or Victor set M 689; **LP**: in EMI set 2906043; **CD**: in Testament vol. 2, SBT 4056.

1937: November 17 (Wed), Abbey Road, Studio 3
FRANZ SCHUBERT (1797–1828): Trio in B-flat Major (D. 898). Alphonse Onnou, Robert Maas, Karl Ulrich Schnabel. 2EA 5586–93: Victor 14807–10, set M 689, or HMV DB 3387–90 [assigned but not issued]; **CD**: Japanese EMI SGR–8207. [NB: This recording was made for and is owned by Victor, not EMI].

1938: November 5 (Sat), Abbey Road, Studio 3
JOSEPH HAYDN (1732–1809): Quartet in B–flat Major, op. 1, no. 1, "La Chasse" (Hob. III:1). 2EA 7213–14; HMV set DB 3768; in HMV set HQS vol. 6, DB 3115/21, or Victor set M 528; **LP**: in EMI set 2906043; **CD**: in Testament vol. 1, SBT 3055; in Allegro vol. 1, CDO 4011; in Enterprise/ Strings QT 99–383.

1938: November 5 (Sat), Abbey Road, Studio 3
JOSEPH HAYDN (1732–1809): Quartet in E–flat Major, op. 20, no. 1 (Hob. III:31). 2EA 7215–18; HMV set DB 3769–70; in HMV set HQS vol. 8, DB 3768–74, or Victor set M 595; **LP**: in EMI set 2906043; **CD**: in Testament vol. 2, SBT 4056; in Allegro CDO 4011; in Enterprise/Strings QT 99–380.

1938: November 5 (Sat), Abbey Road, Studio 3
JOSEPH HAYDN (1732–1809): Quartet in B–flat Major, op. 55, no. 3
(Hob. III:62). 2EA 7219–22; HMV set DB 3771–2; HMV set HQS vol. 8,
DB 3768–74, or Victor set M 595; **LP**: in EMI set 2906043; **CD**: in Testament vol. 2, SBT 4056; in Enterprise/Strings QT 99–377.
1938: December 15 (Thu), Abbey Road, Studio 3
JOSEPH HAYDN (1732–1809): Quartet in B–flat Major, op. 76, no. 4,
"Sunrise" (Hob. III:78). 2EA 7246–49; HMV set DB 3773–74; in HMV
set HQS vol. 1, DB 3768–74; **LP**: in EMI set 2906043; **CD**: in Testament
vol. 1, SBT 3055; in Allegro vol. 3, CDO 4013; in Enterprise/Strings QT
99–386.
1938: December 16 (Fri)
LUDWIG VAN BEETHOVEN (1770–1827): Quartet no. 8 in E Minor,
op. 59, no. 2. 2EA 7402–09; HMV set DB 3740–43; **CD**: in Andante set
2970 ("Quatuor Pro Arte," 4 CDs).

## Pro Arte Quartet of the University of Wisconsin–Madison

All recordings are stereophonic, unless indicated otherwise. Note that
data for University of Wisconsin School of Music Records are often
scanty and even confused, while there are no release numbers. The
same abbreviations for days of the week as above are continued here.

Personnel: Rudolf Kolisch, violin; Albert Rahier, violin; Germain Prevost, viola; Ernst Friedlander, cello.

1945: January 26 (Fri), Coolidge Auditorium, Library of Congress, Washington, DC (live concert)
BÉLA BARTÓK (1881–1945): String Quartet no. 5. **CD**: Music & Arts set
CD–1056 ("In Honor of Rudolf Kolisch," 6 CDs, monophonic).
1945: February 2 (Fri), Coolidge Auditorium, Library of Congress, Washington, DC (live concert)
ROGER SESSIONS (1896–1985): String Quartet no. 1 in E Minor. **LP**:
New World Records NW 303 (monophonic: with Walter Piston's Quartet
no. 2, Budapest Quartet).

Personnel: Rudolf Kolisch, violin; Albert Rahier, violin; Bernard Milofsky, viola, Ernst Friedlander, cello.

1950: January 20 (Fri), WOR Studios, New York
ANTON WEBERN (1883–1945): *Five Movements for String Quartet*, op. 5;
*Six Bagatelles for String Quartet*, op. 9. **LP**: Dial 7 (monophonic: with his
Symphony, op. 21; **CD**: Music & Arts set CD–1056 ("In Honor of Rudolf
Kolisch," 6 CDs).

1950: January 24 (Tue), WOR Studios, New York
ARNOLD SCHOENBERG (1874–1951): String Quartet no. 3, op. 30. **LP**: Dial 4; **CD**: Music & Arts set CD–1056 ("In Honor of Rudolf Kolish," 6 CDs, monophonic).
1950: February 2 (Thu), WOR Studios, New York
ALBAN BERG (1885–1935): *Lyric Suite.* **LP**: Dial 5 (monophonic); **CD**: Music & Arts set CD–1056 ("In Honor of Rudolf Kolisch," monophonic).
1952: February 7 (Thu), Coolidge Auditorium, Library of Congress, Washington, DC (live concert)
ARNOLD SCHOENBERG (1874–1951): String Quartet in D Major (1897). **CD**: Music & Arts set CD–1056 ("In Honor of Rudolf Kolisch," monophonic).

Personnel: Norman Paulu, violin; Thomas Moore, violin; Richard Blum, viola; Lowell Creitz, cello.

1968: June 2. 7 (Sun–Sat), Station WHA (Studio A), University of Wisconsin–Madison
HERBERT FROMM (1905–95): String Quartet (1957); SAMUEL ADLER (1928–): Fourth String Quartet (1963). **LP**: Lyrichord LLST 7203.
1972: January 19 (Thu), Hertz Hall, University of California, Berkeley
ARNOLD ELSTON (1907–71): String Quartet no. 3 (1961). **LP**: Composers Recordings CRI SD 289 (with Gordon Binkerd's Sonata for Cello and Piano). **CD**: New World/CRI NWCRL 289.

Personnel: Norman Paulu, violin; Martha Francis Blum, violin; Richard Blum, viola; Parry Karp, cello.

1978: April?, New York, David Hancock
MARTIN BOYKAN (b. 1931): String Quartet no. 2 (1973). **LP**: Composers Recordings Inc. CRI SD 401 (with works by Miriam Gideon); **CD**: CRI CD 841 (with other works of Boykan).
1978: November? [a New York City church]
PAUL LANSKY (1944–): String Quartet (1971/77). **LP**: Composers Recordings Inc. CRI SD 402; **CD**: CRI SD 402 (with Paul Cooper's String Quartet no. 6 [1977] by the Shepherd Quartet); New World/CRI NWCRL 402.
1980: May?, Mills Concert Hall, University of Wisconsin–Madison
LUDWIG VAN BEETHOVEN (1770–1827): String Quartet in F Major, op. 19, no. 1 (original version). **LP**: Laurel LR–116
1980: May?, Mills Concert Hall, University of Wisconsin–Madison
ERNEST BLOCH (1880–1959): Quartet no. 1 (1916). **LP**: Laurel LR–120; **CD**: Laurel LR 820CD (with Piano Quintet no. 2).
1982: May?, Mills Concert Hall, University of Wisconsin–Madison
KAROL SZYMANOWSKI (1882–1937): String Quartet no. 1 in C, op. 37; String Quartet no. 2, op. 56. **LP**: Laurel LR–123.

1982: April/May, Mills Concert Hall, University of Wisconsin–Madison
ERNEST BLOCH (1888–1959): Quartet no. 2 (1945); *Prelude* (1925);
*Night* (1925); *Two Pieces for String Quartet* (1936, 1950). **LP:** Laurel
LR–126; **CD:** LR–826CD.

1983: May 18–19 (Wed, Thu), Mills Concert Hall, University of Wisconsin–
Madison
ERNEST BLOCH (1880–1959): Piano Quintet no. 2 (1957), with How-
ard Karp, piano; FRED LERDAHL (1943–): Second String Quartet
(1981/83). **LP:** Laurel LR–128; **CD:** LR–820CD (Bloch only, with his
Quartet no. 1), LR–848CD (Bloch only, with his Piano Quintet no. 1).

1984?:
LUIS DE FREITAS BRANCO (1890–1955: String Quartet (1911);
ARMANDO JOSÉ FERNANDES (1906–83): Piano Quintet (1952), with
Howard Karp, piano. **LP:** Educo 4113 ("Music of Portugal").

1981/1985?, Mills Concert Hall, University of Wisconsin–Madison
JOHANNES BRAHMS (1833–97): Piano Quintet in F Minor, op. 34,
with Howard Karp, piano. **LP:** University of Wisconsin–Madison School
of Music [no number].

1986: May?, Laurel Studios, Los Angeles
ERNEST BLOCH (1880–1959): *String Quartet No, 3* (1952); String Quartet no. 4 (1954); *Paysages: "North," "Alpestre," "Tongataboo"; In the Mountains: "Dusk," "Rustic Dance."* **CD:** Laurel LR–841CD.

1986: December 16. 17 (Tue, Wed), Mills Concert Hall, University of
Wisconsin–Madison
KAROL RATHAUS (1895–1954): String Quartet no. 5, op. 72 (1927).
**CD:** Composers Recordings, Inc. CRI SD 559 (with other chamber works
by Rathaus); New World/CRI NWCRL 559

1987: June?, Laurel Studios, Los Angeles
MIKLÓS RÓZSA ((1907–95): String Quartet no. 1, op. 22 (1950); String
Quartet no. 2, op. 38 (1981) [composer attending sessions]. **CD:** Laurel
LR–842CD.

Personnel: Norman Paulu, violin; Jae-Kyung Kim, violin; Richard
Blum, viola; Parry Karp, cello.

1989: December 7 (Thu), Bing Auditorium, Los Angeles County Museum
ERNEST BLOCH (1880–1959): Piano Quintet no. 1 (1923), with How-
ard Karp, piano. **CD:** Laurel LR–848. CD (with Piano Quintet no. 2, and
Suite no. 1 for Solo Cello [P. Karp]).

1989: December?, Bing Auditorium, Los Angeles County Museum
ERNEST BLOCH (1880–1959): String Quartet no. 5 (1956). **CD:** Laurel
LR–853CD (with Piano Quintet no. 1).

Personnel: Norman Paulu, violin; Jae–Kyung Kim, violin; Sally
Chisholm, viola; Parry Karp, cello.

1991: December 19–20 (Thu, Fri), Mills Concert Hall, University of Wisconsin–Madison
TAMAR DIESENDRUCK (b. 1946): *Such Stuff* (Quartet no. 1) (1988). **CD**: Centaur CRC–2412 (with her Quartet no. 2).

1993: May 7–8 (Thu, Fri), Mills Concert Hall, University of Wisconsin–Madison [live concert]
ANDREW IMBRIE (1921–2007): String Quartet no. 4 (1969); String Quartet no. 5 (1987). **CD**: GM Recordings [GUNMAR] GMR 2052 (with his Impromptu for Violin and Piano [1960], Paulu and H. Karp).

1995: April 13 (Wed), Mills Concert Hall, University of Wisconsin–Madison
TAMAR DIESENDRUCK (b. 1946): String Quartet no. 2 ("Babel Dreams") (1992). **CD**: Centaur CRC 2412 (with her Quartet no. 1); Centaur CRC 2857 ("Theater of the Ear": with various instrumental works).

Personnel: David Perry, violin; Suzanne Bea, violin; Sally Chisholm, viola; Parry Karp, cello.

1996: May 4 (Fri), Mills Concert Hall, University of Wisconsin–Madison [live performance]
RALPH SHAPEY (1921–2002): String Quartet no. 9 (1995) [written for and premiered by the PAQ]. in University of Wisconsin School of Music "Centennial Commissions" set [no number].

2000: December 29–31 (Fri–Sun), Purchase College Conservatory of Music Recital Hall, Purchase, NY
ROGER SESSIONS (1896–1985): String Quintet (1958), with Samuel Rhodes; SAMUEL RHODES (b. 1928): Quintet (1968), with Samuel Rhodes; Walter Mays (b. 1941): String Quartet in G Minor (1998) [commissioned for and premiered by the PAQ]. **CD**: Albany TROY569.

2001: April 30–1 May 1 (Tue–Wed), Weidner Center, Green Bay, Wisconsin, Studio 2
ANTONÍN DVOŘÁK (1841–1904): String Quartet in D Minor, op. 34; String Quartet in E–flat Major, op. 51. **CD**: University of Wisconsin–Madison School of Music [no number].

2004: December 20–21 (Mon–Tue), Mills Concert Hall, University of Wisconsin–Madison
FELIX MENDELSSOHN (1809–47): Quartet no. 2 in A Minor, op. 13; Quartet no. 3 in D Major, op. 44, No. 1; Fugue in E Major, op. 81, No. 4. University of Wisconsin–Madison School of Music [no number].

2005: May 10–12 (Tue–Thu), Mills Concert Hall, University of Wisconsin–Madison
BERNHARD HENRIK CRUSELL (1775–1838): Divertimento in C Major, op. 9, for Oboe and String Quartet; WOLFGANG AMADEUS MOZART (1756–91): Quartet in F Major, for Oboe, Violin, Viola, and Cello, K. 370; BENJAMIN BRITTEN (1913–76): *Phantasy, op. 2, for Oboe, Violin, Viola, and Cello* (1932). with Marc Fink, oboe. **CD**: University of Wisconsin–Madison School of Music [no number] (with Harbison *Snow Country*).

2005: December 20 (Tue), Mills Concert Hall, University of Wisconsin–Madison
JOHN HARBISON (b. 1938): *Snow Country* (1977) for oboe, string quartet, and double bass, with Marc Fink, oboe, John Clark, bass. **CD**: University of Wisconsin–Madison School of Music [no number] (with Crusell, Mozart, Britten, above).

2005: December 25, 29 (Sun, Thu), Audio for the Arts, Madison
BRIAN FENNELLY (b. 1937): String Quartet no. 2, "Arias and Interludes" (2001). in "Skyscapes: Chamber Music of Brian Fennelly," Albany TROY980.

2010: September 25 (Sat), Mills Concert Hall, University of Wisconsin–Madison [live concert]
WOLFGANG AMADEUS MOZART (1756–91): Quartet in E–flat Major (K. 428); ROBERT SCHUMANN (1810–56): Quartet in A Major, op. 41, no. 3. **CD**: University of Wisconsin–Madison School of Music promotional release [no number].

2011: December 11–12 (Mon–Tue), Mills Concert Hall, University of Wisconsin–Madison
WALTER MAYS (b. 1941): String Quartet no. 2, "Dreaming Butterfly" (2011) and PAUL SCHOENFIELD (b. 1947): *Three Rhapsodies for Piano Quintet* (2011), with Brian Hsu, piano [both commissioned for and premiered by PAQ. **CD**: Albany set TROY1469–70 ("Centennial Anniversary Commissions, The American Premieres 2011–12": with Bolcom, Harbison).

2012: May 25–26 (Fri–Sat), Mills Concert Hall, University of Wisconsin–Madison
WILLIAM BOLCOM (b. 1938): Piano Quintet no. 2 (2011), with Christopher Taylor, piano, and JOHN HARBISON (b. 1938): String Quartet no. 5 (2011) [both commissioned for and premiered by the PAQ]. **CD**: Albany set TROY1469–70 ("Centennial Anniversary Commissions, The American Premieres 2011–12": with Mays, Schoenfield).

2015: May 16–19 (Sat–Tue), Mills Concert Hall, University of Wisconsin–Madison
BENOÎT MERNIER (b. 1964): String Quartet no. 3 (2013), and PIERRE JALBERT (b. 1967): *Howl, for Clarinet and String Quartet* (2014) [both commissioned and premiered by the PAQ]. **CD**: Albany TROY1634 ("Centennial Anniversary Commissions, Volume 2").

## *CD Reissue Collections (QPA)*

JOSEPH HAYDN (1732–1809):

**Testament**
[NB: in the 8–**LP** EMI set, the Quartets were organized strictly by opus-number sequence, whereas in these two Testament CD sets, the Quartets are in totally scrambled order, with no regard for either recording dates or opus sequences.]

Vol. I, SBT 3055 (3 CDs); vol. 2, SBT 4056 (4 CDs):
Vol. 1: Op. 1, no. 1 (1938); vol. 2: no. 6 (1936).
Vol. 2: Op. 3, no. 4 (1937), no. 5 (1933).

Vol. 1: Op. 20, no. 2 (1931), no. 5 (1934); vol. 2: no. 1 (1938), no. 4 (1935).
Vol. 2: Op. 33, no. 2 (1933), no. 3 (1931), no. 6 (1932).
Vol. 1: Op. 50, no. 3 (1934); vol. 2: no. 6 (1937).
Vol. 1: Op. 54, no. 1 (1932), no. 2 (1932), no. 3 (1936).
Vol. 2: Op. 55, no. 1 (1936), no, 3 (1938).
Vol. 2: Op. 64, no. 3 (1937); no. 4 (1936); vol. 2: no. 6 (1933).
Vol. 2: Op. 71, no. 1 (1933).
Vol. 1: Op. 74, no. 3 (1931); vol. 2: no. 1 (1937), no. 2 (1935).
Vol. 1: Op. 76, no. 3 (1934), no. 4 (1938).
Vol. 1: Op. 77, no. 2 (1935); vol. 2: no. 1 (1931).

**Allegro**
Vol. 1, CDO 4011 (2 CDs):
Op. 1, no. 1 (1938).
Op. 20, no. 1 (1938), no. 2 (1931), no. 4 (1935), no. 5 (1934).
Op. 33, no. 2 (1933), no. 3 (1931), no. 6 (1932).
Op. 50, no. 6 (1937).

Vol. 2, CDO 4012 (2 CDs):
Op. 54, no. 1 (1932), no. 2 (1932), no. 3 (1936).
Op. 64, no. 3 (1937), no. 4 (1936).
Op. 74, no. 1 (1937), no. 2 (1935), no. 3 (1931).

Vol. 3, CDO 4013 (1 CD):
Op. 76, no. 3 (1934), no. 4 (1938).
Op. 77, no. 2 (1935).

**Enterprise/Strings**
QT 99–370:
Op. 77, no. 1 (1931), no. 2 (1935) [with Franck]

QT 99–374:
Op. 33, no. 2 (1933), no. 6 (1932).
Op. 74, no. 1 (1937), no. 2 (1935)

QT 99–377:
Op. 55, no. 1 (1936), no. 3 (1938).
Op. 64, no. 6 (1933).
Op. 71, no. 1 (1931).

QT 99–380:
Op. 20, no. 1 (1938), no. 4 (1935).
Op. 33, no. 3 (1931).
Op. 50, no. 6 (1937).

QT 99–383:
Op. 1, no. 1 (1938)

Op. 54, no. 1 (1932), no. 2 (1932), no. 3 (1936)

QT 99–386:
Op. 20, no. 2 (1931), no. 5 (1934).
Op. 76, no. 3 (1934), no. 4 (1938).

QT 99–388 = Tactus TC 99388:
Op. 64, no. 3 (1937), no. 4 (1936).
Op. 74, no. 3 (1931).
Op. 77, no. 2 (1935).

**Gramofono:** AB 78 916:
Op. 64, no. 3 (1937), 4 (1936).
Op. 74, no. 3 (1931).
Op. 77, no. 2 (1935).


FRANZ SCHUBERT (1797–1828):

**Andante:** 1990 ("Schubert Chamber Music"):
"Trout" Quintet (D. 667) (1935)
String Quintet in C (D. 956) (1935)
[with seven other works by other performers]


Miscellaneous

**Andante:** 2970 ("Quatuor Pro Arte"):
Bartók: Quartet no. 1, op. 7 (1934)
Beethoven: Quartet no. 8, op. 59, no. 2 (1938)
Bloch: Piano Quintet no. 1 (1933)
Borodin: Quartet no. 2 in D (1933)
Franck: Quartet in D (1933)
Glazunov: Novelettes, op. 15:5 (1933)
Mozart: String Quintet no. 3 in C (K. 515) (1934)
Ravel: Quartet in F (1933)
Schubert: Quartet no. 10 in E-flat (D. 87): Finale (1933)
Schumann: Piano Quintet in E-flat, op. 44 (1934)


*Composers, Alphabetical*

Quatuor Pro Arte

BARTÓK, BÉLA (1881–1945)
Quartet no. 1, op. 7 (October 31–November 2, 1934)

BEETHOVEN, LUDWIG VAN (1770–1827)
Quartet no. 8 in E Minor, op. 59, no. 2 (November 16, 1938)

BLOCH, ERNEST (1880–1959)
Piano Quintet no. 1 [Casella] (February 8, 1933)

BORODIN, ALEXANDER (1833–87)
Quartet no. 2 in D Major (December 8, 1933)

BRAHMS, JOHANNES (1833–97)
Piano Quartet no. 1 in G Minor, op. 25 [Rubinstein] (October 7, 10, 11, 1932)
Sextet no. 1, op. 18 [Hobday, Pini] (March 8–9, 1935)

DEBUSSY, CLAUDE (1862–1918)
Quartet in G Minor, op. 10 (February 7, 1933)

DVOŘÁK, ANTONÍN (1844–1901)
Piano Quintet in A Major, op. 81 [Schnabel] (February 1, 1934)

FAURÉ, GABRIEL (1845–1924)
Quartet in E Minor, op. 121 (November 19, 1935)

FRANCK, CÉSAR (1822–90)
Quartet in D Major (May 18, 25, 1933)

GLAZUNOV, ALEXANDER (1865–1936)
5 *Novelettes*, op. 15, no. 5. *Orientale* (December 11, 1933)

HAYDN, JOSEPH (1732–1809) [Hoboken Numbers]
Quartet no. 1 in B-flat Major, op. 1, no. 1, "La Chasse" (November 5, 1938)
Quartet no. 6 in C Major, op. 1, no. 6 (December 3, 1936)
Quartet no. 16 in B-flat Major, op. 3, no. 4 [by R. Hoffstetter] (16.XI.1937)
Quartet no. 17 in F Major, op. 3, no. 5, "Serenade" [by R. Hoffstetter] (11.
　　XII.1933)
Quartet no. 31 in E-flat Major, op. 20, no. 1 (November 5, 1938)
Quartet no. 32 in C Major, op. 20, no. 2 (December 2, 1931)
Quartet no. 34 in D Major, op. 20, no. 4 (November 11, 1935)
Quartet no. 35 in F Minor, op. 20, no. 5 (October 29, 1934)
Quartet no. 38 in E-flat Major, op. 33, no. 2, "Joke" (December 11, 1933)
Quartet no. 39 in C Major, op. 33, no. 3 "Bird" (December 1, 1931)
Quartet no. 42 in D Major, op. 33, no. 6 (October 7, 1932)
Quartet no. 46 in E-flat Major, op. 50, no. 3 (October 30, 1934)
Quartet no. 49 in D Major, op. 50, no. 6, "Frog" (November 15, 1937)
Quartet no. 57 in C Major, op. 54, no. 1 (October 6, 1932)
Quartet no. 58 in G Major, op. 54, no. 2 (October 6, 1932)
Quartet no. 59 in E Major, op. 54, no. 3 (November 19, 1936)
Quartet no. 60 in A Major, op. 55, no. 1 (19.XI.1936)
Quartet no. 62 in B-flat Major, op. 55, no. 3 (Novemher 5, 1938)
Quartet no. 65 in B-flat Major, op. 64, no. 3 (November 16, 1937)
Quartet no. 66 in G Major, op. 64, no. 4 (December 3, 1936)

Quartet no. 68 in E-flat Major, op. 64, no. 6 (December 11, 1933)
Quartet no. 69 in B–flat Major, op. 71, no. 1 (December 12, 1933)
Quartet no. 73 in F Major, op. 74, no. 2 (November 18, 1935)
Quartet no. 72 in C Major, op. 74, no. 1 (November 15, 1937
Quartet no. 74 in G Minor, op. 74,. no. 3 "Rider" (November 30, 1931)
Quartet no. 77 in C Major, op. 76, no. 3, "Emperor" (October 29, 1934)
Quartet no. 78 in B-flat Major, op. 76, no. 4, "Sunrise" (December 15, 1938)
Quartet no. 81 in G Major, op. 77, no. 1 (December 1–2, 1931)
Quartet no. 82 in F Major, op. 77, no. 2, "Lobkowitz" (March 7, 1935)

MOZART, WOLFGANG AMADEUS (1756–91)
Piano Quartet no. 1 in G Minor (K. 487) [Schnabel] (January 31, 1934)
Quartet no. 16 in E-flat Major (K. 428) (November 15, 1936)
Serenade no. 13 in G Major, *Eine kleine Nachtmusik* (K. 525) [C. Hobday]
    (November 16, 1937)
String Quintet no. 3 in C Major (K. 515) [Hobday] (November 2–3, 1934)
String Quintet no. 4 in G Minor (K. 516) [Hobday] (November 15, 1934)
String Quintet no. 5 in D Major (K. 593) [Hobday] (November 18, 1936)

RAVEL, MAURICE (1875–1937)
Quartet in F Major (December 8, 1933)

SCHUBERT, FRANZ (1797–1828)
Piano Quintet in A Major, op. 114, "Trout" (D. 667) [Schnabel, C. Hobday]
    (November 16, 1935)
Quartet no. 10 in E-flat Major, op. posth. 125 (D. 87): Finale (May 18, 1933)
String Quintet in C Major, op. posth. 163 (D. 956) [Pini] (March 6–8, 1935)

SCHUMANN, ROBERT (1810–56)
Piano Quintet in E-flat Major, op. 44 [Schnabel] (December 3–19, 1934)

VIVALDI, ANTONIO (1678–1741)
Concerto in A Major, op. 3 (*L'estro armonico*), no. 5 [arr. Pochon] (December
    12, 1933

Pro Arte Quartet of the University of Wisconsin

ADLER, SAMUEL (b. 1928)
Fourth String Quartet (1963) (June 2–7, 1968)

BARTÓK, BÉLA (1881–1945)
Quartet no. 5 (January 26, 1945)

BEETHOVEN, LUDWIG VAN (1770–1827)
Quartet in F Major, op. 18, no. 1 [original version] (1981)

BERG, ALBAN (1885–1935)

*Lyric Suite* (February 2, 1950)

BLOCH, ERNEST (1880–1959)
*In the Mountains*: "Dusk"; "Rustic Dance" (May?, 1986)
*Paysages*: "North"; "Alpestre"; "Tongataboo" (May?, 1986)
Piano Quintet no. 1 (1923) [Karp] (December [7?], 1989)
Piano Quartet no. 2 (1957) [Karp] (May 18–19, 1983)
Quartet no. 1 (1916) (May?, 1980)
Quartet no. 2 (1945) (April–May 1982)
Quartet no. 3 (1952) (May?, 1986)
Quartet no. 4 (1954) (May?, 1986)
Quartet no. 5 (1956) (December?, 1989)

BOLCOM, WILLIAM (b. 1938)
Piano Quintet no. 2 (2011) (May 25–26, 2013)

BOYKAN, MARTIN (b. 1932)
String Quartet no. 2 (1973) (April?, 1978)

BRAHMS, JOHANNES (1833–97)
Piano Quintet in F Minor, op. 34 [Karp] (1984/85)

BRITTEN, BENJAMIN (1913–75)
*Phantasy*, op. 2, for Oboe, Violin, Viola, and Cello (1932) [Fink] (May 10–12, 2005)

CRUSELL, BERNHARD HENRIK (1775–1838)
Divertimento in C Major, op. 9, for Oboe and String Quartet [Fink] (May 10–12, 2005)

DIESENDRUCK, TAMAR (b. 1946)
*Such Stuff* (Quartet no. 1: 1988) (December 19–20, 1991)
String Quartet no. 2 (*Babel Dreams*: 1992) (April 13, 1993)

DVOŘÁK, ANTONÍN (1841–1904)
Quartet in D Minor, op. 34 (April 30–May 1, 2001)
Quartet in E-flat Major, op. 51 (April 30–May 1, 2001)

ELSTON, ARNOLD (1907–71)
String Quartet (1961) (January 19, 1972)

FENNELLY, BRIAN (b. 1937)
String Quartet no. 2. "Arias and Interludes" (2001) (December 25, 29, 2005)

FERNANDES, ARMANDO JOSÉ (1906–83)
Piano Quintet [Karp] (1984)

FREITAS BRANCO, LUIS DE (1890–1955)
String Quartet (1911) (1984)

FROMM, HERBERT (1905–95)
String Quartet (1957) (June 2–7, 1968)

HARBISON, JOHN (b. 1938)
*Snow Country,* for Oboe, String Quartet, and Double Bass [Fink, Clark]
(December 20, 2005)
String Quartet no. 5 (2011) (December 25–26, 2013)

IMBRIE, ANDREW (1921–2007)
String Quartet no. 4 (1969) (May 7–9, 1993)
String Quartet no. 5 (1987) (May 7–8, 1993)

JALBERT, PIERRE (b. 1967)
*Howl,* for Clarinet and String Quartet (2014) (May 18, 2015)

LANSKY, PAUL (b. 1944)
String Quartet (1971/77) (November?, 1978)

LERDAHL, FRED (b. 1943)
Second String Quartet (1981/83) (May 18–19, 1983)

MAYS, WALTER (b. 1941)
String Quartet in G Minor (1998) (December 29–31, 2000)
String Quartet no. 2, "Dreaming Butterfly" (2011) (May 25–26, 2013)

MENDELSSOHN, FELIX (1809–47)
Fugue in E Major, op. 81, no. 4 (December 20–21, 2004)
Quartet no. 2 in A Minor, op. 13 (December 20–21, 2004)
Quartet no. 3 in D Major, op. 44, no. 1 (December 20–21, 2004)

MERNIER, BENOÎT (b. 1964)
String Quartet no. 3 (2013) (May 16–19, 2015)

MOZART, WOLFGANG AMADEUS (1756–91)
Quartet in F Major, for Oboe, Violin, Viola, and Cello (K. 370) [Fink] (May
10–12, 2005)
Quartet in E-flat Major (K. 428) (September 25, 2010)

RATHAUS, KAROL (1895–1954)
String Quartet no. 5, op. 72 (1927) (December 16–17, 1986)

RHODES, SAMUEL (b. 1928)
Quintet (1968) (December 29–31, 2000)

RÓZSA, MIKLÓS (1907–95)
String Quartet no. 1, op. 22 (1950) (June?, 1987)
String Quartet no. 2, op. 38 (1981) (June?, 1987)

SCHOENBERG, ARNOLD (1874–1951)
Quartet in D Major (1897) (February 7, 1952)
Quartet no. 3 (January 24, 1950)

SCHOENFIELD, PAUL (b. 1947)
*Three Rhapsodies for Piano Quintet* (2011) (December 11–12, 2011)

SCHUMANN, ROBERT (1810–56)
Quartet in A Major, op. 41, no. 3 (September 25, 2010)

SESSIONS, ROGER (1896–1985)
Quartet no. 1 in E Minor (February 2, 1945)
String Quintet (1958) [Rhodes] (December 29–31, 2000)

SHAPEY, RALPH (1921–2002)
String Quartet no. 9 (1995) (May 4, 1996)

SZYMANOWSKI, KAROL (1882–1937)
Quartet no. 1 in C, op. 37 (May?, 1982)
Quartet no. 2, op. 56 (May?, 1982)

WEBERN, ANTON (1883–1945)
*Five Movements for String Quartet*, op. 5 (January 20, 1950)
*Six Bagatelles for String Quartet*, op. 9 (January 20, 1950)

# Noncommercial Archive Recordings
# (Mills Music Library, University of Wisconsin)

## Performance Recordings from Tape, 1940s

[NB: These recordings were digitized to compact discs by Seth Winner Studios, New York. Some are concert recordings; some are taken from Carl Bricken's lectures with live performances; some were recorded by WHA Radio for broadcast by the Mutual Network. Original source recordings for Mutual, on 16-inch LP discs, also in the Archives, are marked with an asterisk (*).]

Brosa Years

BACH. *Brandenburg Concerto* no. 4 [mvts. 2–3 only]. December 16, 1940. **CD** 1A: 3–4

BEETHOVEN. *Grosse Fuge*, op. 133. May 6, 1943. **CD** 5A: 5

BEETHOVEN. Quartet no. 1 in F, op. 18, no. 1 [mvts. 1–3, incomplete, with lecture]. March 11, 1943. **CD** 4A: 1–2

BEETHOVEN. Quartet no. 2 in G, op. 18, no. 2 [incomplete, with lecture]. March 25, 1943. **CD** 4A: 3–4, and 4B: 1–2

BEETHOVEN. Quartet no. 6 in B-flat, op. 18, no. 6 [complete, with lecture]. April 1, 1943. **CD** 4B: 3–4

BEETHOVEN. Quartet no. 9 in C, op. 59, no. 3. April 29, 1943. **CD** 5A: 1–2

BEETHOVEN. Quartet no. 11 in F Minor, op. 95. May 6, 1943. **CD** 5A: 3–4

BRAHMS. Quartet no. 1 in C Minor, op. 51, no. 1 [mvts. 1–2 incomplete, mvts. 3–4 complete]. February 16, 1941. **CD** 1A: 5–7

BRAHMS. Quartet no. 2 in A Minor, op. 51, no. 2 [mvt. 1; 2 incomplete]. February 28, 1943. **CD** 3B: 4

BRAHMS. Piano Quartet no. 1 in G Minor, op. 25 [Halleux, Prevost, Evans, Johansen]. March 24, 1941. **CD** 2A: 1–4*

BRAHMS. Quintet no. 1 in F, op. 88 [mvts. 2–4; with Harold Klatz]. March 24, 1941. **CD** 1B: 6 and 6B: 1*

BRAHMS. Quintet no. 2 in G, op. 111 [with Harold Klatz]. February 16, 1941. **CD** 1B: 4–5

BRAHMS. Violin Sonata no. 1 in G, op. 78 [Brosa, Johansen]. February 16, 1941. **CD** 1B: 1–3*

BRAHMS. Violoncello Sonata no. 1 in D Minor, op. 38 [mvt. 1; Evans, Johansen]. March 24, 1941. **CD** 6B: 2*

DVOŘÁK. Quartet no. 12 in F, op. 96, "American" [mvts. 1, 4]. May 13, 1944. **CD** 6A: 5*

HAYDN. Quartet in D, op. 20, no. 4 [mvt. 3 only]. May 13, 1944. **CD** 6A: 4

HAYDN. Quartet in A, op. 20, no. 6. October 4, 1943. **CD** 5B: 1

HAYDN. Quartet in E-flat, op. 33, no. 2. November 11, 1943. **CD** 6A: 1

HAYDN. Quartet in D, op. 64, no. 5, "Lark." November 11, 1943. **CD** 5B: 3

HAYDN. Quartet in B-flat, op. 71, no. 1. December 2, 1943. **CD** 6A: 2–3

HAYDN. Quartet in D Minor, op. 76, no. 2 [mvt. 1 incomplete; 2–4]. November 12, 1942. **CD** 2A: 5

HAYDN. Quartet in C, op,. 76, no. 3 [mvt. 1]. November 19, 1942. **CD** 2B: 1

HAYDN. Quartet in B-flat, op. 76, no. 4. December 3, 1942. **CD** 2B: 2–3

HAYDN. Quartet in G, op. 77, no. 1. December 17, 1942. **CD** 2B: 4 and 3A: 1

HINDEMITH. Quartet no. 3, op. 22 [mvt. 5 excerpt]. February 28, 1943. **CD** 3B: 3

MOZART. Quartet no. 21 in D, K. 575. February 28, 1943. **CD** 3B: 1–3

MOZART. Piano Quartet no. 2 in E-flat, K. 493 [mvts. 1, 2, both incomplete; Halleux, Prevost, Evans, Johansen]. November 3, 1940. **CD** 1A: 1–2

MOZART. Quintet in G Minor, K.516 [mvts. 1–3, 4 incomplete; with lecture]. February 25, 1943.**CD** 3A: 2–3

TCHAIKOVSKY. Scherzo. May 13, 944. **CD** 6A: 4

Kolisch Years:

As the book was going to press, news arrived of a project to make CD releases, from the live and transcribed performances, by Werner Unger for his Archiphon label. The sources were 16" transcription LPs made for broadcast by Mutual Radio Network. Some works are preserved incomplete, and all incude radio announcements. The first transfers to CDs were made by Seth Winner, but these have been considerably enhanced in Unger's restorations. These have come too late for thorough discographic evaluation, but reference is made to them below. The performances are preceded with a dagger (†); the Archiphon releases are then listed after these in systematic order. It is expected that more such Archiphon releases are still to come.

†BEETHOVEN. Quartet no. 1 in F, op. 18, no. 1. October 14, 1945. **CD** 7A: 1–2
†BEETHOVEN. Quartet no. 1 in F, op. 18, no. 1. March 15, 1947. **CD** 11B: 3–4
†BEETHOVEN. Quartet no. 3 in D, op. 18, no. 3 [mvts 1, 2 incomplete]. December 23, 1945. **CD** 8B: 2
†BEETHOVEN. Quartet no. 5 in A, op. 18, no. 5. January 4, 1947. **CD** 10A: 1–2*
†BEETHOVEN. Quartet no. 6 in B-flat, op. 18, no. 6. March 29, 1947. **CD** 12A: 3–4
†BEETHOVEN. Quartet no. 7 in F, op. 59, no. 1 [mvts. 2–4]. May 12, 1946. **CD** 9B: 3–4
†BEETHOVEN. Quartet no. 8 in E Minor, op. 59, no. 2. January 18, 1947. **CD** 10A: 3–4*
†BEETHOVEN. Quartet no. 9 in C, op. 59, no. 3 [with interviews]. April 12, 1947. **CD** 12B: 3–5
†BEETHOVEN. Quartet no. 9 in C, op. 59, no. 3. April 3, 1949. **CD** 19B: 4, and 20:18
†BEETHOVEN. Quartet no. 11 in F Minor, op. 95. October 9, 1947. **CD** 13A: 1–2
†BEETHOVEN. Quartet no. 12 in E-flat, op. 127 [mvts. 1–3]. February 24, 1946. **CD** 9A: 3–4*
†BRAHMS. Quartet no. 2 in A Minor, op. 51, no. 2. February 5, 1947. **CD** 11A:1–2*
BRAHMS. Quartet no. 3 in B-flat, op. 67 [mvts. 1–2]. October 28, 1945. **CD** 7B: 3
†BRAHMS. Quartet no. 3 in B-flat, op. 67 [mvts. 1, incomplete; 2–4]. April 5, 1947. **CD** 12B: 1–2
†BRAHMS. Piano Quintet in F Minor, op. 34 [with Johansen, plus interviews with Milofsky and Johansen]. October 19, 1947. **CD** 13A: 3–5
†DEBUSSY. Quartet in G Minor. April 17, 1948. **CD** 17B: 3–4
†DVOŘÁK. Quartet no. 12 in F, op. 96, "American." October 17, 1948. **CD** 18B: 2–3*

HAGEN, O. Suite for String Quartet. March 7, 1949. **CD** 19A: 3–4*
†HAYDN. Quartet in D, op. 64, no. 5. March 1, 1947. **CD** 11B: 1–2
†HAYDN. Quartet in D Minor, op. 76, no. 2. April 3, 1949. **CD** 19B: 1–2
LUCKHARDT, H. Duo for Violin and Viola [Kolisch, Milofsky]. April 3, 1949. **CD** 19B: 3
MOZART. Quartet no. 17 in B-flat, K. 458 [mvts 1–2; 3 incomplete]. November 11, 1945. **CD** 8A: 2–3
†MOZART. Quartet no. 19 in C, K. 465. October 7, 1945. **CD** 6B: 3–4
†MOZART. Quartet no. 19 in C, K. 465. January 17, 1948. **CD** 14B: 3–4
MOZART. Quartet no. 20 in D, K. 499 [mvt. 3; 4 incomplete]. February 1, 1947. **CD** 10B: 1
†MOZART. Quartet no. 21 in D, K. 575. December 16, 1945. **CD** 8A: 4 and 8B: 1
†MOZART. Quartet no. 22 in B-flat, K. 589. April 10, 1948. **CD** 17B: 1–2
†MOZART. Quartet no. 23 in F, K. 590. February 10, 1946. **CD** 9A: 1–2*
†MOZART. Quartet no. 23 in F, K. 590. March 22, 1947. **CD** 12A: 1–2*
†RAVEL. Quartet in F. April 5, 1947. **CD** 11A: 3–4
SCHOENBERG. Quartet no. 2 in F-sharp Minor, op. 10 [with Betina Bjork-sten]. (February 6 or 15, 1949). **CD**19A: 1–2*
SCHUBERT. Quartet no. 8 in B-flat, D. 112. October 26, 1947. **CD** 13B: 2–3 and 14a: 1
†SCHUBERT. Quartet no. 8 in B-flat, D. 112. January 24, 1948. **CD** 15A: 1–2
SCHUBERT. Quartet no. 13 in A Minor, D. 804. October 21, 1945. **CD** 7B: 1–2
SCHUBERT. Quartet no. 13 in A Minor, D. 804 [mvt. 1, 2 incomplete]. February 3, 1946. **CD** 8B: 3
SCHUBERT. Quartet no. 13 in A Minor, D. 804. February 8, 1947. **CD** 10B: 2–3*
†SCHUBERT. Quartet no. 13 in A Minor, D. 804. January 31, 1948. **CD** 15A: 3–4*
SCHUBERT. Quartet no. 14 in D Minor, D, 810, "Death and the Maiden." October 17, 1948. **CD** 18A: 3–4*
SCHUBERT. Quartet no. 15 in G, D. 887. February 14, 1948. **CD** 15B: 3–4
SCHUBERT. Quartet no. 15 in G, D. 887. February 15, 1948. **CD** 16A: 3–4, 16B: 1–2*
SCHUBERT. *Quartentsatz* in C Minor, D. 703. May 5, 1946. **CD** 9B: 1
SCHUBERT. *Quartentsatz* in C Minor, D. 703. February 17, 1948. **CD** 15B: 2 (end)
SCHUBERT. Quintet in C, D. 956 [mvts 2–4, with Leigh Elder]. March 13, 1948. **CD** 17A: 3–4*
†SCHUBERT. Piano Quintet in A, D. 667, "The Trout" [Kolisch, Milofsky, Friedlander, Ralph Handcock, Johansen]. October 26, 1947. **CD** 14A: 3–4, and 14B: 1–2
†SCHUBERT. String Trio in B-flat, D. 581 [Kolisch, Milofsky, Friedlander]. February 7, 1948. **CD** 15B: 1–2
SCHUBERT. Sonatina no. 1 in D for Violin and Piano, D. 384 [Rahier, Steffens]. October 26, 1947. **CD** 14A: 2

SCHUBERT. Sonatina no. 2 in A Minor for Violin and Piano, D. 385 [Rahier, Carpenter]. February 15, 1948. **CD** 16A: 1–3
SCHUMANN. Quartet no. 1 in A Minor, op. 41, no. 1 [mvt. 2 incomplete, 3–4]. November 4, 1945. **CD** 8A: 1*
SCHUMANN. Quartet no. 2 in F, op. 41, no. 2 [mvts 1–2, 3 incomplete]. 8 March 1947. **CD** 8A: 2–3
†SHOSTAKOVICH. Trio no. 2 in E Minor, op. 67 [mvts 1–2, 3 incomplete]. May 5, 1946. **CD**18B: 4
†WOLF. *Italian Serenade.* February 1, 1947. **CD** 10B: 1
†WOLF. *Italian Serenade.* October 4, 1948. **CD** 17B (end)

## *16–inch LP Discs (for Mutual) not already noted above (no players or dates identified):*

BACH. *Brandenburg Concertos* nos. 2, 5, 6
MOZART. Quintet in C Minor, K.465
PISTON. [miscellaneous]

## *Archiphon Releases to Date:*

BEETHOVEN. Quartets, op. 18: no. 1 (October 14, 1945, March 15, 1947); no. 3 (December 23, 1945, incomplete); no. 5 (January 4, 1947); no. 6 (March 29, 1947). ARC-WU 192–93
BEETHOVEN. Quartets op. 59, no. 1 (May 5 and 12, 1946); no. 2 (January 18, 1947). ARC-WU 194
BEETHOVEN. Quartets op. 59 no. 3 (April 12, 1947); op. 95 (October 19, 1947). ARC-WU 195
BEETHOVEN. Quartets op. 127 (February 24, 1946, incomplete); op. 133 (May 6, 1943). ARC-WU 197
BRAHMS. Quartets op. 51 no. 2 (February 5, 1947, incomplete); op. 67 (April 5, 1947). ARC-WU 199
BRAHMS. Piano Quintet op. 34 (October 19, 1947). ARC-WU 200
DEBUSSY. Quartet (April 17, 1984); Ravel. Quartet (February 23, 1947). ARC-WU 202
DVOŘÁK. Quartet op. 96 (October 17, 1948); Wolf, Italian Serenade (February 1, 1947, October 4, 1948); Shostakovich. Piano Trio op. 67 (May 5, 1946). ARC-WU 204
MOZART. Quartets K. 575 (December 16, 1945), K. 465 (January 17, 1948). ARC-WU 208
MOZART. Quartets K. 589 (April 10, 1948), K. 590 (**). ARC-WU 210
SCHUBERT. Quartets D. 112 (January 24, 1948), D. 804 (January 31, 1948). ARC-WU 216
SCHUBERT. Piano Quintet D. 667 (October 26, 1947), String Trio D. 581 (February 7, 1948). ARC-WU 221

In addition to the foregoing, and what may come after, Archiphon has released several of the recordings by the earlier Kolisch Quartet, including the 2-CD set of the four Schoenberg Quartets (103–4) as well as their recordings of music by Schubert (107), and Mozart, Schuman, and Wolf (108). There are two volumes of "Kolisch in USA" (130–31, 132) plus a Schubert collection (044); there are also performances of music by Schoenberg (045), including the Violin Concerto, plus *Pierrot lunaire* and the Chamber Symphony (061), as well as the rare Quartet in D of 1897, as performed at the Library of Congress on February 7, 1952 (number not yet known). From Kolisch's Madison years on his own, there are collected performances of music by Liszt and Busoni (048); by Bach and Mozart (058, by Schubert (057); by Webern and Bartók (060); and by Debussy and Ravel (061). Further, there is a recording, made with René Leibowitz, of the Beethoven Violin Concerto (056). Finally, there are two lectures by Kolisch, in German: "Tempo und Charakter in Beethovens Musik" (010) and "Interpretationsprobleme bei Arnold Schönberg" (011). For any serious study of Kolisch's career, as well as of the Pro Arte Quartet under his leadership, these documentary recordings are of great importance. All of the Archiphon releases are available commercially from the company itself at Grossherzog-Friedrich-Strasse, D–77694 Kehl, Germany; email: unger@archiphon.de.

## Reel–to–Reel Tapes (All Paulu years, mostly concert performances):

ADLER. Quartet no. 5 [world premiere]. June 11, 1970
BARTÓK. Quartet no. 2. May 5, 1968
BARTÓK. Quartet no. 6 [open rehearsal, 2 tapes]. December 13, 1978
BARTÓK. Quartet no. 6. February 24, 1979 (with Mozart K. 575)
BEETHOVEN. Quartet no. 3 in D, op. 18, no. 3. January 7, 1968
BEETHOVEN. Quartet no. 5 in A, op. 18, no. 5. November 12, 1967
BEETHOVEN. Quartet no. 10 in E-flat, op. 74. February 8, 1968
BEETHOVEN. Quartet no. 11 in F Minor, op. 95. May 1, 1970
BEETHOVEN. Quartet no. 13 in B-flat, op. 130. May 1, 1970
BEETHOVEN. Quartet no. 16 in F, op. 135. May 5, 1968
BEETHOVEN. *Grosse Fuge* in B-flat, op. 133. May 1, 1970
BERG. Quartet, op. 3. February 9, 1969 (added to Haydn op. 76:2)
BLACKWOOD, E. Concertino for Five Instruments, op. 5. May 16, 1969
BRAHMS. Quartet no. 1 in C, op. 51, no. 1. March 2, 1973
BRAHMS. Quintet no. 2 in G, op. 111. February 24, 1979
DEBUSSY. Quartet in G Minor, op. 10. November 12, 1967

DEBUSSY. Quartet in G Minor, op. 10. March 2, 1973
DEBUSSY. Quartet in G Minor, op. 10. February 21, 1976 (with Stravinsky)
DOHNÁNYI. Serenade, op. 10, for Violin, Viola, and Cello [Paulu, R. Blum, Downes]. December 3, 1972
DVOŘÁK. Quartet no. 13 in A-flat, op. 105. February 9, 1969
FOSS. Quartet no. 1 in G (1947). January 7, 1968
HAYDN. Quartet in D, op. 20, no. 4. February 21, 1976 (with Korte)
HAYDN. Quartet in D Minor, op. 76, no. 2, "Quinten." February 9, 1969 (with Berg)
HINDEMITH. Quartet no. 3, op. 22. February 8, 1968
IMBRIE. Quartet no. 2. March 14, 1969
IMBRIE. Quartet no. 4. March 12, 1973
KORTE. Quartet no. 2. February 21, 1976 (attached to Haydn op. 20:4)
LANSKY. Quartet [open rehearsal]. November 10, 1978
LUCKHARDT, H.. Quartet no. 3. May 5, 1968
LUCKHARDT, H.. Quartet no. 4. December 4, 1971 (attached to Mozart Adagio and Fugue)
MARTINŮ. Trio in D Minor for Violin, Viola, and Cello [Jeanette Ross, Paulu, Downes]. December 3, 1972
MENDELSSOHN. Octet in E–flat [with Fine Arts Quartet]. April 18, 1969
MOZART. Adagio and Fugue in C Minor, K. 546. December 4, 1971 (with Luckhardt)
MOZART. Quartet no. 21 in D, K. 575. January 11, 1970
MOZART. Quartet no. 21 in D, K. 575. February 24, 1979 (with Bartók Quartet 6)
MOZART. Quintet in D, K. 593 [with Fine Arts Quartet member]. April 18, 1969
RAVEL. Quartet in F. January 7, 1968
RAVEL. Quartet In F. November 9, 1978 (attached to Schoenberg Qt. 1)
SCHOENBERG. Quartet no. 1. November 9, 1978 (with Ravel)
SCHOENBERG. *Verklärte Nacht* [with Fine Arts Quartet members]. April 18, 1969
SCHUBERT. Quartet no. 13 in A Minor, D. 804. January 11, 1970
SCHUMANN. Quartet no. 3 in A, op. 41, no. 3. December 4, 1971
SESSIONS. Quartet no. 2. November 12, 1967
STRAVINSKY. Double Canon. February 21, 1976 (attached to Debussy Quartet)
THIMMIG, L. *Seven Profiles* [with Thimmig]. March 2, 1973
WITT, R. Quartet no. 1. February 8, 1968

# SELECTED BIBLIOGRAPHY

Barr, Cyrilla. *Elizabeth Sprague Coolidge: An American Patron of Music.* New York: Schirmer, 1998.

Blum, Martha. "The Pro Arte Quartet: 50 Years." In *The Pro Arte Quartet: 50 Years; The Wingra Woodwing Quintet: 50 Years,* by Martha Blum and Nancy Becknell. Madison: University of Wisconsin–Madison, School of Music, 1991.

Brandt, Nat. *Con Brio: Four Russians Called the Budapest String Quartet.* New York: Oxford University Press, 1993.

Day, Timothy. *A Century of Recorded Music: Listening to Musical History.* New Haven, CT: Yale University Press, 2002.

Dubinsky, Rostislav. *Stormy Applause: Making Music in a Worker's State.* Boston: Northeastern University Press, 1989.

Eisenberg, Evan. *The Recording Angel: Explorations in Phonology/The Experience of Music from Aristotle to Zappa.* New York: McGraw-Hill/Penguin Books, 1987.

Gaisberg, Frederick William. *The Music Goes Round.* New York: Macmillan. 1942. Republished as *Music on Record.* London: Robert Hale, 1948.

Gelatt, Roland. *The Fabulous Phonograph: The Story of the Gramophone from Tin Foil to High Fidelity.* Philadelphia: 1954. Rev. ed., London: Macmillan. 1977.

Hart, Philip. "The Budapest String Quartet Recordings: An Annotated Discography: Part 1: His Master's Voice, 1924–40; Part 2: Columbia Masterworks, 1940–54; Part 3: Columbia Masterworks, 1955–66." *ARSC Journal* 28, no. 2 (1997): 155–73; vol. 24 no. 1 (1998): 85–104; vol. 29, no, 2 (1998): 183–201.

Malderen, Anne Van. "Historique et réception des diverse formations Pro Arte (1912–47)." PhD. diss., Université Catholique de Louvain, 2012.

Moore, Jerrold Northrop. *A Matter of Records: Fred Gaisberg and the Golden Era of the Gramophone.* New York: Taplinger, 1977.

Potter, Tully. *Adolf Busch: The Life of an Honest Musician.* 2 vols. Woodbridge, UK: Toccata Press, 2010.

———. "Budapesters Betrayed." *Classic Record Collector,* Autumn 2003, 36–47.

———. "Bringing Smetana to Life." *Classic Record Collector,* Autumn 2012, 24–33.

———. "The Busch Quartet." *The Gramophone,* November 2013, 20–21.

———. "Czechs and Balances." *Classic Record Collector,* Summer 2006, 40–45.

———. "Poirot lunaire." *Classic Record Collector,* Spring 2001, 30–37.

———. "Pro Arte Quartet." *The Gramophone,* February 2013, 18–19.

———. "Virtues of the Virtuoso Four." *Classic Record Collector,* Summer 2011, 24–28.

Rosseels, Gustave. *A Remembering Journey.* [Private] 1981.

Ruttencutter, Helen Drees. *Quartet: A Profile of the Guarneri Quartet.* New York: Lippincott & Crowell. 1980.

Schwarzkopf, Elisabeth. *On and Off the Record: A Memoir of Walter Legge.* New York: Scribners, 1982.

Steinhardt, Arnold. *Indivisible by Four: A String Quartet in Pursuit of Harmony.* New York: Ferrar-Straus, 1998.

Temianka, Henri. *Facing the Music: An Irreverent Close-up of the Real Concert World.* New York: McKay, 1973. Reprint, Sherman Oaks, CA: Alfred Publishing, 1980.

# INDEX A

# Composers

# INDEX B

# General

First organized in Brussels in 1912 by precocious young Belgian musicians, the Pro Arte String Quartet has survived two world wars and is still performing more than a century later—a durability unique in the annals of such ensembles. Its membership has included such extraordinary musicians as founding first violinist Alphonse Onnou and his successor, Rudolf Kolisch. The Pro Arte was the first string quartet to be affiliated with an American university, a significant and much-imitated status, and the group continues to function in residence at the University of Wisconsin.

This book traces the Pro Arte Quartet's history from its beginnings to the present, highlighted by portraits of the diverse, fascinating, and colorful personalities, musicians and others, who have been a part of that history. The phases of its repertoires are analyzed, and the legacy of its recordings, many of pioneering significance, is reviewed. As a whole, the volume offers a panoramic window into a century of musical life.

John W. Barker is emeritus professor of history at the University of Wisconsin–Madison. He is the author of *Wagner and Venice* (2008) and *Wagner and Venice Fictionalized: Variations on a Theme* (2012), both available from the University of Rochester Press.

"In this detailed account of the Pro Arte Quartet's one-hundred-year existence, the generous appendices are almost worth the cover price alone. . . . The main text is a meticulously researched chronology, tracing the main phases of the quartet's existence, changes in personnel . . . interpretative profile, repertoire, concert appearances and recordings . . . for quartet devotees this is something of a must."
—*BBC Music Magazine*

"John Barker's *Pro Arte Quartet: A Century of Musical Adventure on Two Continents* offers a thorough and informative account of one of the most influential and celebrated string quartets of the twentieth century. Barker's command of the factual data is superb. The book should appeal to anyone interested in string quartets and quartet literature."
—Rob Haskins, University of New Hampshire

www.ingramcontent.com/pod-product-compliance
Lightning Source LLC
Chambersburg PA
CBHW070403100426
42812CB00005B/1618